CHURCH AND STATE IN ITALY
1850–1950

CHURCH AND STATE
IN ITALY
1850–1950

A. C. JEMOLO

Translated by
DAVID MOORE

PHILADELPHIA
DUFOUR EDITIONS
1961

Original Italian Edition 1949
Chiesa e Stato in Italia negli
Ultimi cento anni

English Revised and Translated Edition
© BASIL BLACKWELL 1960

Library of Congress No. 60—16882

Printed in Great Britain

PREFACE

This is not a translation of the complete work published in Italy in 1948 under the title of *Chiesa e Stato in Italia negli ultimi cento anni* (which subsequently ran into several editions) but of an abridgement published in 1955, under the title of *Chiesa e Stato in Italia dal Risorgimento ad oggi*. It neglects the earlier part of the period to concentrate on those aspects which have most bearing upon current political life, and therefore upon the crisis of the secular State (which, together with that of the liberal State occurred immediately after the first world war), upon the years of Fascism with its indefinable church policy (the confessionalism of veteran, unconverted Jacobins, or the clericalism of unbelievers, as one might describe it), and upon the years since 1945, characterized by the continuous predominance of a confessional party, the Christian Democrats. For the translation slight changes have been made, and a final page added to bring the work up to 1959.

As is well known, Italy is a country which has practically no religious minorities; the problem of relations between Church and State assumes, therefore, a form quite different from what is found in countries where two or more denominations exist. During the nineteenth and early twentieth centuries powerful parties of Liberals, and later of Socialists opposed every attempt of the Church to mould or to direct the course of civil society, and this opposition was violent enough to arouse intense resentment which has never died down. But the situation has changed radically since the exhaustion of liberalism and the growth of the sharp contrast between Socialist parties not clearly aligned against Communism and other parties—a contrast which has characterized much of the political life of Europe since the declaration of Communism in Russia; and Italy both in its constitution and laws and also in its custom and practice appears, as far as confessional matters go, to have much more in common with the Iberian countries than with other Catholic countries such as France and Belgium.

Hitherto the different confessional standpoints found in Western countries have aroused little interest in the public mind; we live at a time when economic problems assume a much greater importance than do those of religion. It is impossible to know whether we shall witness a revival of old passions as often happens in history. A collapse of Communism, or simple a lessening of tension which could induce the West to regard Communism as no longer constituting an imminent peril might well open the way for the resurrection of several old disputes.

I feel an obligation to pay homage to the memory of Mr Moore, a very able and diligent translator. Right from the beginning of his work I admired his scrupulousness in preparation, his maintenance of contact with the author so as to clarify thoughts sometimes obscurely expressed, his diligence in quest of exactness of detail. I retain the deepest respect for this most valuable collaborator who would still have been able to contribute much to the understanding in England of recent Italian writing in the field of political history.

CONTENTS

CHAPTER I

THE RISORGIMENTO TO 1861

(BEFORE THE UNIFICATION OF ITALY)

A T the time of the death of Pope Gregory XVI (June 1st, 1846) it was already possible to discern those trends which would eventually be recognized as typifying the history of the Church in the nineteenth century. These were: internally, an absence of theological controversy and strife, a steady growth of the tendency to centralization, and the imposition of an ever more rigid discipline; externally, acute friction with the States and with the parties that continued to embrace those anti-Catholic ideologies which in Catholic countries had already asserted themselves in the course of the eighteenth century.

The nineteenth century had revealed itself as an age characterized by a lively clash of political ideologies. There was a fundamental conflict between the liberal conceptions of power as the prerogative of the people and of Man's inalienable right to propagate new ideas, and the monarchic-absolutist conception, according to which everything that had happened in the Catholic countries since the death of Louis XIV was a mistake. Round about 1820 the future had seemed to be personified by men like Chateaubriand and Friedrich Schlegel, and it had appeared likely that the younger generation would base its hopes for the years to come on the mirage of an alliance between Throne and Altar, on the prestige of the aristocracy, and on the revival of the old mediaeval corporative forms. But ten years later the philosophical, not to say accommodating, attitude of the great absolutist Powers to the liberal revolution of July, 1830, to the constitution of the Belgian Monarchy, and to the defeat of the Spanish Carlists gave grounds for the belief that the trend of the age had radically altered.

Meanwhile, through the medium of the four Popes who had reigned since the beginning of the century, the Church had laid the foundations of its policy.

In the first place, it had given the lie to the dangerous suggestion that it possessed legitimist sympathies. (And in this it was
merely conforming to its traditions: Clement XIII and Clement
XIV had refused to maintain the fiction of a Stuart King of
England after the death of the Old Pretender.) Invoking as ever
the principle of 'the welfare of souls', Pius VII had conducted the
memorial service for Napoleon; and his successors, in order to
ensure that the new South American republics would not be left
without bishops, had studiously ignored the claims of Ferdinand
VII.

Again, although Catholic propaganda invariably tended to
support the principle of absolute monarchy, the Holy See had
not pronounced officially in favour of any particular form of
government. True, it had condemned liberalism; the *Mirari vos* of
August 15th, 1832, did not confine its strictures to the specific
attitude of the French liberal Catholics, who were hostile to the
Concordats and to the traditional alliance between Throne and
Altar, but condemned freedom of thought, the freedom of the
Press, and *rerum novandarum cupiditas*. Yet the traditional method of
condemnation by means of maxims and precepts deliberately
couched in the most virulent terms (a method which made it
possible for men and parties to assert that the doctrines condemned were not their own) was not likely to hinder the future
development of an ecclesiastical policy rendered the more flexible
by the adoption of such liberal formulas as *tolerari potest*. For the
moment, however, the sympathies of the Curia rested with the
champions of absolutism.

Ever since the day when the armies of the French Revolution
had crossed the Alps, the problem of the temporal power had been
in the forefront of men's minds. Sovereign Pontiff or Bishop of
Rome?—that had been the question up to 1814. And even after
the Restoration there had been discussion as to whether the
Papal States should continue to exist in their traditional form or
whether it did not behove the Pope and his advisers to introduce
those reforms which the absolute rulers of Europe had introduced
in their own States. In particular, men had asked themselves
whether the Papal States should not be secularized—that is to say
whether, without prejudice to the sovereignty of the Pope, they
should not be administered by laymen rather than by ecclesiastics;
and the idea had gained ground that this was a problem on whose

solution the preservation of peace in Italy might well depend, and that consequently it was one on which all those rulers who were interested in the maintenance of the political order that had emerged from the Treaty of Vienna were entitled to express an opinion. The currect preoccupation with the question of the temporal power had the effect of focusing the attention of the Holy See more and more on the political conflicts of the time and of making it almost unthinkable that the Church should fail to concern itself with their outcome.

In Italy the longing for unity, at first vague and inarticulate, had suddenly found expression after 1814 in the work of a small group of writers and thinkers. The disturbances of 1830–31 had widened the circle of those who favoured unification, even if this involved federation.

In his book *Dell'Italia* (1835) the Dalmatian Nicolò Tommaseo demanded unification, the expulsion of the Austrians, and a 'marriage of Christianity and liberty'.

A few years later Italy became the battle-ground of the neo-Guelph movement. A number of influences are usually considered to have played their part in this development, chief among them the example allegedly provided by the Spanish resistance of 1808–12 and by events in Greece and Belgium of what can be achieved by a union of religious and patriotic feeling; the expectation of a tightening-up of discipline and morals within the Church; the reformative zeal of the Italian princes; the formation of denominational parties in France and Belgium; and, finally, historical considerations (the memory of the civilizing work of the Church in the Middle Ages and of the resistance offered by Italian Guelphism to the Suevian Emperors, which inspired many with visions of a Papacy pledged to assist in the country's liberation from the Austrian yoke).

Spiritual father of the movement, and chief architect of the Italian Risorgimento in the realm of ideas, was the Piedmontese priest Vincenzo Gioberti, who after the disorders of 1830 became a political exile and was for several decades a highly esteemed philosopher. Towards the end of 1842 Gioberti published the volume *Del primato morale e civile degli italiani*, in which, while extolling the Italian genius and the Italian people's contribution to civilization, he claimed that Italy could achieve unity and independence by means of a confederation of the various States, under the presidency of the Pope; for the Church was the fountain-head of Italian unity—a national fountain-head inasmuch as it had created the nation and had been rooted in it for eighteen centuries. Gioberti did not advocate the introduction of constitutional régimes in the individual States. Instead, he would have been satisfied with consultative assemblies of their rulers. The book had an enormous circulation and found much favour among large sections of the clergy. The future Pope Pius IX was much impressed by it.

During the years that followed, enlightened Italian opinion was shaken by the publication of a series of books, all of which posed the problem of unification.

In 1844 Cesare Balbo, member of a great family of the Piedmontese nobility, published *Le speranze d'Italia*, in which he indicated the various combinations of circumstances that could lead to the withdrawal of Austria from the peninsula. Two years later Luigi Torelli brought out his *Pensieri sull'Italia di un anonimo lombardo*, a violently anti-Austrian publication which called for the division of Italy into three kingdoms—Savoy, Central Italy, and Southern Italy—with Rome, the traditional seat of the Pope, a free city. In his *Della nazionalità italiana*, also published in 1846, Giacomo Durando maintained that in the coming age of Italian resurgence the Kingdoms of Naples and Piedmont could not possibly survive without representative government. The Pope must be made to realize how much the hegemony of Austria interfered with his freedom as Head of the Church. He must be physically isolated from the influence of the various potentates of Europe. Let him keep, if he must, Rome and Civitavecchia and exchange the rest of his territory for Sicily and Sardinia. The year 1846 saw the publication of two diatribes, the one severe in tone, the other more moderate, against the pernicious administration of the Papal States. These were: *Degli ultimi casi di Romagna*, a short work by Massimo d'Azeglio (a Piedmontese nobleman who was also a painter, a novelist and, after 1849, a leading statesman), and Leopoldo Galeotti's book *Della sovranità e del governo temporale dei Papi*.

Conflicting opinions were voiced by a number of priests of the Society of Jesus, who did not believe that the unification of Italy would add to the prestige of the Holy See.

In his *Saggio teoretico di diritto naturale* (1840–43) Father Luigi

Taparelli, brother of the Massimo d'Azeglio just mentioned, had already taken his stand against the 'idol of stones and earth, set up by certain fanatical exponents of the patriotic ideal. In his short work *Della nazionalità* (1847) he maintained that national individuality was possible without independence, and that subjection to a foreign prince was by no means tantamount to servitude, at any rate so long as the prince respected the national characteristics of the people in question. In 1845 the Jesuit Carlo Curci engaged in a polemic with Gioberti, denouncing his attempt to accomplish through the spread of religious ideas 'revolutions of a kind that in former times the savage, bloodthirsty masses had brought about by armed violence'.

A special place among the propagandists of these years must be assigned to Antonio Rosmini-Serbati of Rovereto, a devout priest and the founder of a flourishing religious community. In 1848 Rosmini negotiated with the Holy See on behalf of the Piedmontese Government with a view to the formation of an Italic League; but his efforts to persuade that Government to offer the Pope the bait of a concordat under the terms of which the State would renounce its old jurisdictional weapons, were signally unsuccessful.

In the same year Rosmini published *Delle cinque piaghe della Chiesa* and *La Costituzione secondo la giustizia sociale*. In the first-named book, which must in fact have been begun several years earlier, he deplored the separation of the people from the clergy in the practice of their religion; the clergy's ignorance; the lack of a truly corporate body of bishops; the fact that bishops were appointed by temporal rulers instead of by clergy and people acting in concert (as a result of this criticism the book was placed on the Index); and, finally, the abandonment of the old rule whereby the clergy could retain only so much of the income from Church property as was necessary to provide them with the means of life.

The *Costituzione* is the work of a man who abhors the doctrines thrown up by the French Revolution, and who thus regards the maintenance of the rights of humanity and of the Church as the first essential in any constitution. Rosmini would have liked to see the franchise denied to non-Catholics, and he would have liked to see the principle of the property-qualification rigidly enforced. He believed that the poor should be assisted, but that they had no right to exercise any political power. The granting of such a privilege would be detrimental to the public weal. In France, Thiers was propagating the same idea.

More than a hundred years after the event the 'miracle' of Pope Pius IX remains shrouded in mystery.

It may be said that at the time of his accession there was in Europe, and especially in Italy, a widespread and confident expectation of change. Men longed above all to see the conflicts which loomed so menacingly on the horizon peacefully resolved, in an atmosphere undisturbed by grave crises and internecine strife. (Unlike certain dictators of our own day, no one then would have extolled the glories of war.) All were anxious that a series of aspirations which none wished to regard as conflicting should be speedily satisfied. Thus, the Italians wanted to effect a substantial political unification of their country without being forced to abandon the traditions of the separate States or to depose individual princes. They wanted to retain the benefits of their religion and at the same time to enjoy the advantages of freedom; they wanted reforms; they wanted the whole country to aspire to a more modern economic and administrative system. Most of all, they wanted to be rid of the Austrians, and this despite the fact that Austrian methods of administration were the best the various States had ever known.

And now there came on the scene a Pope of singular goodness and singular charm, which earned him the fervent admiration of millions to the end of his days. A sincere Christian, passionately devoted to the welfare of the Church, convinced of the necessity of carrying out reforms and righting wrongs, he too shared to some extent in the general expectation of favourable developments. So it was that when, on July 16th, 1846, he granted a limited political amnesty and intimated his desire to remedy abuses in the Papal States—as a beginning, in 1847 he formed a Council to assist in the public administration, enthusiasm knew no bounds. Men became convinced that a Pope had arisen who was destined to set the seal on the unification of Italy, to reconcile and satisfy unitarian and anti-Austrian aspirations, and at the same time to manifest his devotion to the religion of his forebears and to the ideal of representative government.

The Pope was a prisoner of the enthusiasms he had aroused. His spontaneous reforms were succeeded by others introduced solely for reasons of expediency—among them the civic guard and, most important of all, the constitution, which was approved only because its rejection after it had been adopted by other Italian princes would have provoked a storm of protest, with the result that Austrian troops would have had to be called in to maintain order. But when the question arose of going to war with Austria, of seeming to endorse the proclamation of one of his generals who had spoken of a 'holy war', the conscience of Pius IX said 'No'. In his address of April 29th, 1848, he declared that the Pope would never make war on Austria, that he would never listen to the advice of those who wanted to see him 'president of a new Republic that would include all the peoples of Italy'.

After that, Pius IX's position in Rome became ever more precarious, and following the murder by Jacobin elements of his minister Pellegrino Rossi he was obliged to flee to Gaeta. Driven to side with opponents of constitutional government, at last he was convinced that the Papacy had need of the temporal power in order to preserve its spiritual independence and that it was impossible to govern the Papal States by methods other than those employed in the past, methods which in effect were reintroduced as soon as the Holy See had recovered its territories through the intervention of the French and Austrian armies.

The one Italian state in which the constitutional forms introduced in 1848 were destined to survive was Piedmont—the state which, in virtue of its adherence to the new order, was ultimately to achieve the miracle of Italian unification. It was here, too, that from 1848 onwards anti-Austrian feeling found its most vigorous expression.

In every age political trends have a logic of their own. This logic is none the less genuine in that it is not that of the abstract reasoner, and it is wont to bring together in an indissoluble unity of purpose men who at any other time would find that they had little in common.

By the beginning of 1848, anti-Austrian feeling and the ideals of national unity and representative government were closely associated in the minds of men representing every shade of political opinion. Within a short time the same had become true of certain problems of ecclesiastical policy. Already those who longed for the advent of the new order were thinking in terms of the emancipation of the Jews and the Waldensians. (In point of fact, in any of the free countries—those countries north of the Alps which Italians regarded with so much admiration—the very idea of withholding political rights from religious dissenters would have been unthinkable.) Moreover, the attitude of the Society of Jesus, which was at variance with the prevailing mood, had caused a wave of anti-Jesuit feeling to sweep through Italy. Indignation reached such a height in Piedmont that in 1848 laws were passed granting political rights to non-Catholics and suppressing Jesuitism.

No further progress could be made for the time being. But already men of liberal convictions had raised questions which in the years that followed were destined to lead to sharp clashes with the Church.

Except in Piedmont, the Italian parliaments were ephemeral. The parliament of Tuscany had no anti-clerical bias; but the Tuscan constitution had already guaranteed the rights of religious dissenters. In Sicily, on the other hand, Parliament showed no mercy to dissenters (though here the problem was purely theoretical, for only Catholics were allowed to enter the island); but it voted in favour of the suppression of the Jesuits and adopted a number of jurisdictional measures.

By the end of 1848, even before the guns had ceased to speak, the neo-Guelph ideal of an Italian federation presided over by the Pope had lost its attraction, even though in circles close to Napoleon III efforts were to be made in 1859–60 to revive it. Men no longer believed in the idea of modernizing the Papal States. Liberals and Catholics eyed one another with suspicion: the former were convinced that the Holy See would be opposed to constitutional government and to any European political initiative which aimed at expelling Austria from the peninsula; and the Catholics for their part were quite certain that in Italy constitutional government, because of its ideological origins and also because of the antecedents of the men who advocated it, could only harm the cause of religion.

The events that followed the disorders of 1849 confirmed these forebodings. There was, as is well known, a strengthening of the bonds uniting Throne and Altar which revived memories of the Restoration itself. One thing only was entirely lacking: such a concentration of intense popular feeling—of young men's expectations and hopes for better times—upon the ideal of an absolute Catholic Monarchy as had occurred between 1815 and 1820.

So far as Italy was concerned the most notable by-products of this renewal of the alliance between Throne and Altar were the accord of April 25th, 1851, between Tuscany and the Holy See, which, though opposed by liberal and moderate opinion and even by the ministers of Leopold II, was nevertheless insisted upon by the Grand Duke, egged on in turn by Austria; and the Austrian Concordat of August 18th, 1855, likewise willed by the Emperor in face of resistance on the part of bureaucrats and university professors, who were still sensitive to any suggestion of a surrender of Austrian influence.

The Tuscan accord of 1851 provided for a renunciation by the State of the old jurisdictional weapons, but it did not revive the ecclesiastical courts: the Church merely retained its absolute authority in all matrimonial questions. The Austrian Concordat of 1855—which had wide repercussions in Europe and was judged with extreme severity by all liberal opinion—was negotiated mainly by the Papal Nuncio Viale Prelà and by von Rauscher, spokesman and former tutor of Franz Josef, who while the talks were in progress became Archbishop of Vienna. It did not proclaim a State religion, but it repealed the whole of the Emperor's legislation, promised the episcopate complete freedom of communication with the Pope, the clergy and the Faithful and left the episcopate as final arbiters in all religious matters. It modified the general civil code of 1811 to the extent of acknowledging the jurisdiction of the ecclesiastical courts in matrimonial disputes. It did not grant the Church any juridical privileges, but it recognized the inviolability of sacred places, and it incorporated an undertaking that the State would help the bishops to ensure that the sanctions which they imposed on members of the clergy were duly enforced. Finally, ecclesiastical organizations were left free to add to their material possessions.

Relations between the Kingdom of the Two Sicilies and the Holy See were already so cordial as to leave little room for further improvement. Nevertheless, a number of long-standing differences were now composed.

This development of cordial relations between the absolutist states and the Holy See, coupled with the eulogies which the Pope in his allocutions was forced to bestow on their rulers, inevitably exerted an influence on liberal opinion.

Only one Italian state, Sardinia, still flaunted the national tricolour, only one kind remained faithful to the constitution—and by this time it was sheltering political refugees from the various absolutist states. Yet its king, Victor Emmanuel II, had to combat Jacobin distrust and the suspicions of the hotheads who would have liked to see the war with Austria indefinitely prolonged even if in the meantime defeat became inevitable.

Political logic, which is governed by its own peculiar laws, now demanded that King Victor and his Government should give proof of their continuing fidelity to the ideal of a free and united Italy by adopting even in ecclesiastical matters a policy diametrically opposed to that pursued by the absolutist states. And the same logic required that Pius IX for his part should hesitate before making any concession to Piedmont, including that which he had made to all the other Catholic states by renouncing the Church's juridical privileges. For in virtue of its unitarian aspirations Piedmont presented a covert threat to the integrity of the Papal realms; and, possessing as it did a free Press and a parliament from which even Jacobin elements were not excluded, it was the one Italian state in which voices hostile to religion and to the Holy See were able to make themselves heard.

Statesmen and political theorists alike appreciated the necessity of Piedmont's policy, realizing that while on the one hand an *entente* with the Papacy would have involved a reconciliation with Austria and the extinction of political liberty, the path of unity and complete freedom of thought would have led just as inevitably to increasing friction with the Holy See.

During the years that followed the military defeat and the return to the *status quo* of 1814 the leading political writer in Italy was still Vincenzo Gioberti. In his book *Del rinnovamento civile d'Italia*, written in 1851, Gioberti passed judgment on the men of 1848–49 and predicted with remarkable accuracy the course of the Risorgimento, even to the extent of anticipating the position in which the Pope would find himself after being deprived of his temporal power and forecasting the passage of the national law that was to give him the status of a free prince without a principate. Violently opposed to the concordats, Gioberti favoured the separation of Church and State, but he believed that the State should exercise control in all matters pertaining to education, marriage, burial, holidays, and also mortmain. And he applauded Piedmont's first laws relating to ecclesiastical affairs, asserting that through them the Government had won the confidence of the people and the goodwill of the most militant exponents of the liberal ideal.

King Victor's two great Prime Ministers, Massimo d'Azeglio, who set the State finally and decisively on a liberal course, and Camillo Benso di Cavour, the miracle-worker who made national unity a reality, shared the same convictions as Gioberti. As a result, after they had failed in their efforts to reach an understanding with the Pope,[1] Parliament in 1850 approved laws suppressing the ecclesiastical courts and making it illegal for ecclesiastical organizations to acquire new property without the consent of the Government. These laws drew lively protests from Catholics and provoked even more violent reactions on the part of liberals. The Archbishop of Turin, Mgr. Luigi Franzoni, denied the privilege of a religious funeral to Pietro di Santa Rosa, the Minister of Agriculture, because he had refused in his last illness to disavow his work as a deputy and a minister. As a result of this action the Archbishop was expelled from the Kingdom. He spent his years of exile at Lyons, and until his death was regarded with veneration by all the 'ultramontanes' of Italy, France and Belgium. Penalties for failing to abstain from work on religious feast-days were subsequently abolished; but the bill proposing the introduction of civil marriage did not go through, the Senate rejecting it by a single vote. In reality the King had schemed for its rejection; he was in constant communication with the Pope, and, although resolved to keep faith with the constitution, to abstain from anything in the nature of a *coup d'état*, and to govern in consultation with Parliament, he was anxious to avoid a break with the Holy See.

Nevertheless, he failed to prevent the Cavour-Rattazzi Cabinet (a coalition of the Centre and the moderate Left) from presenting, and Parliament from approving, a bill providing for the withdrawal of statutory recognition from religious organizations which

---

[1] The Pope would have welcomed a general concordat, but, convinced as he was that a liberal régime could only be disadvantageous to the Church, he was decidedly ill-disposed towards Piedmont, even if personally friendly towards the King.

neglected their work of educating, preaching and tending the sick, as well as from minor ecclesiastical bodies.[1] In accordance with a scheme devised by the Emperor Joseph II, the property of the organizations suppressed went into an ecclesiastical pool, which, after the sale of immovables, guaranteed a minimum stipend to priests whose benefices yielded them an income below the figure named. The Government justified the project on the ground that the State was entitled to distinguish between useless ecclesiastical organizations, which should be suppressed, and those which were necessary and should be helped, adding that a liberal State could not subsidize any religious body with the taxpayers' money and that subsidies hitherto given by the State to needy parish priests would have to be discontinued. Underlying this measure was a desire to strike a blow at the religious associations, whose hostility to the new order was greater than that of the secular clergy. During the debate on this bill the possibility—from the liberal point of view, the danger—that the Crown would reverse its policy was revived for the last time when a senator, Bishop Nazari di Calabiana, promised in the name of the episcopate that if the bill was withdrawn the bishops would assume the responsibility hitherto borne by the State of subsidizing impoverished incumbents. Cavour praised the bishops' generosity and offered his resignation, believing that if the way to agreement could be found, someone else less unacceptable to Rome might more suitably fill the office of Prime Minister. Liberal opinion criticized his action: it foresaw the danger of a concordat and of a *rapprochement* with Austria, which, it maintained, would lead inevitably to an ever more ruthless persecution of elements of the Left and to a restriction of freedom. Mass demonstrations were held. Massimo d'Azeglio, who, while at odds with Cavour on many points, was a resolute champion of liberal ideas, wrote an impassioned letter to the King in which he warned him of the error he was about to commit. The King, who had already asked a successor to form a new Cabinet, saw his mistake in time and refused to accept Cavour's resignation. The bishops' proposal was rejected, and on May 29th, 1855, the bill to suppress religious organizations became law.

---

[1] At the same time the Government continued to respect the principle of 'freedom of association'.

Thereafter the Monarchy was able to pursue its liberal and unitarian course without opposition.

Naturally, the adoption of such laws as this prompted many Catholics, who in 1846–48 had supported the neo-Guelph movement and had joyfully saluted the tricolour, to oppose the idea of unification. The fact of the matter was that the whole of Catholic and conservative Europe regarded Piedmont as a hotbed of revolution and a menace to the peace of the Continent.

A review destined to express the hostility of orthodox Catholics to Piedmont and the liberal ideal was founded by members of the Society of Jesus. Christened *La Civiltà cattolica*, it is still flourishing to-day. The idea of such a publication was conceived by the Neapolitan Jesuit Father Curci and was warmly welcomed by Pius IX, in spite of warnings from the General of the Order, Father Roothan. It first appeared in Naples in 1850, but almost immediately its headquarters were transferred to Rome because by its failure to proclaim the virtues of absolute government it had given offence to Ferdinand II.

The review's leading political writer was Father Taparelli. A rigid doctrinarian, he judged politics, and in particular governments and their social systems, by strictly logical standards—the standards of what he felt *ought* to be: a specific form of government *ought* to produce certain specific effects. He seemed not to realize that human beings, and hence political movements, are characterized by an illogicality which sometimes proves salutary, that allowance must always be made for the effect of sudden inspirations which cannot be accounted for in terms of cold reason. A series of articles published in *Civiltà* provided the material for Father Taparelli's book, *Esame critico degli ordini rappresentativi nella società moderna* (Rome, 1854), which, if they had been more cultured, the dictators who appeared in Europe after 1920 might have had reprinted and circulated as propaganda against those institutions which they were at such pains to destroy by their own efforts.

Father Taparelli bases his thesis on the concept that Man cannot be guided by his own reason. The opinion of the majority cannot replace Catholic certainty. The nation itself cannot change a fallacy into a truth. Whence it follows that the foundation of human society is authority. The various freedoms—educational freedom, freedom of the Press and so forth—ignore the existence of a number of unalterable truths. Those who object that religious conviction cannot be inculcated by force forget that 'the man who ensnares the monster of error, like the man who muzzles a bear, does not claim to have converted the beast, but merely to have saved innocent men from its clutches.' The Church not only has the right to keep a check on moral opinion; it is entitled to exercise control in political and economic matters as well. Above all, it should be responsible for the people's education.

Among the evils of a 'modernized society', and hence of a liberal régime, Father Taparelli regards as fundamental the refusal to recognize the principle of authority and the claims of Catholic truth. In addition, he deplores the idolization of the State and the material conception of the Country as a separate entity circumscribed by 'natural boundaries'; centralized government, which ignores the rights of natural units such as the commune and the family; military conscription, which violates the right of all men to choose their professions; and, finally, the principle of the division of power, which is contrary to nature, since all power is vested in the head of the family. The peoples of the world (apart from the few that are cursed by an overweening ambition) are not conscious, writes Taparelli, of any need for political freedom: they are quite content with their domestic and civic liberties. And he goes on to defend those princes who, having sworn in 1848 to adopt constitutional forms, subsequently re-established absolute governments. 'How stupid and unjust' he says, 'are those charges of bad faith brought against a prince who has freed his subjects from a Voltairian tyranny by wretches who believe that, having extracted a promise by dint of heaven knows what subterfuges, they are entitled to exploit the wealth, restrict the freedom, interfere with the religion, dominate the conscience, and enslave the citizens—men, women and children alike—of an entire nation.'

Gioberti was the last writer who truly personified Italian liberalism. This triumphant doctrine continued to inform all political propaganda up to 1920, and it was, moreover, expounded, in its philosophical and historical rather than in its political aspect, by the greatest Italian thinker of the first half of the present century, Benedetto Croce. Like all dynamic and virile doctrines, it gave rise to a number of variants, schools of thought and political parties, all of which, however, were characterized by an unshakable fidelity to its basic principles.

There were always liberals to be found who desired a reconciliation with the Holy See, convinced that it was possible for a liberal State to live side by side with the respected, pervasive religion that dominated the consciences of men; but for them the period extending roughly from 1855 to 1870 was a particularly difficult one, in which the realization of their dreams came to appear more remote than ever. At the other end of the scale were the unbelievers, latter-day disciples of Voltaire, for whom religion was merely an irrational form of superstition. There were also a number of obstinate jurisdictionalists, who would have welcomed the revival of the type of régime prevalent during the seventeenth and eighteenth centuries, Gallican or 'Josephine' as the case might be.

The two most popular men of the Revolution, Giuseppe Garibaldi and Giuseppe Mazzini, were both resolute opponents of the Church. The first-named, in his speeches and writings, abandoned himself to a vulgar anti-clericalism. But he was not without political intuition, and during his prodigious campaign of 1860, in the course of which he conquered the whole of Sicily and the South, he took care not to offend the religious susceptibilities of the people, offered prayers in churches and sanctuaries, and even witnessed the miracle of St. Januarius at Naples. Subsequently, however, his Government sought to restore as much as it could of the legislation originally introduced by Tanucci.

Mazzini was a man of very different temper. 'Much more devoted to the Christian tradition than he himself imagined . . . he felt that God was the hypostatic realization and the substantial vindication of those unwritten moral laws by which communal life is governed. The Illuminists saw God as an abstract category, untrammelled, one might say, by any living ties with the reality of human society. Mazzini felt that mankind needed something more than a mere code of ethics . . . he was convinced that without religion any kind of social discipline was impossible. . . . If in the eyes of Giuseppe Mazzini the existing confessional forms were all equally inadequate to the new task which religious faith had to assume in the world, if his confidence in established traditions tended to diminish with every day that passed, at least it may be said that his reverence for the Christianity of the Gospels was always profound, not to say sublime. . . . '[1]

Like all mystics and those whose actions are conditioned by feeling, and like a great many of his fellow revolutionaries, Mazzini, who believed in a personal God but was certainly not a Catholic and perhaps not even a Christian, displayed not the slightest interest in juridical forms. Such a man, in fact, would never have felt called upon to attempt to regularize relations between Church and State or to dictate an ecclesiastical code of laws.

The Risorgimento gave to the world the man to whom Paléologue dedicated a volume subtitled *Un grand réaliste*, the man who was the true artificer of national unification: Camillo di Cavour. And Cavour, who had become set in his ideas well before 1848 as a result of his frequent contacts with political circles in Geneva, England and the France of Louis Philippe,[2] was devoted to the ideal of liberty. In his philosophy, true liberty is compounded of a number of individual freedoms, all of which are interdependent, so that if one is violated all the others suffer in consequence. It is worthy of note that among these freedoms he accorded a by-no-means insignificant place to freedom of trade.

We do not know a great deal about Cavour's religious beliefs. When he was little more than eighteen years of age he passed through a spiritual crisis which prompted him to embrace a crude rationalism.[3] Did he later revert to the faith of his fathers? On numerous occasions he declared himself to be a Catholic, and we know that on his death-bed he was at pains to obtain the consolations of religion. But it is doubtful whether his Catholicism signified an acceptance of the Church's dogmas and a belief in its sacraments—whether, in fact, it signified anything more than a belief in a personal God and an adhesion to the Church regarded as an organized institution with a high civilizing mission. And we may well ponder whether his anxiety not to die a reprobate was not merely the anxiety of a statesman, unwilling that his death should confirm in the eyes of the many the impossibility of remaining in the Church while disobeying the Pope in the political field.

---

[1] E. Buonaiuti, *Storia del cristianesimo*, III, pp. 490–495 (Milan, 1942–43).

[2] F. Ruffini, *La giovinezza di Cavour*, 2nd ed. (two vols., Turin, 1937–38).

[3] F. Ruffini, *Ultimi studi sul conte di Cavour* (Bari, 1936).

What we do know is that it was Cavour's sincere belief in freedom that inspired his plan for the regularization of relations between Church and State—a plan which finds its epitome in the formula 'a Free Church in a Free State'.

In 1842 the Protestant pastor Alexandre Vinet had published his *Essai sur la manifestation des convictions religieuses et sur la séparation de l'Église et de l'État,* based on the concept that the acquisition of a religious faith is a spontaneous act, from which it follows that a State religion is inadmissible. From this source, as well as from his passionate belief in freedom, Cavour derived the idea that the State should renounce all control over the Church, which in its turn should not lay claim to any special privileges, but should be subject to the law of the land. Accordingly, all the fundamental institutions of civil life should be secularized, although the Church should be left free to expand, to win souls, to persuade an ever-increasing number of people to submit of their own free will to its discipline. But even an overwhelming majority of believers must never be allowed to impose its will on a minority or otherwise to embarrass it, just as a majority of unbelievers must never transform the State into an instrument of atheistic propaganda or in any way weaken the position of the Faithful.

Here is the essence of Cavour's thought. In effect, he always offers an equally stout opposition to clericals and Jacobins, to attempts on the part of the Church to interfere in the life of the State, and to measures aimed at the persecution of Catholics and clergy.

Utterly absorbed as he was in political life, Cavour wrote no books. Anyone who wishes to make a closer study of the separatist doctrine which inspired his policies should consult *La Chiesa e lo Stato in Piemonte* (1854–55), written by one of his most faithful followers, Pier Carlo Boggio. The author bases himself on the assumption that the State has jurisdiction only over the external acts of the individual and then only in so far as they affect the security and well-being of the community; whereas the Church has jurisdiction only over men's consciences, with special reference to the health of the individual soul. It follows that Church and State ought to exist side by side, each being independent of the other within its own sphere. Later, we read: 'The religious spirit seeks to make the individual perfect. The translation of this principle into the realm of politics invariably provokes a whole series of measures which are more or less vexatious and oppressive according to the intensity of their sponsor's conviction that he is acting in the interests of those against whom they are directed ... there is no more inflexible and pertinacious tyrant than he who believes that he has a mandate from God to seek to promote by his rule the spiritual welfare of his subjects ... as a general rule, the fruits of hieratical government are not freedom of thought, the advance of learning, industrial progress and commercial prosperity, but prostration, ignorance, poverty and enfeeblement.'

The student would also do well to read Marco Minghetti's twelve letters *Della libertà religiosa* (1855). Minghetti had represented Bologna in Pius IX's Council of State (to which reference has already been made), and in 1848 he had been a Papal minister. Subsequently he collaborated closely with Cavour in the negotiations which the great minister conducted with Rome during the last months of his life, and after Italy's unification he was twice Prime Minister of the Kingdom.

Minghetti denies that the spirit of Christianity is incompatible with religious freedom. The Gospel, he says, makes no reference to civil government nor to relations between Church and State. And he adds that nothing emerges more clearly from the Christian doctrine than the primacy of spiritual freedom. 'When Church and State forged their alliance and temporal punishments were combined with spiritual ones, or at least the exercise of civil rights was made conditional upon the profession of a State religion, then violence was countered by deception, to which even governments were party.' Like Cavour, Minghetti affirms the interdependence of all the freedoms. The separation of Church and State does not make a conflict between the two inevitable, rather does it establish between them a harmony no longer inspired by self-interest, fear and passion, but 'resulting from the fundamental unity of the spiritual and temporal orders, and indeed of all orders, whether of thought or life, speculation or action.'

If their theoretical concepts and basic principles are crystal-clear, the same cannot be said of the manner in which Cavour and his followers set about putting them into practice. They do not advocate the separation of Church and State, as exemplified in the U.S.A., where the idea of government legislation in the realm of ecclesiastical affairs is unknown. Nor, for that matter, do they express themselves in favour of the Belgian system. Indeed, they often point to it as an illustration of the axiom that the granting of freedom to the Church is the first step to a clerical dictatorship. Cavour was a man of action, and he was not deaf to the voices of those who sought to remind him that what might be done with impunity by a great State, a State not torn by internal dissensions, whose citizens were of one mind on all fundamental questions—on the need for the renunciation of any form of State supervision of ecclesiastical activities—could not be done by a State like Sardinia. For in the Kingdom there was still a deep division of opinion between those who wistfully recalled the peaceful days of the absolute monarchy and those who yearned for the gradual introduction of liberal measures, between those who desired the preservation of the *status quo* and looked askance at the political exiles from other Italian States to whom the Government had offered hospitality and in many cases employment—a considerable part of the Kingdom, to wit Savoy, made no secret of the fact that it felt completely extraneous to the rest of the peninsula—and those who would have liked to see the Kingdom of Sardinia absorbed into a united Italy.

All Catholics instinctively realized that separation would be more injurious to the principles to which they were pledged than the most rigorous jurisdictional measures, inasmuch as it would give the State complete control of the law and of the external life of the people, leaving the Church to keep watch over men's consciences and denying it any authority other than that voluntarily conceded to it by the Faithful. And old jurisdictionalists and Jacobins were equally dismayed by the idea of a disarmed State, powerless to punish bishops, to protect priests who were faithful to national ideals—'patriot' priests—from the wrath of their superiors, to prevent the formation of countless new religious associations, to prohibit the latter from giving instruction, and to prevent ecclesiastical bodies from receiving legacies. And, as always in politics, there were the prudent ones, those who accepted the idea in principle, but who felt that they must needs await a suitable moment to translate it into action, and who would willingly have left it to their successors to work out the practical details.

But there came a time when it seemed to Cavour that the moment was ripe to carry the idea into effect. It came on the morrow of Italy's unification, when he felt he would be justified in offering the Church her freedom—which he sincerely believed would be as beneficial to the Church as to the State—in exchange for the renunciation of her temporal power.

In 1859 the French Army crossed the Alps. The battles of Magenta, Solferino and San Martino were followed by the armistice of Villafranca. It seemed that Piedmont must surely annex Lombardy, that all Italy must revert to the *status quo* of 1814. But on the proclamation of war the States of Parma, Modena, Tuscany and Romagna had risen in revolt, and in order to restore their lawful governments it would have been necessary to use force. Austria was in the throes of a crisis; France announced that she did not propose to intervene. On May 5th, 1860, Garibaldi left Quarto with a thousand volunteers. First Sicily, then the continental part of the Kingdom collapsed. To the accompaniment of the rallying-cry of 'Italy for Victor Emmanuel' preparations were made to annex the territories in question. Finally, the regular army occupied Umbria and the Marches. France accepted the situation, claiming as the price of her acquiescence the surrender of Savoy, cradle of the dynasty, and Nice.

Napoleon III would have liked to help Italy and to avoid giving too much offence not merely to Catholic opinion throughout the world, but to almost all shades of French opinion, which regarded the unification of Italy as contrary to France's interests.

On December 22nd, 1859, there was published in Paris a pamphlet entitled *Le Pape et le Congrès*. Although unsigned, it was known to reflect the views of the Emperor. The author declared that the Pope must be allowed to retain his sovereignty, but that an authority which derived from God Himself could not be imposed on the peoples by force. The smaller the Pope's domain, and the more his position resembled that of the father of a family, the less likelihood would there be of any trouble in the future. The Pope should be content to keep Rome and a very small piece of the surrounding territory. All the Catholic Powers would combine to ensure the permanence of the Holy See. It was highly desirable that a meeting of those Powers should be held in Paris before the end of 1860 to guarantee the integrity of Rome and the Papal territory, as well as their economic security.

The pamphlet caused much indignation among French Catholics. Veuillot likened it to the kiss of Judas. Mgr. Dupanloup, Mgr. Pie and other French bishops, various eminent laymen, Catholics,

Orleanists and even Protestants seized their pens and rushed to the attack. De Broglie, Falloux, Cochin, Corcelles, Guizot, Thiers, Cousin, Villemain and Montalembert all expressed themselves in vehement terms. After a campaign which bore the appearance of a protest against the Emperor's policy, Father Lacordaire was elected a member of the Academy. (In spite of this, the old champion of Catholic liberalism also took up his pen in defence not only of the temporal authority of the Pope but of the recent reforms and of the idea of an Italian Confederation.)

In Paris there was much talk of establishing an Italian Confederation under the honorary presidency of the Pope. But Pius IX made his agreement to such a proposal conditional upon his recovery of Romagna; and at the same time he made it clear that he was opposed to the idea of appointing Victor Emmanuel to be vicar apostolic of the territory. For their part, neither the Government of Turin nor the liberals would hear of the suggestion that Umbria and the Marches should be restored to their former ruler. In February, 1861, another pamphlet entitled *La France, Rome et l'Italie* made its appearance. It was written ostensibly by the Vicomte de la Gueronnière, but in fact by Persigny, who extolled Napoleon III's work on behalf of the Church and laid emphasis on the Roman Curia's numerous manifestations of intransigence, and even of hostility to the Emperor. Peace, he declared, must be established between Italy and the Pope, for the bonds that united them were indissoluble. The Emperor, 'fidèle à son double devoir de souverain élu par la volonté national et de fils aîné de l'Église, ne peut sacrifier l'Italie à la cour de Rome ni livrer la Papauté à la révolution.' The publication provoked a fresh flood of polemics and pastoral letters.

Naturally, the period of transition to Italian unity, characterized by the military occupation of vast areas of the peninsula and the setting up of various provisional governments, was not devoid of incident. The ecclesiastical legislation adopted by Piedmont was wholly or in part extended to those regions of Italy which had been annexed or were in the process of being annexed. In the provinces that had risen against their lawful rulers the episcopate declined to recognize the new governments, and in face of this intransigence the latter reacted violently. For refusing to allow his clergy to take part in the nation-wide celebrations Cardinal Corsi, Archbishop of Pisa, was arrested and banished to Turin, where he was confined to a monastery. So corrupting are the effects of inflamed passions coupled with the empty pretence of *salus populi* that even so great a champion and exponent of the ideals of liberty as Cavour approved this measure, although he was aware of its doubtful legality. In addition, Mgr. Ratta, vicar capitular of Bologna, was arrested and tried.

The immediate preoccupation of Cavour and the Piedmontese Government was to remain outside the conflict; to ensure the elimination from the 1859 peace treaty of those clauses which provided that the banished rulers should return to their lands and that, apart from the incorporation of Lombardy in the State of Piedmont, there should be no change in the country's political structure; to induce the Powers to recognize the fact of Italy's unification (the Government's fears on this score grew daily less, for the situation was undoubtedly favourable to the cause of Italian nationalism); and—since a permanent state of conflict was not without its disadvantages—to arrive at a *modus vivendi* with the Pope. In the meantime, however, another problem had arisen—the problem of selecting a capital for the new Kingdom of Italy, which had been proclaimed on March 17th, 1861. Now that Savoy had been ceded to France, Turin was almost a frontier town. Cavour, who was tortured by the memory of the dissension that had arisen between Milan and Turin in 1848, feared that the new Kingdom might be plunged into a serious, possibly a fatal crisis over this question of a capital. Neither Naples nor Florence would be willing to play second fiddle to Turin, while deputies hailing from Sicily and Calabria would not take kindly to the idea of having to travel the whole length of Italy in order to sit in a Parliament whose headquarters were situated at the foot of the Alps.

It seemed to Cavour that the only possible solution to the problem was to make Rome the capital. Before the splendour of that name, with all its great associations, the claims of all other Italian cities paled into insignificance. Realist that he was, Cavour was acutely conscious of the problems of his time, and he was by temperament utterly disinclined to glorify the memory of a greatness that had ended more than fifteen centuries before. A true European, he was completely absorbed in the events that were unfolding in the north of the Continent, and he had never in his life had any desire to visit the city of the Caesars. It is therefore all the more remarkable that, by a strange combination of circumstances, he should have come to regard the question of Rome's future as the most important of all the problems that beset Italy at the moment of her unification, and that he should have associated the question of the annexation of Rome by Italy, and hence the question of the Church's loss of her temporal power, with the question of the relations between Italy and the Holy See. The consequences of this linking of two seemingly unrelated problems were alike incalculable and enduring; and it is not without interest that the great statesman's contemporaries, save for a few shrewd spirits who regarded it as a mistake on his part, completely failed to appreciate its significance.

In the parliamentary debate of March, 1861, Boncompagni, a loyal supporter of Cavour, declared that the Pope could no longer be allowed to retain his temporal power and that Rome must now become the capital of Italy. In his reply Cavour rammed home this point, adding that the Government hoped 'to solve the Roman problem by convincing the more responsible section of the Catholic community that the reunion of Rome with Italy would be in no way prejudicial to the independence of the Church'. And he went on to quote part of the message which the Government intended to address to the Pope: 'Holy Father, for you the possession of temporal power is no longer a guarantee of independence. Renounce it, and we will give you that freedom which you have sought in vain for three centuries from all the great Catholic Powers. You have endeavoured to secure a part of this freedom by means of concordats, in consideration of which you, Holy Father, have been forced to concede privileges—nay, worse than that, you have been compelled to surrender your spiritual weapons—to those temporal Powers which have accorded you some small degree of freedom. But now we come to offer you in full measure something that you have never been able to obtain from those Powers which boasted that they were your allies and your devoted children. We are ready to proclaim throughout Italy this great principle: A Free Church in a Free State.' He then proceeded to remind his audience that the programme of the Government, of the political party in whose name he spoke, was 'to imbue all sections of society, both civil and religious, with the ideal of liberty. We desire economic liberty, we desire administrative liberty, we desire full and absolute liberty of conscience. We desire all the political liberties that are compatible with the maintenance of public order. And therefore, as a necessary consequence of this order of things, we deem it essential to the harmony of the edifice which we seek to raise that the principle of liberty should be applied to the relations between Church and State'.

Enemies of Cavour declared at the time, and more especially later on, that he had worked a clever parliamentary trick, that the expression 'a Free Church in a Free State' was one of those resounding but empty phrases which political parties often insert in their programmes, but that in the mind of the statesman it carried no precise significance. It seems certain that these allegations do not correspond to the truth. There can be little doubt that Cavour sincerely believed in the possibility of establishing a dual régime, calculated to benefit the Church as much as the State, and indeed that he believed such a system must surely prevail in the future. It is necessary to add, however, not only that he had to have a basic plan, if not a detailed programme, but that here too the politician, the man of action, he who was confronted with the task of solving day-to-day problems, took precedence both of the theorist and of the visionary, who, alike as an Italian and as a citizen of the world, had his eyes constantly fixed on a dim and distant future.

During the winter of 1860–61 Cavour secretly opened negotiations with the Roman Curia through the medium of two trusted liegemen, Father Carlo Passaglia and the Professor of Medicine in the University of Rome, Diomede Pantaleoni, who for his part was convinced that the Pope must be persuaded to renounce every particle of his temporal power, retaining only the trappings of sovereignty, together with absolute jurisdiction over the Church.

Both Passaglia and Pantaleoni had influential contacts in Rome, and both enjoyed the acquaintance or friendship of a number of cardinals (Pantaleoni was medical adviser to Cardinal Wiseman). Slowly and painfully the negotiations got under way. What Cavour offered was to all intents and purposes a Concordat: in return for the Pope's renunciation of his temporal power the State would renounce all its jurisdictional weapons. The Pope would retain all the outward and visible signs of sovereignty, and the administrative offices of the Church would enjoy a privileged position. In Italy no official recognition would be accorded to religious organizations, but the State would allocate property, both movable and immovable, for the maintenance of the episcopate, of ecclesiastical chapters and seminaries, and of those members of the clergy having the cure of souls. The number of the dioceses would be reduced to eighty, and bishops would be appointed by means of an electoral system to be decided upon at some time in the future, the State renouncing all rights in the matter, save that it would be entitled to exercise a veto in controversial cases.

The news of the conference spread to Paris, where it was received with suspicion and scepticism. It was also revealed to the Austrian ambassador by Cardinal Antonelli. Suddenly, however, the negotiations were broken off. On March 18th, 1861, Pius IX in his consistorial address reminded the assembled prelates of all the wrongs which the Church had suffered at the hands of the Piedmontese liberals, and declared that he could never permit 'the unjust aggressor to remain peacefully and honourably in possession of that which he had wrongfully seized'; for to do so would be to 'establish the false principle that wrong-doing is justified by success'. The Pope 'can in no wise consent to such a vandalic act of piracy without violating the basis of that moral discipline of which he is recognized to be, as it were, the prototype and exemplar'. The emissaries were accordingly obliged to leave Rome.

It is probable that in any event the negotiations would have had an unfavourable outcome. Pius IX would never willingly have assumed the enormous responsibility of renouncing his temporal power; while his mistrust of liberalism, of Piedmont, and even of Napoleon III, whom he regarded as a treacherous ally, would have made him even less inclined to take such a step. It must, however, be added that the veiled reproaches which the two emissaries, Pantaleoni and Father Passaglia, cast upon Cavour in their letters were not without justification. The actions of the Government, as well as of the governors of the annexed provinces, who abrogated the old concordats, extended Piedmont's anti-Catholic legislation, and seized numerous monasteries, could not but diminish still further the Holy See's already scant enthusiasm for an agreement.

Cavour, the great architect of Italian unity, died less than three

c

months after the proclamation of the Kingdom. Napoleon III, who had such a great regard for the Piedmontese minister, even though he was at times embarrassed by his policies, and who appreciated his greatness better than did King Victor Emmanuel,[1] generously availed himself of the opportunity to recognize the new Kingdom unconditionally. Nevertheless, in a letter to the King, written on July 12th, 1861, he declared that France could not evacuate Rome so long as the Holy See remained at odds with the Kingdom, and the Pope ran the risk of seeing what was left of his State invaded by regular or irregular forces.

Bibliographical Note.

The whole of the abundant literature of the Risorgimento and of the subsequent period—including all relevant dictionaries, repertories and reviews—is of interest to students of the relations between Church and State in Italy from about 1845 to the end of the nineteenth century.

The following two essays have a special bearing on our subject: F. Ruffini, *Lineamenti storici delle relazioni fra lo Stato e la Chiesa in Italia*, Turin, 1891, reprinted as an introduction to the Italian translation (ed. Ruffini, Turin, 1893) of E. Friedberg's *Trattato di diritto ecclesiastico cattolics ed evangelico* and A. Della Torre, *Il Cristianesimo in Italia dai filosofisti ai modernisti*, appended to the Italian translation (Milan, 1912; pp. 653–1077) of S. Reinach's *Orpheus, Storia generale delle religioni*. The last-named book has an excellent bibliography.

Among more recent works the following are particularly deserving of attention: L. Salvatorelli, *Il pensiero politico italiano dal 1700 al 1870*, 5th ed., Turin, 1949 (Chapter VI onwards); *id.*, *Pensiero ed azione del Risorgimento*, 3rd ed., Turin, 1951 (Chapters V–VII); E. Buonaiuti, *Storia del cristianesimo*, Vol. III, Milan, undated [1943].

An enormous number of books have been written on the Roman question, which occupies such an important place in the history of relations between Church and State in Italy, especially during the period 1861–1929. Particularly worthy of mention are: F. Scaduto, *Guarentige pontificie e relazioni fra Stato e Chiesa*, 2nd ed., Turin, 1889 (this book contains an ample bibliography); A. Piola, *La questione romana nella storia e nel diritto da Cavour al trattato del Laterano*, Padua, 1931; G. Mollat, *La Question romaine de Pie VI à Pie IX*, Paris, 1932; V. Del Giudice, *La questione romana e i rapporti fra Stato e Chiesa fino alla Conciliazione*, Rome [1948]; G. Quazza, *La questione romana nel 1848–49*, Modena, 1947; *La diplomazia del regno di Sardegna durante la prima guerra d'indipendenza*, II: *Relazioni con lo Stato Pontificio (marzo 1848–luglio 1849)*, ed. Carlo Baudi di Vesme, Turin, 1951 (Istituto per la Storia del Risorgimento, Comitato di Torino).

[1] The King had a kind of inferiority complex towards Cavour. The relationship between the two men was not unlike that which later existed between the German Emperor Wilhelm I and Bismarck.

The student of relations between Church and State in Italy during the last hundred years will find much useful material in the files of *La Civiltà Cattolica* (founded in 1850) and of the *Nuova Antologia* (founded in 1866).

Of special importance for their bearing on the period studied in this first chapter are the numerous books on Gioberti, among which mention must be made of A. Anzilotti, *Gioberti*, Florence, 1922 (reprinted, Florence, 1931); *id., La funzione storica del giobertismo*, Florence, 1924; *id., Dal neoguelfismo all 'idea liberale*, in *Nuova rivista storica*, I, 1917; A. Omodeo, *Vincenzo Gioberti e la sua evoluzione politica*, Turin, 1941. Among the many writings on Charles Albert the student should consult A. Omodeo, *La leggenda di Carlo Alberto nella recente storiografia*, Turin, 1940 (reprinted in *Difesa del Risorgimento*, Turin, 1951).

Also to be consulted are the *Discorsi parlamentari* of Camillo di Cavour, 11 volumes, Turin, 1863–72 (new edition, prepared by A. Omodeo and L. Russo, Florence, 1932 *sqq.*) and the *Scritti* of Mazzini, Imola, 1906 *sqq.* On Pius IX and his pontificate *v.* F. Hayward, *History of the Popes*, 1931, R. Aubert, *Le pontificat de Pie IX*, Saint-Didier, 1952.

For the history of this period *cf.* C. Spellanzon, *Storia del Risorgimento e dell 'unità d'Italia*, Milan, 1933 *sqq.*, Volumes II-V; L. Salvatorelli, *Prima e dopo il Quarantotto*, Turin, 1948.

CHAPTER II

THE YEARS OF STRESS 1861–78

(FROM THE PROCLAMATION OF THE KINGDOM OF ITALY TO THE
DEATHS OF PIUS IX AND VICTOR EMMANUEL II)

THE death of Cavour found the whole of Italy except
Venice and Rome united under a single flag. Although the
new Kingdom was not yet officially recognized by the
Great Powers, there was little danger that the latter would make
any attempt to meddle in its internal affairs. Relations with the
Holy See had been broken off, and there was no immediate
prospect of a reconciliation. The King, his ministers and the
members of the Italian Parliament were the object of ecclesiastical
reprobation—a circumstance which had the effect of disrupting
the religious life of the Catholics among them, who often found
themselves excluded from the sacraments and, unless they
retracted on their death-beds, denied the consolation of a religious
funeral. From 1849 onwards Rome was policed by a French
garrison as well as by the official Papal army. In the main the
city's population took the part of the Pope, but it was no more
than lukewarm in its allegiance. Its attitude in no way resembled
that of the Spaniards of 1808–12 or the Neapolitan mendicants of
1799, and certainly it was altogether opposed to any suggestion of
revolt. In the Papal States, now reduced to Rome and a few small
towns and large villages, together with the surrounding country
districts, which at that time were practically uninhabited,
Mazzinian and liberal elements flourished side by side; but, as a
number of incidents clearly demonstrated, the first-named were
too few in number to cause the Holy See any alarm, while the
liberals were moderate in their views and likewise gave the Papal
Government no grounds for anxiety. There was, however,
Garibaldi, with his great influence over the people; Garibaldi,
who with his volunteers had but lately accomplished the miraculous feat of conquering the Kingdom of Naples; Garibaldi, whose
men were fretting at their enforced idleness and thirsting for new

adventures; Garibaldi, over whom the King alone exerted any influence, and that not always sufficient to hold him in check.

An armed attempt by Garibaldi on Rome, followed by the city's occupation, would have entailed a clash with the French garrison. As a result, everything—the question of the annexed territories, the question of Italian unity—might have been thrown once more into the melting-pot. Only a politician possessed of extreme daring and extreme confidence in his country's destiny could have believed that such an adventure would culminate in the peaceful withdrawal of the French and the incorporation of Rome in the Kingdom. Nevertheless, in 1862 Garibaldi mustered an army of volunteers and set out from Calabria to make the attempt; but the Government had the courage to stop him at once and to forbid him to approach the Eternal City. In the event, there was a brief armed clash, in the course of which Garibaldi was slightly wounded. The Government inflicted severe punishments on those members of the regular army who had deserted in order to enlist in the general's forces.

Napoleon III wanted to reconcile the irreconcilable—namely the Pope, French public opinion, and Italy—to ensure the maintenance of the Pope's sovereignty, and to respect the principle of non-intervention. In 1862 he announced his plan for an agreement. The existing Papal territory would be slightly enlarged, but it would be governed on a municipal basis and would send deputies to the Italian Chamber, while the Pope would appoint a certain number of senators. The Holy See and the Kingdom would pool their financial resources and would have a common army. A customs union would be established. After some difficulty the French ministers succeeded in persuading the Emperor that his plan did not provide a basis for serious negotiations.

Far more realistic was an idea—originally formulated by Thouvenel—which had been the subject of discussion during the last days of Cavour. This provided for a withdrawal of the French garrison from Rome in return for an undertaking on the part of the Kingdom to prevent any attack on what was left of the Papal States. The plan formed the basis of the 'September Convention' of 1864, approved by the Minghetti Government in which Emilio Visconti Venosta filled the role of Foreign Minister. Under the terms of the agreement Italy would undertake not to attack the Papal States and to use force if necessary to prevent any third party from launching an attack upon them from her territory. France would gradually withdraw her troops. The Papal States would raise an army, in which they would be permitted to enrol foreign volunteers.[1] But the most unpalatable clause in the whole agreement was reserved for the protocol. It provided that the convention would only come into force after the King had arranged for the capital to be transferred from Turin to another city.

Why was this clause inserted? According to the Left, represented by the Piedmontese, who were distressed at the thought of losing the capital, its inclusion signified that the Government had accepted the thesis first propounded in 1861 by Massimo d'Azeglio that the place best suited to become the capital of Italy was not Rome but Florence. The Government denied the accusation; but it is difficult to believe that, on the French side at least, the clause was not intended to pave the way for such a development.

In Turin the announcement that the convention had been signed provoked grave disorders—in the course of which many people lost their lives—as well as numerous demonstrations of hostility to the House of Savoy.

The capital was in fact transferred to Florence and the new Kingdom, in spite of many internal difficulties, gradually established itself on a firm basis. Legislation proceeded along liberal lines. The new civil code of laws, promulgated in 1865, provided for the secularization of marriage. Church marriages, though not subjected to any oppressive regulations (unlike other countries, Italy never insisted that civil marriages should take precedence of religious ones), were not officially recognized by the State. The suppression of religious bodies became general, not to say universal. Religious remained free to form communities and to take vows, though many of the most ancient monasteries and convents were taken over by the State. Numerous other ecclesiastical organizations were suppressed. Those that survived, with the exception of the various parishes, were not allowed to retain any immovable property other than their actual headquarters. Everything else had to be sold and the proceeds invested in Government securities. Members of the clergy were no longer exempted from military service, and the army ceased to employ chaplains.

---

[1] In the event the volunteers—comprising Frenchmen, Belgians, Irishmen and Spaniards—became known as the Papal Zouaves. The Frenchmen among them formed the nucleus of La Charette's corps of Zouaves which fought in the Franco-Prussian war of 1870–71.

Naturally, these measures were vigorously opposed by Catholics, who felt that they were being excluded from the life of the new State. For several years champions of the old order continued to raise their voices—men who hoped for the disruption of Italian unity and for the return of the King of the Two Sicilies, the Grand Duke of Tuscany, and the Dukes of Parma and Modena. These were outnumbered by men of more modest ambitions who would have been content with a fundamental reorientation of Italian policy, a limited desecularization of the State, and the repeal of anti-Catholic legislation. But circumstances were no longer the same as in the years prior to 1859. Then, it had been possible to think in terms of a concordat. Now, this was ruled out by the Pope's refusal to recognize the new Kingdom on the ground that its Sovereign had no legal standing except in his traditional domains and in Lombardy, which had been ceded to him by formal treaty.[1]

The attitude of the Holy See had likewise been steadily hardening. In his address *Maxima quidem laetitia* of June 9th, 1862, the Pope declared that he could not be free unless he exercised temporal power. The encyclical *Quanta cura* of December 8th, 1864 (the so-called *Syllabus*), condemned all the errors of liberalism, denounced freedom of worship, and insisted on ecclesiastical immunity and privilege, the *potestas directa vel indirecta* of the Pope, and the Church's right to supervise State education and to administer the sacrament of marriage.

Thereafter Pius IX constantly proclaimed the rights of the Church. He sincerely believed that it was not his duty to compromise or to exercise tolerance. The publication of the *Syllabus* was followed by the episode of the boy Mortara, a child of Jewish birth living in the Papal territory who, following a servant-girl's disclosure that she had baptized him, was taken away from his parents and brought up in the Catholic faith. The Vatican Council of 1869–70 proclaimed the doctrine of the infallibility of the Pope. All these things, in varying degrees, were symptomatic of the attitude of the Papacy, and they increased the reluctance of Catholic constitutional governments and of moderates to work for an understanding with the Holy See. In Austria the proclama-

---

[1] In the same way, the Pope acknowledged the King's jurisdiction over Venetia following the signature of the Treaty of Prague (1866).

tion of the doctrine of Papal infallibility led to the denunciation of the Concordat of 1855.

If the truly fundamental, as distinct from the ephemeral, problems of the age were those which had to do with relations between Church and State, and still more with relations between Catholicism and freedom, the general public in Italy, and perhaps in Europe as a whole, continued to concentrate the bulk of their attention on the Roman question.

In 1867 the Government was weak enough to allow a brigade of Garibaldini to penetrate into the Papal States. Its entry coincided with a series of fruitless attempts on the part of some Roman Republicans to stir up revolution. A French division was hurriedly dispatched by sea to the Papal States and the Garibaldini were defeated at Monterotondo and Mentana. The effects of the September Convention had been nullified: Rome once more had a French garrison. The Papal Government proceeded with all the rigour of the law against the ringleaders of the conspiracy, and two of the revolutionaries, Monti and Tognetti, ended their days on the scaffold.

The years that followed were extremely difficult for the Italian Government. The parties of the Left—which ought to have felt morally responsible for the return to Rome of the French garrison —were incensed with the Government of moderate liberals which now held office, and they demanded that stern measures be taken against Church and clergy. During this period passions rose to fever-heat.

In 1870 the Franco-Prussian war broke out. The Italian ministers restrained the King from taking the field at the side of Napoleon III, pointing out to him how unpopular Italy's great benefactor, who was also one of the chief architects of her unity, had become after Mentana and Monterotondo in the eyes of large numbers of Italians (nor was he on that account any more beloved by the Catholic masses). The French Government was obliged to recall the division that was garrisoning the Papal States. On this occasion the Italian Government, at France's request, declared that it still regarded the Convention of September, 1864, as valid. But when, on September 4th, 1870, the Empire collapsed, it felt, not without reason, that it was no longer bound by the agreement. In point of fact, not only had

Napoleon III's rule been largely personal in character, but in all matters pertaining to Italy the Emperor had acted against the convictions of his people, and almost always against those of his ministers. He had been spurred on by the memories of his youth, by his humanitarian principles, and by his natural sympathy with the ideals of liberalism. But even now the Romans did not rise; accordingly, the occupation of their city could only be justified if it were the result of spontaneous and irresistible pressure from large sections of public opinion. In fact, the entire Left Wing, and a not inconsiderable portion of the moderate Right, would have regarded it as an unpardonable crime for their leaders to neglect this unique opportunity, which would never occur again.

And so, after the King had dispatched yet another message to Pius IX asking him to consent to the city's occupation, the deed was accomplished by force. The Pope offered only a token resistance, but some dozens of men lost their lives before the fighting came to an end.

The instructions given to the general commanding the expedition were to leave the Pope with a fragment of his territory and to refrain from occupying the Vatican. After the Papal forces had been disarmed, however, Cardinal Antonelli, under the pretext that public security would be threatened if the zone in question were left unguarded, appealed to the general to occupy it. In this he was, perhaps, merely conforming to that 'policy of despair' which had so often inspired his actions—in other words, he probably felt that the worse the Pope's position could be made to appear, the more reason would there be to hope for intervention on the part of the Catholic Powers. However that may be, the general acceded to his request.

Pius IX's domain was now restricted to the apostolic palaces, from which he was never again to emerge.

The abolition of the temporal power, with which was associated the idea of granting the Church absolute freedom in its own sphere, had been duly brought about; and it remained for Italy to solve—as she was to succeed in doing—the new problem, now posed for the first time, of demonstrating to the Catholic world at large that the Pope could rule the Church without interference and without any loss of prestige, even though he no longer possessed any territorial sovereignty.

So much for the bare facts of history. In the present context, however, events would seem to be of less immediate interest than ideas. During the years 1850–75, and more especially in the years between the unification of the Kingdom and the passing of the Law of Guarantees, which established the legal position of the Holy See as it was to remain until the signature of the Lateran Treaty in 1929, Italy was a veritable workshop of ideas bearing upon the relations between religion and politics, between Catholicism and freedom, between Church and State—a work-shop in which methods were evolved for the improvement of relations between the two powers. During this period the liberal idea, the concept of liberty as something intrinsically good which is universal in its application and which refreshes and invigorates everything it touches, inspired a new scheme for the internal reform of the Church. This scheme, though it represented the logical conclusion of a process begun long years before, was nevertheless quite original. Certainly it owed nothing either to French Jansenism or to that other philosophy from which, a little later, the 'old Catholics' of Germany were to derive their inspiration.

One feels that Italian thought and Italian propaganda play a singularly important part in the whole question, and that they must needs be accorded a prominent place in any history of nineteenth-century European culture.

Cavour's successor as head of the Italian Government was Bettino Ricasoli, a member of a great Tuscan family. Thus the responsibilities of government were assumed by one who personi-fied the finest traditions of the intellectual aristocracy, of a ruling class which thought of power in terms of duty and responsibility to God and Man. Ricasoli was a worthy exponent of that trend of thought, that concern for cultural values, that supreme regard for intellect which Tuscany—homeland of Dante and cradle of the Renaissance in the fields of art, letters and, remembering Galileo, science—had encouraged for centuries.

He was, moreover, a Catholic, although, some years before, he had for a brief moment inclined towards Protestantism. But he was typical, as Gentile put it, of 'those liberal Catholics who adhere not, indeed, to the Catholic Church as it is, but to the Catholic Church as it ought to be; seeking a faith that stands for complete spiritual freedom and at the same time for social order, albeit not of the kind that, through the State, disciplines and regiments individual men with a severity which is a limit imposed by freedom on itself; and therefore tending to waver between the ideas of separation and unity, alike in what is termed social and practical life and in the life of the spirit, which is regarded as individual and wholly interior'.[1]

With the advent of Ricasoli Italian politics became concerned not only with the freedom *of* the Church, but with freedom *in* the Church. The new Prime Minister's great desire was to see the administration of ecclesiastical property and, if possible, the appointment of bishops and parish priests entrusted to religious communities.   1182049

There was never the remotest likelihood that this project would come to fruition—a statement that applies equally to the bill which Ricasoli's second Government presented to the Chamber in January, 1867, under the title 'Freedom of the Church'. In effect, this bill envisaged the complete realization of the separatist programme. It provided for the ending of State control of the Church and of State participation in the appointment of clergy, as well as for the abolition of ecclesiastical privilege and immunity. It stipulated that the Church should be governed exclusively by canon law. The Church would not, however, be allowed to own immovable property; and it would therefore have to sell all its inherited estates, handing over the proceeds to its bishops, whose duty it would be to distribute them among the ecclesiastical organizations of their dioceses.

Ricasoli's ideas were elaborated at meetings of a small discussion-group, the moving spirit of which was his friend Raffaelle Lambruschini, a nephew of Pius VII's secretary, who had himself been banished to Corsica during the last two years of the Napoleonic Empire. Lambruschini and his friends and correspondents, among them Ricasoli, were for many years diligent students of every aspect of Christianity. In many of their ideas they anticipated by more than half a century the pioneers of modernism. Among other things, they desired radical alterations in the constitution of the Church—alterations which, if Lambruschini had had his way, would even have included the abolition of the rule whereby the clergy were forbidden to marry and the

---

[1] G. Gentile, *Gino Capponi e la cultura toscana nel secolo decimonono*, 2nd ed., Florence, 1926 (pp. 102–112).

adoption of the vernacular as the language of religious services.

Once having come to power, Ricasoli wavered between the idea that the State should passively await the reform of the Church, which he regarded as inevitable, and the idea that it should, rather, take the lead in promoting it. Nevertheless, he was convinced that the State ought not to compromise what he and his circle regarded as the rights of the Faithful, by recognizing the Pope as sole representative of the Church in any future negotiations. The State 'should have but one object: to restore to its citizens their religious liberties, in other words the right to administer the temporal inheritance of the Church. Inasmuch as the people have a controlling interest in all affairs of a municipal or national character, it is only reasonable that they should once again enjoy this privilege.' The State should restore 'to Catholic communities' 'those rights of which in the unhappy days of despotism and barbarism they were wrongfully deprived ... freedom to administer their religious inheritance' and 'freedom to elect their bishops.'[1]

What seemed impossible to Ricasoli and his circle was that the structure of the Church could remain unaltered, that, in fact, the process of centralization and the tightening-up of discipline could continue and be intensified without fatal results to the Church and to religion.

At a distance of a hundred years, and in the light of subsequent events, it is difficult for us to understand how a man of such genuine talents could so have deluded himself as to put reforms of ecclesiastical legislation, which other Catholic States had carried out and which were in no way utopian in character, on the same plane as the idea of a civil constitution of the clergy such as had eluded even the great reforming zeal of the men of the French Revolution. Catholics would never have consented to become, in defiance of the Pope, the administrators of ecclesiastical property and the electors of their priests. Ricasoli's sense of impending religious revolution was wholly illusory; the problem of how political leaders should comport themselves when such a revolution began did not exist.

And yet we should not judge Ricasoli by the yardstick of our own experience. Such ideas as the election of bishops and priests by clergy and people and that ecclesiastical property should be

[1] B. Ricasoli, *Lettere e documenti*, Florence, 1887–95 (vol. vii, pp. 260 *sqq.*, 303 *sqq.*).

administered by a duly elected body of laymen were common
enough between about 1830 and 1880. Even Rosmini accepted
them.

Moreover, too many people, fundamentally hostile to the idea
of abandoning the old jurisdictional weapons, yet afraid to defy
the *idola fori* and to proclaim their opposition to the idea of
separation and to the emancipation of the Church, liked to escape
from their dilemma by advancing some such argument as follows:
'Freedom for the Church, by all means—so long as the Pope is
not left free to oppress the bishops, or the bishops to oppress the
Faithful. Freedom for a regenerate, democratic Church in which
all power is vested in the rank and file. Until the religious revolution has been accomplished let the State continue to guard that
which was entrusted to it by the Faithful many centuries ago and
not allow the Pope to usurp it.'

Ricasoli certainly did not subscribe to these opinions. Always
the sincerest of men, he had the special virtue of being sincere
with himself. But as a political thinker he was inclined to hesitate
between action and temporization; between accepting the Church
as it was and aspiring to that ideal, original Church which all
reformers end by taking as their model; between recognizing
freedom as the Church's right and regarding it as a generous
concession on the part of the State; between denying the State all
authority over the 'true Church' and maintaining that it was for
the State alone to judge which ecclesiastical organizations should
be preserved and which suppressed, to decide what property the
surviving organizations might retain, and to ensure a fair distribution of incomes among the clergy.

Ricasoli is the most significant figure of the period. He embodies
the aspirations and the fundamental contradictions which
characterize the whole of Italy's ecclesiastical policy between
1855 and 1870.

There are, however, other names worthy of mention. Among
these is the name of Marco Minghetti.

Minghetti was a devout Catholic, a man of great moderation
and a profound realist. His outlook was very similar to Cavour's,
even to the extent that he regarded the Roman question and the
question of the Church's freedom as inseparable.

He was a sincere advocate of the Church's emancipation. To

the arguments of the jurisdictionalist deputy Mancini he retorted: 'I have defended the freedom of the Church just as I have defended administrative freedom, educational freedom, freedom of trade and, in fact, all freedoms, because, in my opinion, they are all interrelated and interdependent, because each helps to sustain the others, and because I believe that freedom is the rock on which every strong and conservative Government is founded.'[1] The State is neither atheistic nor secular; 'it is without competence in religious matters. The Church is a free organization existing within the State, and it should not be subject to any restrictions that do not apply to other organizations. The rights of the Church are not prescriptive in character; they are compounded of the individual rights of all its members.' It is not true that the State and the Church are 'equal and parallel powers which accept mutual limitations and make mutual concessions . . . there is not, and there cannot be, more than one true authority, in the legislative and coercive sense of a power to impose laws by force—in a word, of *imperium*; and this authority belongs to the State. . . . If we think of the State as possessing only juridical authority the concept of separation becomes perfectly intelligible. With its powers so restricted, the State is bound to recognize the rights of the individual and the principle of freedom of association, and moreover it is seen to be entirely without competence in religious matters. . . . The State does not create rights. It recognizes them, upholding the principle of equal justice for all.'[2]

Understanding the Italian people as he did, Minghetti knew that it was useless to think of internal reforms or to hope that the Faithful would claim the right to elect their bishops. He knew too, that Italians would oppose any form of sectarianism prejudicial to the Church as well as any extension of secularism, such as the exclusion of the clergy from participation in civic functions. He advocated the retention of Article I of the Statute, which proclaimed the Catholic religion as the religion of the State, observing that the accepted interpretation of that article in no way conflicted with the principle of religious freedom.[3]

[1] Speeches of January 24th and 30th, 1871, in M. Minghetti, *Discorsi parlamentari*, Rome, 1888–90 (vol. v, pp. 140, 145 *sqq.*).

[2] Parliamentary speeches of March 11th, 1871, and May 8th, 1873, op. cit., vol. v, pp. 161, 301 *sqq.*

[3] Parliamentary speeches of January 2nd and March 11th, 1871, and May 7th, 1875, op. cit., vol. v, pp. 141, 148–160; vol. vi, pp. 559 *sqq.*

In his book *Stato e Chiesa* Minghetti, himself a practising Christian, affirms his belief in the possibility of establishing a purely secular code of morality and justice. He reiterates the argument that the State has no competence in religious matters since divine revelation 'lies outside the sphere of earthly things and transcends the natural and the rational'. It follows that, although the State is responsible for public education, it cannot be allowed to provide religious instruction; moreover, it must exclude from its teaching anything that might encourage unbelief or a contempt for religion. In his eagerness to see the Church accorded true freedom he even urges that religious organizations be legalized and given the right to own property, subject to certain conditions which would have to be embodied in a new and comprehensive law.

He looks at the Italy of his day and finds that the moral standards of the clergy have improved, but that their culture is mediocre. He decides that the Italian genius 'was never ascetic or mystical; but certainly in the present century the religious sentiment is almost non-existent'. Among the Catholic masses 'habit counts for more than faith. The latter has little influence on thought, and even less on action'.[1]

Carlo Boncompagni, several times a minister, President of the Chamber, and in 1859 Governor General of Central Italy, invariably drew his inspiration from the memory and teaching of Cavour.

He too saw the emancipation of the Church as part of a larger settlement. 'I want the Church to be free, just as I want all other dissident communions to be free. I want Catholics to be free, and unbelievers too. I want the Church to be free, just as I want the State to be free, just as I want the parish to be free, and the school, and industry—in fact, everything that represents a great interest or a great principle.'

Vigorously opposed to any extension of Cavour's legislation, he defends the Church's right to own property voluntarily assigned to it by the Faithful. He believes that after the Pope has lost his temporal power he will be unable to find any worldly support except 'among the Catholic laity, to which nearly all Italian liberals belong'. He may then become reconciled to modern

[1] M. Minghetti, *Stato e Chiesa*, 2nd ed., Milan, 1878.

civilization and to the march of progress, and may even approve the election of bishops by clergy and people and the granting of wide powers to the provincial Councils. But the State cannot make changes in the Church's constitution. In temporal matters the Anglican Church is guilty of abuses no less shocking than those perpetrated by Italians. Yet the British Government 'knows that interference in the affairs of a Church that is and should be independent is a greater evil than the toleration of the gravest abuses'. The question of reforming the administration of Church property should be left over for discussion at some future date.

Like Cavour, Boncompagni considers that the Roman question is intimately connected with the direction of Italy's ecclesiastical policy. So long as the temporal power survives, it will be impossible to apply in its widest sense the principle of 'a Free Church in a Free State'.

Looking to the future, he utters these prophetic words: 'All those Catholic peoples that entered the paths of liberty came into conflict with the Pope. Then, after they had achieved their ends, they made peace with him. One day Italy will be forced to do the same. But an observation is necessary: these reconciliations were brought about neither by the same men nor by the same parties as had provoked the original conflict. In most cases, during the time that elapsed between the break and the reconciliation a sort of reaction set in, as a result of which power fell into the hands of men with a less jealous regard for freedom. I too am certain that a reconciliation between Italy and the Church will take place. I am anxious that it should be brought about by men who are not prepared to abandon any of the principles of freedom.'[1]

This last hope was not destined to be realized.

Pasquale Stanislao Mancini, known to historians of international law as a champion of the nationalist principle, was an heir to the jurisdictional tradition of Naples, where he had in 1861 been Councillor of the Lieutenancy for Ecclesiastical Affairs.

Mancini sought to reconcile a sturdy traditionalism with a sincere desire for the political unification of the Kingdom with the rest of Italy. A brilliant jurist and a great parliamentary orator, he was politically a member of the Left. He, too, approved

[1] C. Bon-Compagni, *La Chiesa e lo Stato in Italia*, Florence, 1866 (especially pp. 128 *sqq.*, 148 *sqq.*, 289 *sqq.*, 458–462).

of the emancipation of the Church, with the proviso that the Church's freedom should be 'compounded of the individual liberties of believers in the field of religious doctrine'. He advocated the 'independence of all communions in matters of faith' and affirmed 'the incompetence of the State to interfere in the spiritual life of the community, saving always its right to maintain public order in accordance with the guarantees and safeguards of common law'.[1] No restrictions should be placed upon the freedom of the Faithful and of the clergy to believe in and to practise their religion; but religious societies, like all other societies, should be subject to the authority of the State. Moreover, the official recognition of such societies should be regarded as a concession, liable to be withdrawn if the public interest so demanded.

A free Church would still be subject to common law. Its emancipation would not place it in a privileged position entitling it to create official organizations of its own with substantial rights of possession. Nor would senior members of the hierarchy be able to oppress their inferiors in the knowledge that the latter could not turn to the State for protection.[2]

But Mancini lacks the contempt for the old jurisdictional weapons which characterizes the disciples of Cavour. Bishops are not ordinary citizens, and the Government is undoubtedly entitled to prevent them from abandoning their sees.[3] It is fitting that the State should have the right to appoint bishops. There is justice, too, in the *Exequatur* and the *Placet*. Certainly the Pope should be allowed to publish his edicts; but the *Exequatur* serves 'to invalidate any papal ordinances that encroach upon or violate the rights of the civil authority, and to make it impossible for them to be carried into effect'.[4]

In the debate on the Law of Guarantees which followed the capture of Rome, Mancini insisted that the law in question should be purely domestic in character, that it should not be the subject of international negotiations, and that the Pope should be made to understand clearly that even though he had been the object of

---

[1] Parliamentary speech of December 8th, 1861, in P. S. Mancini, *Discorsi parlamentari*, Rome, 1893–97 (vol. i, pp. 26–30).

[2] Speeches of January 28th, 1871, and July 11th, 1867, ibid., vol. iii, pp. 460–463, and vol. ii, pp. 497–501.

[3] Speech of March 15th, 1862, ibid., vol. i, pp. 126 *sqq.*

[4] speeches of May 13th, 1871, July 11th, 1867, March 16th, 1871, ibid., vol. iii, pp. 643–659; vol. ii, pp. 548–557; vol. iii, pp. 666–670.

D

manifestations of obedience and respect, nothing now remained to him of his former sovereignty. Mancini considered that it would be dangerous to declare the Pope legally irresponsible, the more so as, unlike the King, he had no responsible ministers to whom he could turn for advice. He was opposed to the suggestion that the State should renounce the majority of its old jurisdictional powers—a measure which the Right would have liked to see adopted then and there.

Mancini it was who uttered the Ghibelline *cri de cœur*: 'Throughout the ages the national spirit of Italy has been instinctively anti-papal and anti-clerical. . . . This is the immortal spirit which our greatest minds, the trustees of Italic civilization, have handed down from one to another since the beginning of our era.'

Ever a jealous guardian of Left-Wing interests, Mancini sponsored a bill designed to put an end to the abuses perpetrated by ministers of religion. In the course of his speech he declared that the Church should be held to account for its invasion of the political field—an act prejudicial and injurious to the State's laws and customs, its political structure, and its free institutions.

Quintino Sella was a Piedmontese and a man of the Right. A mineralogist by profession, he had wide interests which extended to every branch of culture. He attained special fame as Minister of Finance, as the man who restored the nation's economy—a task which he selected for himself because his moral sense told him that even States should accept responsibility for their debts, while his political sense warned him that the State which becomes involved in financial difficulties cannot but have a bankrupt policy, both at home and abroad.

He was a theist rather than a Catholic, but he believed in the indestructibility of religion. If he accepted Cavour's formula 'a Free Church in a Free State' he, like Boncompagni and Mancini, saw in it above all a guarantee of freedom of thought and conscience, for organized communities as for individuals. Basically he was not far removed in outlook from Mancini, and like him he insisted strongly on the rights of the State. He was, however, a moderate, who sought to justify the poverty of the secular clergy and condemned all manifestations of Jacobin extremism.

In August, 1870, he acted as intermediary between the Left Wing and the Government in an attempt to persuade the latter to occupy Rome. In fact, he was anxious for the capital to be moved without delay. He wanted Rome to be a cultural metropolis, a renowned centre of free discussion.

A man who enjoyed great prestige during the years in which Florence was the capital of Italy was Francesco Crispi, the Sicilian exile of 1849 and legal adviser to Garibaldi during the expedition of the 'Thousand'. Faced at that time with the necessity of choosing between Mazzini and Garibaldi he decided in favour of the General, inventor of the formula 'Italy and Victor Emmanuel'.

Crispi expressed himself in extremely caustic terms on the subject of Catholicism. In fact, he did not believe in the possibility of a reconciliation between Church and State; but at the same time he was one of the few men who felt that a mistake had been made in attaching so much importance to the Roman question. However, it was too late to reverse this policy now, and one could only hope that the Romans would stage a revolution.

Crispi was a convinced jurisdictionalist: during his exile in Malta he had even written approvingly of the British Crown's domination of the Anglican Church. He believed that the State was justified in exercising the most rigorous control over the organized Church—this, he emphasized, was not the same thing as faith and worship, which should be completely unrestricted— and he defended the authority of temporal rulers with uncompromising vigour. The Church's inheritance had originated as a reward given to the Church by States and private individuals for its work of educating the people, administering what was later to become the civil State, and dispensing justice. Now that the State had resumed these functions the Church's inheritance should revert to the laity.

In the debate on the Law of Guarantees Crispi, like Mancini, opposed the idea of granting the Pope an immunity which would extend to his conduct outside the immediate sphere of his ecclesiastical ministry. He also opposed the clause in the bill which provided for the State's renunciation of certain of its jurisdictional powers.

In 1850–52 Rosmini had as his guest at Stresa a young exile from southern Italy named Ruggero Bonghi. As a result of his contacts with Rosmini, Manzoni and Gustavo di Cavour, Bonghi without actually accepting Catholic doctrine, did acquire a religious sense, a conviction of the importance of the religious phenomenon.

For all his versatility—he was a prolific writer and journalist as well as a deputy and minister—Bonghi lacked a strong personality, and just as he never succeeded during the course of a fairly long life in arriving at any definite conclusions, positive or negative, on the subject of religion, so too he never pursued a consistent line in the matter of ecclesiastical policy. And yet he must be mentioned as a disseminator of ideas who, though the seeds he sowed were of widely differing kinds, could claim credit for the fact that the Italian liberal bourgeoisie of the period following the Risorgimento did not tacitly accept the conventional view that religion was steadily declining in importance, that faith would be ousted by science, and that the school would take the place of the Church.

He too succumbed to the common illusion (to which Ricasoli had fallen victim some years before) when he expressed the belief that Italy might one day become the battle-ground of a movement analogous to that initiated by the 'old Catholics' of Germany—a movement calculated to give currency to 'the view that Roman Catholicism should be judged by the same criterion, at once liberal and conservative, in other words that it should be discussed in the light of the rules which guide the Pope and the Curia and subjected to reforms not dissimilar to those which are now being attempted in Germany'; and again when he expressed his confidence that, under pressure from the Faithful and the clergy, the Church would ultimately consent to the appointment of bishops by clergy and people without State intervention.

He was more successful when he came to define the essentials of a moderate policy towards the Church. The Government, he declared, should not seek to achieve a reconciliation of ideas, for the ideas of the two societies, ecclesiastical and civil, were irreconcilable. Instead, it should pursue a policy of justice. Such a policy would have the effect of detaching large numbers of Catholics from the extreme clerical party, which was inciting them to rebel, and of bringing them closer to the Government.

His most conspicuous achievement as a politician was the new draft, which he prepared in his capacity as chairman of the specially constituted parliamentary committee, of the text of the Law of Guarantees. This embodied a compromise between the Government's aim, which was to give the fullest independence to the Pope and to grant the Church the maximum amount of freedom, and the aim of the Left Wing, which sought to make the Pope a true citizen of Italy and to preserve intact the State's jurisdictional powers.

As a parliamentarian he insisted, without success, that the State, which had adopted a liberal policy towards the Church to the extent of allowing it to run schools for the children of the laity in competition with Government-controlled schools, should not, on the other hand, cease to interest itself in the teaching of the seminaries. Above all, it should not abolish the theological faculties in the State universities, but should rather encourage the clergy to attend them, making a degree in theology an essential qualification for certain ecclesiastical offices. It seemed to him that this would be to create a window through which the clergy could look out on the world of modern culture.

As to the question of religious organizations, he favoured the suppression of those which depended for their survival on charity, for they comprised uncultivated elements, and, moreover, they enjoyed a great ascendancy over the people. He would, however, have made an exception in the case of those which concerned themselves with education, philanthropic activities, and missions abroad.[1]

If the project of 'Freedom for the Church', regarded as a renunciation on the part of the State of all the means of repression and control with which the law provided it, had always been effectively resisted by liberal opinion, it was not until about 1870 that it met with open opposition from men who believed that the State ought to retain its jurisdictional powers, at the same time revising and bringing up to date the instruments which positive law placed at its disposal. In virtue of their new proposals these men came to be known as neo-jurisdictionalists.

The most conspicuous among them was Giuseppe Piola, a deputy and senator, a sincere Catholic, and author of *La libertà della Chiesa* (Milan, 1874).

---

[1] Cf. the essay *Chiesa e Stato in Germania* (1871), in R. Bonghi, *Ritratti e studi di vita religiosa*, Florence, 1937; and parliamentary speech of March 14th, 1871, in R. Bonghi, *Stato e Chiesa*, ed. W. Maturi, Milan, 1942 (vol. i, pp. 233 *sqq.*).

The thesis propounded in this work is that the case for separation rests on the false assumption that the Church is a *private*
institution, whereas it is by its very nature a *social* institution and
as such should be subject to civil law. It is therefore only just that
the State should have a say in the appointment of beneficiaries,
inasmuch as the latter fulfil a function which is eminently
propagandist in character; that it should supervise meetings of
Church councils, just as it orders and supervises those of communal councils; and that it should subject new regulations drawn
up by the Church to a form of censorship (*exequatur*). The ecclesiastic is fully entitled to appeal from the spiritual to the temporal
authority, whether his action means that the civil application of
the penalty inflicted on him by his superiors will be suspended
until the State has recognized the legality of the disciplinary
procedure, or that decisions of the ecclesiastical authority will be
declared null and void in the temporal sphere because they
infringe State laws or ecclesiastical laws which the State has
already recognized as valid. The State has a right of inspection
embracing all types of educational establishment, seminaries
included. In Government-controlled schools it is necessary to
distinguish between the teaching of natural religion (i.e. of
principles common to all creeds) and the teaching of specific
religious dogmas. The first should be included in the curriculum
(for this reason Piola would like to see atheists and even simple
deists debarred from teaching), but the second should be omitted.
Unlike Bonghi, Piola considers that theology should not be taught
by the State.

He would not deprive the Church of its right to own property,
but he would force it to abolish the mediaeval type of benefice.

A neo-jurisdictionalist of quite a different stamp, and a resolute
anti-clerical to boot, was Guido Padelletti. A professor in the
University of Rome, he, like many dons of his own and the
succeeding generation, was an enthusiastic admirer of post-1870
Germany—the Germany of the *Maigesetze*.

He too maintained that the cardinal error of the separatists was
their failure to appreciate that religion is not simply a personal
matter, but that it has a vital bearing on the external life of a
nation. The belief that freedom is a spear of Peleus which first
wounds, then heals, is a liberal prejudice; the example of Belgium

shows how easily the emancipation of the Church can lead to the domination of the State by the clergy. He defends the right of appeal from the spiritual to the temporal authority. Not without reason, he observes that it is easier to persuade the Church to continue to obey the time-honoured laws of the State than to make it accept innovations. He accordingly believes that it is useless to think of entrusting the task of electing bishops and parish priests to the Catholic laity, nor does he see any real reason for abolishing the benefice, which still constitutes a by no means negligible bond of union between the secular clergy and the State. Like Bonghi, he believes that the suppression of theological faculties would be a mistake. He maintains that the clergy have a legal status of their own which, while entitling them to special protection, also justifies the adoption of special repressive regulations and sanctions.

If Padelletti took as his political ideal the Germany of the years around 1873, other university professors of the period were dominated by the influence of Hegel, which was particularly strong in the University of Naples.

A notable philosopher of the time was Bertrando Spaventa. Connected by ties of blood with the *élite* of Neapolitan liberalism, he was originally intended for the priesthood. He was no at separatist. 'The Church', he wrote 'has never even considered the possibility of separation. In this, I feel, it has not only safeguarded its own interests but has probed and discerned rather more successfully than a number of statesmen the essence of the modern State. . . . It believes that godliness is its prerogative, that it alone possesses it and can dispense it, and that the State should receive it from its hands. In this it is mistaken. On the other hand, the State itself has a false and muddled conception of godliness, the true nature of which it completely fails to appreciate. In the State's eyes godliness is not the spirit of human society—the universal ethical force—but rather an external and spontaneous element in the service of something higher than itself. Yet its deep sense of the divine, which has not yet developed into a distinct consciousness of its infinity, lies at the root of its new struggle with the Church.'[1]

As early as 1851 Spaventa, writing in a Piedmontese periodical,

[1] B. Spaventa, *Saggi di critica filosofica, politica e religiosa*, Naples, 1867 (pp. 222–227).

had defended the privileged position of the State school and had contradicted those who maintained that the Church should be accorded a wide measure of freedom in the sphere of education.

In 1871 another disciple of Hegel, the Neapolitan Augusto Vera, published a book now, like its author, quite forgotten. The work, which evoked a mention from Treitschke and was destined to have a considerable circulation, is based entirely on the Hegelian philosophy and is animated by the writer's scarcely veiled contempt for Cavour. Vera begins by extolling the Germanic races—which know that religion is the foundation of the State and that a political revolution is only possible if it is accompanied by a religious revolution—at the expense of the Latin races, which, because they cannot aspire to spiritual unity, believe exactly the opposite. The separation of Church and State is bound to destroy the unity both of the individual spirit and of the national spirit. Again, just as the Germanic races are superior to the Latin, so Protestantism is superior to Catholicism. The Catholic's thinking is done for him by the Pope; the much-vaunted unity of Catholics is purely disciplinary and external. On the other hand, the faith that finds expression in Protestant unity is a true faith, because it is a faith of the spirit.

A complete separation of Church and State would make conciliation and freedom impossible. The peace implicit in Cavour's formula is the peace of the tomb; as well might he have said 'a free soul in a free body'. In fact, conciliation can exist only in the midst of conflict; freedom thrives on struggle. Religion is a social institution, not a mere relationship between Man and God. Religion and the State constitute two exalted spheres of reason, above which—though not outside them—there is only philosophy. They are grounded in a nature or reason that is absolute, determining their relationship and embodying at one and the same time their conflicts, their virtues and their objective reality.[1]

This brief review of Italian thought on the vitally important question of relations between Church and State during the period of the Risorgimento has included a number of references to the Law of Guarantees. Not only was the latter Italy's truly great

[1] A. Vera, *Cavour et l'église libre dans l'état libre*, Naples-Paris, 1874.

achievement in the field of legislation, but it had world-wide and lasting repercussions. It was, indeed, thanks to this law and to the régime which it inaugurated that not only the world at large, but also the Papacy itself, became convinced that the temporal power had been too heavy a burden for the Holy See to bear, and that the latter's prestige, its ability to rule the Church effectively and to work for the diffusion of Catholicism throughout the world, had been materially increased by the loss of that power. The accords of 1929 marked a decisive turning-point in Italy's domestic policy, signifying as they did the final elimination of all that remained of her liberal institutions. But so far as the Roman question was concerned they marked only a change of formula. For the Holy See has continued to lack any territorial base other than those apostolic palaces over which the Italian Government had never claimed to exercise any jurisdiction, and ambassadors accredited to the Holy See have continued to reside in Italian territory.

The law of May 13th, 1871, known as the Law of Guarantees, was divided into two parts.

The first part related to the Holy See. Under its provisions the Pope was to be deprived of all his sovereign rights, retaining possession only of the Vatican and Lateran Palaces and the villa of Castel Gandolfo. He was, however, to be accorded all the honours of a sovereign, including the rights of precedence conceded to him by Catholic rulers, and he could not be arraigned under Italian penal law even for acts not immediately connected with his ministry. This provision, which was in part opposed by the Left, constituted the crux of the whole matter. History afforded no precedent for the case of a citizen who could declare the State unlawful and even incite men to destroy it without being punished or restrained by the State, and who could make any accusation against foreign States with the knowledge that if they protested his own State would have to reply: 'We can do nothing.' Moreover, under the law those who attacked or wronged the Pope would be liable to the same penalties as were prescribed for similar offences against the King. The diplomatic corps accredited to the Holy See would be entitled to the same immunities and privileges as the diplomatic corps accredited to the King. The Pope would be allowed to maintain his traditional armed forces, consisting of Mobile Guards, Swiss Guards, Palatine Guards and gendarmes. All cardinals would be left free to take part in conclaves, even those who at the time were undergoing punishment for crimes against the State, and no ecclesiastic could be persecuted for having assisted in the drafting and dissemination of Papal bulls. In addition, the State agreed never to expel from Rome any ecclesiastic whose work lay in the city. The Pope was to be allowed to have his own telegraph office and to make use of the 'diplomatic bag'; and the State promised to make him an annual allowance of 3,225,000 lire. (It is a well-known fact that the Pope did not recognize the Law of Guarantees, protesting that it did not guarantee his independence—the tone of his protests changed with the passage of time. While the law remained in force he never emerged from the Vatican. He did not claim his allowance of 3,225,000 lire, nor did he establish his own telegraph office.)

The second part of the law, concerning relations between Church and State, represented no more than a very timid attempt to put the principles of separatism into practice. The State renounced all control over the promulgation of new ecclesiastical laws and in general over acts of the ecclesiastical authorities. It ceased to require bishops to take an oath of allegiance, and it gave up the right to appoint them in regions where the King claimed that prerogative. It repudiated the King's claim (which the Pope regarded as invalid) to fill the office of Papal Legate in Sicily by right of inheritance. Meetings of Church Councils could in future be called without previous Government assent. But nominations to ecclesiastical benefices (not to non-beneficiary offices, however important) and transactions relating to the property of officially recognized ecclesiastical organizations remained subject to Government control.

As has already been stated, the Pope did not recognize the Law of Guarantees. All orthodox Catholics shared his view that it did not guarantee the independence of the Holy See and that the measure of freedom accorded did not compensate for the loss of the temporal power. And yet, among these Catholics, it became more and more necessary to distinguish between the few who continued even after 1870 to hope for a return to the *status quo* of the years prior to 1859, and the remainder who, while they regarded the present situation as bad or even calamitous, cherished no such illusions as this. Already the Italian State had weathered one major storm in the shape of the guerrilla war, conducted in part by Bourbon sympathizers and in part by armed brigands, which had raged for years over a large part of the former Kingdom of Naples. It had survived the military defeat of 1866 and the disappearance from the scene of its great protector, Napoleon III. There was as yet no sign of the emergence of a Catholic monarch who would be willing to unsheathe the sword for the purpose of restoring the temporal power to the Papacy. Accordingly, men began to consider the possibility of bringing about a Catholic revival by lawful means, of winning over the Kingdom of Italy, now an inescapable reality, to the Catholic faith and of reforming its legislation. So far as the Law of Guarantees in particular was concerned, it was not long before those who moved even in Vatican circles, while insisting on its inadequacy, began to weigh its advantages. As a result, there was consternation whenever it seemed likely that the reins of government would fall into the hands of elements which might be expected to consider the law anew.

Guglielmo Audisio was a Piedmontese theologian who, as a result of demagogic persecution, had taken refuge round about 1850 in Rome, where he became a university professor and a canon of St. Peter's. In 1876, having fallen out of favour with Pius IX because of his lukewarm attitude towards the dogma of Papal infallibility, he wrote his book *Della società politica e religiosa, rispetto al secolo decimonono*, which is essentially the work of an advocate of conciliation. In it he affirms that Catholicism is by no means inconsistent with freedom, nor even with a reasonable measure of religious freedom—though this latter does not imply a toleration of atheism, which is a prime cause of immorality. The autonomy of the State and that of the Church are separate, but not opposed. It is only proper that Italy, the home of the Pope, should have especially cordial relations with the Church. 'The Italian Government, abandoning all negative ideas of revolution and separation, should freely embrace and actively pursue the three positive and vital forms of activity represented by *politics, religion* and *education*. Politically, the Government should assume the role of an incorruptible administrator, not of an overbearing tyrant. . . . To the practice of politics the Government should add that of religion.'

Propaganda of this kind steadily increased in volume as the

years went by. Very different from that of the 'societies for the emancipation of the clergy' which had flourished a few years before, paying little regard to the Pope, eager for the abolition of the Temporal Power, devising schemes, albeit vague ones, for the reform of the Church, and sometimes even hinting at the evils of clerical celibacy, it emanated from devout Catholics who, even if in their hearts they did not regret the loss of the Temporal Power, side-stepped the question by declaring simply that they submitted themselves to the Pope's will. They did not envisage the internal reform of the Church; all they desired was a clergy distinguished for its piety, culture and high moral standards. They repeated that they left it to the Pope to decide when and how Catholics should participate in the political struggle in Italy. But they felt in their hearts that Catholics ought to resign themselves to the advent of national unity and to the abolition of the Temporal Power and that they should seek to gain the ascendancy by the democratic processes of party rivalry and free elections.

Bibliographical Note.

In addition to the works mentioned in the preceding chapter, students of the Roman question should consult: V. Del Giudice, *La questione romana e i rapporti fra Stato e Chiesa fino alla Conciliazione*, Rome, 1948; A. Piola, *La questione romana nella storia e nel diritto*, Padua, 1931; S. Jacini, *Il tramonto del potere temporale nelle relazioni degli ambasciatori austriaci a Roma*, Bari, 1931. The principal documents relating to the question are embodied in A. C. Jemolo's volume *La questione romana*, Milan (undated).

Still of fundamental importance for the light it sheds on the policy of the Italian state is the inaugural address of M. Falco, *La politica ecclesiastica della Destra*, Turin, 1914. The student should also consult S. Jacini, *La politica ecclesiastica italiana da Villafranca a Porta Pia*, Bari, 1938.

For the ecclesiastical policy of Napoleon III, which had such an important bearing on the Roman question, see J. Maurain, *La politique ecclésiastique du Second Empire de* 1852 *à* 1869, Paris, 1930.

On the *Syllabus* and the proclamation of the Pope's infallibility see A. Quacquarelli, *La crisi della religiosità contemporanea*, Bari, 1946, and the first chapter of G. Spadolini, *L'opposizione cattolica*, Florence, 1954.

CHAPTER III

THE AGE OF LEO XIII AND HUMBERT I

NO one who looks back on the years 1878–1900 after the lapse of half a century can fail to appreciate that they saw the completion of the physical process of Italy's recovery from the wounds she had sustained during the period of the Risorgimento, the acceptance on the part of a growing body of Catholics of what was now a *fait accompli*, and the purging of a steadily increasing number of Italians from the poison of anti-clericalism and Jacobin rhetoric.

And yet, while acknowledging these facts, one should equally recognize that, during the selfsame period, the political life of Italy was characterized by a peculiar bitterness, and the nation's law-makers took further steps along the road to secularization.

Pius IX had taken up the clearest possible theoretical position in defence of the temporal power against the forces of liberalism and had repeatedly insisted that the State should respect the traditional rights of the Church. Nevertheless, his great goodness, his constant goodwill towards King Victor and his unwavering affection for Italy, coupled with his advanced age and his un-willingness to tie the hands of a successor whose advent could not long be delayed, made it unthinkable that he should even consider adopting a policy of revendication. In fact, his policy after 1859 was essentially a negative one. It was based on the principle of *non possumus*; the Pope sought merely to keep his doctrinal positions intact, leaving it to his successor to reap the fruits of his wholly theoretical resistance.

His successor was at pains to gather in this harvest of hopes which had been bequeathed to him. Indeed, throughout his pontificate, except during the years of his extreme old age, he was essentially a political Pope.

To-day, perhaps, the figure of Pius IX stands out more boldly in retrospect than that of Leo XIII, just as the cardinals,[1]

[1] Antonelli, Pie, Rauscher, Schwarzenberg, Ledochowski, the 'ultramontanist' Manning, Pitra, Bonnechose, etc.

prelates[1] and religious[2] of his time are more clearly remembered than the men who served under Pope Leo. And yet Leo XIIIs' contemporaries—indifferents and political opponents as well as Catholics—found his personality extremely attractive. Zola, who failed to obtain an audience with him, has drawn in *Rome* a physical portrait of the man which should surely be included in any concise anthology of the prophet of realism.

Modern opinion does not accord with the judgment of those of his contemporaries who believed that the great achievement of the humanistic Pope was the merging of two traditions—the tradition of Papal diplomacy and that of the old Italian diplomacy of the Renaissance and the Counter-Reformation. In fact, it appears that the Pope was frequently inclined to hesitate, that he was one of those diplomats who trace out grandiose plans but do not bother about the details nor concern themselves overmuch with the practical aspect, who establish and develop ideal positions but are subsequently not averse to bequeathing them to their successors, without having first carried their ideas to a logical conclusion. Truth to tell, during these years the Papal Curia and moderate Italian opinion often revealed an implicit mutual confidence in the *vis sanatrix* of time. Both believed that the wounds of the Risorgimento would ultimately heal, but that it would be dangerous to substitute the surgeon's knife for the therapeutic power of nature.

Leo XIII continued to insist that the temporal power was necessary to the Pope as a guarantee of his independence. But he no longer talked of recovering the whole of the former Papal territory. Instead, he limited his explicit claims to Rome, leaving it to be clearly understood that he no longer desired to reopen the question of Italian unity.

The first nine years of Leo XIII's pontificate were notable for two outstanding achievements of Vatican policy. First of all, the Holy See, following the bitter struggles of 1873, succeeded in achieving a reconciliation with Germany, sacrificing the 'old Catholics' and the leader of the 'Centre', Windthorst, in the cause of the universal Church. Secondly, it disavowed the aspirations of

---

[1] Including Darboy, Dupanloup, Mgr. de Ségur, Ketteler and above all Newman, who was raised to the purple by Leo XIII at the beginning of his pontificate but whose work and books which enabled Lord Howard to describe him as the greatest Catholic of his generation had been finished during the reign of Pius IX.

[2] For example, the Oratorian Gratry.

other loyal Catholics, of those Frenchmen—bishops like Cardinal Pie, as well as laymen—who believed that the well-being of France, her return to the Catholic fold, could be assured only by the restoration of the Monarchy. The sacrifice of these loyal elements favoured the creation of that robust French Catholic party which, even when it ceased to be the party in power, even when it appeared to have been defeated, still exerted much influence, alike in the Army, the Diplomatic Service and the administration, and was still dominant in the Academy and the University. One might also make out a flattering case for the Pope's policy towards a number of other States; but these isolated successes did not merge into a grand political strategy of a kind which would have enabled the Pope to assume the role of mediator between the European Powers. There were times when this must have seemed almost within his compass—for example, when he acted as arbiter in the dispute over the Carolines. In the event, such a supreme court of appeal might well have constituted a guarantee of peace.

Certainly both the attitude of Italy and the Roman question were obstacles to the realization of this great European policy. The fact that the Pope was not invited to the conference which preceded the Peace of Aja was entirely the fault of Italy—or, if one prefers, of the short-sighted and pusillanimous policy of the Italian Government, which constantly suffered from an inferiority complex and which, even after national unity had been consolidated and it had become certain that no State would take action to restore the temporal power, was terrified—alike in 1899 and 1914—lest the Roman question should be brought up at the international conference-table.

In the event, Francis Joseph's devotion to the Holy See prevented him from visiting King Humbert in Rome and led him to insist on the adoption by the Triple Alliance of a formula which would make it possible for him to assure the Pope that the three Powers had not entered into any agreement that could be interpreted as a guarantee of Italy's territorial integrity or as a recognition of her right to annex the Eternal City. But the guarantee existed in fact by virtue of the Austro-German pledge to defend Italy if she were attacked by France, that is to say by the one country in which Catholics, legitimists and upholders of the political tradition which opposed Italian unification would

have been willing to take up arms in the cause of the Holy See—
though the people would have risen in revolt if the outcome of the
war had been in any doubt. The danger for Italy of such a war,
already lessened by the events of 1876—by the shattering of
Henry V's hopes of kingship and the resignation of MacMahon—
had in effect disappeared completely with the formation of the
Triple Alliance.

Germany had a low opinion of her Italian ally and of the
latter's military forces. But William I's sense of chivalry and
William II's respect for the hierarchy, coupled with Bismarck's
assessment of the possible value of the Holy See's support in his
dealings with the Poles and with the Centre, ensured the triumph
of the forces of moderation. As a result, Germany was content to
hope that Italy would pursue a policy of restraint, but that even
so the parties of the Left would remain in a wholly subordinate
position.

It is difficult to establish whether, as has been said, the Holy See
did in fact consider the possibility of promoting a Franco-
Austrian alliance, or a grouping of Austria, France and Germany
which would have had the effect of isolating Italy. Certainly there
is no evidence that it took any positive step in this direction.
Moreover, the political balance-sheet at the end of Leo XIII's
pontificate was by no means an imposing one. The Triple
Alliance was by this time firmly established. Italy had overcome
fresh trials without showing any signs of disintegration, and by the
turn of the century her prestige on the Continent was beginning
to increase. No European Power appeared disposed to include in
its political programme so much as an offer to mediate with a
view to the internationalization of the Italian Law of Guarantees.
In France all religious organizations had been disbanded and
disestablishment was already in sight.

On the other hand, the position of Catholicism in the world,
especially in the Protestant countries and in missionary territories, showed a marked improvement. The mass emigrations
from Ireland to the United States were gradually bearing fruit as
the new Americans achieved a higher standard of living. Even an
untrained ear might detect, above the ranting of the materialists
and the positivists, signs that educated men were abandoning
their belief that science could discover and explain everything,
that it could, in fact, take the place of faith. The new philosophies

which were beginning to emerge all represented a reaction against positivism. Several of them, in one way or another, even accorded a place in the scheme of things to the Infinite.

In a religious sense the pontificate of Leo XIII developed along traditional lines, following the course already mapped out by Pius IX. The new Pope's policy was to continue the work of centralization and the tightening up of ecclesiastical discipline; to disseminate Thomistic culture and ensure that Thomism was accepted as the only official theological doctrine; and to create in Rome great institutes of ecclesiastical culture for the training of future bishops and the future rectors of the great seminaries which were springing up in every Catholic State.

The Pope's policy of allowing Catholics comparative intellectual freedom in the fields of historical and New Testament research and biblical exegesis yielded notable results, which the anti-modernist reaction completely failed to nullify.

Both religious and political in its implications was the Pope's attitude towards the social question, crystallized in the encyclical *Rerum novarum* (1891). To be sure, this did not set forth any concrete programme of reform; it did, however, represent a timely complement to the uncompromisingly anti-socialistic propositions of the *Syllabus*. It formally approved and theoretically co-ordinated the manifold schemes which certain eminent ecclesiastics of Central Europe had adopted in order to meet the needs and fulfil the aspirations of the poorer classes, and to prevent the airing of their grievances from becoming a socialist monopoly. The Church declared that the worker's wage was not a commodity like any other, subject only to the law of supply and demand; it rededicated itself to its traditional task of upholding the principles of justice and protecting the poor; finally and most important, it threw a bridgehead into the future—a bridgehead that would permit the growth of a Christian democracy and the formation of trade associations able to resist the tyranny of capitalist employers.

Italian historiographers of recent years have devoted much of their time and energy to the study of the personalities, systems, and Catholic organizations of the period extending roughly from 1870 to 1910.

Now that Italy was once more ruled by Catholics it was natural

E

that historians should concern themselves with the fortunes of the
Catholic political party. During the period of the Risorgimento
this party had suffered a temporary eclipse. After the seizure of
Rome the Pope had banished it from the political scene, inasmuch
as he had ordered its members not to vote in elections, and still
less to accept office as deputies or senators. In taking this step he
was not necessarily recognizing the legality of the new order of
things; but this knowledge was little consolation to the party, and
in the circumstances it is remarkable that it should have retained
so much of its vitality.

Such curiosity on the part of contemporary historians was
amply justified. Moreover, their method of going to work was to
be welcomed as a healthy reaction to the convention which
decreed that the history of any period of struggle should be written
exclusively by the victors and that it should concern itself solely
with the victors' personalities. Yet this same method carried within
it the seeds of a fallacy. *Post hoc, ergo propter hoc*: there was a danger
that the new school of historians would seek to ascribe recent
victories to remote causes, forgetting the vast, world-wide up-
heavals in every sphere of politics and thought which had provided the true impulse for the Catholic reconquest of Italy. In
this story of Italian Catholic resistance and organization between
1870 and 1900 there is much to admire: faith in a good cause;
trust in God; the selflessness of men who knew that they were
defending not their own interests, but their children's and perhaps
even their grandchildren's; the renunciation of many advantages,
ambitions and high responsibilities for the sake of a principle; the
refusal to be discouraged by a series of disappointments. Like all
resistances of the kind, this one was made possible only by the
most rigorous self-discipline. In every city Catholics went into
voluntary isolation, constituting separate communities which
boycotted schools and clubs, refused to collaborate in any way
with other confessions and, as soon as circumstances permitted,
even formed self-contained economic units. Such a prolonged
resistance, almost always continuing into the second generation,
with very few defections even within whole families, would have
been impossible had not Catholics deliberately isolated themselves
from the rest of the community.

The organizations which kept the Catholic world united were
the *Gioventù Cattolica* and, in particular, the *Opera dei Congressi*.

The last-named steadily increased its influence, forming a capillary organization whose ramifications embraced every kind of activity and which never allowed its cultural and economic aspects, its work in the field of municipal elections and its efforts to gain the support of charitable institutions to overshadow its religious mission. Thus, its meetings were invariably attended by an ecclesiastical observer possessing a right of veto. This cult of organization was a remarkable phenomenon in an age in which it is true to say that the various political parties did not even know the meaning of the word. Incidentally, from the structural viewpoint these Catholic bodies are closely paralleled by the Communist Party of to-day.

Later on, about the time of the *Rerum novarum*, the Church formulated a new sociological and economic theory which subordinated the interests of the individual to moral and religious considerations and which, therefore, opened the way to a settlement of all social questions in accordance with the principles of charity, solidarity and neighbourly love propounded in the Gospels. The greatest exponent of the new economic doctrine was Professor Giuseppe Toniolo of the University of Pisa, whose name is still much revered by Italian Catholics, while there is even talk of his beatification. (On the other hand, the doctrine is held in small regard by adherents of other economic systems, which are based on the principle that economics and ethics are mutually independent.) As has already been indicated, a number of economic organizations were established independently of these developments in the doctrinal field. They included savings banks and co-operative societies, and their activities were for the most part confined to single provinces or to even smaller areas. There were, however, a few that operated over a wider field. Thus, the Bank of Rome, founded during this period, was from the first essentially national in character, allegedly financing the economic projects of the Holy See.

The problem of trade unions cropped up rather later in Italy than elsewhere. The question whether it was permissible for Catholics to belong to mixed unions did not arise until after the First World War. Moreover, it arose in a form very different from that in which it had arisen in pluriconfessional countries during the nineteenth century, inasmuch as in Italy the Church's principal concern was to prevent Catholic workers from joining organizations in which socialist elements predominated. During the pontificate of Leo XIII there was considerable argument as to whether it was permissible for Catholics, firstly, to establish confessional trade unions organized and controlled by ecclesiastics, and secondly, to insist on their rights as employees and if need be to resort to the strike weapon in order to enforce their legitimate demands. To many leaders of the Catholic movement, aristocrats or members of the upper middle class, such methods were profoundly distasteful. They were much less so to the clergy, who were in closer touch with the needs of the people and were more concerned with countering the effects of socialist propaganda. In the event, a number of trade unions were formed, and there were a few isolated instances of clashes between Catholic factory-workers (especially women) and their employers. But the Catholic trade-union movement never approached its socialist counterpart in importance. Only after the First World War did it assume a momentary significance, and it never introduced any suggestion of bitterness into its struggles with capital. The Catholic ideal was always a corporative system in which all disputes between capital and labour would be solved by the persuasive reasoning of an influential priest or, if really necessary, by arbitration, without the workers' having to resort to the weapons of the strike and the lock-out. The most fanatical organizers of labour and the most ardent champions of the workers ended by becoming socialists. But such defections were exceedingly rare.

As already stated, recent Italian writers have devoted a great deal of attention to the history of Catholic organization since 1870, reproaching their more diffuse predecessors for having woefully neglected it, for having failed even to record the names of its greatest exponents—for example, the barrister Casoni and Count Acquaderni.

Here it should be noted that the significance of this movement—which flourished chiefly in northern and central Italy, that is to say in the more advanced areas, where the effects of socialist infiltration were already becoming apparent—was that it united and fortified those elements whose loyalty to Catholicism had been established beyond argument. But it did not make any contribution to the history of doctrines and ideas. It always complied unquestioningly not only with the Pope's directives, but with his wishes. By no stretch of imagination can it be said to have followed in the wake of those Catholic movements which ended by gaining the allegiance of the ecclesiastical hierarchy, by making it feel that its opposition would have alienated numbers of good Catholics, by imbuing the mass of believers with new sensibilities. The preoccupation with the social problem which becomes apparent at a certain moment in the teaching of the Church manifested itself abroad long before it did in Italy, and it was everywhere the result of the propagation of the first socialist doctrines and also, in a less degree, of the idea that in its campaign against the rationalist bourgeoisie the Church could bring pressure to bear on the proletariat, which was not interested in the former's ideals of a moral, secular State; and in particular on the rural masses. To be sure, it is impossible to give credit for this preoccupation to Italy's Catholic organizers, who in the matter of social reform did not lead the way but merely swam with the tide. Still less is it possible to distinguish in those same organizers any particular talent for religious disputation. They were merely good, pious, practising Catholics, and for this very reason their religious life was a tranquil one, and they took absolutely no part in religious controversies, such as that which arose when the Holy See condemned certain propositions drawn from the works of Rosmini.

Alluding both to the period of the Risorgimento proper and to these years, upholders of that Italian Catholic tradition, which was largely created by Fascism, describe liberal Italy as a witch-hunting, sectarian and factious country dominated by freemasons. The impartial observer notices in the first place that under this liberal régime no Italian ever received more than a token punishment for a political crime or for conspiring against the new State; I believe it is a fact that the maximum sentence ever passed for an offence of this type was six months' imprisonment. (The repressive measures taken in the south roughly between 1861 and 1867 were prompted by an outbreak of genuine brigandage which, even if its causes were political, even if it was sponsored largely by elements of the disbanded Bourbonist army, even if it received the blessing of the ex-King of Naples, assumed from the first such a blatantly criminal character that no Catholic historian has ever dared to defend it.) On the other hand, it is undeniably true that Catholics were constantly assailed by pin-pricks, that they were frequently wounded in the most sensitive part of their being.

These were the years in which Christianity was subjected to violent attacks by materialists, who scoffed at every manifestation of religious feeling, regarded the saints as half-wits and miracles as gross impostures, and respected none of the things that Christians hold sacred. Not only this, but Italian Catholics were actually tormented by their adversaries with the syllogism: 'If you are Catholics, you obey the Pope; and if you obey the Pope, you desire the dissolution of Italian unity; you are enemies of your Country.' It is a crude syllogism, one that will admit no *distinguo*, and after 1866, the last year in which large groups of Catholics expressed their desire for the overthrow of the régime, it was unjust even to those of the strictest political orthodoxy. Yet it was used to torment Catholics until about 1912. It must, however, be realized that the Government, always on the pretext that they were dealing with groups and organizations which did not recognize national unity nor the legality of the new constitution, and which considered it a crime to take any part in political elections, showed scant respect for their freedom and afforded them little protection from the assaults of their enemies. The history of Catholic congresses down to 1900 is full of tales of prefectorial bans on meetings and processions, of raids on clubs or violent dispersals of meetings carried out by anti-clerical students or Left-Wing associations. Politically-minded Catholics had withdrawn into isolation and were living a life apart. Anti-clericals were unwilling to let them participate along with other Italians in celebrations commemorating ancient Italian glories such as the Lombard League against Barbarossa. In 1892, during the celebrations in connection with the quater-centenary of the discovery of America, a demonstration was held in a Rome square for the purpose of preventing a Catholic association from placing a wreath on the bust of Christopher Columbus in the Pincio. (The ribbons on the wreath, naturally enough, were not in the national colours but were blue and yellow, the colours of the association: Catholics tended to avoid even single colours of the national flag.) On the other hand, all evocations of the nation's past glories were given an anti-clerical bias, even if this entailed gross distortions of historical fact. A case in point was the special celebration held to mark the six-hundredth anniversary of the expulsion of Charles of Anjou from Sicily.

Freemasonry, which in Italy as in all the Latin countries has a

distinctly anti-clerical flavour, was everywhere strongly en-
trenched. It was responsible for the appointment of countless
nonentities to university chairs and to high positions in the State.
But the picture would be misleading if one did not add that, so
far as the records show, not one Catholic of any note was excluded
from the teaching profession, the Bench, the Army or the administration on the score of his freely-avowed religious convictions.
Mention has already been made of Toniolo, who taught at Pisa.
At Pavia, the Chair of Roman Law was occupied by Contardo
Ferrini, who to-day is numbered among the saints. Catholic
philosophers filled posts in universities (Francesco Acri at Bologna,
Giuseppe Allievo at Turin). Other faculties included among their
members such intransigents as the criminal jurist Carrara (Pisa),
Abbot Pertile, a survivor from the Austrian era (Padua), and the
irascible Vallauri (Turin); not to mention Catholics like Federico
Persico (Naples) and Carlo Francesco Gabba (Pisa), who, though
they made no secret of their devotion to the Church, were nevertheless in favour of conciliation.

In an entirely different category from the intransigents were
those avowed Catholics who, while declaring themselves openly
and unreservedly in favour of a unified Italy with Rome as its
capital, longed for a reconciliation between Church and State
and opposed any further move in the direction of secularization.
(They succeeded in preventing both the legalization of divorce
and the adoption of a measure whereby civil marriage would
have taken precedence of its religious counterpart; but they failed
to prevent the passage of a bill relating to benevolent institutions,
by the terms of which the assets of all confraternities were to be
seized and used for charitable purposes.) These advocates of
compromise would have welcomed the repeal of some of the
ecclesiastical laws passed during the period of the Risorgimento.
Above all, they would have liked to see the Government attaching
greater importance to religious values and adopting a more
respectful tone towards the authorities of the Church. Although
described by their opponents as 'clericals', they were accorded
full rights of citizenship; and the Government, far from being
able to exercise a restraining influence upon them, was forced to
take full account of their attitude.

Naturally, these unitarian Catholics did not all represent the
same shade of opinion: some laid chief emphasis on their

Catholicism, others on their nationalism. Their common meeting-ground was the *Rassegna Nazionale*. The conservative editors of this publication, which first appeared in Florence in 1879, declared themselves in favour of reform and claimed to be both good Catholics and good Italians. The review's animating spirit was Augusto Conti, a celebrated philosopher of the time, who in 1866 had spoken in Parliament against the bill to suppress religious organizations; but its editorial staff also included the theologian Audisio;[1] the historian Cesare Cantù; Carlo Francesco Gabba,[2] an eminent jurist, who taught in the University of Pisa; Domenico Carutti, another historian; Federico Persico,[3] Professor of Municipal and International Law in the University of Naples; and, at a later date, the well-known novelist Antonio Fogazzaro and Ermenegildo Pistelli, a priest in the Scuole Pie.

In 1885 Fogazzaro published a novel, *Daniele Cortis*,[4] in which the hero is a candidate for Parliament. In his electoral address he advocates the formation of a non-confessional party not subject to the authority of the Church; but 'the people must be permitted to receive religious instruction from the clergy as and when they desire; the State must not foolishly imagine that it is damaging the cause of liberty by refusing to employ self-confessed atheists; it must officially recognize those religious associations whose aims do not conflict with the laws; it must, in principle, guarantee to all its citizens the right to the peaceful exercise of their religion both in public and in private; and it must abstain from any interference, whether lawful or violent, in the internal affairs of the Church, saving always that it has the right to protect its own property.'

Was it permissible for a Catholic to offer himself as a candidate in a political election? That was the question on which Catholics as a body were divided. Those who declared themselves to be 'conservatives', and unreservedly supported the claim of Rome to be the capital, were regarded by their orthodox co-religionists not merely as bad Catholics but as traitors to the Holy See. Sometimes they were contemptuously referred to as sowers of tares or

---

[1] See p. 51.
[2] See p. 124.
[3] See p. 63.
[4] This book is still widely read in Italy and, in fact, was only recently made into a film.

were openly accused of spreading treason (the term 'fifth column' had not yet been invented). But even orthodox Catholics were not genuinely united, except in their allegiance to Rome. For some, in whom memories of the Risorgimento still rankled, their subjection to the Holy See was a source of joy; for them it would have been painful beyond words to be compelled to recognize the unity of Italy as legal, to have to swear fidelity as deputies to the King and the Constitution. But for others, who became more numerous every year, it was a burden. These were not only conscious of their strength, they were inclined to overrate it; and it distressed them to see their rulers pursuing an anti-clerical policy; they found it humiliating to be governed by men who in calculating their parliamentary majorities did not have to take account of any Catholic groupings. Why should they let these men continue to dechristianize the country when they could prevent them? Why did they persist in their futile protests, when they knew that they had no hope of disrupting Italian unity, that they could never restore the Temporal Power, that probably the Pope himself would be terrified if he found himself one day in 1890 confronted with the problem of governing several millions of Italians, who by that time would have grown accustomed to forms of freedom and ways of thinking which the Church could never tolerate?

The old Jesuit Father Curci, who in 1848 had carried on a campaign against Gioberti, and who even after 1870 had denounced Italian unity in fiery language, hoping all the time that Henry V would launch a crusade for the restoration of the temporal power, was unable ten years later to find a satisfactory answer to these questions. He accordingly left the Order, and was severely taken to task—though his religious orthodoxy remained completely above suspicion—for asserting that, in the moral and religious interests of the country, Catholics should henceforth play a full part in its political life. In his view, Italy's best hope for the future lay in an alliance between Catholics and conservatives.

Orthodox Catholics repeatedly declared that they would continue to obey the Pope's orders. But the younger men had found a new battle-cry: 'Let us in the meantime prepare for the day when the Pope commands us to throw ourselves into the political struggle.' Moreover, they even succeeded in gaining the support of a priest, Don David Albertario, a violent and uncompromising opponent of liberalism who until then had always desired the restoration of the temporal power.

From 1876 onwards Italy was governed by the party of the Left, the party which had reproached Cavour's successors for the undue moderation of their ecclesiastical policy, had rejected the separatist formula of 'a Free Church in a Free State', and had preserved its faith in the jurisdictional weapon, which its opponents declared to be illiberal, and in any case outmoded. The members of this party had at the time opposed the Law of Guarantees, feeling that it made too many concessions to the Pope and the Church.

But adherents of the old Right-Wing party could derive some satisfaction from the fact that, once in the saddle, the Left had not substantially altered the broad lines of the nation's ecclesiastical policy. Not only had it declared that the Law of Guarantees could not now be modified, but it had added very little to the existing legislation, although in 1887 a measure was passed freeing those farmers to whom the old law still applied from the necessity of handing over a tenth of their produce to their parish priest. (In point of fact, the new law was so badly worded that parish priests are able to claim tithes even to this day.) The penal code of 1889 omitted all mention of a State religion but continued to refer in general terms to religious creeds and ceremonies and to the ministry. It prescribed penalties for ministers who abused their position by inciting the people to flout the laws and Government decrees or to treat officialdom with less than proper respect or who compelled or persuaded anyone to perform actions or to make statements contrary to the laws or prejudicial to the rights which these conferred on the citizen. (This measure was directed particularly against those who acquired property formerly belonging to the Church.)   The law of July 17th, 1890, relating to charitable institutions, was finally approved. This was not a Jacobin measure, and in principle it respected the intentions of the founders.[1] But it provided that the State should exercise a stricter control over the institutions in question. It aimed to ensure that the parish priest should not be a member of the Con-

---

[1] Thus, where the founder of a new charitable institution decreed in his will that it should be reserved exclusively for Catholics his wishes were generally observed.

gregation of Charity, and that the State should be able, by altering
their terms of reference, to transform the character of those
institutions which were no longer able to fulfil their charitable
purpose. Above all, it hit a number of institutions (notably the
confraternities[1]) whose objects were partly religious and partly
benevolent, stipulating that, with rare exceptions, the property of
those that were primarily religious in character should be devoted
to charity. The minister who proposed the law, Francesco Crispi,
was a Sicilian, and as such was well acquainted with the life of the
confraternities. He declared that, owing to bad administration,
their vast possessions yielded a very modest income, and he
emphasized that this income was wrongly distributed. Too little
was allocated to charity, while too much was spent on celebrations, illuminations and firework displays. The ministerial report
on the project drew attention to the passions which these confraternities sometimes aroused in villages, involving questions of
precedence in processions and the priority to be accorded to
different sacred images.

When the bill was submitted to Parliament it encountered stiff
opposition, and it may be said that the Conservative Party treated
the issue as an opportunity to pit its strength against that of the
Government. In the course of an extremely lively debate a
distinction was drawn between State charity and charity inspired
by religious zeal. In particular, the question was raised of the
extent to which the State was entitled to tamper with the wills of
founders of benevolent institutions. On the one hand it was
asserted that not even legislators could overrule the dispositions of
a testator; on the other, the argument was put forward that had
the testators involved been able to foresee the present turn of
events they would have arranged things differently. Senator
Massarani justly observed that during the two thousand years
that divided Quiritarian and Praetorian Law from the modern
codes, with their adherence to the principle of legitimate inheritance, the legal significance attached to wills had steadily
diminished.

Although the Senate approved the law in substance, it refused
to accept the principle that the character of those religious
organizations which did not satisfy a public need should be
modified to serve the ends of charity. A conflict ensued bet-

---

[1] Lay associations which flourished particularly in the south of Italy.

ween the Chamber, which supported this clause of the bill, and the Senate, and in the event the latter was compelled to give way.

Among the ministers of Humbert I the one best remembered to-day is Francesco Crispi. He is remembered chiefly because of his African venture (in reality it was not initiated by him, and it served to precipitate his political downfall, even though he was not to blame for its failure); because he took every opportunity to build up Italy's prestige as a Great Power; because he concerned himself with the welfare of his countrymen abroad, urging the building of schools that would help their children to retain their identity as Italians; and, finally, because he always sought to justify the powers of the Executive in Parliament.

For all these reasons the Fascists liked to regard this disciple of Garibaldi as a prophet of their creed; but such a claim was certainly arbitrary, for Crispi invariably respected the rights of Parliament, and his conception of the State was such that he would never have approved of a party that endeavoured to impose its will by force. Yet it cannot be denied that, whereas the previous rulers of Italy, both of the Right and of the Left, had always subscribed in international affairs to a policy of 'clean hands'—in other words, they had refused to launch out into any adventures unless some vital national interest were at stake—Crispi initiated Italians in the dangerous game of 'prestige politics' and persuaded them to accept the thesis that a Great Power should make its voice heard in all international disputes, even though its own interests were not directly involved.

On the question of the relations between Church and State Crispi revealed himself as a Garibaldian of Mazzinian origins. He was, moreover, a masonic dignitary—though in a Sicilian this meant less than it would have done in the case of a north Italian. But unlike so many of his contemporaries, who regarded religion as a superstitition that would soon be discredited by science, he was not a materialist. He refused to take part in the inaugural ceremony of the Giordano Bruno Society because the latter proclaimed itself to be atheistic, whereas he stood for liberty of conscience and was opposed 'to all those who display intolerance, whether in the field of religion or of reason, for they are enemies of the human spirit and partisans of despotism. . . . I believe that religious ideas should always be tolerated, whatever form they

may take. Giordano Bruno was not an atheist . . . the martyr[1]
believed in God. . . . All our great men have been deists. Dante,
Michelangelo and Galileo believed in God. So did Mazzini and
Garibaldi.' And in his speech of September 20th, 1895, at the
unveiling of the memorial to Garibaldi, he said: 'Religion is not
and should not be a function of the State. It comforts those who
believe by offering them the hope of an eternal future. It nurtures
the spirit of faith, and for that reason it is holy.'[2]

Although he made no secret of the fact that as a deputy he had
opposed the Law of Guarantees, he did not now advocate its
repeal. Indeed, a quarter of a century after the event we find him
somewhat reluctantly singing its praises. Thus, in a speech to the
Senate in 1895 he declared that 'to-day the Pope is independent,
he exercises his functions without let or hindrance, he communicates with the whole world, he prays, he dominates the consciences
of men. . . . In what part of the world does the Pope enjoy more
freedom than he does in Italy?'[3] And again: 'The autonomy of
the spirit, which we defend and guarantee, is a fortress in which
the Supreme Pontiff can take refuge, in which he will be immune
from all attacks. Material power eludes him, and it will be to his
credit if he can put it behind him; but the souls of men are his,
and he rules them, to such effect that all the powers of the Earth
have cause to envy him. By the law of 1871 Italian genius succeeded in solving a problem which in earlier times would have
appeared insoluble. In a land where there is liberty both of
thought and conscience the Head of the Church was granted
unlimited freedom within the sphere of his sacred ministry; he was
made unaccountable for his actions and immune from their legal
consequences. The Pope is subject only to God, and no human
power can touch him. Surrounded by all the honours and privileges of a monarch, freed from the embarrassment of the temporal
power and from all the hatreds, resentments and anxieties that go
with it, he exercises a sovereign authority over those who put their
trust in him—and they are numbered in millions. No prince on
earth resembles him or is his peer; he is unique. He has no

[1] Bruno (1550–1600) was burnt at the stake as a heretic. (D. M.)

[2] Speech in the Chamber, November 28th, 1895, in F. Crispi, *Discorsi parlamentari*,
Rome, 1915, iii, pp. 360 *sqq.*; *id.*, *Ultimi scritti e discorsi extra parlamentari*, Rome [un-
dated], pp. 217 *sqq.*

[3] Speech in the Senate, July 17th, 1895, in *Discorsi parlamentari* (op. cit.), iii, pp.
838 *sqq.*

territory under his jurisdiction—and, if he had, it would be narrow—but all the world forms part of his celestial empire; and with that he should be content. As a temporal prince his authority would be diminished, because he would be equal to all other princes, and could not be first among them. All would oppose him, just as they have opposed him for several centuries past, to the prejudice of the Faith and of the Church's spiritual authority. But in virtue of the sovereignty that we have conferred upon him he transcends all the rest of mankind, and therein lies his power. He exercises his functions in complete independence, he communicates with all the world, he prays, he dominates men's consciences, he protects others yet himself has no need of protection, because the territory of Italy serves him in the office of a shield.'[1]

Violently opposed as he was to the concordats, Crispi declared that in his view the ideal relationship between Church and State was that prevailing in America, where 'the State is sovereign, the various confessions are all free within the orbit of the State and are under the latter's protection. If this relationship could be established in the Old World—which still seems to me scarcely within the bounds of possibility—a great step would have been taken along the road to freedom.'[2]

To anyone who views the situation from a distance, and in the light of subsequent events, it is evident that during these years an open reconciliation between Italy and the Papacy was virtually impossible. Italian public opinion was not yet prepared to renounce even a narrow strip of territory, to repudiate even a fraction of the legislation of the Risorgimento. The Holy See could not have renounced the temporal power without giving grave offence to many Catholics, and in particular to French Catholics, who in these years had set themselves up as somewhat arrogant and obnoxious champions of the Papacy. It seemed, however, that, once the new Italian State had overcome its initial trials and proved its vitality, the two sides would inevitably arrive at a *modus vivendi*, which might in fact be preferable to a formal accord. Probably the Holy See, without explicitly renouncing its

[1] Speech at the unveiling of the memorial to Garibaldi, in *Ultimi scritti* (cited above), pp. 217 *sqq.*

[2] Speech in the Chamber, June 6th, 1885, in *Discorsi parlamentari* (op. cit.), ii, pp. 749 *sqq.*

claims, would cut its losses in respect of the temporal power just as it had done years before in the case of Avignon, while Italy would drop that part of her ecclesiastical legislation—for example, the law suppressing religious organizations—which was most closely identified with the passions of the Risorgimento. It seemed that the realization of a *modus vivendi* had been brought nearer by the growth of the European socialist movement, the effects of which had already been seen in France in 1848–50 and were now visible all over the Continent, where the cultured bourgeoisie, the politically-minded middle class, were withdrawing to conservative positions, and even abandoning certain rationalistic convictions. Europe, in fact, was witnessing, *mutatis mutandis*, a repetition of the processes which had been set in motion a hundred years before by the French Revolution.

So much would have been apparent even to a contemporary observer, so long as he viewed the situation objectively and did not indulge in any wishful thinking with regard to the immediate future.

But neither Crispi nor, at bottom, Leo XIII was one of those far-seeing statesmen who strive to prepare the ground for future generations, untroubled by the thought that they will not live to see the fruits of their labours. And between 1848 and 1870 Italians had seen too many prodigies accomplished to believe that the age of miracles was past. Thus was born a strange hope of immediate reconciliation, which faded rapidly, leaving behind it a legacy of bitterness.

At Christmas, 1886, the Bishop of Cremona, Mgr. Geremia Bonomelli, a man highly esteemed in moderate Catholic and conservative circles, wrote to the Pope in the following terms: 'Within the short space of little more than eight years You have accomplished many notable things. You have corrected a number of false ideas, and, through the medium of Your immortal Encyclicals, You have given a powerful impulse to scholarship. But Your greatest achievement consists in the fact that You have peaceably composed so many of the serious differences that had arisen between the temporal States and the Holy See. You have shown Yourself to be in a true sense the Vicar of Him Who was heralded as *Princeps pacis*, and of Whom the Apostle wrote that He came *reconciliare omnia*. O Holy Father, in this most auspicious year of Your Jubilee there is one blessing that I crave above all others—namely, that You may accomplish that most difficult and most necessary of all tasks, the pacification of our Country. If this work is delayed for many more years I tremble for the future. Let us not delude ourselves—intellectual Youth, which one day will be the mainstay of society, is steadily detaching itself from the Church and in so doing is setting an example which sooner or later will be followed by the entire nation. What will then become of the Holy See, alone in the midst of an unbelieving and fiercely hostile society?'

This letter marked the resurgence of that confidence in the possibility of reconciliation which had never been more than momentarily shaken by Leo XIII's demands—repeated at intervals ever since his accession to the throne of St. Peter—for the restoration of the temporal power. This renewal of hope was inspired by the Pope's diplomatic successes, which men chose to regard as evidence of his spirit of conciliation, and above all by the cordiality of the relations which the Holy See had succeeded in establishing—through the good offices of Cardinal Luigi Jacobini, Secretary of State, and in particular of the surrogate Mgr. Luigi Galimberti, who himself was subsequently raised to the purple—with the Germany of Bismarck. Failing to perceive the profound difference between the two sets of circumstances, and arguing that it was impossible for the Holy See to exploit the cordial relations established with the powerful German Empire so long as it condemned the very existence of one of the members of the Triple Alliance, Italians saw in this *entente* between the Vatican and Germany a good omen for reconciliation. A majority of the Italian bourgeoisie was, perhaps, encouraged also by the baseless hope of a personal intervention on the part of Bismarck, who during these years was regarded by those elements which supported the Triple Alliance (in other words by the majority of the politically conscious middle class) as a *deus ex machina*, well disposed towards Italy and in favour of conciliation.

Replying to Mgr. Bonomelli, Leo XIII declared himself to be in complete agreement with the sentiments expressed in his letter, adding: 'Moreover, that you should call upon the Father of Light to help us bring peace to Italy also, stricken as she is by this war [against the Church], corresponds perfectly to Our own aspirations, Who, perceiving the immense difficulties of the present situation, place Our trust solely in God's help.'

The Bishop's letter to the Pope and the latter's reply were published in the Press.

In his address of February 28th to the Sacred College the Pope said, *inter alia*: 'But if men were willing and finally able to satisfy our just claims, the first to feel the great benefits of such a course would be that country which had the good fortune to be chosen as the seat of the Papacy and which is indebted to the Papacy for so much of its greatness and glory.' Claims, but they are unspecified. No reproaches, no vituperation. In a word—*nil desperandum*.

The funeral services which were held in many churches for the victims of Dogali—a lamentable episode of colonial warfare in the course of which five hundred Italians were massacred—prompted the authorities of Church and State to make new and unprecedented efforts to compose their differences. From pulpits all over Italy bishops extolled the Army and its virtues and heaped blessings on the common homeland, expressing themselves in language that had not been heard for many a long year. The leader of the national Catholic organization, Augusto Conti, was responsible for the inscription on the plaque which was put up in Santa Croce in memory of the five hundred.

Father Tosti of Cassino published a pamphlet, *La Conciliazione*, which quickly ran into several editions. Father Tosti had already shared, in spirit and through the medium of his pen, in the enthusiasms of 1848, and he was noted for his ardent and unwavering patriotism, as well as for his strict orthodoxy and his absolute submission to the discipline of the cloister.

In his pamphlet he extolled Leo XIII, the prince of peace, and dwelt on the evils of the division between Pope and people. 'Can a single day, September 20th, erase from the calendar of the Roman Church nineteen centuries of devotion and service?' he wrote; and in rather solemn tones he went on to prophesy that 1888, the year in which Leo XIII would celebrate the fiftieth anniversary of his entry into the priesthood, would be a year of miraculous events: 'We shall see the gestatorial chair carried on the shoulders of thirty million Italians; we shall see Leo XIII raised so high by those sturdy shoulders that, when he lowers his eyes, he will no longer see any sign of the disputes and dissensions which now rack the world. His eyes will come to rest on the gates of a new Empire—the dominion of the consciences of all those who

F

are weary of strife and who thirst for peace, a dominion to which every man will be free to submit. Those gates will open wide as he approaches; and at his passing a shout of triumph will burst forth like a torrent of joy from the Alps to the sea: *Ave, princeps pacis.*'

This almost visionary note was sustained throughout the pamphlet, which contained no concrete proposals and nothing of a juridical character.

It seems certain that prior to its publication the proofs were submitted both to the Holy See and to Crispi.

On May 23rd, almost simultaneously with the appearance of the pamphlet, the Pope delivered his address *Episcoporum ordinem*: 'May the prayers which We offer for the peace of all nations avail the land of Italy in the way that We should wish; for God has bound this land to the Roman Pontificate with indissoluble bonds, and because of her special character she is especially dear to Us. Of a surety, as We have said more than once ere now, We have for long earnestly desired that Italians should enjoy a stable peace and that their tragic dispute with the Roman Pontificate should finally be composed, without prejudice to the sacred rights and dignity of the Apostolic See, which are violated not so much by popular calumny as by the machinations of the various sects. In other words, the parties concerned must agree to re-establish a system of things whereby the Roman Pontiff will be subject to the authority of no man and will enjoy the true and complete liberty that is his by right. Such a system of things, if men will but judge truly, would not only do no injury to the Italian State, but would add greatly to its security and prosperity. . . .'

The Pope no longer referred to the State of Piedmont; instead, he spoke of the Italian State. He made no mention of any territorial claims, but merely asked for complete liberty. He refrained from casting any stones, except to deplore the machinations of the sects. . . . There were, he averred, solid grounds for hope.

On May 27th Augusto Conti wrote in *L'Opinione* of the moral, political and economic necessity of a reconciliation: this was desired by the Pope, by the King, and by a majority of the people and clergy.

Writing in the *Rassegna Nazionale*, R. Mazzei took a somewhat longer view. The Holy See, he declared, should not demand the restoration of the Papal States, and Italians should not expect the Pope to approve the Law of Guarantees. The Government should give a first proof of its goodwill by exempting student missionaries from military service, with a view to exempting the whole of the clergy at a later date. If it did not forbid anti-Catholic teaching, at least it should relax all the present restrictions on education. It should scrupulously refrain from confiscating the property of charitable institutions and from adapting it to uses for which it had never been intended. It should accord legal recognition to duly-registered religious marriages. The Church should abolish the *non expedit*; the Government would then cease to ingratiate itself with radicals and would no longer neglect Catholics, as it was wont to do at present by reason of the fact that they did not vote at elections and therefore were of no account politically.

Until the archives of the Vatican are opened it will be difficult to decide whether all this talk of conciliation had any concrete basis; whether Crispi, and others too, albeit far removed from him in outlook, were right in believing that French diplomats and prelates were urging the Pope to draw in his horns, feeling that their countrymen would have regarded a reconciliation at this juncture as a grave scandal; or, conversely, whether it was the Holy See that was disappointed, and the Italian Government that was obliged to give way in the face of masonic pressure. Perhaps, after all, the most likely explanation is that the men of 1887 realized that they had been the victims of a great illusion, not unlike that which, forty years before, had led men to hope that Pius IX would go to war with Austria over the question of Italian unity. Perhaps the two sides had never really intended to come together, and this was merely the bursting of the bubble.

On June 10th the anti-clerical republican Giovanni Bovio made a speech in the Chamber in which he sought an explanation of the Government's policy towards the Vatican. The speech was relatively moderate in tone. Bovio did not speak disrespectfully of the Pope, but he asserted that the time was not ripe for a reconciliation. Good could come only from a struggle, of a kind that would compel the State to press forward in the fields of science and legislation and the Holy See to vindicate its traditions and to crystallize its dogmas. 'Reconciliation would mean stagnation. It would be tantamount to a pact of mutual mediocrity between the State and the Church. A Pope who was only half a prince and a State that was only semi-Catholic would meet on a common ground rotten with half-baked institutions, half-baked men and half-baked religion. . . .'

To this Zanardelli, Keeper of the Seals, replied: 'Reconciliation is essential. Surely it is preferable to discord, to schism, to internecine strife between Church and State. I visualize a patriotic clergy, seeking to promote the well-being of our country, imbued with a sense of its greatness, at pains not to stir up social dissension. But in order that these aims may be achieved, I, Zanardelli, conscious that Italy . . . has through her laws given the Church a wider measure of freedom than any other nation in Europe, am in duty bound . . . to see to it that those same laws are faithfully and scrupulously observed. . . . I certainly cannot allow the State to abdicate its inalienable rights, its immutable duties, its indefectible mission to spread enlightenment, to foster progress, to advance civilization.' And Crispi in his turn made a reply that was a clarion-call: 'We do not seek reconciliation, nor do we need to, for our country is not at war. We neither know nor care what they are thinking in the Vatican. Leo XIII is not an ordinary man. Events are moving towards a climax: those which have the effect of damping down, even of extinguishing the fiercest antagonisms may also bring Church and State closer together. For our part, however, we shall not violate the nation's sacred rights, long since established by the plebiscites. Italy belongs to herself, to herself alone, and she has but one ruler: the King.'[1]

This reply certainly does not contain any hostile criticism of the Holy See; indeed, it includes a favourable reference to the person of the Pope. Yet we can detect in it not the slightest gesture of conciliation. There is no admission that a majority at least of the Italian people is disturbed by the continued dissension between Church and State, no hint of the smallest concession on the part of the latter, nothing to offset that reference to the plebiscites, which signifies that no territorial concession will be made. Again, the final passage amounts to a rejection of the thesis that those same Italians who make up the political society headed by the King also form part of a religious society headed by the Pope.

After these replies it was virtually certain—however much the advocates of reconciliation might seek to delude themselves—that there could be no *rapprochement* between Church and State.

---

[1] *Atti parlamentari* (Chamber of Deputies, 14th Parliament, 1st Session, Debate of June 10th, 1887, pp. 3,414 *sq.*).

On July 26th the Holy See published a letter from Leo XIII to his new Secretary of State, Cardinal Rampolla, bearing the date June 15th (though there is reason to suspect that it was ante-dated). Simultaneously there appeared in the Press (as a result, it was said, of an indiscretion on the part of certain foreign diplomats) the text of a circular which represented Cardinal Rampolla's first attempt since his preferment to clarify the Church's policy. Addressed to the Nuncios, whose task it was to communicate its contents to the Governments to which they were accredited, it sought to explain the Pope's address of May 23rd and was clearly intended to reassure those Governments which were most at-tracted by the idea of a reconciliation between the Pope and Italy. In fact the circular was merely a paraphrase or amplification of the pontifical letter, in which the Holy Father had tried to explain what was in his mind.

Many times, wrote Leo XIII, we have expressed 'Our desire for a final settlement of the differences ... between Italy, as now officially constituted, and the Roman Pontificate.' He had expressed the same desire in his address of May 23rd; but this time he was more specific. 'In order,' he went on, 'to establish peace and concord [in Italy] it is not enough, as it would be elsewhere, to make certain concessions to the Church, to modify or repeal hostile laws, to abolish contradictory regulations. It is necessary, in addition and above all, to regularize the position of the Supreme Pontiff, which for many years, as a result of violence and injustice, has been unworthy of Him and incompatible with the freedom of His Apostolic office. . . . [It is] an indispensable condition for the restoration of peace and harmony in Italy that the Roman Pontiff be invested once more with true sovereignty. ... An institution that was brought into existence by means at once so lawful and so natural' was the civil Principate of the Popes, 'which has behind it a tradition of peaceful and undisputed dominion stretching back twelve centuries, which has contributed so much to the spread of the Faith and to the progress of civiliza-tion, which has earned for itself so many titles to the gratitude of the nations, has more than any other the right to be respected and sustained. Nor can it be said that the designs of Providence in its regard have changed merely because it has been subjected to a series of injustices and rude assaults. Indeed, the very fact that attacks on the civil Principate of the Popes have always been made by enemies of the Church, and in recent times mainly by the various sects, which, by destroying the temporal power, hoped to make it easier for themselves to assail and combat the Pope's spiritual authority, clearly demonstrates that, in the intention of Providence, the temporal sovereignty of the Popes is still to be regarded as a means to the regular exercise of their Apostolic power, inasmuch as it constitutes an effective guarantee of their freedom and independence. What We have said in general of the civil Principate of the Popes applies even more, and in a special way, to Rome. The city's entire history clearly proclaims its destiny. . . . The fate of Rome has been linked, divinely and indissolubly, to that of the Vicar of Jesus Christ. . . . Spontaneously, without inflicting any injury or encountering any opposition, and by the most lawful means, the Popes became not only her spiritual but her temporal overlords, and as such they have continued to rule her down to our own days. . . . It would be foolish to pretend that the Popes willingly sacrificed, along with their temporal sovereignty, that which was their most sacred and precious possession—We mean their freedom to govern the Church, for which their Predecessors had always fought so gloriously. With God's help We certainly shall not fail in Our duty, and unless We are invested once again with a true and effective sovereignty, consistent with Our independence and with the dignity of the Apostolic See, We can envisage no clear way to agreement and peace. The Catholic Church, supremely jealous of the freedom of its Head, will never rest until it sees His just grievances redressed. We know that politicians, compelled to recognize what is obvious, namely that present conditions militate against the Roman Pontificate, are devising new plans and expedients to improve them. But these attempts are vain and useless; and so will be all others of a similar kind, which under the pretence of restoring the Pope's sovereignty leave Him in fact in a state of utter subjection. . . . Hitherto the only effective means that Providence has devised in order to protect the freedom of the Papacy has been the temporal power.' Leo XIII then proceeded to refute the arguments of those who opposed the restoration of the Pope's sovereignty and to deny that national unity was either necessary or desirable. He cited instances of 'extremely prosperous nations—nations [that were] powerful and glorious' despite the fact that they had not been combined with others into a single

State—and appealed to that common sense which demanded that justice should prevail—'justice, foundation-stone of the happiness and the stability of nations'. He also made it clear that he regarded the restoration of the temporal power as a practical possibility, pointing out that if the Popes were to regain possession of their civil authority they would not fail 'to enrich it with all the perfections of which it is capable, taking into account the problems of the age and the new needs of the people'. They would 'lighten the burden of taxation', behave 'with the utmost generosity towards charitable organizations and benevolent institutions' and take 'special care of the needy and of the working classes, whose lot they would be at pains to improve. . . . In a word, [they would make] of the civil Principate one of those institutions that are best calculated to promote the welfare of the people'.

The advocates of conciliation took note of this letter and expressed their confidence in the future. Stefano Jacini, who had been a junior minister in Cavour's Government and who in 1871 had voted in Parliament against the proposal to transfer the capital to Rome, now admitted that to place the city once more under the jurisdiction of the Holy See would be to destroy the whole fabric of the Italian State. He spoke of the satisfaction that would be felt throughout the Catholic world if all the nations were to recognize the Law of Guarantees, according the Pope all the honours due to a sovereign, permitting him to exercise his authority without let or hindrance, and leaving him free to communicate with the Faithful and with the governments of temporal states. Carlo Francesco Gabba, one of the greatest jurists of the day, took a similar line to Jacini.

In face of the Pope's letter the Italian Government at first adopted a non-committal attitude.

In a telegram to the Mayor of Rome (September 20th) Humbert I, alluding to Leo XIII's forthcoming jubilee, which was to be marked by an exhibition in the Vatican and by a rally of pilgrims, expressed himself in the following terms: 'On an auspicious occasion in the near future Rome will prove to the world that, besides all the refinements of modern civilization, she can offer to those who visit her in order to pay homage to the Supreme Pontiff the assurance of her gracious hospitality, at the same time maintaining to the full her dignity as the capital of a country that is both strong and free.'

Zanardelli, Keeper of the Seals, rejected the proposal of Bonghi, a deputy, that the signatories of petitions advocating reconciliation should be brought to trial.

Thereafter, however, the situation deteriorated rapidly.

When the Mayor of Rome, Duke Torlonia, called on the Cardinal Vicar and asked him to convey to the Holy Father the good wishes of his fellow-citizens and himself on the occasion of his jubilee, Crispi called a meeting of the Council of Ministers at the end of which he submitted to the King for signature a proclamation to the effect that the Mayor had been relieved of his post. This document was at once accorded the widest publicity. It provoked vigorous protests on the part of Catholics, but liberals were for the most part content to reserve their judgment.

At the municipal elections in Rome on June 19th, 1887, the Roman Union party, a coalition of Catholics and conservatives, had gained a notable victory. After the dismissal of Mayor Torlonia the Government used all its influence in an effort to ensure that the Commune of Rome would be controlled by a liberal administration; an electoral committee composed of a number of exalted personages—it included the son of Garibaldi as well as a member of each of the two most ancient Roman families, the Caetani and the Colonna—announced a programme which made it plain that the election was to be fought on political issues. In the event the liberals won the contest by a handsome majority.

In 1891 F. S. Nitti, a young professor who was destined to become a noted statesman,[1] published a slender volume entitled *Il socialismo cattolico* which contains the following passage: 'If the Papacy were to follow the lead given by so many of its clergy, if it continued steadfastly along the road that it has chosen, if it had the courage to proclaim peace between capital and labour, recognizing that the second has the same rights as the first and promoting an accord between them, it would find itself at the head of a movement which no man could check and which would perhaps enable the Church to realize its ancient Catholic dream.'

Without repeating what we have already said about Leo XIII's social policy and Catholic initiatives in the same field, we may

---

[1] President of the Council in 1919, Nitti spent the period of the Fascist régime in exile. He returned to politics after the Second World War, and as a member of the Constituent Assembly of 1947–48 showed that he had lost none of his skill as a parliamentarian.

mention that liberal reaction to the first indications that the Church was proposing to concern itself with the welfare of the people, and perhaps even to espouse the cause of the workers, was vigorous in the extreme. One would almost say that the clerical organizations of the time had had a vague premonition of the return of the confessional State, of the growth of the popular party and of Christian democracy.

There were, meanwhile, those who continued to look back upon the past, unable to dismiss from their minds the fear of a disruption of Italian unity, to rid themselves of the obsession which had haunted the men of 1861–66, namely that the Vatican was scheming for the return of the King of the Two Sicilies and of the Dukes. Every sign of unrest, every popular disturbance, every national setback, great or small, evoked the cry: 'Behold the hand of the priest.' The Vatican was behind everything—behind the Government's failure to conclude commercial treaties, behind the tariff-wars, behind the setbacks of the Italian Consolidated Fund, behind the labour agitations. On the morrow of the first desultory uprisings of the Sicilian *Fasci*—clearly the unorganized, unplanned protest of men driven to desperation by poverty—Crispi accused the leaders of the movement of having acted in collusion with clerical associations of other European countries.[1] Writing in his newspaper, *La Riforma*, Jessie White Mario, in an article entitled *I veri sobillatori*, insisted that the disturbances in Sicily were clerical in inspiration.[2]

In an article published in 1897 the young Right-Wing deputy Sidney Sonnino—a future President of the Council and Italian Foreign Minister throughout the First World War—pointed out that, if on the one hand 'socialism wishes in the name of equality to suppress all individual liberties ... on the other hand the clerical organization, which, opposed as it is to all freedom of thought and conscience, tends in reality towards the most intolerant obscurantism and believes in the suppression of disorder through the suppression of progress and of every manifestation of the human spirit, is making giant strides as much in the name of the loftiest ideals of the human fraternity as of good order and the maintenance of the social traditions of the past'.

In May, 1898, socialist disorders occurred all over Italy, reach-

[1] F. Crispi, *Discorsi parlamentari*, III, p. 687, session of February 28th, 1894.
[2] No. 11, dated January 12th, 1894.

ing their climax in Milan, where the declaration of a state of siege, the severity of the repressions, and the sentences passed by the military tribunals provoked a popular reaction which was to determine the character of Italian liberalism for the next seventeen years. These disturbances were the signal for unprecedented outbursts of hostility to Catholic organizations. Among those arrested in Milan was Don Davide Albertario, writer of impassioned articles and pamphlets in defence of the temporal power. Was it blindness or merely considerations of expediency that led the authorities to accuse such a well-known personality of Catholic intransigence in order to make people believe that the Vatican was profiting by the labour unrest to further its own anti-Italian political designs?

Writing in *La Nuova Antologia*, the deputy Ugo Pisa named among the causes of the disturbances in Milan 'a vast and intricate network of committees, brotherhoods and clerical conventicles, all of which refuse to recognize the unification of Italy with Rome as her capital and are extremely active in advocating and plotting, under the cloak of electoral organizations and Catholic congresses, the restoration of the temporal power. This is not to speak of the numerous other cells of the pseudo-Catholic party, whose activity consists in propagating collectivist principles and imbuing the masses with the idea that, if such principles are to be put into practice at an early date, the State must be compelled to restore to the Church, sole champion of morality and social equality, those rights which it has wrongfully appropriated'.[1]

The Rudinì Ministry could not withstand the pressure which was brought to bear upon it from every side, and among the many organizations which it dissolved in those days were the Catholic associations. In an encyclical of August 5th Leo XIII formally protested against this policy.

But the reaction was not long delayed.

The same great review of the liberal middle class, *La Nuova Antologia*, sprang to the defence of the associations, declaring that they represented an admirably compact network of provident societies unobtrusively constructed by the Church in an extremely short space of time, and that they were attuned to the modern age and to the needs of the people, especially of those living in the country.

[1] *La sommossa di Milano*, in *La Nuova Antologia*, vol. 159, June 16th, 1898, pp. 674 *sqq.*

The sympathies of the majority went out to these associations. Few believed that they were in league with the rebels, with the builders of the barricades. The good sense of the people (tempered with a suggestion of mental laziness, which made it impossible for them to imagine the Catholic association in any guise other than that of the confraternity or the benevolent society) protested against all expressions of sectarian feeling. The orders to disband were revoked, the associations revived. The episode had done them good. That brief experience of martyrdom had surrounded them with an aura of nobility, had helped to discredit some of the prejudices of those workers who had already half embraced the philosophy of the class struggle.

Bibliographical Note.

Essential for the understanding of Italian trends of thought, and in particular the attitude of politically-minded Italians of this period, is F. Chabod, *Storia della politica estera italiana dal 1870 al 1896, Le premesse*, Bari, 1951.
For the pontificate of Leo XIII in all its aspects v. C. Crispolti and G. Aureli, *La politica di Leone XIII da Luigi Galimberti a Mariano Rampolla*, Rome, 1912; E. Vercesi, *Tre papi: Leone XIII, Pio IX, Benedetto XV*, Milan, 1929; E. Soderini, *Il pontificato di Leone XIII*, Milan, 1923–33; F. Hayward, *Léon XIII*, Paris, 1937.
On the Catholic political and social movement in Italy v. E. Vercesi, *Il movimento cattolico in Italia* (1870–1922), Florence, 1923; F. Fonzi, *I cattolici e la società italiana dopo l'unità*, Rome, 1953; G. de Rosa, *L'Azione cattolica, Storia politica dal 1874 al 1904*, Bari, 1953; F. Magri, *L'azione cattolica in Italia* (1775–1951), two volumes, Milan, 1953 (especially the chapters relating to the post-Fascist era); G. Candeloro, *Il movimento cattolico in Italia*, Rome, 1953; G. Spadolini, *L'opposizione cattolica*, Florence, 1954.
There are no biographies of King Humbert. For the feeling at Court during this period, the religious fervour of Queen Margaret, contemporary politicians, and the lingering distrust felt by anti-clericals for 'Risorgimentalists', even for those without any definite Jacobin affiliations, the student should consult D. Farini, *Diario*, Milan, 1942.
On Crispi v. G. Castellini, *Crispi*, Florence, 1915; G. Salvemini, *La politica estera di Francesco Crispi*, Rome, 1919; A. C. Jemolo, *Crispi*, Florence, 1921; V. E. Orlando, *Crispi* [lecture], Palermo, 1923; F. Ercole, *La personalità storica ed il pensiero politico di Francesco Crispi* [lecture], Palermo, 1928; G. Volpe, *Francesco Crispi*, Venice, 1928.

CHAPTER IV

THE NEW CENTURY

ON the morning of December 24th, 1899, the bells of all the churches in Rome rang out in jubilation. The city was filled with a joyous medley of sound.

In St. Peter's Leo XIII was inaugurating the Holy Year. The words conjured up a vision of festivities of which few had any personal recollection. For in the last Holy Year, 1875, there had been no public celebrations; and it had been the same in the Holy Year of 1850, which had been inaugurated while Pius IX was still in exile at Gaeta. Thus, even for the oldest among the Romans, the Holy Year that was opening with a series of pilgrimages whose ordered dignity nothing could disturb was destined to be unique of its kind.

But when the Holy Year was over the bells would ring in a new century, one to which Italians looked forward with anxiety, though not with any undue pessimism. Indeed, there were not a few who believed that the new century would be completely dominated by economic questions and that, with new scientific techniques placing more and more resources at the disposal of mankind, even the problems of the class war would admit of a peaceful solution. Such optimism was inspired by the knowledge that for thirty years past none of the great European Powers had taken up arms except for the purpose of embarking on colonial adventures, and that the two age-old rivalries, between England and Russia for the hegemony of Asia and between England and France for the possession of the African colonial territories, had been reconciled, or were in the process of being reconciled, without recourse to arms.

So, too, in the matter of relations between Church and State in Italy, those who looked beneath the surface would have discerned a general feeling of confidence.

Catholic journalists might continue to write that thirty years represented, after all, an insignificant period in the history of the

Papacy, which was measured in terms of centuries, and that, indeed, it was comforting to note that after a lapse of thirty years Catholics were more than ever alive to the importance of the Roman question, as was evidenced by the fact that no Catholic congress ever assembled anywhere in the world without expressing hopes, freely endorsed by royal princes and influential parliamentarians, that the intolerable situation in which the Papacy found itself would soon be remedied. But this did not alter the fact that no member of the College of Cardinals, none of those—prelates or laymen, Italians or foreigners—who counted for most in the Catholic world, could any longer seriously visualize the papal gendarmes stalking the streets of Rome. Such an idea was inconceivable outside the realm of fantasy or dreams.

In its turn, the anti-clerical Press might continue to talk of the papal she-wolf lurking in the heart of Italy, of the Pope as Italy's arch-enemy, of the necessity of repealing the Law of Guarantees; but no one in his heart of hearts thought, and few certainly desired, to see the Pope exiled from Italy or even expelled from the Vatican and reduced to living in a monastery.

In the minds of most there was a deep-seated conviction—based on a variety of considerations and prompted by a number of motives—that on many questions the last word had already been spoken. The abolition of the temporal power and the Law of Guarantees, the formal suppression of the monasteries and the tolerance that enabled them to survive in the form of free associations and to continue their religious, scholastic and philanthropic activities, the substantial secularization of State institutions and in particular the non-recognition by the State of religious marriages—these things were regarded by nearly everyone as established and irremovable features of the Italian scene. But there were some who believed, and justly, that within the limits defined by these landmarks there was still room for a great number of divergences of opinion, less clamorous, less substantial than those which had arisen in the nineteenth century. These nevertheless were still likely to arouse the passions of Catholics and anti-clericals alike, having regard to the continuing uncertainty as to the fate of those *summa bona* which the former identified with the salvation of souls and freedom of conscience, the latter with freedom of speech, liberty of thought, and the sovereignty of the State. These divergences of opinion centred on the following questions: the legalization of religious instruction in State schools and Government recognition and inspection of free schools; the legality or otherwise of juridical measures designed to guarantee endowments to religious communities not recognized by the State; the continued secularization of the confraternities as opposed to the abandonment of this policy, which in fact deprived the ecclesiastical authorities of capital that still had considerable value by contemporary standards; the status (equal or inferior) to be accorded under the new social legislation to confessional organizations (co-operative societies, banks, friendly societies or workers' associations) in comparison with secular bodies. To this list might perhaps be added the law according civil marriage precedence of religious marriage, a measure that was still bitterly defended by the parties of the Left.

But younger Catholics, who were less attached to the past with all its regrets and rancours, did not visualize future relations between Church and State in terms of a list of battles that must be fought and if possible won. They did not look at the problem as they might have looked at a lake whose waters were gradually subsiding after being lashed to fury by a gale. Instead, they felt that slowly a new situation was arising, that new trends were becoming apparent which might bring unexpected developments, not only in the relations of Church and State, but also in those of believers and unbelievers, of militant Catholics and Catholics who were such merely in virtue of the fact that they had been baptized and that they had recourse to the sacraments in the more solemn hours of their lives—perhaps only when they were married or had suffered bereavement—and who at the same time were heedless of all the efforts of the educational authorities to initiate them in the mysteries of politics and economics.

In every country where socialism had taken root a new ingredient had been thrown into the melting-pot of internal politics, an ingredient which produced unexpected divisions and groupings. That which the Catholic Church's desperate appeal for the defence of moral values had failed to accomplish—partly because right-thinking people had never felt, especially and with good reason in Italy, that liberalism offered a serious threat either to the integrity of the family, or to the indissolubility of marriage, or to the traditional relationship between children and their parents —was to-day being brought about by the threat to economic

values. One of the reasons for this was that even those who
professed to be violently opposed to historical materialism felt in
some obscure way that many moral values were much more
closely related to the economic values in question than to religious
values. A society in which there was no private property, in which
fathers did not bequeath their possessions to their children, in
which the State owned all lands and industries and the factories
belonged to the workers, seemed far more chaotic than a society
whose code of laws provided for the affiliation of illegitimate
children and even for divorce, and whose educational legislation
had moved in the direction of the monopoly of the State school.
Hence that necessity long proclaimed by moderate Catholics
especially, who were by no means obdurate in their demand for
the restoration of the temporal power, and with equal fervour by
those conservatives who did not identify themselves with the
tradition of the Risorgimento, and its legacy to succeeding
generations, and with the secularization of charitable institutions,
of schools, of the law: the necessity, namely, of an alliance of all
conservative forces, of men who could be relied upon to bury old
controversies, and to work together in the future in a spirit of compromise and mutual trust. The Church would never again fill its
ancient, historic role; but some of its aspirations, relating to
educational legislation and charitable institutions, would certainly
be fulfilled; its economic organizations, subject to the control of
parish priests and bishops and no longer regarded with hostility
by the State, would be able to reveal their true potentialities;
above all, it would have the satisfaction, within a single generation,
of seeing posts of authority filled by men who were among its
most devoted followers.

Now, only those who are far removed from the world of politics
and government make the mistake of overrating the significance of
the law and underrating the significance of its practical application. In the opinion of all expert judges, the Church had good
reason to be satisfied. Not only was it free to carry on its work of
winning souls without interruption, but it enjoyed the full protection of the State. Moreover, even though the laws remained
unchanged, a large number of Ministers, senior magistrates,
directors of great financial organizations and of the great railway
companies, were themselves practising Catholics; and, most
important, non-Catholics tended to regard even militant Cath-

olics, as well as those with political affiliations, as necessary partners in an alliance which, like all firm and active alliances, was based on the principle of *do ut des*. Written laws are mere words on a printed page: it is men who give them life when they apply them; and hermeneutics, the broad or narrow interpretation, the jurisprudence which, once it has been perfected, may well obscure the law, the ministerial circular defining the principles that must be observed in a particular case—all these things can twist the law to suit a purpose, making it signify one thing when its authors intended it to signify something quite different.

The joyful sound of the church bells ringing out on that morning of Christmas Eve, 1899, must surely have found an echo in many a Catholic heart. True, the ship of conciliation had struck a rock, and much of its cargo had been lost. Yet all that was essential had been saved; and now the vessel, its hull intact, was in sight of a new land—a land that offered to those on board a fairer prospect than any of them had imagined in their wildest dreams.

Political writers laid emphasis on the factors most likely to contribute to a practical understanding between Church and State, and even more between Catholics—trammelled by Church-controlled organizations and obedient to the directives of their bishops and parish priests in regard to the use and non-use of the political and administrative vote—and conservatives. Justly, they pointed out the futility of continuing to debate theoretical principles or questions which had long ceased to have any contemporary significance. With even greater wisdom, some of them asserted that it was impossible to eradicate from the hearts of men their sense of religious values. An enormous number of people continued to respect such values and to order their lives accordingly, even though intellectually they professed to accept what appeared to be an utterly contradictory set of universalistic conceptions and philosophical principles. It was therefore useless for any State to pursue a policy that was likely to antagonize those whose inner life was dominated by the religious factor. All these observations were just. But the factor which seemed most likely to operate in favour of a reconciliation was the rapid reduction in the number of convictions sincerely held by either side: on the one hand, the growing indifference of the secular world not only to everything connected with the internal working of the Church, but also to everything that savoured of abstract thought, general rules and formulas, and to that tremendous world of principles which had been the scene of all the great verbal clashes of the nineteenth century; on the other hand, the historic indifference of the Church to political forms, which it judged solely by the criterion of whether or not they were consistent with the maintenance of ecclesiastical liberties, and whether or not they respected the natural rights of man.

In point of fact, the sort of conciliation which came to be regarded as more and more possible of achievement was a conciliation rooted in indifference. The two sides were impelled to accept this idea by the necessity of facing together a number of very real dangers, of being able to count on each other's support in the battles which those dangers would make inevitable—in short, of building up confidence in each other's reliability as an ally in case of need. But Catholics and conservatives alike displayed a marked indifference to all that was unrelated to the purpose of the alliance. Catholics remained indifferent to problems of administrative organization, of constitutional reform, of codification, of tariff policy, of monetary policy, unless some incidental consideration led them to discern in their solution one way or another possibilities of success or failure for their own party. More radical and more profound was the indifference of the conservatives, and of politically-minded Italians in general, to what transpired within the Church: so that the condemnation of certain principles of biblical exegesis or ecclesiastical history or of some interpretation of Christian dogma, the reform of the seminaries, the codification of canon law, the intensification of the ecclesiastic's subjection to the authority of his superior (involving the introduction of a regulation providing for the dismissal of recalcitrant parish priests), the condemnation of every philosophy that constituted a deviation from Thomism—all these things were regarded by the politically-minded Italian as if they were happening on another planet, and could in no way endanger the values by which he set most store.

Anyone free from prejudice and unattracted by outmoded systems of thought, who looks at those who still called themselves liberals—the politicians who constituted a majority at Montecitorio and at the Palazzo Madama round about the turn of the century, and the eminent university professors who wrote in the

G

political dailies with the widest circulations—and compares them with the men who had filled their shoes a generation earlier, at the time of the seizure of Rome and the Law of Guarantees, cannot but regard this cleavage as a factor of paramount significance.

In the political world of 1900 a man of the type of Ricasoli, who regarded the religious problem as essentially a social and political problem, and who felt that the spirit which dominated the internal life of the Church was of vital concern to the State and its rulers, would have been considered an anachronism. Those rare politicians who, in the eyes of their contemporaries, tended to exaggerate the importance of the problem of relations between Church and State, were already beginning to assume a slightly ridiculous, not to say grotesque appearance. Italians well understood the sentiments of the politician of the Right who, in pursuit of his conservative aims, insisted on the necessity of cultivating the Church, which was, or could be, such a powerful ally, of making every concession to it, above all of not exasperating it by attempting to revive anti-clerical feeling. They adopted a considerate attitude towards the university professor who stressed the importance of the religious sentiment, of its individual and collective manifestations, both ordinary and abnormal. But after the death of Ruggero Bonghi the internal life of the Church had become, so far as the secular and liberal world was concerned, the private preserve of a few journalistic 'specialists'. To them the small talk of the Vatican, the prospect of this or that cardinal's succession to the papacy, the petty scandals of the Black aristocracy, the strictures of the Congregations of the Holy Office and of the Index were as significant as the disciplinary reforms which were so important in the eyes of canonists and of future historians of the Church.

Thus the most essential conditions for a reconciliation had already been largely fulfilled, and would so continue as the politically-minded class altered in character, as it ceased to consist primarily of lawyers and professors, men of humanistic or philosophic culture who attached great importance to abstract principles. The most solidly-based reconciliation would be one that enabled each to offer the other something that would be much prized by the recipient and of little value to the donor. I speak of the conditions for a reconciliation rather than of reconciliation itself: for history is made by human beings, and nothing is achieved or completed automatically, but rather by the concentrated endeavours of resolute men; so at every moment the situation presents ways that are open and ways that are barred, ways that no individual will, no personal effort can ever succeed in opening up, and a multiplicity of broad highways, between which a choice can always be made.

If a referendum were held among Italians to nominate the two greatest personalities of the last fifty years, without regard to the nature of their activities, I believe that most—with the exception of an inconsiderable number of Fascists—would put their crosses against the names of Benedetto Croce and Giovanni Giolitti. Of very different types—they had a wholesome respect for each other—Croce was a minister in Giolitti's last Government and as a historian of the twentieth century reassessed Giolitti's work: the one a thinker, a front-rank figure among European intellectuals, a man of vast culture, but who for the greater part of his life remained on the fringe of politics, and only in his old age played an active part in them, and even then only a minor part; the other a man whose culture, though considerable, was nevertheless limited, who devoted all his energies to political life and saw everything through the eyes of a parliamentarian, who in politics was not a theorist but an empiricist with a special flair for dealing with problems of finance and administration.

Cultivated people outside Italy know of Benedetto Croce the idealistic philosopher and the historian; but it is impossible for those who have no direct experience of Italian life to realize what he has meant to Italians. It is not enough even to say that he was the philosopher and teacher of at least two generations, from the eighties onwards, for Croce, who never occupied a university chair, not only had a decisive influence on the intellectual development of those who knew him, who read his books and adhered to his philosophy, but, as happens to the very few who for a time completely dominate the intellectual life of a country, he made an essential, if indirect, contribution to the education of those who did not come under his immediate influence, did not read his works, or remained for ever hostile to his teaching.

Neither the Catholic anchored to the teaching of the Church, with its traditional philosophy founded on Thomism, nor the Communist intellectual enslaved by dialectical materialism, could ever claim to be a disciple of Croce. But among the exponents of Catholic culture it is necessary to distinguish between the many who have read Croce, absorbing his doctrines if only later to repudiate them, who have continually revised their traditional beliefs in the light of Crocian idealism, and who have constantly reconsidered and brought up to date almost all their literary and historical judgments in the light of what Croce wrote: and the few who, shut away in monasteries or languishing in remote villages, have remained in fact inaccessible to Croce, and in some cases have never even heard of him. Between them there is a great gulf fixed. The first are contemporaries with whom one can talk and argue; they differ from us in outlook, but their world is the same. The second belong to a different world, and with them no argument is possible; they exert no influence, nor are they amenable to any, because all the channels of communication between themselves and the outside world are blocked.

In the same way, one cannot adequately explain Italian Communism to-day, or the fact that it is still possible for intellectuals of opposite convictions to achieve a limited measure of agreement, unless one reflects that the Communist intellectual who has hitherto stolen most of the limelight is not the man who has been brought up exclusively on the standard texts of Communism, but the man who has matured in the grammar schools and universities of Italy and who, however much he likes to cite only those standard texts as his sources, is in reality also of Crocean derivation.

In this sense, I believe, Croce's influence was far greater than that of Gioberti and Rosmini, whose work covered a much narrower field and who, moreover, could not claim to have set a whole generation talking and arguing about their doctrines. It may be compared (although his work made a far less profound social impact, and—as the formative element of two generations, not as a contribution to European philosophy—it had a purely domestic significance) with that of the great precursors of the French Revolution, Voltaire and Rousseau, or with that exerted over a similar period by Goethe.

What was Croce's contribution to Italian thought about the relations between Church and State?

During the early years of Fascism there were some who accused Croce of having been one of its originators. This ridiculous accusation was prompted perhaps by the recollection that, at the beginning of the Fascist era and of the period of nationalism that preceded it, the Italian people had found themselves without the means of combating the anti-Risorgimental, anti-illuministic, anti-humanitarian doctrines which those movements proclaimed. For Croce had dispelled many of the animosities, exposed the baselessness of many of the ingenuous beliefs, and exploded many of the myths which, though they represented the dross of the thought of the Risorgimento, were nevertheless the medium through which it imposed itself on the humbler classes, on those who were no more than half educated.

In 1905 Croce published in his review, *La Critica*, his 'personal recollections' *A proposito del positivismo italiano*, in which he wrote: 'Among the imbecilities which the man who concerns himself with philosophy and with the pursuit of learning in general may commit in the course of his life, there is one which I can boast that I have always avoided, even in my earliest youth: I have never been a *positivist*.' And he describes the adherents of positivism—students, lawyers, doctors—who read nothing, repeat the usual parrot-cries, and quote at second and third hand without even bothering to check their facts. What depresses Croce is the vulgarity of the masses, of the half-educated people who crowd the universities and leave them with the regulation diplomas and degrees, and the sight of so much vulgar anti-clericalism, compounded of ignorance and incomprehension, nurtured on legends which no self-respecting historian would ever dream of discussing, and incapable of discriminating between the various branches of the Church's activity. What offends him is the average man's superstitious, fetishistic attachment—the fruit of mental laziness much more than of enlightened enthusiasm—not to the doctrines of the Risorgimento but to its dross, to its incomprehension of all that went before, of the centuries of history that preceded it (an attachment which, he feels, incidentally casts a slur on the traditions of his native province and of his family, on the judgments which he as a historian has passed on the Kingdom of Naples). What pains him is the puerile negation of the whole life of the spirit, the puerile belief that chemistry and physiology can take the place of philosophy.

But even the great positivists do not escape his censure. Herbert Spencer is described as 'one of the most jejune philosophers who ever lived'. 'The only philosophers recognized as legitimate and treated with respect [by the positivists] were those who promised, with the gestures of quack dentists haranguing the crowds from the top of their barrows laden with medicine bottles and tins, to pursue their philosophical researches in the laboratory, with the aid of scientific instruments and mechanical gadgets.'

Are we still in the realm of pure philosophy? Yes and no.

With his usual candour Croce continues: 'My horror of positivism . . . became so intense that for several years it stifled even the democratic sympathies which I have always possessed. . . . For some reason unknown (unless, perhaps, it was that blind adulation of popularity which is almost inevitable under this form of government), Italian democracy was positivistic in character; and my stomach refused to digest it until it had been seasoned with Marxian socialism, which, as everybody now knows, is impregnated with classical German philosophy. Even to-day the positivistic phraseology of certain Italian democrats gets on my nerves and makes me almost wish I were a conservative . . . and many more or less worthy democratic agitators would be well-advised to refrain from discoursing upon science and philosophy, of which they lack the expert knowledge with which one must credit them in other fields of human activity.' From this position he never retreated.

If we turn to *La filosofia della pratica* we read: 'This function of an idealistic ethical symbol, this affirmation that the moral act is an expression of the love and the will of the universal Spirit, is characteristic of the religious and Christian Ethic, the Ethic of love and of the anxious search for the divine presence, which, as a result of narrow partisanship or lack of insight, is spurned and vilified to-day by vulgar rationalists and intellectualists, by so-called free-thinkers and similar riff-raff who frequent masonic lodges. There is hardly any truth of Ethics that cannot be expressed in the words of traditional religion, which we learned as children and which rise spontaneously to our lips because they are the most sublime, the most appropriate, and the most beautiful of all: words that are, to be sure, still redolent of mythology, yet at the same time instinct with philosophy. Between the idealistic philosopher and the religious man there is undoubtedly a deep rift; but it is no different from that which appears in ourselves on the eve of a crisis, when we are mentally divided, and yet very close to inner unity and harmony. If the religious man cannot help regarding the philosopher as his adversary, indeed as his mortal enemy, the philosopher for his part sees in the religious man his younger brother, himself as he was but a moment before. Hence, he will always feel more strongly attracted to an austere, compassionate, allegorical religious ethic than to one that is superficially rationalistic.'

This page forms a prelude to the better-known essay published in 1942, *Perché non possiamo non dirci 'cristiani'*.[1]

Even before Croce we can discern, in the cultured bourgeoisie of liberal traditions—we need not here attempt to define the sentiments of the Catholic middle class—an impatience both with the exponents of positivistic pseudo-philosophy, who actually believed that physiology and the other positive sciences could dispel all shadows, leaving no further room for speculation, and with the pseudo-history which sought to substantiate slanderous tales about Popes or kings, devoid of any documentary foundation, as well as with those who evinced an intense and unqualified admiration for all the personalities and events of the Risorgimento.

Croce used his influence to encourage these still half-hearted and sporadic tendencies.

The old anti-clericals, who saw the hand of the 'Jesuit' in every disaster, and regarded the great saints merely as impostors or eccentrics or even as madmen, gradually degenerated into figures of fun; and the old patriotic rhetoric, based on invective and on evocations of Italian glories, became equally insupportable.

All this helped in no small measure to increase the seriousness of our outlook, to purify our culture; it had a powerful educational effect on the Italian middle class and on university students. But it is none the less true that a first defensive barrier against a revival of anti-illuministic doctrines—the weakest of all, but the one that protected the least-cultured classes—had now fallen. When men of fervent piety and lofty sentiments take up the axe and proceed to demolish legends and superstitions, truly religious spirits take heart of grace and breathe more freely: they cleave to their Church, which becomes stronger than ever; but men of

---

[1] Anyone who wishes to obtain an idea of the vehement reaction on the part of convinced positivists to Croce's writings should read the little-known posthumous essay by the economist Achille Loria, *Una crociera eccezionale* (Milan, 1947), in which it is asserted (p. 72) that it was Croce's 'undisguised intention to rebuild religion on the ruins of positivism. In spite of everything, he is still no more than an archpriest of the *Scuole Pie*. . . . '

smaller minds, who are more numerous, the mentally lazy, incapable of abandoning their routine or of reasoning, quickly lose their bearings; beneath the outer crust of superstition and legend that has fallen away they fail to discern the vibrant pulse of faith. So it was that those who taught men to regard the Risorgimento with a dispassionate eye, to venerate it for its truly good qualities, for the currents of thought which had inspired it and run through it, for the virtues of its most illustrious figures, contrived in the process to educate a certain number of enlightened spirits, inveterate anti-totalitarians whom Fascism could never have deflected from their course. At the same time, however, they imbued the minds of ordinary men with the idea that it was permissible to criticize the followers of Garibaldi, that one need not be a Jesuit to maintain that there had been some good in the world before the Risorgimento, that the latter had even destroyed a number of excellent institutions. And so for many mediocre intelligences, for certain indolent minds, the Risorgimento, ceasing to be above criticism, ceased also to constitute a safeguard against the temptation to return to the cult of the despot which relieves the individual man of the necessity of thinking for himself, to the cult of blind obedience to the ruler, in which the voice of conscience is silenced.

There was, moreover, running through the whole of Croce's work, a vein of anti-illuminism, which certainly represented an intellectual achievement on the part of the philosopher, and which influenced even minds more acute than those whose judgment might have been warped by a too-realistic vision of the Risorgimento.

Croce's philosophy is a-religious, and there is no place in it for the infinite. It lays due emphasis on the ethical and social values of Christianity, but all meditation and speculation on a possible supernatural world are held to be outside its province. It is not concerned with effecting compromises, with tracing out lines of demarcation, with allocating spheres of influence. The worlds of thought and reason, all the possible achievements of the human intellect—these are the province of philosophy, which is sovereign and independent in its own field. Beyond is the realm of poetry, the realm of mythology; beyond, too, in accordance with a poetic convention, is the realm of religion. But the compromise which other philosophies have attempted, the consideration of an aspect of reality which cannot be explored by reason and which represents the special province of religion, the legitimate domain of a faith not subject to rational controls, remains extraneous to the philosophy of Croce.

It is well known that certain thinkers, following in the wake of this philosophy, have believed in the possibility of reaching a compromise with Catholicism: a compromise which, however, in the best-known attempt, that of Giovanni Gentile, entails the complete subordination of the traditional Catholic doctrine, which is left with only a nominal independence, to the idealistic philosophy, which appropriates its substance.[1]

Personally, through *La Critica*, Croce was always a champion of lay culture and of the secular State. His writing was frequently anti-clerical in tone, and he deprecated the way in which Catholic writers falsified history and the tendency of men with religious prejudices to reassess and disparage literary epochs and periods. This anti-religious strain is even more pronounced in the man who, after the dismissal of Gentile, collaborated with Croce in the work of editing *La Critica*: Adolfo Omodeo.

However, among the ways in which the political world might have exploited Croce's thought was the possibility that, basing itself on the clear-cut distinction between religion, which belongs to the realm of poetry, and the Church, which represents social power, with aims that are realized in every sphere of practical life, it might have discerned no inconsistency of conduct in a State which described itself as secular and claimed to preserve the autonomy of its own ethical life, but which at the same time made all sorts of concessions to the Church in the juridical field—which, no less than the economic field, is a sphere of practical life—and bound itself to the Holy See through concordats giving the latter a privileged position.

Giovanni Giolitti was a minister during Italy's years of prosperity (1900–15)—the era of her industrial development, of the conquest of Libya, of the paper lira which more than held its own against the gold currency.

He belonged to a generation which in its adolescence, when it

---

[1] See also the last published writing of G. Gentile, a lecture entitled *La mia religione* (Florence, 1943), where there is an echo of Lambruschini in the references to the negativity of religious dogmas and the restrictive character of the authority responsible for their maintenance as also for their formulation.

was too young to participate in military or political events, had seen the unification of Italy completed as if by a miracle within the space of two years; a generation which could not recall the conspiracies, the political trials, the Mazzinianism of the heroic period, even though its members must have been fully conversant with the history of such recent events and in their early childhood may even have heard them described by their parents. This generation had grown up in the years following 1861. It may therefore be said (speaking generally) that it had not experienced the dissatisfaction and indignation which so many of the pre-1860 liberal middle class had felt at the corruption and the inadequacy of the infant State and at its failure to reflect the renewed national consciousness. It had, however, been considerably influenced in its most formative years by that feeling of disappointment which always follows the realization of plans long prepared and contemplated—of designs hitherto regarded as the key to a substantial betterment of conditions—and in particular the institution of new political régimes: a feeling which was in fact widespread in Italy during the years that followed the country's unification.

Giolitti belonged to the Piedmontese middle class—which, although it had furnished the extreme parties with supporters, for the most part had continued to regard the conflicts of parties with suspicion and had remained hostile to and contemptuous of platform orators and extremists. This class was convinced of the necessity for the State (but for its horror of strong words it might, even have spoken of its 'sanctity'), convinced that it was every man's duty to see that the country was well governed. It did not share that distrust of all forms of State control and intervention which was apparent in other provinces; but its confidence in the State was fixed upon the administration, and did not extend to the various political organizations. Those who have known Piedmontese of Giolitti's generation are aware that in most cases —especially when they talked freely—they revealed an extreme bitterness towards the Garibaldini and the old radicals and an intense dislike and distrust of priests who dabbled in politics. For the most part they pursued moderate political ideals. Thus, they envisaged a separation of Church and State free from all rancour and unmarred by legalistic quibbling, together with a just administration, an irreproachable civil service, and a prudent financial policy, designed to keep taxes low and the market value of consolidated stock high. They were, accordingly, opposed to all adventures in the realm of foreign policy and, later on, to all colonial enterprises.

The middle class of that generation had one dominating characteristic (shared, incidentally, by all North Italians): a profound horror of advertising their feelings, which they felt should in no circumstances be exposed to public view.

Italians younger than himself who came from other provinces often disliked Giolitti for those characteristics which he shared with his fellow Piedmontese and with the rest of his generation of the provincial middle class. They disliked his persuasive but restrained oratory, sometimes witty and challenging but un-rhetorical, never appealing to sentiment, yet, when the necessity arose, he did not hesitate to invoke the great moral principles, making frequent references to the importance of a sense of duty and to the sanctity of the plighted word. They disliked the roughness of his style, which in his speeches was masked by a certain persuasiveness, a certain liveliness in debate, as well as by occasional flashes of wit, but which was fully apparent in his infrequent writings, and which in a literary sense placed him on a lower plane than such of his contemporaries as Crispi, Luzzatti, Sonnino, and even the modest Boselli. They disliked his seeming disregard for culture. In office, however, he strove to satisfy the educational needs of the people at all levels, formed a complete and accurate picture of the leading figures in every branch of Italian art and science and honoured in the most fitting ways those of his countrymen who had distinguished themselves in the literary, scientific and artistic fields. But it was completely foreign to his nature to adorn his conversation with literary quotations or in any way to reveal the extent of his knowledge and of his interests outside the sphere of politics and government. Again, even in the years of his greatest triumphs the majority of Italians were displeased by his ostentatious preference for internal politics, particularly for questions relating to finance, public works and departmental administration. But his apparent indifference to foreign affairs did not prevent him from bringing Italy's most auspicious colonial enterprise to a triumphant conclusion and from clearly defining in 1913 the limits of his country's obligations under the Triple Alliance, thereby nipping in the bud Austria's plans for a Serbian adventure. They disliked his way of considering

every question from the point of view of Parliament, his profound
conviction that the only 'country' of which it was necessary to
take account was the legislative body. Finally, they disapproved
of what was in fact his supreme virtue—his great sense of proportion, which led him to discourage excessive hopes and over-bold
aspirations.

Was Giolitti a religious man? Did he believe in God? The
Piedmontese of his generation had a great horror of displaying
their feelings, particularly in the matter of religion. They did not
flaunt their beliefs, however fervently held; their religion, in fact,
was devoid of any lyrical quality. On the question whether or not
they were practising Christians they always maintained a discreet
silence. (For that matter, history does not record whether Cavour
himself was in the habit of attending Mass and partaking of the
sacraments: all we know is that he received the consolations of
religion on his death-bed.)

To the best of our knowledge, even in conversation within
Giolitti's family circle the subject of religion was never mentioned.
He had the deepest respect for the beliefs of others. He considered
it natural that the great events of life—birth, marriage, death—
should be signalized by a religious ceremony. But he took no
intellectual part in religious discussions, even in those which
concerned the external life of the Church, its basic policies. On his
death-bed he found it natural to receive the consolations of
religion, and to no one did it seem that his attitude represented
the return of one who had strayed from the fold. But certainly he
had remained in a corner of the fold, showing little curiosity about
what took place elsewhere within it.

If there is one conviction which seems clearly to underlie the
whole of Giolitti's work—alike as Minister, as President of the
Council, and as leader of the party in power—in so far as it
concerns the relations between Church and State, it is this: that
the past is dead and buried; that Italy, united as never before,
has nothing to fear from the by now platonic demands of the
Holy See—whether propounded by Leo XIII, who, clearly, still
cherished territorial ambitions, or by Pius X, who merely deplored
the conditions imposed on the Papacy. That the possibility of a
formal reconciliation did not exist was the opinion of all clear-
sighted Italians, at any rate after the disappointment of 1887 and
until 1918. But Giolitti considered that such a reconciliation was

not even desirable. In character he was the antithesis of Crispi and—to compare him with a more recent figure—of Mussolini. By no means inclined to underrate the importance of personal success and prestige, he was attracted not by their superficial glitter but by their value as a means to an end. Thus, he loved to dominate the Chamber, but every so often he himself provoked crises which enabled him to retire for a period from the direction of public affairs. In his eyes they were to be measured in terms of concrete results achieved, not of interminable parliamentary ovations in which deputies joined with the spectators in the public galleries, and still less of popular acclamation, which would merely have irritated him. Like all the parliamentarians of his generation he tended to identify the country with the legislature, and so was inclined to underrate the significance of any manifestations of opinion which did not culminate in parliamentary divisions and in alterations of parliamentary majorities and minorities. (What view, incidentally, did the politicians of the early 1900s take of irredentist feeling, which counted for nothing in Parliament?) Because of this he considered that his great achievement in the matter of the relations between Church and State lay in the fact that he had succeeded in inducing Catholics to participate in political life without constituting a party of their own, which would have provoked reactions and revived controversies that might have proved embarrassing. In this way he had strengthened what he regarded as the *pars sanior* of the country, that which favoured enlightened and moderate progress. Unwittingly, too, he had realized the ideal of the statesman who makes the most effective contribution to reconciliation by never speaking of it, never setting a term for it—knowing that it will come about after he has descended into the peace of the grave, yet creating the spiritual atmosphere necessary to ensure that the work of time, which heals all wounds, shall not be impeded by controversies or by incidents that may inflame wounds not yet healed. But in truth we do not know whether in his heart of hearts he ever envisaged a formal reconciliation, however long delayed, whether he thought fit to work for it, if only in the interests of his own generation's children and grandchildren. He was, we must remember, always a man of the Left, and he was always the bureaucrat of the Piedmontese provincial middle class, with their characteristic horror of any manifestation of feeling, particularly religious feeling, and their aversion to any form of theatricality. I think he would have been not a little shocked to be shown the scenes so often depicted in popular oleographs, of the Pope arm-in-arm with the King, or of cheering crowds lining the route between St. Peter's and the Quirinal. His formula, almost certainly not premeditated, and not intended to be an amendment of Cavour's famous dictum, of the State and the Church advancing along two parallel lines, and hence never destined to meet, certainly expressed his true sentiments. And well did it epitomize the liberal creed, which a well-known German publicist had expressed many years before when he asserted that never in the course of his journey from the cradle to the grave should the citizen be asked by the State to expound his religious beliefs. Nor did his formula make it necessary for the State to adopt the dangerous procedure of blinding itself to facts, to remain in ignorance of the ways in which religious feeling found expression, of what the Faithful expected from the State in the way of moral leadership, and above all of the nature of the political forces that were arrayed on the side of the Church. Instead, it signified—and in this respect Giolitti's policy conformed to it—that legislation, which represents only a small part of a Government's activity, should never concern itself with religious matters, nor seek to give statutory effect to decrees or interdicts or sanctions designed to weaken the authority of the Church.

Humbert I had been a constitutional monarch; he had not revealed the hardihood of the first King of Italy, who had negotiated, over the heads of his ministers and even against their wishes, with Napoleon III, Pius IX and Garibaldi. But he had always taken an active interest in the development of the broad lines of his country's policy, had declared himself to be a fervent supporter of the Triple Alliance, and had opposed his ministers when they sought to effect economies at the expense of the army.

Even greater—though the significance of the fact should not be overrated—had been the interest shown in public affairs by Queen Margaret. The *Diario* of Domenico Farini, who was for a long time President of the Chamber of Deputies and later of the Senate, and who was a true child of the Risorgimento (his father had been 'Dictator' of Emilia in 1859 and he himself had taken an active part in the struggle for Italy's independence), contains some rather severe references to certain actions of 'this Bourbon Queen', as when, on meeting a procession, she alighted from her carriage and joined the throng, or when, on emerging from a religious ceremony, she lavished praises on a city councillor, known as a papalist and as an advocate of the restoration of the temporal power, who had resisted a proposal that the cross should be removed from the Capitol.

There had been much talk in those years of a 'Court party', with which it was alleged that Crispi had more than once come into conflict; and those elements which had enjoyed the true friendship of the King and Queen had been conservative in outlook.

The new King Victor Emmanuel III, who ascended the throne at the age of thirty-one, was a taciturn man; he was never to rid himself of the inferiority complex caused by an unfortunate physique and by a very strict, militaristic upbringing. He had no friends. Although he had never expressed any opinions it had always been said, at the time when he was Crown Prince, that he was hostile to Crispi's policy; and it was rumoured that he was a freemason.

The Court always counted for less in Italy than in other monarchies. After the death of King Humbert, it had been in some ways democratized—for example, it was now less difficult than it had been to obtain admission to the presence of the Queen and to Court balls—in others it had become even more remote from the people. The Queen, who was a good wife and mother, but who up to the last spoke Italian with a Balkan accent, did not seek, as Queen Margaret had done, to surround herself with men of letters, artists, and the most fashionable personalities of the day; she always remained indifferent to the country's intellectual life; and, like her husband, she had no friends. The King, who also suffered from an inability to remember faces, received visitors with strictly formal courtesy, asking questions which often revealed his culture and embarrassed his listener, but never permitting the latter to make any attempt to start a conversation. Politicians called into consultation at times of crisis were heard out in silence. The King's tutors must have instilled into him the principle, to which he adhered with a rigidity verging on the ludicrous, that a constitutional monarch 'never reveals his true feelings'; and, while he was cordial towards ministers in office, he would never have dreamed of showing the smallest sign of friendliness to the minister who had been defeated in Parliament. A politician who was for a long time one of his ministers—a former President of the Council and a member of the Order of Annunziata—used to say that the cordiality with which the King welcomed his new ministers was only equalled by the indifference with which he received those who had come to submit their resignation.

In these circumstances one could not really have described the King and Queen or the Court as dynamic forces in Italian life, the less so that the Court had always been organized on a strictly military basis: the King had never had a civilian staff, and he could only be approached through his chief aide-de-camp. And yet, during the first fifteen years of his reign, King Victor was often spoken of as a socialist or as a socialist sympathizer. Certainly he enjoyed the support of radicals and freemasons; and, by contrast, he was regarded with deep suspicion by ultra-conservative elements—a suspicion masked by an atavistic reverence in the older men, somewhat more overt in the young. On the occasion of an election a few conservative-nationalist journalists dared to suggest that the lackeys of the Quirinal had spared no pains to ensure the return of the social-reformist candidate in the second College of Rome, the one in which the royal palace was situated; and in the election of 1913 a number of young nationalists, preferring the less of two evils, surreptitiously voted for an old socialist-anarchist in order to keep out the retiring deputy, who was reputed to be the King's man.

Although the King was by nature taciturn, and the cordiality which he displayed on rare occasions was only relative—it was in no way comparable to the effusive friendliness, I will not say of a William II, but of an Edward VII—it appeared that he was favourably disposed towards Leonida Bissolati, a socialist deputy formerly identified with the extreme Left[1] who had later become a social-reformist, taking a line very similar to that of the radicals. In point of fact, Bissolati was a man of great integrity, a most noble patriot and humanitarian. A minister during the first war, he faded from the scene before his time after trying to oppose the bombastic nationalism of D'Annunzio and Mussolini, which was to mar for ever relations between Italy and Jugoslavia. It was said that the King was well disposed towards coalitions of parties of

---

[1] Bissolati was one of those who in the time of Crispi had cried 'Hands off Africa!' and 'Long live Menelik!' in token of protest against Italy's colonial enterprise.

the Left, in which anti-clericalism was the strongest unifying element and which asserted themselves principally in municipal elections. Certainly he seemed to maintain the most cordial and intimate relations with successive mayors of Rome, who in those years were nearly always frankly secular in outlook, and in particular with the mayor who modernized the capital, Ernesto Nathan, formerly a masonic Grand Master and still the *bète noire* of clerical sympathizers. On the other hand, the King's relations with the high clergy were extremely frigid (no one ever heard of a priest, or even of a Court chaplain, with whom the royal pair were on terms of any familiarity, with whom they were in the habit of holding long conversations). In all the cities of the realm— excepting only the province of Rome—to which the King went on official visits he was accorded the homage of the Bishop, and sometimes that of the Cardinal Archbishop. But the conversations which took place on these occasions were brief, and they were confined to neutral subjects. Sometimes the King made no secret of his annoyance when an indiscreet prelate alluded to his family's Catholic traditions or to the piety of his august mother. He never attended divine service even when he was on holiday. The only place of worship he ever opened was the synagogue in Rome. His children were for the most part entrusted to the care of Protestant nursemaids, both foreign and Italian (Waldensians).

As for the Queen—a Montenegrin princess who had embraced the Catholic faith for dynastic reasons—her philanthropic activities, which were principally concerned with the fight against certain infantile diseases, were always rigorously secular in character, and of the doctors who assisted her in her work not all were Catholics. She was never seen in the company of an ecclesiastic.

It may be added that in foreign affairs also, which in Italy as in every other country, but perhaps to an even greater extent there, have always been largely subordinated to considerations of domestic policy, the King did not reveal himself to be such a resolute champion of the Triple Alliance as his father. His reign began with a tour of military establishments which marked the end of the long period of tension between Italy and France, with visits to St. Petersburg, Paris and London, where Humbert I had never set foot—in short, with an orientation of foreign policy calculated to bring joy to the hearts of all radicals and republicans.

H

It is, I repeat, impossible to maintain that the Court initiated any movement having as its object the transformation of society, or even of the broad lines of Italian domestic policy. It was merely noted at the time that the death of Humbert I had removed an obstacle to the release and the operation of new forces.

When the Saracco Ministry, which Victor Emmanuel had inherited from his father, was overwhelmed by a parliamentary vote, the new King called upon Giuseppe Zanardelli to form a government. Zanardelli was, unequivocally, a man of the Left. As Keeper of the Seals he had sponsored a bill for the abolition of tithes (which had become law) and a divorce bill (tabled in 1884 and promptly rejected), and he was the author of the penal code of 1889 which embodied the laws suppressing the abuses to which ministers of religion were at that time particularly prone. Of his sympathy for irredentism he had given positive proof in his capacity of Keeper of the Seals, in the course of the legal proceedings which had followed the abortive gesture and the conviction of Oberdan. He was alleged on all sides to have masonic connections. The Church could not expect to find any support in this quarter.

In the Speech from the Throne of February 20th, 1902, it was announced that the Government proposed to submit a bill on the subject of divorce and affiliation. The question of divorce had already been raised in a bill sponsored by Berenini and Borciani and submitted to the Chamber by the former on December 6th, 1901. This bill sanctioned divorce on legal grounds (condemnation of husband or wife to not less than ten years' penal servitude, or legal separation dating back five years if there were children, three years if there were none); on moral grounds (*de facto* separation for a long period, or a combination of circumstances such as to preclude all hope of a reconciliation); and on physiological grounds (judicial interdiction due to an incurable mental infirmity of more than three years' standing, or to permanent impotence confirmed since marriage). Cocco Ortu, the Keeper of the Seals, requested the Chamber to give the proposal its earnest consideration. This it did, and the bill was subsequently accorded eight votes out of nine in committee. But the termination of the legislative session caused it to be dropped before it had come up for debate.

The government bill foreshadowed in the Speech from the Throne was submitted to the Chamber under the title of 'A Bill Relating to the Organization of the Family'. It was sponsored by the President of the Council, Zanardelli, and the Keeper of the Seals, Cocco Ortu.

A highly influential minister named Giusso, who represented with much distinction the conservative tradition of the South, saw fit to disclaim any moral responsibility for the bill by handing in his resignation. By contrast, Giolitti, Minister of the Interior, appeared indifferent to the fate of the proposal.

The bill sanctioned divorce only if the couple in question had obtained a judicial separation on the ground of adultery, wilful desertion of the conjugal roof, excesses, cruelty, or grave threats and injuries, or because one of the partners had been sentenced to penal servitude for a period of not less than twenty years. The proviso that the necessary application could not be made less than one year—three years if there were children of the marriage—after the court had confirmed the decree of separation made it difficult to get a divorce. A husband or wife divorced on the ground of adultery could not marry the co-respondent.

The report insisted that the bill should not be regarded as an attack on the integrity of the family, still less as an act of hostility to religion and the Church, but rather as a necessary act of social justice designed to relieve the sufferings of too many unhappy people who were united by a bond which, usually through no fault of their own, had become intolerable. It was puerile, said the report, to blame divorce for a disintegration of the family of which it was the consequence and for which it sought to provide a remedy. The question of divorce was not a religious question. In other Catholic countries where divorce had been introduced Catholics had not experienced any qualms of conscience. If it had been considered permissible to give the family, through civil marriage, a legal status founded on the law of the State, then it was logical that the State should also be able to provide for the dissolution of marriage. If, moreover, the Catholic conscience had regarded civil marriage as a form of concubinage, why should it be dismayed by its dissolution?

Opposition to the bill came, of course, principally from Catholics, but not from them alone: a firm stand was taken against it by the leader of the liberal conservatives, Sidney Sonnino.

All the forces of Catholicism were mobilized against the proposal. The list of petitions presented to Parliament for its rejection is also interesting as showing the distance travelled in a few years by Catholic organizations of an economic character, including co-operative and friendly societies and rural banks. Petitions against the bill were circulated for signature in all parishes. The Church, from the Holy See down to the last cathedral chapter, and the Press, from *La Civiltà Cattolica* to the weekly paper of the smallest cathedral town, resisted the proposal by every means in their power, as did vast numbers of individual men and women, without distinction between traditionalist Catholics of the old school and democratic Christians.

It was defended as a matter of course by the radicals, and less strenuously by the socialists, who had fought more whole-heartedly the year before for Berenini's bill, for which they had assumed a certain measure of responsibility. Leonida Bissolati declared in *Avanti* that the Socialist Party did not insist on the legalization of divorce, since, if the social system founded on capitalism and private ownership were replaced by a system based on collective ownership, the institution of marriage, which owed its origin to woman's need to be supported, would be transformed. The question of divorce primarily concerned the middle classes. Owing to the prohibitive cost of the litigation involved it was of no more than academic interest to the proletariat. A few papers of the extreme Left, such as *Il Tempo*, derided the bill for its extreme moderation, for the fact that it did not sanction divorce by mutual consent.

Early in December the bill entered the committee stage. A committee of nine was appointed, of whom five opposed the measure and four supported it. It was observed that not a few ministerial deputies voted against it, fearing the reactions of their constituents. The committee accordingly rejected Clause 1 of the bill. Turati, in an article published in *La Critica Sociale* under the title of 'Guelfismo italico', noted how opposition had grown during the interval between the rejection of Berenini's bill and the submission of the Government's more moderate proposals. 'I would point out,' he wrote, 'that the dispassionate anti-clericals of the past summer have wisely and opportunely returned to the more decorous and comfortable paths of orthodoxy, and that the strict morality of Italian conjugal and family life is no longer in

such acute and imminent danger of subversion.' The rejection of
the bill was an indication of the continuing power of the Church.
The socialist cause was harmed rather than helped by the superficial, vulgar, violent anti-clericalism which found its highest
expression in *L'Asino*, a weekly paper with a wide circulation
edited by Guido Podrecca. This periodical, which made a feature
of its highly offensive coloured cartoons of priests, often trans-
gressed the bounds of decency and was frequently prosecuted for
making libellous accusations against ecclesiastics, which it failed
to substantiate in court. The clergy did not consist exclusively of
priests of the kind depicted by Podrecca. It included also men of
intellect, men distinguished for their culture and their industry.
In order to combat the Guelph power it was necessary to study
the structure of the Church and of the party which it dominated,
to seek out their various instruments of propaganda. Among the
Church's most formidable weapons were the private schools, both
primary and secondary, which were invariably controlled by
religious organizations.

With the closure of the twenty-first legislative session the bill
sponsored by Zanardelli and Cocco Ortu was dropped before
even the part relating to affiliation had been debated. Zanardelli,
now in the last years of his life, resigned his post as President of
the Council on October 29th, 1903, and was succeeded by
Giolitti.

On August 4th, 1903, Pius X ascended the pontifical throne.
Twenty-five years younger than his predecessor, and not, like
him, a native of the Papal States, he had no nostalgic longing for
the restoration of the Temporal Power. The protests which he
uttered on his accession, and the fact that he remained shut up
in the Vatican, seemed to represent no more than a formal
gesture, a mark of respect for the tradition established by his
predecessors. As Bishop of Mantua and Patriarch of Venice the
new Pope had formerly exercised his authority in those regions of
Italy where Catholic organization was strongest and most vigorous, where Catholics had undisputed control of the municipal
councils and, in many districts, of virtually the whole of public
life. It was therefore natural that he should be conscious of the
regret and the ill-concealed impatience with which so many
militant Catholics viewed their inability to enter into the political

struggle, to assure the Church of those successes, of that voice in Italian affairs, which they felt to be no more than its due.

A Pope never abruptly reverses the policy of his predecessor. Theoretically, the Church's rule forbidding Catholics to vote in political elections remained in force throughout Pius X's pontificate; but in the three general elections of 1904, 1909 and 1913 it was ignored to an ever-increasing extent, and its infringement, even when not sanctioned by special dispensations, was treated with ever greater indulgence.

The celebrations in honour of the jubilee of Italy's unification, the Rome Exhibition, the acid comments evoked by the participation of foreign sovereigns in the festivities—by the tone of their telegrams, by their failure to visit the Pope—might well have produced a recrudescence of the old wound caused by the Risorgimento and a resumption of violent controversies. Happily, the danger was averted.

On September 20th, 1910, Ernesto Nathan, Mayor of Rome, in a speech at the Porta Pia affirmed the superiority of secular civilization, for which, he said, the Rome Exhibition would represent a great victory, as millions of visitors would flock to see this triumphant expression of Italian industry and unity and of the moral values which they symbolized. The speech aroused the ire of Catholics. And indeed, the sentiments expressed were not those of a man free from prejudice, even if they could not be described as offensive either to the Pope or to the Church.

Two days later the Pope lodged a formal protest. Practising Catholics would probably have abstained on principle from participating in that part of the jubilee celebrations which was scheduled to take place in Rome; but had they sought a pretext, it was provided by Nathan's speech. This enabled them to base their abstention not so much on their opposition to Italian unity— an attitude of mind which continued to be unpopular—as on the fact that the Government had chosen to invest the Rome Exhibition with an anti-religious character, to make it a symbol of the superiority of secular ideas. Hence, their abstention was not only legitimate, but natural. Yet the papal protest of September 22nd, 1910, was not solemnized by inclusion in the *Acta*. The *Acta* of 1910 and 1911 contain no reference to the jubilee celebrations.

In 1911 *La Civiltà Cattolica* published two important articles. 'Le commemorazioni patriottiche del 1911', spoke of 'the numerous violations of the moral law' by means of which the Risorgimento had been accomplished and which made all attempts to justify it inadmissible; of the failure of the policy of Cavour, who had hoped to enter Rome by agreement with the Pope; and of the impossible position of the latter. The second article (the first in order of publication), 'Anno di lutto', was a fierce reply to the speech delivered by Giovanni Pascoli on January 9th at the University of Bologna. It described the jubilee celebrations as 'a frenzy of sectarian joy reminiscent of that vote of March 27th, 1861, by which the deputies of the Turin Parliament, some knowingly, others unwittingly, stimulated the desire of international freemasonry to see the capital of the Catholic world transformed into the capital of a neo-pagan Italy. This is the palingenesis which they wish to celebrate. . . . No Catholic worthy of the name can but regard this year as a year of religious mourning, nor can he do other than oppose festivities which are an insult to his faith through the medium of Christian atonement. In particular, we Catholics of Italy mourn also as citizens, by reason of the shame which such a senseless manifestation of virulent anti-papal feeling brings upon our nation and our country.'

Indignation was aroused not only by these articles, but even more by the resolutions which came from Catholic associations and congresses abroad deploring the intolerable position of the Pope, to which the celebrations of 1911 had once again drawn attention. There was not an Italian university in which the students did not hold at least one anti-clerical meeting.

But the fires of anti-clericalism were by now burning low. They glowed red for a while, then died out one by one. Certainly neither Prime Minister Luzzatti, nor Giolitti, who succeeded him in March, desired anything other than reconciliation.

October saw the launching of the Libyan enterprise, which, on the initiative of D'Annunzio, at once assumed the aspect (wholly literary and symbolical, it goes without saying) of a crusade, of a struggle between the Cross and the Crescent, of a return of Christian civilization to the East. De Felice and other socialist deputies protested in vain against such attempts to invest the war with a religious character. Towards the end of the year *La Civiltà Cattolica* was able to announce in its columns of Italian news that many bishops had ordered the prayer *Tempore belli* to be offered up in their churches, thereby intimating that they wished the expedition success; that the Battle of Lepanto had been commemorated with great solemnity; and that even the Sacred Order of Malta was participating in the war by contributing a hospital ship.

On the Roman question, therefore, the pontificate of Pius X was characterized by a substantial change of policy. (The idea of recovering the Temporal Power by means of a European conflict, viewed with equanimity by Pope Leo XIII, would have horrified Pope Pius X, who, with much greater realism, envisaged the possibility that at some time in the not-far-distant future the Italian Parliament would come to be dominated by Catholics.) But there were changes of policy in other directions also. In the history of the Church Pius X is remembered as the anti-modernist Pope (though it should not be forgotten that on the occasion of his beatification and canonization (1954) emphasis was laid rather on his personal virtues—which during his lifetime earned him the unqualified respect even of non-Catholics and of his enemies— than on the mark which he had left on the history of the Church, a mark that has proved less enduring in some ways than in others); and we may recall how he rounded off the work of his predecessors by formulating the *Codex*, thereby completing the Church's authoritarian structure. The *Codex* contains one characteristic article, providing for the dismissal of parish priests by decree of their bishops, which half a century before would have scandalized those who maintained that it was the duty of the State to watch over the liberties of the minor clergy and to protect them from the possible high-handedness of their superiors. We may recall, too, how the introduction, during his pontificate, of communion for children and of confirmation at the age of seven, and the recommendation of frequent, even daily communion, for laymen as well as clergy, fulfilled aspirations which for a very long time had given rise to conflicts within the bosom of the Church. This appeared to represent a further victory for what had been known as the Jesuitical school of thought over that other school of thought which had originally been termed Jansenistic and later Gallican, even though it had by no means been confined to French territory.

This is not the place to define the nature of modernism or to evaluate the significance of its condemnation. Here it must suffice to recall that there were in fact several kinds of modernism, having little or nothing in common one with another. There was, for example, the dogmatic and philosophical kind, of which the principal exponent was George Tyrrell. This was based on the concept of the evolution of dogma, regarded as the means of bringing home a religious truth to believers who live in a given period of civilization and have the knowledge, the preoccupations, the spiritual needs, the curiosity, characteristic of that period. According to Tyrrell and his followers dogma was constant inasmuch as it represented a divine answer to those preoccupations; but its actual formulation was bound to vary in accordance with the intellectual capacity and the needs of a particular generation. There was also a historical modernism, the outstanding exponent of which was Loisy, who, without concerning himself with questions of dogma, without worrying about the revolutionary conclusions to which he might be led—and so virtually rejecting the idea that the Bible was Holy Writ, divinely inspired —sought to reassess the significance of Christ's preaching, the state of mind and the expectations of the earliest Christian generations, examining the Gospels and the Pauline epistles as objectively as if they had been ordinary historical documents, and challenging the traditional theory as to their authorship and the dates of their composition. Again, there was a political modernism, seeking reconciliation with democracy and, if possible, with socialism, dreaming of a Church that would not base its practical policy on an alliance with the wealthy classes, but would champion the poor against the rich, insisting on their rights instead of begging for charity. There was a modernism which, surveying the internal structure of the Church, envisaged a democratic reformation, and which re-echoed the old slogans—abolition of ecclesiastical celibacy, and election of bishops by clergy and people. Finally, there was a modernism which sought to eliminate the conflicts between science and faith, and thus to offer an interpretation of *Genesis* consistent with the doctrine of evolution, with the findings of geology, of palaeontology, of history.

These spiritual aspirations were all very different; but they all postulated the abandonment by Catholics of their policy of rigid adherence to tradition, of unconditional and servile obedience to the teaching of the supreme religious authorities, and they all sprang from a fervent, at times somewhat ingenuous, belief in contemporary science—viewed in all its aspects, including those of historical criticism and ethnology—from the certainty that it could not be wrong, that there could be no retreat from some of the positions which it had established.

Pius X's reaction to modernism in all its forms was uncompromisingly hostile; nor is this the place to consider which of the affirmations and aspirations of the one side and which of the strictures of the other are still valid after more than forty years, what influence modernism has had on orthodox teaching, what attitudes the Church has been forced to adopt by the anti-modernist reaction. Here it is only necessary to note that modernism was a clear indication of the change that had come about in the attitude of politically-minded Italians to those problems which concerned the Church.

Who can remotely imagine what would have been the reaction not merely of Bettino Ricasoli and his Tuscan circle, who had ardently and vainly hoped for such a development, but of P. S. Mancini and, for that matter, of Ruggero Bonghi, to a movement so complex and important as modernism, which had originated in the very bosom of the Church and was common to all the countries of Europe, and which in Italy boasted champions of the calibre of Ernesto Buonaiuti, Salvatore Minocchi, Romolo Murri and, as an exponent of the feeling of the Catholic laity, perhaps the most popular novelist of the day, Antonio Fogazzaro? Such a movement would have provoked a veritable *crise de conscience* among politicians, who would have been compelled to ask themselves whether it was not the State's duty to encourage a modernism that had originated in the very bosom of the Church, and to protect it from the attacks of the Roman Curia—a question to which all the opponents of clericalism would undoubtedly have replied in the affirmative. In fact, the condemnation of modernism in 1907 left Italian laymen completely unmoved.

By this time the nation envisaged a form of separation very different from, and far more radical than, the juridical separation defined in Cavour's formula.

Ernesto Buonaiuti never forgave Croce for the pages he wrote on the occasion of the condemnation of modernism. In a very different sphere, a precisely similar attitude was adopted by the socialists. Turati and Treves, the two greatest exponents of radical and reformist socialism, thought as Croce did on this question. Modernism held no more interest for idealists and for educated laymen in general than it did for Left-Wing politicians. The Church had acted logically in condemning those who had rebelled against its discipline and its law. That law, which demanded obedience, adherence to tradition, and the repudiation of free discussion and of the living forces of disputation and free thought, was essential to the preservation of a society based on the Catholic *mythos*, a society which could not expose to the disintegrating effects of criticism and free discussion that heterogeneous and gradually-assembled collection of principles on which it was founded. Modern thinkers could not utilize any of the ideas inherent in a doctrine based on supernatural premises; to them modernized theology meant no more than the orthodox theology of Thomism had done.

The interests of the proletariat in no way coincided with the interests of these discontented and rebellious priests, whose unsatisfied intellectual desire for the creation of a new theory of dogma or of a new history belonged to a completely different order of ideas. As for scientific truths, they were what they were, they were self-affirming and self-evident, and the approval or disapproval of ecclesiastical circles could neither arrest nor hasten their affirmation. If, moreover, certain Catholics saw fit to adhere to socialism, the Socialist Party did not on principle close its doors to anyone on the grounds of his religious beliefs. Yet it remained suspicious of those who continued to submit to an authority which openly declared its hostility to socialism and which condemned all its achievements, and could not but be somewhat puzzled by those who persisted in practices which it regarded as superstitious, in beliefs irreconcilable with those scientific dogmas which lay at the root of socialist teaching. But there was no place among the allies of socialism for organizations that wished to retain their religious character, whose members intended to act, in the context of the class struggle, not as proletarians but as Catholics.

A similar indifference prevailed throughout the ranks of Italian liberalism, even if here signs of passive sympathy were occasionally apparent. The general feeling among liberals was that the State could not possible intervene in what was a domestic affair of the Church. Wisely it was pointed out that the State could not allow the secular arm to be used for the purpose of sequestrating writings, dissolving associations, or dismissing modernists from posts in Government-controlled schools and universities, and that it could not undertake to create or to help a schismatic Church, conscious as it was of the fate that had overtaken all such Churches. Those who had been nurtured on liberal thought could also note with satisfaction that many of the clergy, it might well be said the best among them, were manifestly dissatisfied with the teaching imparted in the seminaries and the pontifical universities and longed for something better, and that the need for free discussion, for a genuine form of inquiry that would not be subordinated at the outset to the necessity of reaching a foreordained conclusion, was making itself felt even in circles that had not hitherto been conscious of it. But it was not possible to do more than note these facts; it was not possible to undermine the foundations of the Church, in which all power, even that of determining what were and what were not questions of faith, what should and what should not be taught, proceeded from above.

It was said that for modernists there were only two possible courses: either to submit or to leave the Church. But there were to be cases of personal solutions, of individual *crises de conscience*. It was pointed out that the strictures of Pius X might even have been a mistake, and that this mistake might adversely affect the future course of the Church's history; but the fact remained that anything in the nature of an organized revolt was out of the question. And yet, as more and more laymen proceeded to make their submission, cases of anti-clerical intolerance became quite frequent.

Was it right that Antonio Fogazzaro, who had submitted after the condemnation of his modernist novel, *Il Santo*, should continue to be a member of the Supreme Council of Public Education? Or that the priest Ernesto Buonaiuti should be elevated to the chair of Religious History in the University of Rome? Was not the State entitled to insist that its university chairs should be filled by men who enjoyed complete freedom in the realm of speculation, and to exclude from membership of the Supreme Council of Education those who had voluntarily restricted their freedom of discussion and decision in accordance with the dictates of the Church? These were the questions which men were to ask themselves a few years later.

But this intolerance never assumed an active form. No bill

designed to impose a preventive censorship, an *accessit* to public
offices in the name of free thought, would have had any likelihood
of finding its way into the statute-book. Rather, a profound,
innate love of freedom would have deterred even the most
resolute opponent of these acts of submission from presenting
such a bill.

In the secular world modernism had only a literary aftermath.
For a few years the figure of the modernistic priest, gentle and
cultured, devoted to the poor, devoted to his country, persecuted
by bishops and Jesuits, continued to appear in novels and plays.
But this pale shadow of the literary anti-clericalism which had
been so widespread in the late nineteenth century was destined
soon to vanish in its turn.

In his attitude to specific issues—for example, administrative
questions, the participation of Catholics in elections, the appointment of bishops, or the dispute, in abeyance since 1873, as to what
proportion of the liquid assets of the religious organizations
suppressed in the city of Rome should be placed at the disposal
of the Holy See for distribution among the various religious
Orders—Pius X could be accommodating. But where questions of
principle were involved he was always uncompromising to a
degree. He was indifferent to unpopularity. In a world in which
the various socialist parties were continually growing in strength,
in which humanitarian ideas were spreading unopposed, he did
not fail to assert the rights of ownership in their entirety, nor to
insist that, while the poor man might aspire to the rich man's
charity, he had no moral title to any of the rich man's possessions.

Not without justice his contemporaries observed that he always
based his policy on the authority of the Church. This he conceived in such abstract and general terms that he invoked it at
every turn; thus, in his encyclical *Editae saepe* he asserted that the
Church should teach Catholics not only what they must believe,
but also what they must do. He wanted the Church to pervade
the political life of all the nations and to dominate all religious
parties, which should conform to a single type and should be
frankly and exclusively confessional in character, being governed
directly by the ecclesiastical authority or else predominantly by
bishops. In Italy the *Non expedit*—the ecclesiastical decree forbidding Catholics to take part in political elections—was still in

force. Officially Catholics did not go to the polls, officially there were no Catholic deputies (though it was gradually beginning to be admitted that the man who sat at Montecitorio might still call himself a Catholic in a religious sense: for the first time a number of deputies had been received, in their private capacity of course, by the Pope). Less than ever was it possible to speak of a Catholic Party; but Catholic organizations, which were springing up and flourishing on an ever-increasing scale, were under the direct surveillance of the Holy See, which intervened at every suggestion of policies it did not approve.

In his autograph letter of November 22nd, 1909, addressed to Count Medolago Albani, President of the Social Economic Union, the Pope condemned the plan for a federation of professional unions and leagues which would include even non-Catholic organizations, provided that they were imbued with the idea of 'social justice'. In general, Catholic organizations should be subject to the jurisdiction of the Holy See. Under the terms of the new statute of the Union of Italian Catholics, approved by the Vatican for a period of three years and transmitted by the Cardinal Secretary of State to Count Della Torre on December 17th, 1912, provision was made for a mixed system of elections and co-options, but the choice of the general president was reserved to the Pope. In the meantime the electoral system would not apply: the statute provided that for the first time the episcopate would appoint the presidents of the diocesan councils, and the latter the incumbents of the parishes within their jurisdiction.

The Pope's indifference to unpopularity, even in an Italy in which anti-clerical feeling was still strong, was revealed in the episode of Mgr. Bonomelli, Bishop of Cremona. Among conservative Catholics, among the advocates of an accord, even if not a solemn and formal one, between Church and State, the Bishop had been for many years the most popular prelate in Italy, while his activities on behalf of Italian emigrants had earned him the respect and gratitude of an even larger section of the community. But when, in a pastoral letter written in 1906, he repeated the old refrain which had been the first battle-cry of the French liberal Catholics, namely that it was better for the Church to detach itself from the State than to consent to accept the latter's uncertain protection, the Archbishop of Milan and the Bishops of Lombardy, allegedly in response to an invitation sent from Rome, addressed a joint letter of protest to the Pope, whose reply contained some harsh strictures on Mgr. Bonomelli. As a result the Bishop retracted, but on visiting Rome he was not received in audience by the Pontiff; on the other hand, he was warmly welcomed in Milan by Cardinal Ferrari, who at a meeting of the Lombard episcopate appointed him the official spokesman.

Although Catholic organizations were now flourishing on an ever-increasing scale, the Church could count on forces far more numerous than those represented by the members of these bodies. There were, however, a number of defections on the part of families which for many decades had served in the Guelph ranks, and whose younger members were not disposed to submit indefinitely to what they regarded as an excessively harsh discipline, to live for ever in an atmosphere which frequently seemed to them somewhat musty.

There were comparatively few whose indignation got so much the better of them that they openly rebelled. The most vociferous rebels were priests: for a priest there could be no compromise between revolt and total submission to superiors who sought to regulate his life, who would name the city in which he must live, the functions which he might or might not discharge, and who, after he had drawn public attention to himself and had created a scandal, would as a rule no longer permit him to write, except perhaps on neutral subjects and under the watchful eyes of numerous censors. A layman, on the other hand, could join a political party condemned by the Church without being expelled from the fold or incurring the penalty of excommunication provided that he did not play a leading part in its activities.

In 1906 Romolo Murri saw his review, *Cultura sociale*, placed under an official ban, partly because he had published in its columns an open letter from Tommaso Gallarati Scotti[1] which was a clarion-call to revolt. The Church, declared Scotti, was entitled to a reasonable measure of respect and obedience; but

'to-day there is nothing which the ecclesiastical authorities regard with so much suspicion as unfettered intellectual progress in a field which to them is sacrosanct. . . . Since the death of Pope Leo the Roman Curia has assumed towards the world of thought a reactionary attitude reminiscent of the days

[1] The future Ambassador in London of the Italian Republic.

of Pius IX, when the Church was at war with everything and everybody. . . . There are very many of us in Italy to-day who, having an ardent faith, feel unable to adapt ourselves to a clerical policy which seriously threatens that Catholic intellectual progress for which we desire to work energetically so long as God grants us life. . . . We cannot in all sincerity uphold official Catholic policy. An open struggle would be useless, since rebellion is merely a waste of energy. It is better for us to continue to work and meanwhile to await our hour. And that hour cannot be long in coming.'

This was the most uncompromising position that a layman could take up; but if an ecclesiastic associated himself with such opinions he would have to resign himself to seeing his life completely revolutionized.

In his inaugural address to the Congress of the National Democratic League (September 15th–18th, 1906), Tommaso Gallarati Scotti expressed himself as follows:

'I know that people from all walks of life will seek to brand us as rebels; I know that they will refuse to take account of our open profession of the Catholic faith, of the integrity of our lives, of the honesty of our words and deeds. . . . Rebels? Perhaps: words mean so little. But we are rebelling not against the Church's dogma, not against the hierarchical authority in its divine mission on Earth, not against the prescribed forms of worship—we declare ourselves to be united in a single faith with the most ignorant old woman in Christendom—but against a false concept of authority which corrupts men's souls and seeks to penetrate even into the life of the nation, against a religious ignorance that invests profane, transient and conjectural things with the character of eternal truths, and would compel a people to observe outmoded and threadbare forms without permitting it that spontaneous development which alone can create new institutions and new forms of Christian civilization.'

And on the subject of the relations between Church and State he added:

'With an ingenuous satisfaction that is a sign of the modesty of their aspirations devout folk may rejoice in the courteous relations that exist between the civil and the ecclesiastical authorities and may point with emotion to the advantages deriving from the fact that the Catechism is taught in many Italian State schools. But anyone who looks beneath the surface of things must feel how precarious all this is, how fragile are the grounds of political expediency on which it is based. No— for us it is not enough that an Archbishop should pay lip-service to the King, that a priest should be elected to a university chair on a show of hands. We desire not superimposition but integration. The nation's religious faith must be rebuilt on a foundation of new ideas. It must revive naturally as the result of an intense spiritual longing. It must inform the lives of the whole people. . . . '

He recognized the desire for justice which animated the Socialist Party; but the adherents of the League were deterred from joining it by its anti-Christian character, by its 'vulgar and even ignorant reaffirmation of paganism, its one-sided view of the economic problem, its artificial negation of Man as he is. . . . '

In 1908 the National Democratic League held its congress at Rimini. In a report on ecclesiastical policy Tommaso Gallarati Scotti advocated freedom of education at all levels; State control of elementary and secondary teaching in all schools as a means of ensuring the fulfilment of the current educational programmes; the abolition of religious instruction in elementary schools (this would be imparted instead, together with moral instruction, in private or confessional schools); State-controlled examinations for would-be teachers; the reorganization of the teaching of the comparative history of religion, the philosophy of religion and the history of Christianity in the largest State universities. He also advocated the separation of Church from State in the economic and administrative spheres; the abolition of the royal patronage, of State administration of Church property, and of the *placet* and *exequatur*; the consignment of ecclesiastical property, converted into transferable securities, to Catholic organizations officially recognized by Church and State, which would have the right to administer them as they saw fit; freedom of associations for religious communities (associations depositing their statutes would be able to obtain legal recognition and to possess immovable property for their own immediate use); and the revision of the Law of

Guarantees. He insisted on the abolition of religious instruction in elementary schools: for 'as this is reduced through gradual curtailments to the status of a concession to the religious feeling of majorities, so it becomes an illusion and perpetuates an equivocal situation'. In any case, the State could not afford to let the teaching Church survive without keeping it under surveillance and re-examining its teaching from the viewpoint of official education.

These democratic Catholics were rebels; but so long as they did not mingle with other parties, so long as they felt the need to remain united among themselves as Catholics, so long as this religious bond continued to transcend all others, nothing was lost: the majority would return to the fold.

Having entered on the path of rebellion, Murri could not, as a priest, content himself with half-measures. He renounced his cloth, married, and became radical deputy for Monte Giorgio. He did not return to the fold—which, it must be emphasized, he had not left in consequence of any wavering of faith—until late in his old age, when death was imminent. But even during his years of revolt he was tormented by the problem of the social function of religion. In an article entitled *Le vie nuovissime del socialismo*[1] he wrote that socialism had come almost by chance to constitute a general conception of the world, a philosophy of life, an ethic which challenged the old conceptions. In Italy its effects had been ruinous: 'It fosters egoisms, it glorifies, in the individual, not the universal and immortal humanity which he embodies, but his transient material and external existence. It does not foster faiths that exalt and dominate human life, compelling it to pursue aims and ideals whose realization is desirable *per se* and not for the practical and immediate advantages which it offers to opportunists dominated by the tyrannical instinct of *principium individuationis*.' Socialism, 'at one in this with the whole of human society, should help men to liberate themselves from that which has long tormented and oppressed their consciences: from religious hypocrisy, from religion viewed as an instrument of government, as a form of political privilege. It should restore religion to its true dwelling-place, which is the conscience, allowing it to flourish and expand as a personal sense of the supreme mysteries of being, as a free creation of faiths and

[1] *Nuova Antologia*, vol. 157, 1912, pp. 476 *sqq.*

religious ideals, as the symbol of a spontaneous association of free men intent on fostering such ideals and on realizing them in their lives. This is a work of true secularity; and it is the solemn duty of a democracy to promote, on behalf of all its citizens, a genuine and complete religious freedom'.

Others withdrew from the Catholic organizations, from the ranks of political Catholicism, rather in the spirit of colonists who go forth to hoist their country's flag in new territories.

I refer to the retirement of a number of young Catholics, sprung from families with sturdy Guelph or even legitimist traditions, who helped to form the first nationalist groups, of which they soon constituted such an overwhelming majority that at the first congress they were able to overthrow those Left-Wing liberal or radical elements whose nationalism was inspired by Irredentist sympathies.

Those who remained tied to confessional political organizations, from which non-Catholics were excluded, were gradually closing their ranks despite the dissensions which continually flared up between intransigents and progressives and the frequent clashes between *Civiltà Cattolica* and the minor journals that echoed its views on the one hand and *Rassegna Nazionale* and its satellites on the other—clashes even about religious questions, for the *Rassegna*, while not openly rebellious, nevertheless remained progressive in outlook.

The *Rassegna* persisted in its cult of Savonarola and continued to draw its inspiration from Rosmini. In its attitude to spiritual questions it allowed itself to be guided by Cardinal Capecelatro. In defiance of papal policy, it gave weight to the opinions of those French prelates who approved of their country's recently enacted law of separation based on the formation of Church societies. Even when the bill was rejected it continued to call attention to the evils that had sprung from the illusion of an alliance between Throne and Altar and to emphasize the good that could result from such a law—closer contact between clergy and faithful, veneration of the priest in virtue of his poverty, and so forth. Moreover, it not only shared tendencies common to Catholics of the other camp, such as a desire for measures aimed at suppressing immorality in the Press, but it tended rapidly to become an organ of the conservatives.

Among the most assiduous writers on the problem of Church

and State was a great Sicilian landlord, Senator the Duke of Gualtieri. Gualtieri was a man in whom conservatism was tempered with a barely-concealed regret for the disappearance of the *ancien régime*. In his view universal suffrage was contrary to the natural order. Representative government had been proved a failure, and in its place Italy was likely to have, not democracy on the Jacobin model, but either a revival of personal rule, as in the United States, or a 'direct' form of democracy, whereby questions of major importance would be submitted to a popular referendum, as in Switzerland. Expressing a paternalistic conception, Gualtieri taught that the welfare of the humbler classes is dependent on that of the landed gentry, and that

'a greater share in the running of the State' should be the prerogative of 'those who make greater sacrifices to maintain it and who clearly have a greater interest in good administration, wise government and the maintenance of law and order.' Taxes should not be imposed on personal property, but only on real estate, for taxes imposed on personal property strike a blow at outward signs of wealth that are in fact illusory. Most unjust of all is the progressive tax, which represents a misapplication of the principle that all should be equally conscious of the burden: for 'if the origin and the extent of men's needs are attributable to their upbringing, to habits acquired in their early childhood, to the fortune which they possess, to the environment in which they have always lived, as well as to heredity, it should be recognized that the wealthy classes have a much greater number of needs than the lower classes, with the result that the burden of the progressive tax, by depriving them of the means of satisfying certain of those needs, is likely to entail for most of them sacrifices proportionately far greater than the classes less favoured by fortune will be called upon to bear.'

In 1908 the *Rassegna Nazionale* welcomed the 'reformist conservative programme' launched by a group of senators including the venerable member of the Order of the Annunziata, Genova Thaon di Revel; the jurists Buonamici, C. F. Gabba and Filomusi Guelfi; the Duke of Gualtieri; and others bearing illustrious aristocratic names; General Fiorenzo Bava-Beccaris, hated by the Left for his military repression of the socialist riots in Milan in

1898 (his name recalled the military tribunals, the sentences—subsequently revoked by an amnesty—and the rigours of martial law); and a number of old university professors, one of whom, Carlo Calisse, could not however reconcile himself to the new party's repudiation of that species of password, so typical of the age, represented by the adjective 'democratic'.

The programme, couched in extremely stately language, began with an attack on free-thinkers and pseudo-liberals. It urged that the State should intervene by taking preventive action, not limiting itself to repression but

> 'forbidding all, without distinction of political colour or party, openly to spread hatred, error and immorality, and keeping a reasonable check on the campaign at present being waged against *ownership* and *personal interest*, which, so long as they are not allowed to conflict with the public weal, constitute precious springs of sure progress; against the *family*, which, in its present inviolable monogamic form, has reached the apogee of its development; and against the *country*, which certain tragically deluded spirits would to-day wish to see destroyed. . . . '

Here in essence are the ideas which fifteen years later were to lead so many Catholics to become enthusiastic disciples of the Fascists, who set themselves up as protectors of religion, property and the family, and who at the same time revived the sentiment of patriotism. Although the authors of the programme protested against the Government's failure to intervene in conflicts between capital and labour, and reminded it of its duty to protect the free workers summoned to replace the strikers, they were already looking forward to the day when such conflicts would be resolved by arbitration. Moreover, they declared that too much thought had been given to the distribution of wealth, whereas it was on the problem of production that the emphasis should have been laid. But they struck an openly paternalistic note which Fascism lacked:

> 'Deceived by those who woo them, the workers of our day have ceased to concern themselves with anything except their own rights, which they conceive to be absolutely limitless. They are in danger of falling under a new form of despotism and of being plunged into even greater misery by men who, often

from ulterior and undisclosable motives, persuade them to put forward absurd claims and to devise and carry into effect criminal and futile projects. Only when they have learned to appreciate their duties as wage-earners, citizens and human beings will the workers be able to formulate their claims wisely and with the certainty that they will not be ignored.' And, contrary to what Fascism would later practise, they declared that they would always combat the 'irresponsible urge to indulge in colonial adventures'.

They wanted to see emigration encouraged, they recommended an honourable foreign policy which would respect the pledged word, they complained that the nascent industries were embarrassed by exorbitant taxes and that 'in the greater part of Italy landed proprietors were crushed by the enormous weight of supertaxes which provinces and communes had increased beyond all reasonable measure'.

'Italy is a Catholic country', declared the programme, 'and it was from Catholicism (which must not be confused, as some would wish, either with devout superstition or with a blind obedience to every prescript of imperious clericalism) that Italy derived the basic elements of an ethic which is admired and imitated by those same men who try in vain to replace it. . . . This faith and this ethic must be able to exist, and to propagate themselves, within the limits of common justice, without being persecuted, whether by the moral constrictions of thoughtless outrages and calumnies, or by legal constrictions which would establish odious privileges for other creeds. If a minister of the Catholic religion, exceeding the bounds of his authority, ventures to make any attempt on our free institutions, let him be restrained forthwith. But so long as he confines himself to teaching and defending his own doctrine he is entitled, like the Jewish rabbi, the Protestant pastor, the Buddhist fakir, and the atheist, not to have the free expression of his thought impeded by special measures.' And the authors of the programme call for 'the most complete abstention from all ill-considered assaults on the freedom which parents still enjoy to provide for the education of their children. . . . If the State were so imprudent as to usurp this supreme authority it would weaken the most deeply-cherished moral and intellectual bonds of family life, and a country which had become a tyrant in the home would assume for many the guise of a cruel stepmother'.

The programme was amply discussed in the pages of the *Rassegna* itself. Domenico Zanichelli, a writer of constitutional history, was by no means pleased with what the programme had to say about foreign and colonial policy. It seemed to him that a conservative programme ought to have advocated a scheme of colonial development and the pursuit of 'peace with honour, not peace alone: that must be our goal, and to that end we must be strong and active.' Francesco Filomusi Guelfi, one of the great teachers in the Roman Faculty of Law, emphasized the Catholic character of Italy and the significance of Article 1 of the Statute; nevertheless, he considered that the Law of Guarantees was incapable of further improvement. But the editor of the review accepted an article—to which, however, he replied in a leader— by a member of the opposite camp, the radical Massimo Fovel. This writer severely criticized the programme, which, he said, provoked

'very bitter reflections on the ever-widening gulf between our political classes properly so called and those social classes which form the bulk of the population and which represent the country's true strength. . . . Before the first assaults of organized labour our fragile party system has collapsed like a house of cards, and since the general strike of September, 1904, we have witnessed in municipal and political circles such a panic-stricken closing of the ranks that our *glorious* secular traditions have been thrown overboard and some have spoken—*risum teneatis!*—of a capitalist blockade. From that day to this it has been impossible to find in Italy a respectable working man who has not claimed to be, and indeed who has not been, a conservative.'

Thus did the review which had always stood for conciliation ride the storm provoked by Murri and the Democratic League, turning its bows resolutely in the direction of conservatism.

With complete orthodoxy it spoke now of the failure of State education, of the offence that would be given to those with religious susceptibilities if such religious instruction as was still provided in the schools were to be abolished. It opposed Gabelli's idea that the State should teach only Christian ethics, leaving the teaching of dogma to the clergy: the danger that the lay teacher, 'speaking without conviction of doctrinal matters, may sow in the minds of children the fatal seed of scepticism, which dries up the source of every lofty sentiment, could easily be averted if religious instruction were left to priests'.

Public anxiety about the army took the form of an aversion to the introduction of two-yearly engagements and of the system of territorial recruitment. Emphasis was laid on the necessity of armaments, on the principle *si vis pacem para bellum*. Many deplored the fact that the Government did not dare ask Parliament for the financial means necessary for a complete solution of the military problem. As early as 1908 votes were cast in favour of intervention in Tripolitania.

Meanwhile, the popular attitude towards the extreme Left became more and more hostile. After one of the periodic clashes between demonstrating workers and police in the Piazza del Gesù in Rome, Borgnini proposed in the Senate that a message of sympathy should be sent to the wounded of both sides. But his suggestion met with violent opposition from Carafa, who declared that those who had been injured while discharging their duty could not be placed on an equality with men who were the victims of their own criminal folly. And Senator Colonna, worthy descendant of the ancient family, added: ' I cannot find it in my heart to send a message of sympathy to the representatives of a party which recognizes neither God, nor King, nor Country!' (In the elections of 1887, however, the same Senator Colonna had led a secular group avowedly hostile to the Catholics.) Moreover, a large body of opinion deplored the fact that the bad example came from men of rank, who set the Phrygian cap atop of the patrician coronet, regardless of the fact that the people 'often look for a lead to those whom they are accustomed to hold in consideration on the score of wealth, title and the lustre of their name'.

Not only was the national Democratic League denounced on the ground that it sought to justify alliances with the socialists to which Catholics could not accede, but Catholics were put on their guard against the celebrated exponent of Catholic economy and sociology, Toniolo. This man was an idealist who sought in democracy remedies which it could not provide. It was largely due to his teaching that the Christian Democrats had been induced to follow a course which was not free from pitfalls—such as that of ignoring the interests of all except the proletariat.

Thus did the non-conformist Catholicism of the traditional advocates of conciliation draw ever closer in its political orientation to that of the old intransigents. Naturally, the intransigents too had travelled a long way. During the past twenty years the tone of *Civiltà Cattolica* had undergone a radical change. Now, the review expressed confidence in certain front-line figures of the old liberal world—such as Luigi Luzzatti, Jewish by birth but vaguely deistic in outlook, with pronounced Buddhist sympathies —while it applauded many of the initiatives taken in Parliament and praised certain decisions of the judiciary.

More and more it came to be felt that divergent opinions about the past should not lead to disunion, that those who allowed such divergences to influence their personal conduct were playing into the hands of the anti-clericals. Anyone who, in glancing through the files of *Civiltà Cattolica*, happened to skip a few years would think he was reading a different review when he came upon a complacent reference in 1910 to the fury of the anti-clericals at the news that a majority of the Catholic and moderate members of the municipal council of Genoa had approved the commemoration of the expedition of the 'Thousand'.

The patriotic and military note became ever more strident.

'Two institutions continue to offer stout resistance to the attacks that are being made, in the name of new ideas, the democratic spirit and social justice, on all those things which in the past were held most sacred,' declared *Civiltà Cattolica* in the same year. 'The institutions in question are the religious Orders and the Army. Each in its own way represents a most formidable obstacle to the spread of the menace of subversion as well as a sure defence of the existing social order. Consequently, the fury of the subversive parties is directed against both with growing intensity.'

The article constituted a reply to those in the opposing camp who disapproved of the Church's ministrations to the needs of the military and of the construction of Catholic recreation-huts and assembly-rooms to which efforts were made to attract soldiers during the hours when they were free to leave their barracks. The writer accordingly emphasized the practical advantages which the

religious spirit offered the military: not only did it keep them out
of mischief, but

> 'it confers upon the Army as a whole an inestimable boon by
> maintaining a more vigorous discipline. The days have passed
> when an army was assembled or disbanded according to the
> circumstances of the moment. In Italy the Army is now a
> permanent institution which stands in need of stable unifying
> principles and discipline. . . . Once religion has penetrated into
> the ranks of the military, soldiers become not merely comrades
> but brothers; their officers become not merely commanders but
> fathers; and the flag in which the national colours were blessed
> would be doubly sacred: to such a flag the devout soldier would
> dedicate not only the blood in his veins but all the highest
> aspirations of a spirit burning with faith—with that faith which
> has always created heroes'.

Were such sentiments as these inspired by the Italian patriotic
tradition? Assuredly not: for 'to-day the Catholics of Italy, far
from conspiring among themselves, exercise such self-restraint and
proceed with such circumspection that their prudence and
discretion can be called excessive—if, indeed, it does not at times
amount to a capitulation to their adversaries'. Every effort is
made to 'imbue' soldiers who frequent Catholic recreation-huts
with the utmost respect 'for the King, the leaders of the hierarchy,
and the laws and customs of the country'.

But the questions debated during these years were of minor
importance. A few old, neglected threads were taken up anew.
Two further attempts were made to push through a bill designed
to give the civil marriage ceremony legal precedence of its
religious counterpart. On February 3rd, 1914, Finocchiaro Aprile,
Keeper of the Seals, a Sicilian with numerous masonic connections,
presented in the Chamber a bill which sought to impose the
mildest of sanctions—a fine ranging from a hundred to a thousand
lire—on the husband and wife, as well as on the priest, in cases
where a religious marriage had not been preceded by a civil
ceremony; the action to be withdrawn if the couple contracted a
civil marriage before the sentence was ratified. The bill was
preceded by a long report on the subject in which we read that
'the State does not concern itself with religious rites, and no one
questions its incompetence to deal with such matters; on the other

hand, it has the specific duty of ensuring the harmonious and orderly coexistence of all the forces that operate in the life of the community.' However, adds the report, day-to-day experience teaches 'that in the majority of cases these illegal unions do not result from ignorance of the civil law but merely reflect the desire of the parties involved to acquire, or to continue to enjoy, material advantages which would be denied to them under the terms of civil marriage.'

Keeper of the Seals Scialoja sent a circular to the procurators general requesting information about the revolution in arrangements for the training of priests which the Holy See was effecting by the establishment of regional seminaries. Scialoja affirmed that the civil authorities could not disinterest themselves in this reform; and his successor, Fani, also affirmed the State's right to keep a watchful eye on the seminaries. But the affirmations were wholly theoretical, for no government inspector ever crossed the threshold of a seminary. Equally unrealistic was the demand from numerous anti-clerical newspapers, and resolutely opposed by the *Corriere della Sera*, that the minimum age for admission to seminaries should be eighteen.

A new problem concerned the right of Catholic organizations to be represented on the Council of the Ministry of Labour. Luzzatti, the Minister, was in favour of the idea, but in February, 1910, the Council rejected it on a motion by the socialist Maffi, who asserted that 'the exclusion of all religious and political elements from our deliberations is the guarantee that the economic interests of employers and workers alike will be studied calmly and objectively.' Meanwhile a great war of words was going on in the legal reviews about the legitimacy of 'ecclesiastical frauds'. The debate, which, for all its vehemence, aroused strong feeling only among the interested parties and the jurists, hinged upon the question whether there was any law by which rightful heirs could prove that the *De cuius*, while ostensibly allowing property to pass to an individual, was really designed to ensure that it fell into the hands of a religious community, existing *de facto*, and, if so, whether the heirs in question could legally prevent the *De cuius* from taking effect.

Exerting his great influence as a writer and a magistrate, Ludovico Mortara, formerly a university professor and now a procurator general, urged his fellow-jurists, among whom opinion on the matter had long been divided, to accept the view that 'ecclesiastical frauds' were illegal. In January, 1911, after the Court of Criminal Appeal had already upheld this interpretation, Fani, Keeper of the Seals, caused considerable dismay in Catholic circles by a speech in the Chamber which expressed the hope that the legal profession would stand firm against these frauds, and promised consideration of the possibility of governmental decision in individual cases of unlawful inheritance.

Once more, the primary school question was one of the most important topics. Religious teaching in these schools was accorded a great deal of space in the newspapers, and all manner of compromises were suggested by thoughtful men who were anxious to see the whole problem settled once and for all. In the municipal councils battle was joined between the champions of religious education and those who desired its abolition. The newspapers of the two factions published letters deploring the fact that parents were being dragooned into signing petitions for its continued inclusion in the curriculum or protesting against the obstructionism practised by this or that local authority in an attempt to evade its obligation to provide at any rate a hall for religious teaching.

Of far greater moment was the question of control of the primary schools by the State. Such a possibility was regarded with horror by Catholics of all classes, partly because they were traditionally opposed to centralization, partly because during these years their hopes of securing enough seats in the Chamber to form a government were non-existent: this despite the fact that a considerable number of communes were Catholic-dominated, while there were others—exactly how many it is hard to determine —in which the indifference of the municipal council and the powerful influence of wealthy citizens whose personal interests were involved enabled the local school to remain under the control of Catholic elements. The President of the Catholic Association of Schoolteachers, Niccolò Tommaseo, had to resign because he was in favour, not of the nationalization of the schools but of their 'provincialization', which some regarded as a first step towards nationalization, others as nationalization itself under a different name.

In May–June, 1910, the Chamber debated the bill for the nationalization of primary schools in the smaller communes (chiefly those whose economic resources did not allow them to make adequate provision for the maintenance of such schools). Prime Minister Luzzatti, when confronted with 1,200 petitions all urging that the schools should remain under municipal control, refuted the charge that the bill was contrary to the principle of 'freedom of conscience' and that it constituted a threat to the independence of the communes. The bill was supported by all the most eminent figures in the Liberal Party. Deputies and republicans insisted that provincial boards of education should be dominated by civil servants and that State control of private schools should be made effective. Only twenty-five members opposed the passage of the bill to its second reading; but on the following day the extreme Left, whose determination to resist any modification of the original text of Article 1 had hardened overnight, was heavily outvoted in the Chamber. The republican deputy Comandini deplored the Government's indecision; and the vote enabled Catholic writers to claim that it was uncertain which side had won, the more so as the Government did not insist on an immediate debate in the Senate.

In the event, the bill did not become law until June 4th, 1911, and was couched in extremely moderate terms. In general, the chief towns of the provinces and of the various administrative districts were to retain control of their primary schools, but the second group could renounce the privilege if they wished. Elsewhere, primary schools were to be administered by the provincial Board of Education, though communes might continue to administer their schools subject to certain guarantees and provided that the 1911 census showed that not more than twenty-five per cent of the population aged six years and over were illiterate. Each provincial Board of Education would comprise fifteen members, some of them civil servants, but the majority nominated by local teachers and school governors or by the municipal councils.

None of the Governments which held office after the defeat of Zanardelli pursued an anti-clerical policy, not even the two short-lived administrations headed by Sonnino, who, more than any other member of the Italian Parliament, personified the old tradition of the Risorgimento. Because he supported the view that Catholic organizations should be represented on the Council of the Ministry of Labour, and because of his pamphlets denouncing obscene publications and plays, Luzzatti came near to winning the support of the Catholics. Fortis, a Prime Minister of the extreme Left, included in his Cabinet the Marchese Nerio Malvezzi, a Catholic in the tradition of Stefano Jacini, who dared to assert that the Law of Guarantees did not represent the last word on the Roman Question, and whose undisguised clericalism was attacked by the radicals and the republicans in the debate that led to the resignation of the second Fortis Ministry. The latter, incidentally, numbered among its most influential members several men to whom the Catholic world looked with confidence— for example, Tommaso Tittoni.

As we have seen, the dominant figure of the period was Giovanni Giolitti. He too enjoyed the confidence of the Vatican and of the Catholic leaders, who well knew that he would never adopt an anti-clerical policy and that he was naturally opposed to all forms of sectarianism. They knew also—and if they had momentarily forgotten the fact he would have reminded them of it—that his was pre-eminently a middle-of-the-road policy; they knew that, profiting by the experience of Crispi and the other Prime Ministers who, in the closing years of the nineteenth century, had had recourse to a number of extreme anti-socialist measures which had aroused much indignation in the country, he would never adopt a policy hostile to the extreme Left; and they knew that so long as he remained at the helm there would never be any danger of a drift towards a Guelph monarchy.

The so-called 'Gentiloni Pact' and the Government's attitude in the years 1913–14 were an indication of what Catholics might expect from Giolitti.

At the beginning of 1913 a group of extremely influential Italian Catholics unanimously decided to put up Catholic candidates only in the few constituencies in which they felt absolutely sure of their ground or in which there would be opposition —however overwhelming—from anti-clerical candidates alone. In general, they pledged their support to the liberal candidate, provided that he gave certain undertakings with regard to the problem of the schools (he must not discredit the private school, nor must he challenge the right of fathers to make arrangements for the religious education of their children), the question of divorce, and the right of religious organizations to equality under the State with non-religious organizations; and provided also that he promised to oppose any bill directed against the religious Congregations. Candidates who accepted these conditions had to sign a written undertaking to that effect.[1]

The pact, which was named after Count Gentiloni, President of the Catholic Union of Electors, was officially supported by the Government. Its implementation was the responsibility of the prefects. Certain concessions were made on both sides. Thus, while the Catholics encountered no governmental opposition to their demand that the rebel priest Romolo Murri should continue to contest his constituency, the Marca d'Ancona, they themselves respected Giolitti's wish that Cuneo should be contested by Tancredi Galimberti, who was free of any taint of anti-clericalism, but who had rebelled against Giolitti himself after being one of his most loyal supporters.

The pact, which had not been kept strictly secret (the *Corriere della Sera* had spoken of it long before the elections), duly took effect, and the Catholics were able to claim, not without justice, that but for it the liberals would have lost a large number of seats. But it provoked a good deal of criticism among the public. It continued to be opposed by the more influential liberal newspapers, those not suspected of coalitionist tendencies, such as Albertini's *Corriere della Sera*.

The Catholics were also able to claim that in the same year (1913) they had taken another great step towards asserting themselves not as a dominant party, but as one with some prospect of holding the balance in the parliamentary struggle. This development was destined to make nonsense of the absurd argument embodied by anti-clerical polemics in the following dilemma: 'Either you are against the Pope and count for nothing, or you are for the Pope and do not recognize or desire the unity of Italy, maintaining that the temporal power is still a paramount necessity.'

Towards the end of the year—to be precise, from November 30th to December 6th—the eighth Social Week was held in Milan. The inaugural address, consisting of an analysis of the Constantinian Edict, was delivered by the Archbishop of Udine,

[1] These facts are recorded in an article, 'I cattolici italiani e le ultime elezioni politiche,' written by one of the Catholics in question, Filippo Meda, and published a year later in *Nuova Antologia* (vol. 169, 1914, pp. 295 *sqq*.). The article makes no mention of any *nihil obstat* emanating from the Secretariat of State; but it can safely be assumed that the Vatican approved the programme in advance.

Mgr. Antonio Rossi. It is inconceivable, said the Archbishop, that the Church should be free unless the Pope is free. The Pope's freedom should be, above all, international in character. Essentially it implies a recognition and, as it were, a guarantee by all the nations over which the Pontiff's spiritual authority ought to extend. Its maintenance should be a matter of deep concern to all States on amicable terms with the State in which the Pontiff has his seat. These assurances have nothing to do with the Law of Guarantees. Mgr. Rossi added that he lacked the authority or the competence to propose an alternative solution of the Roman Question; but he let it be understood that he would regard the internationalization of the Law of Guarantees as both feasible and sufficient. In the course of the Social Week there was also talk of a reassessment of Article 1 of the Statute of the Realm—the 1848 Statute of Charles Albert, which declared the Catholic religion to be the religion of the State.

No one doubted—and here the extreme reticence of even the most authoritative Catholic journals is significant—that the Archbishop's remarks had been authorized by the Vatican, and that what his speech meant in effect was that Italian Catholics no longer made any territorial claims on behalf of the Holy See but only demanded that the latter's status as defined in the Law of Guarantees should be internationally recognized. As Carlo Ottavio Cornaggia, an exponent of Catholic opinion, wrote shortly afterwards,[1] the declarations formulated during this Social Week by Count della Torre made it no longer possible for any man of good faith to repeat the old insinuations about 'potential threats to the integrity of the Italian State and to its independence in the realm of foreign policy'.

Moreover, during the period of the election Catholic candidates had once again made the most explicit declarations respecting their attitude towards the country's unification and their devotion to its institutions.

Nevertheless, the Social Week, like the Gentiloni Pact, provoked a considerable amount of hostile criticism. The great liberal newspapers, Albertini's *Corriere della Sera* and Frassati's *La Stampa*, protested that the Roman Question had been settled once and for all. Luigi Luzzatti wrote two letters to the *Corriere*; Pompeo Molmenti published an article in the Trieste *Piccolo*. On the

[1] Liberali e cattolici, in *Nuova Antologia*, vol. 169, 1914, pp. 138 *sqq.*

Catholic side, the *Difesa* of Venice distinguished itself by the fervour with which it presented its case, while even the venerable Professor Toniolo entered the lists.

In the early days of the new Parliament, during the debate on the Speech from the Throne, Antonio Salandra, a Right-Wing liberal and an opponent of Giolitti, declared that his liberal friends had made a mistake in seeking the support of the Catholics, who had been greatly emboldened by their action. It was the duty of the liberals, without lapsing into anti-clericalism, to defend the State no less against the Catholics than against the extreme Left. Unlike the Catholics, who were obliged to venerate a power that was not national, a power that, indeed, proclaimed itself to be supra-national, and the socialists, who subscribed to a doctrine of humanitarianism which imposed a limit on their patriotism, the liberals were free to concentrate first and foremost on what was the rightful task of all political parties—namely, the affirmation of the patriotic ideal.

Giolitti believed that he could rectify the situation by introducing a bill designed to give civil marriage legal precedence of religious marriage and by instituting an inquiry into the question whether the laws providing for the confiscation of Church property had been fully implemented.

But, while his policy caused pardonable indignation among Catholics (on whose lips the popular saying 'after the holy day the vow to the saint is forgotten' was frequently to be heard) it also had the effect of alienating the radicals, or at any rate the most combative elements among them, who demanded the resignation of the radical ministers from his Government.

Filippo Meda, in the article already mentioned, stoutly defended the electoral compromise, which was adopted wherever a contest arose. Italian Catholics, he declared, regarded adherents of the pact not as political weaklings but as men who had accepted a programme formulated and propounded with the sole object of creating a rallying-point for all who were genuinely anxious to ensure that the first experiment in universal suffrage would not culminate in a victory for anti-clericalism. Without Catholic support the liberals would have had fewer than two hundred representatives in the new Parliament. In the provinces, they would, but for their alliance with the Catholics, have found difficulty in maintaining control of the local councils. But did

K

they, rationally speaking, still constitute a party? That was open to question, seeing that they no longer manifested a complete and constant uniformity of opinions and aspirations: thus, some of them favoured the legalization of divorce, while others opposed it.

Salandra 'misjudged the historical and psychological moment—if the expression is permissible—when he insisted that it was necessary for the Liberal Party to set itself up in the Chamber as the defender of the State *even against another party*, i.e. against the Catholics, without, however, adopting a policy of anti-clericalism. And he misjudged it . . . if only because of the lack of proportion between the two poles from which he insisted on remaining equidistant: I am thinking, to be sure, not of numerical but of ideal proportion.' Replying to Salandra, Meda declared that, whatever a man's nationality, membership of the Church could in no way detract from his patriotism. 'To-day, the fact that a man is or is not a militant Catholic no longer signifies that he is hostile to or in favour of the unitarian, monarchical, constitutional régime. . . . It merely reflects his desire that modern society should be guided by Christian or by anti-Christian principles in the sphere of legislation and administration.'

The Catholics were conscious of their strength, but when it came to participating in electoral and parliamentary life they proceeded very cautiously for fear of provoking hostility. They well knew that few people had a clear vision of the manifold ways in which, by adding to the political heritage of the country their own inheritance of Catholic ideals and discipline, they were able and willing to work not for the establishment of a Catholic hegemony, but for the defence of society, in the fullest sense of the term. In Italy, the regimentation of Catholics was necessary not only for the defence of religion 'but also for the normal and progressive evolution of the nation's life'.

The liberals were mistaken if they thought the Catholics could always be relied upon to come to their rescue merely because they feared the socialists and the coalitionists. Politically united, the Catholics were a valuable asset to the liberals. Disunited, far from gravitating for the most part towards the Liberal Party and allowing it to absorb them, they would have been induced, by a perfectly natural reaction, to follow different, even opposite paths.

Cornaggia too, in his almost contemporaneous article, asked

himself why the liberals had recently adopted this defensive attitude, this attitude of hostility to the alliance with the Catholics.

'In the Liberal Party there are anti-clericals, and their voice has prevailed amid the silence—let us not mince matters—of the great majority, who nevertheless realize how absurd and unfair are these renewed feelings of mistrust.' Left-Wing elements were given full credit for services, for acts of loyalty, that were insignificant compared with those performed by the Catholics, who for their part had to reckon, now as always, with 'anti-religious prejudice', with 'the *aeterna auctoritas* of the Twelve Tables. The political luggage of a section of the Liberal Party undoubtedly includes a hostility to religion, varying in its forms and manifestations, but always such as to rule out the possibility of co-operation with those who, by contrast, have the interests of religion at heart. In reality, popular *blocs* have never had any realistic basis apart from anti-clericalism. This alone has had the power to unite the middle-class radical and the socialist. Moreover, it is wont to exert its influence even in the liberal camp, seeking to substitute alliances with radicals and worse for those alliances with moderate Catholics which have yielded such happy results in the past.'

With the passage of time Catholics would organize themselves better, both politically and socially. In Italy they had come late into public life;

'but they can still do much, provided that they display reasonable enlightenment and prudence. They will not constitute a political party, which would be an absurdity in a country that is essentially Catholic, a country in which a socialist remarks upon the cross on the voting-paper in order to win votes; but they should put forward a programme advocating freedom for all and respect for religion. This will command widespread support even among the working masses, all of whom are to-day called upon to vote. For the workers can easily be convinced that Catholic traditions, because of their moral and material superiority, are more substantial and efficacious than socialist promise.' It was, however, essential, Cornaggia added, 'that no one should be alarmed by the democratic tendencies which to-day command such a wide measure of approval among Catholic organizations.'

But the radicals were dissatisfied with the outcome of the election, even if there was no other reason for their discontent.

'Giolitti', wrote the distinguished economist De Viti de Marco, 'has conceded to us the will-o'-the-wisp of "legal precedence for civil marriage" '—and a will-o'-the-wisp it was, indeed, to prove —'but to the steel magnates, the sugar-manufacturers, and the great landowners he has conceded the reality of import duties, thereby benefiting the parasitic industries which represent the stronghold of conservative interests.'[1]

The sixth radical congress found the parliamentary group eager to continue its collaboration with the Government; but the constituencies prevailed through the medium of their four hundred delegates, who, although for the most part favourably disposed towards the policy of popular *blocs*, nevertheless insisted that the party should assert its independence. And so the radical ministers were forced to resign.

The Government retained a large majority, but it was part of Giolitti's normal strategy not to prolong his administrations unduly. He had directed the electoral campaign; the next election was a long way ahead. Better, then, that another politician should assume the responsibilities of government for a while: Giolitti could return whenever he wished.

But not everything can be foreseen. As a result of the episode of the radical congress, and to a certain extent of the Gentiloni Pact, Giolitti was not destined to find himself in control of Italian policy on the outbreak of the First World War.

A comparison between the attitudes of the various parties to problems of ecclesiastical policy in 1871 and in 1911, to take two representative years—the year of the Law of Guarantees, and that of the jubilee of Italian unification—would be necessarily incomplete, owing to the fact that during the intervening forty years several groups disappeared and a number of entirely new forces emerged in their place.

Among the former were those that opposed national unification and were in favour of a return to the conditions that had obtained up to 1859. The new forces included the great Socialist Party, which, though already divided into reformists and revolutionaries,

---

[1] Congresso e programma radicale, in *Nuova Antologia*, 1914, vol. 169, pp. 197 *sqq.*

retained the unity of a complex ideological movement—some would have said of a new religion.

The Italian—and in general the Latin—socialist of the first ten years of the century was totally different from his brother of to-day. He would never have admitted, for instance, that any question of wages was of greater moment to him than a great abstract question. He longed for the moral and material redemption of the poorer classes, but he believed that this should be achieved by a transformation of the world. Depending on his school of thought and the particular concepts of the section of the Party with which he identified himself, he might differ from his fellows as to the manner in which he hoped to effect his regeneration, but his true aim was the complete obliteration of the past. He even had his special forms of dress, used the appellation 'Comrade', and wore a distinctive flower—a red carnation—in his buttonhole. If he was a fanatical believer in the new ideas he did not even observe the rites of civil marriage, but openly lived in 'sin'. To his ideal system a fundamental reorganization of the economy was no less essential than a humanitarian outlook, anti-clericalism, internationalism, anti-militarism, an aversion to all that had its origin in the military spirit or was infected with that spirit—whether it was a question of decorations, even for valour, or of duels.

If we look a little closer, however, we see that this socialism was characterized by a rift more fundamental than the formal division, sanctioned by the Party congresses, between reformists and revolutionaries. I refer to the rift between a socialism founded on humanitarianism—rich in sentiment and poetry, but woefully lacking in doctrinal principles, constructive aims and clear ideas— and another socialism, having very different origins and very different objectives.

It was the humanitarian aspect of socialism that had induced Garibaldi to embrace the philosophy when it was in its infancy. It was this aspect, too, that had had the best-known and most significant literary manifestations, on the one hand in the short stories and sketches written during the last ten years of his life by the extremely popular children's author Edmondo De Amicis, on the other in the ardent poetry of youth which made the reputation of Ada Negri and which contained a note of humanity destined never to be repeated in any of her subsequent work. Aside, however, from the humanitarian passages which occur in all the poetry of the last few decades of the nineteenth century, a great part of the literary and scientific world of the 1890s—personified by men such as Giovanni Pascoli and Cesare Lombroso, Arturo Graf and Corrado Corradino—had identified itself, albeit vaguely, with the Party proper. This socialist humanitarianism, based on the concept of sympathy for the underdog, was still far from being a spent force, even though nearly twenty years had elapsed since the original formulation of the principles of Italian socialism, and more than fifteen since the publication of Antonio Labriola's essay in commemoration of the Communist Manifesto—in other words, since Marxist ideas had first been widely disseminated among Italians. Many called themselves socialists solely in the name of this humanitarianism, which alone prompted them to vote for socialist candidates at elections.

At the opposite end of the scale another form of socialism was already emerging. This claimed to be based entirely on the philosophy of Marx, but had the support of writers and intellectuals of far more recent—to wit, Sorelian—derivation and was completely free of humanitarian dross. It was a socialism in which Marxism was contaminated by a series of transitions and deviations on the part of its exponents: necessity of the class struggle—love of the class struggle—love of the struggle *per se*—the cult of violence.

As early as 1911 a close observer would have discerned that conflict of ideas between the most venerated figure of Italian socialism, the sexagenarian Filippo Turati,[1] and the twenty-eight-year-old Mussolini which was to become fully apparent twelve years later.

Beneath its seeming order, its division into parties and trends, its bureaucracy, its possession of great newspapers, socialism was in reality a party-system still in the process of formation, the battle-ground of an ever-increasing number of doctrines and trends, of which it was not always easy to say which were mutually compatible and which were not. Such were historical materialism and syndicalist doctrine; Marxist procedures and Sorelian procedures; absolute confidence in an economic system concentrating

---

[1] Founder of *Critica Sociale* and a confirmed anti-militarist who was sentenced by the Milan military tribunal of 1898. Though always averse to joining the Government, he was strictly objective. in his judgment of the advantages which the policy of Giolitti offered to the working class.

property in the hands of a diminishing number of landowners, thus facilitating the final expropriation of the landed class; faith in the general strike as a weapon capable of shaking the structure of the old world to its foundations; a continuing adhesion to the old positivism, to the ancient faith in science, to the secular canons of scientific probity, to that pragmatism which was ever ready to sacrifice truth to the practical aim in view and which the economist Achille Loria, a professor in the University of Turin and chief Italian exponent of historical materialism, denounced in prophetic and passionate terms in the revolutionary trade-unionists—willing slaves of intuitionism and of the anti-scientific movement which marked the essential difference between the new century and the old.[1]

But other phenomena too were apparent in that world: a rapid senescence (did not the heroic socialists of 1898 already seem venerable in 1911?) and a growing power of adaptation. At war with the governmental machine, faced with the necessity of assuring their co-operatives of contracts and special facilities, the destroyers became frequenters of ministries, adept at twisting laws and regulations to suit their ends, conversant with all the intricacies of State accountancy.

But when one looked at the Church, at the priesthood, at religious freedom, at the relationship between politics and religion, all this revolutionary ferment which was discernible in socialism as a whole, all this liveliness of thought and argument seemed to vanish away, leaving behind the inheritance of those Romagnole republicans who drew their inspiration from the Carbonari, of those Piedmontese and Tuscan liberals, dabblers in freemasonry, who maintained intact the spiritual heritage of the Jacobin phrase-makers of the assemblies of 1848.

Notwithstanding several authoritative warnings, the socialists showed a tendency to revert to the formulas of the most antiquated and most banal anti-clericalism. In general—whether or not they were men of learning, and excluding those few intellectuals in the trade-union movement whose pragmatism in any case did not extend outside the sphere of the politico-social disciplines—they revealed, like the positivists of the preceding generation, a blind faith in 'science'. They were quite unaware of the purely relative value of certain of its teachings, of the provisional or transitory

[1] 'La filosofia contro la scienza', in *Nuova Antologia*, 1913, vol. 168, pp. 553 *sqq.*

character of certain of its enunciations, of the series of conditions which conspired to limit the validity of certain of its laws. They had a scant sense of the difference which, even in the sphere of the strictly positive sciences, separates the law which defines the relationship that exists from the hypothesis, which purports to be the rational explanation of the law or seeks to widen its application to a field of relationships whose actual existence is as yet unconfirmed; and an equally scant sense (justified in only very few by an intuitive belief in a unity of science and history, of the material world and the spiritual world, that permits a community of vision and subsumption under all-embracing laws) of the difference that exists between the respective values of the law enunciated in the sphere of the experimental sciences, of the economic law or the demographic law, and finally of the laws enunciated in other social spheres, where it is no longer possible to represent, or at least to measure, relationships of quantity. In this scientific faith they imagined that they perceived the justification of that aversion to religion which on closer scrutiny was seen to be rather the reflection of their political yearning for a coalition of liberal and Catholic forces, for the creation of a great moderate party in which all the forces of conservatism should give the measure of their power, and which would have barred for many years the road to the fulfilment of all the aspirations of socialism.

Certain it is that all the old anti-clerical slogans became commonplaces in socialist newspapers, pamphlets and speeches, in the conferences of the labour councils and of the popular universities, where the Party was dominant, and in the electoral manifestos and contests. It was an intemperate anti-clericalism, whether directed at religion, at history, or strictly at politics. It is very probable that the lofty intellects, the generous and exquisitely sensitive spirits that were to be found even in the ranks of socialism, were more than once constrained to recognize its dismal, shameful character, and certainly more than one champion of socialism contrived to abstain from this base anti-clericalism. But party discipline or fear of the masses forbade violent reactions. Guido Podrecca, editor of *L'Asino*, was expelled from the Party in 1912 for his support of the Libyan enterprise; but no one in his Party had dared to protest against the scurrilities, the vulgarities, the base falsifications of history, the calumnies against priests and nuns, the demoralizing misrepresentations of the true nature of religion with which he filled his widely-read journal each week, and which had excited the disgust of so fierce an anti-clerical as Gaetano Salvemini. Benito Mussolini could conduct in the pages of *Avanti!* his campaign against freemasonry and ensure the triumph of this campaign at the Ancona Conference of 1914, which proclaimed the incompatibility of socialist and masonic principles. But his object was merely to strengthen discipline within the Party, to make it impossible for socialists to submit to another hierarchy—and, moreover, a clandestine hierarchy, extraneous to the Party—and to bar the way to a policy of popular *blocs*, which in the opinion of himself and his associates was leading the socialists to renounce the most effective of their weapons—those battles in the economic field which should have constituted their *raison d'être*. There was, however, in this no opposition to anti-clerical excesses. Indeed, it was felt necessary to dispel every shadow of the suspicion which, as a result of this attitude, might arise with increasing bitterness against the Church and its men—a suspicion which in Mussolini's case was to last at any rate until 1919.

Thus the advent and triumphal progress of socialism, which was one of the most striking reasons why the Italian political scene of 1911 differed so greatly from that of 1871, had brought with it no new development in the field of ecclesiastical policy.

As has been indicated, however, the Catholics had profoundly modified their attitude. And this modification would have appeared even more remarkable to anyone remembering that, if one wished to understand the position thoroughly, one could not think only of those Catholics who were members of ecclesiastical organizations, but must take account of the few who, while politico-Catholic in sentiment, had at a certain point broken the bonds of discipline and gone to swell the ranks of the moderate party or, more recently, those of the young nationalist party. This was not the result of any *crise de conscience*—because they could no longer accept any part of the teaching of political Catholicism—but from a desire to carry on the fight more effectively. They wished to be free from embarrassing doctrinaire principles in which no one believed any longer and which owed their survival partly to tradition and partly to apathy, and to fight for those concrete aims which Catholicism set before itself without offering gratuitous advantages to their enemies. Long before 1911 no bishop or parish priest would have thought that the deputy, senator, or minister of liberal convictions was exposing himself to the risk of censure, or have feared for the salvation of his soul. The term 'liberal' no longer had a frightening sound, save perhaps in a few remote provincial or rural areas or among families of the most unimpeachable Catholic orthodoxy. It was therefore not surprising that Catholics of firm religious faith, sincerely respectful towards the Holy See, and convinced that Italy could not be great and happy except as a Catholic nation, believed of course, that they could better serve their convictions by becoming mayors or provincial councillors or liberal deputies than by accepting defeat merely to deny the support of Catholics to the moderate group in the commune or in the college or to impose one label rather than another on the coalition which was naturally springing up in opposition to the popular *bloc*. In 1911, the jubilee year of Italy's unification, the 'Catholic' mayors obeyed the Pontiff's order and refrained from attending the congress of Italian mayors held in Rome. But among those who did attend, a great number who were Catholics at heart did not fail to worship at the tomb of the Prince of the Apostles. Many Venetian mayors who had come to Rome for the congress presented themselves, either by previous arrangement or with letters of introduction, at the home of the Pope's sisters; and if they could not obtain an audience of the Pope, which was denied to all those who were attending the jubilee celebrations in an official capacity, they were at least able to take home to their families those autographed portraits of His Holiness, those blessed rosaries, those souvenirs of the Vatican on which they had set their hearts.

But what changes were taking place in the camp of those who had always kept the Catholic flag unfurled! The Social Week of 1913 to which reference has already been made was a straw in the wind which forced even the enemies of Catholicism, so long as they were not completely blinded by prejudice, to appreciate the distance that had been travelled and to realize the impossibility of continuing to regard Catholics in the political sphere as the opponents of unity, as men who could assume power only after a military defeat of Italy that would entail its dismemberment.

As we have seen, the internal differences between Catholics were growing less. The patriotism which in the conciliationists of

1870 had been considered a sign of liberal feeling was driving their successors along the road to nationalism—towards the very point at which an understanding with the intransigents of forty years before would have been less difficult to achieve.

No reign of Guelphism was in prospect, only a first negative achievement in the shape of resistance to the parties of the Left and the arrest of their progress in open collaboration with the liberal-conservatives. Agreements with these latter were for the moment based on the maintenance of the *status quo*; what would happen in the future remained to be seen. As to the current situation *de jure*, it was fully realized that not a little of what it is given to administrations to accomplish not *contra legem*, but *praeter legem*, could be achieved in the social sphere, in the sphere of practical activity, and that through the efforts of the prefects the number of Communal administrations, charitable institutions and Catholic-controlled societies could be considerably increased.

No co-operation was forthcoming from the few faithful disciples of Murri, who were disposed to form alliances with parties of the Left; but so long as they remained united among themselves, so long as the designation of Catholics was that which they valued the most, there was reason to hope in their case for that revival of the spirit of solidarity which in fact came about with the rise of the Popular Party.

Without attracting Government support, and without having any visible effect on the policy of the Vatican, the tendency of workers and peasants to enrol in Catholic leagues continued apace. In point of fact, the fate of these organizations depended less on government policy or pontifical directives than on the religious enthusiasm of the masses, on their determination—which was to vary in degree according to the district—to resist the already highly-developed and flourishing Red organizations by forming as a counter-measure less numerous rival organizations, and, finally, on the spirit of initiative revealed by parish priests and other ecclesiastics.

Perhaps this spirit of initiative was the principal reason why, in areas where similar conditions prevailed, White leagues sometimes flourished, while sometimes no trace of them could be discerned. Thus, in Turin, which around 1906–08 was regarded as a 'Red' city, a parish priest, Mgr. Spandre, who subsequently was raised to the bishopric of Asti, created cells of Catholic workers of all

types, including railway and tramway employees, and staged frequent processions in which the White organizations paraded their
forces.

And now the white labara of the Catholic leagues, usually
adorned with tricolour ribbons, and sometimes even the tricolour
itself, began to appear—unostentatiously, it is true, and never in
the same processions, never side by side—as a counter to the red
flags of the socialist leagues. It was, however, only in the Veneto
and in certain isolated districts elsewhere in the peninsula that
these leagues became a factor to be reckoned with in the struggle
between capital and labour. Nevertheless, there were times when
they justified the charge repeatedly levelled by the socialists
against the employers that they were in reality an instrument
designed by the latter for the purpose of breaking the strike-
weapon in the hands of the working class and of securing excessively cheap labour (and here the charge was directed not so much
against the White leagues as against the associations of female
workers controlled by nuns); while in a few cases, even without
forming open alliances—Reds and Whites were ceaselessly at war
with one another—they supported the socialist leagues in isolated
battles or skirmishes between workers and employers.

Anyone who had continued this comparison between the
feelings of the various political groups in the matter of ecclesiastical policy after a lapse of forty years would have asked
himself, as he contemplated the position of the liberals, how far
it was possible to speak of continuity in their case.

As has already been remarked, it would certainly have been
possible to discount that section of the old Right Wing of which
Ricasoli had been the most illustrious representative and which,
faithful to the principle of judicial separatism, had nevertheless
hoped to witness a reform of the Church which would derive its
main impulse and support if not from the State, then assuredly
not from the laity.

At the other end of the scale, the liberals included among their
most active supporters men who ultimately ceased to accord any
place in the scheme of things to the Church. These men had
decided by the light of logic that there was no reason for the
existence of confessional parties, that the sphere of religion was
quite separate from that of politics, that there was in the life of a
believer a time for prayer and for attendance at church and a time

for political activity, that it was easy for a Catholic to distinguish between those spheres in which it was his duty to obey his parish priest and his bishop and those in which it was an abuse of privilege for the dignitaries in question to attempt to impose their authority. The fact that confessional parties were springing up all over Europe, that in Italy as in every other country there were scores of thousands of citizens for whom religious considerations came first and the religious label was the yardstick by which they distinguished friend from foe, did nothing to modify this philosophy. And, as sometimes happens even with historians, a denial of the legitimacy of the abstract idea was finally transformed into a refusal to recognize the reality.

These liberals refused to take account, they consistently underestimated the significance, not only of religious life itself, but of all political activity of a confessional nature. Posthumous evidence of this mentality is to be found in the detailed history of the origins of the First World War by Luigi Albertini, the great editor of the *Corriere della Sera* and a man nurtured in the purest liberal tradition: a history in which the Holy See is never even mentioned, as if the Foreign Ministers of Denmark or Portugal were more important than the Secretariat of State.

The exponent *par excellence* of the liberal tradition, with its concept of the sovereign State that frames its laws with a strict regard for the rights of the various religious denominations yet refuses to come to terms with them, and its distrust of confessional organizations that presume to exceed the bounds of purely religious activity, was that least tractable of Italian parliamentarians, Sidney Sonnino.

In an article in the *Nuova Antologia* entitled 'Il partito liberale e il suffragio universale'[1] Sonnino posed the question: 'Is it possible, is it desirable, to form a liberal *bloc*, made up of so-called elements of the Right, the Centre and the Free Left, that will live a separate and independent life, steadfastly opposing any fusion of moderates and Catholics on the one hand, of progressionists and socialists on the other? I believe that it is. Indeed, I consider that such a development will be not merely useful but necessary if our political life is to evolve along sound lines.' . . . 'The sole aim and ideal of the Liberal Party, the dominant sentiment inspiring all its actions, must be the general interest of the national State, con-

[1] Vol. 155, 1911, pp. 305 *sqq.*

ceived as the sum of all its citizens, regardless of their religious or political creeds or of their social positions. . . . And it is precisely in this that it [i.e. the Liberal Party] differs from the extreme parties, Socialist and Catholic alike.' The existence of the Socialist Party and the Catholic Party, 'both firmly established and organized for the battle . . . is a fact that would to-day render any lasting split in the constitutional Liberal Party extremely dangerous—dangerous, that is, from the point of view of the general interest of the nation.'

These words reflected an unwavering belief in the necessity of a task which liberalism would have abdicated by allying itself with the Catholics. Moreover, they in no way conflicted with the thought of the most eminent liberals, even of those who appeared more tractable than Sonnino: men like Salandra, who had expressed his disapproval of the Gentiloni Pact; Giolitti, who had enunciated the formula of the 'two parallels' and who, if he sometimes tolerated casual alliances for single battles, would subsequently demonstrate his independence of outlook by administering little pin-pricks to the Church; Orlando; and even Luzzatti, who, though favourably disposed towards the Catholics when it seemed to him that their requests did not exceed the bounds of common justice, was destined to write: 'The modern State addresses itself to all those Gods who die only to be born again, to all the philosophical systems, in these terms: "I guarantee to you the necessary freedom to practise your faiths and to indulge in your dreams, whether you curse me or bless me. I am the arbiter: my function is not to vouch for the truth of this or that opinion, but to ensure that equal respect is paid to all those doctrines, and to all the activities inspired by those doctrines, that come within the jurisdiction of the sovereign State and are thus entitled to a share of the respect due to its supreme authority. But in the exercise of this same sovereignty there are some countries, among them this Italy of ours, which have need of a singular and superhuman patience in order to render the serene and necessary coexistence of a liberal Monarchy with the Papacy in Rome ever more secure, ever more widely accepted."[1]'

Luigi Luzzatti's *bonhomie* did not prevent him from taking up an unequivocal position whenever it seemed that the non-

---

[1] 'Le controversie politiche e giuridiche sulla libertà religiosa,' in *Nuova Antologia*, 1912, vol. 157, pp. 501 *sqq.*

confessional character of the State was again in question. In his inaugural lecture at Rome University in 1914 he observed regretfully that he had believed that the secular character of the Italian State was no longer in dispute and that 'the people's silence with regard to the religious tolerance and—pardon the expression—the *non-confessional character* of our régime signified, as in the United States of America, a universal assent accorded either on principle or from motives of prudence.' However, during the Social Week at Milan not only was it proposed to internationalize the Law of Guarantees, but emphasis was laid on the confessional character of the State.

In the course of his lecture Luzzatti recalled the precedent of the Zanardelli penal code, which had sought to place all confessions on an equality; and he reminded his audience that the committees of the Chamber and Senate had been unwilling at the time to admit even the expression 'religions lawfully professed in the State' lest it should be thought that only those religions sanctioned by law were protected, and that they had wished to substitute the phrase 'religions professed in the State'.

'History teaches that of all the freedoms the one that is slowest and most reluctant to root itself in the individual conscience is that which sanctions contradiction and conflict between religious and philosophical ideas, and that the line dividing propaganda, evangelism, proselytism, and gentle pressures from persecution is narrow, often invisible.'[1]

Any suggestion in 1914 of a return to the conditions that had prevailed before the Risorgimento, of a return to the confessional State, would have been unanimously opposed by all the most eminent exponents of liberalism.

By way of compensation, however, the Church no longer had cause to fear any State intervention, even of an indirect kind, in its activities. It could virtually discount the few controls which the law still exercised over its administrative life, controls which in fact caused it no embarrassment.

Cavour's formula was still apparently sacred to all who called themselves liberals. Giolitti's image of the 'two parallels' and Luzzatti's formula, 'freedom of worship in a sovereign State', were merely its modern derivatives, and were not intended to supplant it.

---

[1] La religione nel diritto costituzionale italiano, in *Nuova Antologia*, vol. 169, 1914, pp. 57 *sqq.*

Apart from the formula, however, nothing survived of the thought and spirit of the statesman who lay buried at Sàntena. Nothing survived of that fervent, active faith in freedom which both wounds and heals, which renews all things, which rejuvenates institutions and revivifies the conceptions that are subject to its influence. That faith had been in the truest sense Cavour's religion, the dynamic of his life, the inspiration that lent wings to his oratory, which in itself was devoid of charm and colour. Now it lay dormant; the liberals of to-day were perfunctory churchmen, the kind who profess a religious faith, yet dare not look into their hearts because they are too much afraid that their avowed beliefs will not bear examination and analysis, the kind who prefer to put their faith into cold storage in the hope that they will be able to draw on it in the hour of need. They did not even share Cavour's interest in the Church as a historical institution, as a living, active organization. This interest had certainly been profound, so much so that he had been moved to study the history and law of the Church and to examine closely its institutions. He had distinguished between those which he deemed capable of bearing new and beneficent fruits and those which seemed to him so much dead wood, between those which he perceived as dangerous cankers and those which, by contrast, seemed to him fortunate survivals from a happier age. The history and law of the Church no longer interested the politicians, who tended to regard the great institution as a gigantic monolith, speaking of it—a sure sign, this, of incomprehension and apathy— as of something uniform, compact, impervious to the laws of evolution. Nothing seemed to have survived of Cavour's profound conception of a freedom which, with or without the approval of individual pontiffs, would eventually permeate the body of the Church and rejuvenate it, so hastening the advent of a new era of understanding between an Italy that remained a Christian State and a Church whose spirit and institutions had received a new lease of life.

Neither in the Liberal Party nor elsewhere was there any sign of the emergence of men worthy to be dubbed the spiritual heirs of the jurisdictionalists, old and new. Experience of the Church's powers of resistance, coupled with apathy, had stifled the urge to affirm in a positive way an ascendancy of the State over the Church which would enable the former to exercise a limited measure of authority and control and to ensure that the younger clergy would not remain immune from modern cultural influences.

The Church might be concerned about persecutions, about restrictions on its external activities, about the seizure of its possessions; but it no longer had reason to be concerned about attacks on its internal liberty, about State interference between itself and the faithful, between superiors and inferiors.

If the comparison with the parties of forty years before had been taken a stage further it would have been found that there had been little or no change in the uncompromisingly anti-clerical attitude of the republicans and of those radicals who in 1870 did not yet exist as a group, but who nevertheless had their standard-bearers on the frontier between liberalism and republicanism—in other words, among those liberals who were at once more lukewarm than tradition demanded and more ardent in their desire for social reforms, and among those republicans who now regarded as of minor importance the question whether the Head of the State should be hereditary or elected.

Indeed, much greater emphasis was laid on anti-clericalism in their programmes, in which juridical questions took precedence of economic questions, than in the programme of socialism.

However, these spiritual heirs of the Jacobins of 1848 and 1860 sought to express their anti-clericalism in a different field from the men of the Risorgimento, who had been dominated by their faith in the legislative weapon. They asked little or nothing of the legislator, but pinned their hopes to the executive, to the Communal councils, to the magistrates.

To be sure, they repeated, albeit without conviction, the old complaints about the Law of Guarantees, about the sacrifices which the State had accepted in sanctioning it (complaints which had had some meaning when uttered by jurisdictionalists still wedded to the pre-1789 tradition of the Catholic State, but which had none when they came from the champions of the secular State). To be sure, they repeated the assertion (here again without ever getting to the heart of the matter, without ever heeding the many jurists who were agreed in recognizing the baselessness of the complaint) that out of respect for the principle of freedom of association the law relating to the suppression of religious organizations had never been enforced. But at heart they were content

L

with the legislation directed against ecclesiastical frauds, with the satisfactions and successes of which they were assured by the battles that took place in the Communal councils and by the deliberations of the provincial administrative juntas.

From them the Church could fear pin-pricks rather than rapier-thrusts in the political and administrative field.

Finally, there existed an embryonic party of which it would have been impossible to find any counterpart in the political line-up of forty years before. I refer to the Nationalist Party.

This was never a party with a vast popular appeal. But among the bourgeoisie, especially the intellectual bourgeoisie of the towns, it made rapid and satisfactory progress; and it was a by no means negligible factor in the eclipse of the democratic and liberal ideology by reactionary doctrines (although no one could have foreseen in 1911 the crisis that lay in the not far distant future). The party showed signs of its recent origin; it bore the stamp of a movement that had been nurtured on the most widely-varied ideas. Its birth had been stimulated first and foremost by that desire for military adventures and martial glory, for colonial conquests or a broadening of frontiers, which after long periods of peace and prosperity invariably assails nations that are sufficiently powerful to cherish such aspirations. Irredentism had played its part, that latent yearning for the recovery of Trento and Trieste which has always been widespread among Italians and which was now largely identified with the republicans and the radicals, as well as, in a more general sense, with freemasonry. But there had been a great rush to join the new party, especially in Rome, on the part of young men from families with Catholic traditions, quite often with Bourbonist traditions, in which it was still the custom to accept decorations from the pretender to the throne of the Two Sicilies. Although educated in Catholic schools and colleges, these young men were not disposed to submit any longer to the ban on political activity which the Holy See still imposed on the Faithful. In fact, they wanted to be able to participate freely in the political struggle, without being guided by religious organizations, without being confined to circles in which they were constantly under clerical surveillance. Many flocked to join the new party from the ranks of the liberal-conservatives, eager for a more vigorous prosecution of the war against the political *blocs*, eager to ally themselves with the

Catholics precisely because of their hatred of immoderate and vulgar anti-clericalism.

Socialists, republicans and radicals were at one in their opposition to clerical influences. But anti-clericalism, which was the chief unifying element in the *blocs*, did not find expression on the political level alone. The Italians of 1911 were far less prone than their successors of to-day to join political parties, or even to look to them for a lead. In the towns, sons of bankers or agrarians or great landowners who were bitterly opposed to the socialists in the economic field voted for the *blocs* in virtue of their anti-clericalism. In the South more than in the North, and especially in the smaller centres of the South, anti-clericalism was still synonymous with nonconformity; the young man who wanted to rebel against tradition, to escape from the tyranny of the family, was invariably anti-clerical in outlook.

This widespread anti-clericalism, which constituted the main theme of conversation in the corridors of the universities, in the rooms of the ministries, in the second- and third-class compartments of railway-trains, must be constantly borne in mind. No one who underestimates its importance—regarding it merely as an abortive movement which accomplished nothing, and which for that reason history can afford to ignore—will succeed in achieving a balanced view of the conduct of the clergy and of Catholics under Fascism.

As a movement it was essentially unorganized. It spent itself in daily demonstrations, in continual pin-pricks aimed at the clergy and the faithful without any constructive intent, without any differentiation of objectives, rejecting *en bloc* all the values affirmed in the opposite camp, striking wherever the opportunity offered.

It was a negative movement, with disturbing overtones of vulgarity, which in a society now comparatively cultured and refined provoked a reaction far more violent than that which positivism had engendered in Croce round about 1884, when he was a university student.

Ultimately this crude anti-clericalism had the indirect effect of lowering in the esteem of the rising generation the whole doctrinal edifice of the Risorgimento and of causing its noblest figures to appear in retrospect in the grotesque likeness of Flaubert's Monsieur Homais. It opened the way to parties which at heart already repudiated nearly all the values of the Risorgimento, even though they would not yet have dared to proclaim themselves 'anti-Risorgimento'—an expression which was actually to be coined in due course.

The usual arguments were constantly retailed via all the recognized media, from speeches in Parliament to those delivered in the Communal councils of towns and villages—never had ecclesiastical subjects been so freely discussed in the Communal councils—from the great democratic, radical[1] and socialist[2] organs to the innumerable small newspapers which were published in all the administrative centres and of which the most prominent was *L'Asino*, a widely-read weekly, with pages in full colour, founded by Podrecca and Galantara and dedicated *ex professo* to the anti-clerical campaign. In the religious field, a profession of material-ism, an attempt to demonstrate the impossibility and absurdity of a personal God who watches over the destinies of men, a relegation of all miracles and of everything in religious life that transcends human reason to the category of impostures—all this, of course, being characterized by an over-simplification adapted to the ignorance of those at whom such propaganda was directed, together with a reduction to their simplest terms of the words listed in the *Dictionnaire Philosophique*. In the historical field, a demonstration of the thesis that Christ never existed, a rehash of the various anti-papal legends and the various historical contra-dictions encountered by the dogma of Papal infallibility, and, in particular, an evocation of the horrors of Catholic religious intolerance, of the story of the Inquisition and of its most illustrious victims: the whole being treated as it could be only by writers sublimely ignorant of sources, texts and the rudiments of historical criticism, writers who had never heard it said that the historian should try to recapture the atmosphere and the environment in which the events he describes unfolded themselves. In the political field, the constant evocation of a Church that had not renounced a single one of its mediaeval claims, that was only waiting for a suitable moment to proclaim them anew and to try to vindicate them, so that it could reimpose intolerable restrictions on every expression of opinion; of a Papacy plotting in the shadows to destroy the unity of Italy, a Papacy that would have liked to see

[1] *Il Secolo* (Milan), *La Gazzetta del Popolo* (Turin), *Il Messaggero* and *La Vita* (Rome).
[2] *Avanti!*

Italy humiliated and defeated so that it might re-establish the Temporal Power; of a clergy allied to the rich for the exploitation and humiliation of the poor. Denigration of the clergy was incessant in all the anti-clerical journals. The worst passions of the people were constantly inflamed by evocations of the lecherous priest who was for ever trying to seduce women or, even worse, the children entrusted to his care. Whenever possible, scandals were invented which nine times out of ten were shown at the first inquiry to be fictitious. This anti-clericalism found expression largely in the juridical field, where, however, it did not leave a single work, a single book that is still read to-day. In *De iure condendo*, its exponents demanded the abrogation of the Law of Guarantees, the suppression of Article 1 of the Statute, the confiscation of all ecclesiastical property, the legalization of divorce, the passage of a law establishing the precedence of the civil marriage rite over the religious. But they did so with little confidence; and in fact no party pledged itself whole-heartedly to these objectives. When it was a question of concluding agreements with a ministry, of trading support for a majority or fixing a price for the abandonment of a campaign embarrassing to the Government, the parties of the Left or of the extreme Left sought their reward never in the sphere of ecclesiastical policy, but in quite different fields—for instance, in those of social legislation, public works, and State policy in regard to strikes and disputes between capital and labour. In *De iure condito*, the exponents of anti-clericalism demanded that the law suppressing religious corporations should be interpreted in such a way that the latter would lose even their right of free association.

But it was above all in the sphere of Communal politics that a daily struggle was waged. The parents of pupils in elementary schools were to be prevented from availing themselves of the privilege still accorded to them of reserving school halls for the religious instruction of their children; priests and nuns prevented from filling posts in elementary schools; infant-schools staffed by nuns were to be closed down; the display of crucifixes in school halls prohibited; nursing sisters in hospitals to be replaced with lay personnel; religious confraternities and, in general, charitable institutions that still retained a confessional character were to be suppressed; among the regulations imposed by urban police forces was one to restrict the ringing of church bells to a minimum, prohibiting it, for example, during the hours of darkness; ecclesiastics were to be liable to the tax imposed on those who exercised a profession; new crematoria were to be opened in cemeteries so that, by securing a monopoly of funeral transport, the Communes might make it impossible for the confraternities (especially those in Sicily and the South, where this branch of their activity was most in evidence) to conduct the funerals of their own members.

The Catholics defended themselves tenaciously, opposing argument to argument, initiative to initiative. The life of nearly all the Communes of Italy was poisoned by this futile struggle. (Happily the period was one of economic prosperity, and all this squabbling did not prevent many excellent and useful measures from being taken in the popular interest.) But the rift between Catholics and anti-clericals was complete. Mention has already been made of the obstacles to their co-operation even in the sphere of the class struggle. On the one hand, the socialist and republican leagues were intolerant of practising Catholics; on the other, Catholic workers and peasants were beginning to form their own confessional organizations. Naturally, the landowning class tried to profit by the division, stoking up the fires of anti-clericalism by branding the Catholics as 'blacklegs' and 'strike-breakers' and by accusing them of preventing the working class from realizing its just aspirations.

Was all this mere puerility? Was it the result of mental laziness? Was it an example of that method of winning popularity which consists in repeating to the people the same old clichés, in conjuring up before them the same old images, without demanding any mental effort on their part? Could it be that even those men of intellect and culture who participated in the anti-clerical movement were so blinded by prejudice as to suppose that religious faith could be destroyed by such means, that the edifice of the Church could be brought down by such pin-pricks, which irritated but did not wound? Could it be that even men to whom politics were the staff of life, men who had for years represented a constituency at Montecitorio, did not realize the extent to which they were playing into the hands of their adversaries—encouraging the formation of a solid *bloc* of conservatives, united not only by interest but also by the disgust which this crude anti-clericalism, this vulgar intolerance, inspired in the hearts of many, including even non-Catholics, even non-believers?

Or was it rather not puerility, but a premeditated scheme with but a single object—namely, to maintain a semblance of friction, a spirit of hostility, to ensure that, especially in the provinces, no one would be able to escape the obligation of figuring in one group or the other, of being either a sectarian in the eyes of the Catholics or a clericalist in the eyes of those who served in the opposing faction?

And if such a scheme existed, how was it to be judged? Severely, as being designed to prevent men of goodwill from overcoming the historical obstacles to reconciliation, from closing the internal rift between Italians, which had completely lost its *raison d'être*? This scheme to keep Italians divided, to deny the light of the sun, the dignity of a political party, to that section of opinion which had always existed and which continued to ask itself whether the problem of the relations between Church and State had not been exaggerated, whether, in fact, it could not be shelved or at least thrust into the background, so that Italians might work together in one of the countless fields that were open to them—was it a scheme devised by sectarians, by men incapable of aspiring to a vision of their country's higher interests?

Or were these exponents of anti-clericalism merely being astute when they artificially maintained an appearance of dissension, when they refused to recognize what to impartial observers seemed obvious—namely that in the Catholic camp profound changes had occurred, that in the political and social sphere the Catholics, especially in northern Italy, had assumed a new guise, almost indistinguishable from that of forty years before? Did they realize, even dimly, that, as the gap narrowed between the spiritual heirs of those Catholics who, even though they had shared the hopes of 1848, would have renounced everything, even national unity, rather than offend the Church, and the spiritual heirs of those other Catholics who, even if they had disapproved of individual measures, had nevertheless accepted the Risorgimento as a whole and had not regarded it as a disaster for the Church—did they realize that it was the values of liberalism, the values of Camillo di Cavour and of Minghetti, that were being jeopardized by a failure to correlate the vast moral and material forces of Catholicism with those of liberalism? Did they realize that, while the latter presented a beautiful, harmonious, sumptuous façade, its hidden potentialities were almost completely neutralized by a lack

of organization? Did they realize that the collapse of anti-
clericalism would have been followed inevitably by a new era of
Guelphism?

These were the questions that were being asked on the eve of
the First World War by the few observers of the Italian scene who
combined discernment with objectivity.

Bibliographical Note.

The best-known biography of Pius X, R. Bazin's *Pie X* (Paris, 1936)
gives much consideration to the man himself, but is devoid of interest
so far as his relations with the Italian State are concerned.

On the political activity of the Catholics, see the two books by
Vercesi cited in the bibliography at the end of the preceding chapter.

In order to obtain an adequate idea of Italian modernism in the
political field it is essential to read all the writings—published very
sporadically, mainly in reviews—of R. Murri. On the fortunes of
religious modernism in Italy, including its impact on lay public
opinion and on the prevailing philosophy of the time, see the early
pages of E. Buonaiuti, *Pellegrino di Roma* (Rome, 1945).

A highly synthetic picture of the reign of Victor Emmanuel III is
presented in G. Volpe's *L'Italia in cammino. L'ultimo cinquantennio* (Milan,
1927). The Speeches from the Throne are collected in an appendix to
Volpe's other book, *Vittorio Emanuele III* (Milan, 1939).

Of no interest to the student of relations between Church and State,
even though it sheds light on the history of the period, is G. Giolitti's
Memorie della mia vita (Milan, 1922). On the other hand, the early
pages of V. E. Orlando's *Su alcuni miei rapporti di Governo con la Santa
Sede* (Naples, 1930; 2nd ed., Milan-Rome, 1944) furnish some data on
the development of formal relations between the Italian Government
and the Vatican. Some of the closing speeches in the annual debates
on the financial estimates of the Ministry of Grace and Justice, which
were the traditional occasion for the airing of different points of view
on ecclesiastical policy, are included in C. Finocchiaro Aprile's
Discorsi parlamentari (Rome, 1923). The speeches in question give a
concrete idea of the subjects debated during the early years of the
century.

CHAPTER V

THE 1914–18 WAR AND POST-WAR PROBLEMS

ALL those still living who were in Italy during the winter and spring of 1915 will retain indelible memories of one of those gradual ebullitions of popular passion, one of those infectious waves of emotion, to which few, and least of all the isolated individual, can remain indifferent.

Something of the same kind must have occurred in 1789, when even men in whose lives privilege and tradition had played a fundamental part were swept willy-nilly into the ranks of the revolutionaries, and in 1846–47, when even a Father Taparelli was momentarily transformed. Yet it is perhaps true to say that the impact of 1915 was more enduring. The fanatics of 1789 in many cases returned after a few years to the old ideas, to the old patterns of feeling, coming to regard their fanaticisms as an aberration; but I have known no Italian who was caught up in the emotional holocaust of 1915 who has ever regretted his enthusiasms, who has ever repented of what he wrote or said or did at that time in the sacred name of intervention. I have known Fascists and Naziphils who in 1940–43 still recalled with joy that they had once taken up arms against Germany; I have known fervent anti-Fascists who would never have admitted that May, 1915, had been the ominous prelude to October, 1922. With Man's unfailing genius for subordinating reason to the necessity of arriving at a desired conclusion, not one of those who had the joy of being enveloped by that wave of passion ever felt the smallest twinge of regret for what he had said or done in those momentous days.

Nobody who has once shared in one of those collective outbursts of passion in which the individual's interests, predilections and mental outlook of the day before are forgotten can ever again become the dupe of a historical materialism which pretends to explain everything.

Nevertheless, 1915 in Italy was not the same as 1914 in France —a year which saw, for the last time, a pure and sacred union of all elements, an unconditional desire for victory that united Catholics and radicals and socialists, an eruption of national feeling in which all the passions of party were forgotten. In Italy it was possible to speak of genuine unity only after the disaster of October, 1917, which was as fortunate an event from the viewpoint of internal politics as it was inauspicious in the military sense.

In 1915, the pressure brought to bear on the Government by popular demonstrations was only too apparent. No less obvious, even to those with a scant critical sense, was the ideology of the intervention, which, contemptuously dubbed by the Right 'the masonic mentality', might have been described much more respectfully and with equal regard for truth as a modernized version of the illuministic ideology of a century and a half before. Later, under Fascism, an attempt was made, in this matter as in others, to falsify history, to dismiss the interventionist fervour of 1915 as no more than an expression of nationalism. In reality, however, Trento and Trieste (in those days popular feeling did not aspire to Fiume and Dalmatia) had always constituted the synthetic formula that revealed the essence of Irredentism. Not altogether unlike the liberalism of Montalembert, to whom only Catholic nations subject to non-Catholic sovereigns were deserving of pity, worthy of succour, Italian Irredentism—which had never included among its adherents a single influential name that did not bear the stamp of freemasonry or radicalism or republicanism, still less one that was not Jewish—looked upon as 'unredeemed' only those who, Italian by language and tradition, found themselves in subjection to an authoritarian and clericalist monarchy. The sense of nationality resumed here the function which it had exercised in Europe when it had first appeared to the strains of the *Marseillaise*—that of opening the way to a universal idea.

The fact that the Nationalists, who until August, 1914, had been filled with a burning hatred of France, had, with a miraculous intuition of what would inevitably follow the declaration of neutrality, avoided the isolation and the speedy eclipse to which a persistence in their Germanophilia would surely have condemned them and had thrown in their lot with the advocates of intervention on the side of France, Britain and Russia, did not alter the situation one whit. They were few in number, and in any case the people were actuated not so much by a desire to establish their country's natural frontier as by an aversion to the eternal barbarian, to the demon of militarism, to the two Central European Empires, in each of which traces of feudalism were still apparent and an aristocratic clique still held the reins of government, to that order of ideas which came under the general heading or Prussianism, and to the avowed clericalism of the Austrian Empire. One need only refer to the pictures in the illustrated papers, to the posters and propaganda-leaflets of the period, without troubling to delve into the mass of literature dealing with the intervention, in order to appreciate the truth of this assertion.

Indeed, Italian interventionism, not only in 1915 but also in the years that followed, was riddled with anti-clericalism. Contemporary short stories, together with all the articles and commentaries in the Catholic papers, which refute the charges of defeatism levelled against the clergy by interventionists, remain as evidence of the fact.

It was impossible to blame Catholics if they were somewhat suspicious of interventionism, which was championed by nearly all the best-known exponents of Italian anti-clericalism as well as by those newspapers most hostile to the Church. A corrective was provided by the *Corriere della Sera* and by some of the great names of liberalism—men such as Salandra and Sonnino—who constituted a living guarantee of resistance to Jacobin backslidings, but who had nevertheless signified their opposition to any kind of liberal-Catholic coalition, being concerned as ever with the defence of pure liberalism. The only reliable friends the Catholics possessed among the interventionists were the Nationalists. But in 1915 they still counted for little.

The Vatican was opposed to Italian intervention, partly on account of the Pontiff's natural desire to prevent the conflict from spreading, but also because of his concern as to the position of the Holy See should Italy enter the war. This was inevitable, when the first voices that were raised in the interventionist camp on the subject of the Vatican's position advocated that the privileges conferred upon it by the Law of Guarantees should be suspended for the duration?[1]

It is well known that in the event the Law of Guarantees was

---

[1] Cf. G. Quadrotta, *Il Papa, l'Italia e la guerra*, with a preface by F. Scaduto (Milan, 1915); and for the most significant writings on the subject published in 1915 and during the early months of 1916 see M. Falco, *Le prerogative della Santa Sede e la guerra* (Milan, 1916).

not modified; and in view of the fact that its provisions continued to apply even after Italy's entry into the war, liberal writers could justly claim that it had been finally vindicated (Filippo Crispolti had spoken in 1905 of its *pons asinorum*). Actually, however, the Holy See, on being officially requested by the Government to assume moral responsibility for ensuring that the diplomatic representatives accredited to it by the Central Powers would not take advantage of their immunity to harm the Italian cause, had preferred to invite them to transfer themselves to Switzerland. It could thus be said with perfect truth that the Law of Guarantees had been 'vindicated'.

However, after a year of war the situation had already changed substantially.

In general, the Catholics did not rise to the same heights of enthusiasm as the interventionists; and they were to find themselves in a somewhat embarrassing position whenever the Pontiff issued an encyclical appealing for peace. The interventionists described these encyclicals as attempts to rescue the Central Powers from their difficulties; and when Benedict XV, in a phrase whose validity history was to demonstrate, spoke of 'useless slaughter', cries were raised against the defeatist Pope by all those who approved of their country's policy! Nevertheless, they showed themselves to be loyal citizens, who evaded none of the obligations imposed on them by the war; the families of the Black aristocracy and that section of the bourgeoisie which was most faithful to the Holy See provided their quota of fighting men, some of them fanatical in their devotion to the cause. A number of ecclesiastics, notably the already well-known Father Semeria, stressed the patriotic note and applied themselves with great zeal to the task of ministering to the spiritual needs of the troops. The Italian soldier could never doubt that his cause was just, and that it had the blessing of the Church.

On the other hand, the aversion of the official Socialist Party to the war, its undisguised, uncompromising pacificism—reflected in daily demonstrations which caused those in the opposing camp to see red—had the effect of making the great mass of right-thinking people, including all those parliamentarians whose judgment was not warped by party prejudice, aware of the need to maintain their solidarity with the Catholic world, to refrain from embittering it unnecessarily, to make of it an element favourable to the Government, ready to proclaim its moral support of the war and its conduct.

What was more important, the people could appreciate the essential, manifestly sincere neutrality of the Holy See in the conflict. The old anti-clerical assertion that in the event of war the Vatican would conspire to destroy the unity of the nation was patently belied by the facts.

In a speech delivered on November 21st, 1915, at the Teatro Massimo, Palermo, V. E. Orlando, Keeper of the Seals, besides referring to the solidarity of all parties and by means of an anecdote, skilfully evoking, without seeming to do so, the figure of the soldier-priest, specifically mentioned the scrupulous way in which the Government had observed the Law of Guarantees, 'concealing the few weaknesses [in the law] which experience had revealed by a liberal interpretation of its fundamental principle— namely, that the special form of spiritual sovereignty [exercised by the Pope] should be recognized and guaranteed': so that to-day 'the Supreme Pontiff governs the Church and carries out his sublime ministry without let or hindrance, enjoying a freedom, security and prestige appropriate to the truly sovereign authority which is his by right in the spiritual field.'

The second War Cabinet, presided over by Boselli (June 18th, 1916–October 29th, 1917), was able to announce itself as a cabinet of national unity and to receive into its midst a minister who had formerly been a militant Catholic—Filippo Meda. It was this same Meda who, as Minister of Finance, was to play an active part in the seizure of the Palazzo Venezia, property of the Austrian Empire and headquarters of Vienna's mission to the Holy See, when the Government demanded its restoration to Italy. This action evoked a mild protest from the Pontiff, who saw in it fresh evidence that no amount of goodwill on the part of the nation's rulers could eliminate the disadvantages of the situation in which the Papacy had been placed by the loss of the Temporal Power.

Meda continued to serve in the third War Ministry under Orlando. It was during this Ministry's term of office that the Bolshevik Government published details of the clause inserted in the Treaty of London—some said at Sonnino's instigation, others at the King's—with the object of denying the Holy See a voice in any peace treaty for fear that at an international conference it would revive its claims with regard to the temporal power.[1] Although this disclosure caused some indignation in Catholic circles no one took a tragic view of the matter, partly because in 1918 no one any longer envisaged the possibility of the war ending with a sort of Congress of Vienna at which a Cardinal-Legate might utter words fraught with significance for the future of the world, and partly also because American intervention alone had sufficed to put all the secret agreements arrived at in 1915 once more in the melting-pot.

Meanwhile, *necessitate ipsa dictante*, another bastion of liberal ecclesiastical policy fell almost unnoticed—namely, the principle of 'no State-subsidies for religion'. In order that the miserable stipends of parish priests might be slightly increased in recognition of the recent and continuing fall in the value of the currency, the State was forced to make a grant to the Ecclesiastical Fund. When the day of victory arrived the clergy joined in all the public manifestations of joy.

The progress of the peace negotiations in Paris was painfully slow. In May, 1919, a prelate from Chicago, Mgr. Kelly, took the initiative in pointing out to Prime Minister Orlando the desirability of instituting direct negotiations between the Holy See and Italy. Orlando agreed to the suggestion in principle, and Mgr. Kelly proceeded to Rome, whence an official of the Secretariat of State, Mgr. Bonaventura Cerretti, Secretary for Church Affairs, was immediately sent to Paris with a plan drafted by Cardinal Gasparri. The plan sought to confer upon the precincts of the Vatican the dignity of an independent State possessing international sovereignty. Furthermore, it implied that the new State's borders should be extended to include certain neighbouring districts. It did not advocate any financial contribution on the part of Italy, nor any modifications of the Italian juridical system that might affect the rights of the individual; but it spoke in general terms of an eventual Concordat which would restrict the application of the ecclesiastical laws.

Orlando was favourable, but his attitude was in no way comparable to that of Cardinal Gasparri, who had sent Mgr.

---

[1] In March, 1916, Guglielmo Quadrotta had circulated a questionnaire in which he sounded opinion as to the desirability or otherwise of the Pope's participation in the peace conference. The replies are embodied in an appendix to G. Quadrotta's *La Chiesa cattolica nella crisi universale* (Rome, 1921). The book is also of some interest for the details it gives of the subsequent careers of certain of the men who replied.

Cerretti on his mission without twenty-four hours of Mgr. Kelly's arrival in Rome.

Meanwhile, the constitutional formalities were duly observed. It was necessary to inform the King and to refer the matter to the Council of Ministers. Here there was some opposition, but Orlando was prepared if necessary even to re-shuffle his Cabinet. However, he could not stir from Paris, and negotiations conducted from a distance are seldom satisfactory. Moreover, it was necessary to take account of the psychological mood of the country, deeply shaken by its recent ordeal and torn by conflicting emotions. If, Orlando told Mgr. Cerretti, the cataclysmic happenings of the past four years 'are succeeded by such an epoch-making event as the solution of the Roman Question, we may find that the shock administered to an organism already so seriously weakened has brought the patient to the verge of what I would almost describe as nervous prostration. As you well know, to a weakened organism even a joyful experience can be fatal. . . . Therefore, all things considered, it might be better to await the signature of the peace treaty before opening negotiations. In the meantime, however, I will begin to prepare the ground. Within the next ten days I will convene the Council of Ministers either on the frontier or in Rome and will expound the plan to my colleagues.'

But on June 15th the Orlando Cabinet resigned, and the government of the country passed into the hands of the man who during the last months of the war had been Orlando's bitter adversary—Francesco Saverio Nitti. In this first Nitti Cabinet the Catholics were represented by Cesare Nava, who assumed the office of Minister for the Liberated Territories. (In the succeeding Cabinet, formed in June, 1920, the post of Minister for War was destined to be filled by another old Catholic, Rodinò.) However, the new Administration also included, as Keeper of the Seals, a man much hated by the Catholics, Ludovico Mortara.

Although there is no evidence that the negotiations were continued by the new Government, the latter's actions repeatedly bore witness to the radical change in the atmosphere. Cardinal Filippo Giustini, Papal Envoy to Jerusalem on the occasion of the seven hundredth anniversary of St. Francis's journey to the East, left Taranto on September 13th, 1919, in the cruiser *Quarto*, flying the standard of the Royal Princes, landed at Jaffa with the captain of the ship to the accompaniment of the customary salute of guns and was there received by the Italian Consul, who welcomed him on behalf of his Government. At the Franciscan Custodia in Jerusalem a detachment of *carabinieri* formed a guard of honour for the Papal Envoy, who was accompanied on his round of visits by the Italian Consul.

On Cardinal Giustini's death in March, 1920, Prime Minister Nitti went to view his remains.

In his encyclical *Pacem, Dei munus* of May 23rd, 1920, Benedict XV repudiated the one form of protest adopted by the Papacy since 1870 that had caused the Italian Government serious embarrassment—namely, the refusal to receive Catholic Heads of State who had come to Rome to visit the King of Italy. In the spring of 1921 there was much talk of conciliation; and a summary of the arguments which the newspapers had developed on that theme between May 29th and June 20th was published by the Press Office of the Ministry of Foreign Affairs.

Finally, on the death of Benedict XV, the Bonomi Government adopted a form of official mourning that had never been used on any similar occasion in the past. For his part, the new Pope broke with the tradition established by his three immediate predecessors and pronounced his blessing on the people from the outer portico of St. Peter's (February 6th, 1922)—though his gesture was promptly followed by a declaration expressing 'all possible reservations in regard to the inviolable rights of the Church and of the Holy See'. Six days later Pope Pius XI again conferred his blessing on the people massed in the square, among them units of the Italian Army that had come to present arms on the occasion of his enthronement ceremony.

The rise of the Italian Popular Party in 1919 is pre-eminently associated with the name of Luigi Sturzo. Born at Caltagirone, Don Sturzo was a typical Sicilian priest from a well-to-do family whose social background had permitted him from his earliest youth to move about the world of men with some freedom, while his economic position had spared him the necessity of filling ecclesiastical posts in obscure centres. He had always been a most devout priest. In the years of his intensest political activity one heard it said of him that, faced with an unexpected difficulty, with a contretemps, with the necessity of taking a grave decision, he would go into a church and pray at length to the Almighty for guidance. I do not believe that even in his moments of greatest bitterness he was ever assailed by the temptation to rebel, either directly or indirectly, against the authority of the Church, or to publish an anonymous article criticizing the Holy See.

He had, however, always been one of those priests—by no means rare either in Italy or abroad—who have a flair and a taste for administration: one of those priests who are capable of extreme piety, who would never be assailed by the thought that the cloth they wear is the symbol of an ill-chosen vocation, but who, believing that the function of religion is truly universal, taking the precept *instaurare omnia in Christo* absolutely literally, maintaining that there is no field of activity, even among those which to the common run of men appear genuinely 'neutral', in which it is not possible, metaphorically, to plant the Cross, concentrate all their attention not on questions of theology, ethics, liturgy or ecclesiastical organization, but on problems relating to practical life—problems of economics, law or administration. Such men are the founders of political leagues, of savings banks, of organizations which seek to advise on administrative or fiscal matters. In local political battles they are the experts, the dreaded minority councillors who severely criticize the Junta's financial estimates and discover illegalities in every mayoral prescript. Don Sturzo was for many years deputy mayor—the law forbidding a minister of religion to assume the title of mayor itself—in his native Caltagirone; and he is said to have been a Communal magistrate of exceptional excellence. He became highly expert in matters of local administration, and at all national conventions at which representatives of provinces and communes met to discuss their problems, his views were eagerly sought and listened to. Equally, however, his name used to figure in the minutes of Catholic congresses, such as that held at Naples in March, 1910, when he sat alongside some of the most distinguished members of the devout laity—men such as Count Gentiloni, Commendatore Pericoli, Commendatore Rodinò, Mauri, and the celebrated advocate Miglioli.

The ascetic figure of the urbane Sicilian priest quickly became popular in the Ministries of Rome, to which he used to come, armed always with reliable information, knowing well the questions at issue and the legal framework within which they had

M

to be settled, for the purpose of investigating this or that measure, or of advocating this or that solution to such-and-such a problem.

The taste for administration (the importance of which is probably appreciated less in the Anglo-Saxon than in the Germanic and Latin countries) is a specialized taste. Politicians of the most widely varied types—one thinks of Cavour, Crispi, Giolitti—have possessed it in overflowing measure. To others it has been denied, and these have had to rely on expert advisers in all matters pertaining to administration. Luigi Sturzo possessed it in a unique degree.

Don Sturzo came to maturity during the first fifteen years of the century—that is to say, not only in the years of Italian prosperity, but also at a time when public life was essentially peaceful, when right-thinking people might be stimulated from time to time by an election, but never by the spectacle of subversion, of a Parliament invaded and dispersed either by a profane mob or a battalion of grenadiers. Within the framework of this social and political order the party of the extreme Left, constituted by the revolutionary socialists, was continually dominated by men from good bourgeois families, for the most part university graduates who argued in terms of law and economics.

Equally, Don Sturzo's character was moulded in the years of Pius X's pontificate, during which the higher ranks of the Vatican became imbued with the conviction that not only was a restoration of the Papal States impossible—of this they had already become convinced during the second half of the papacy of Leo XIII—but that it would have been a most deplorable event, that with a few juridical modifications, with a less tenuous modification of external conditions, the existing status of the Pope—neither a political subject nor yet a Head of State—might become the ideal status from the point of view of the Church. It is not surprising that a man who grew up in those years conceived the good of the Church in terms of the peaceful capture by Catholics of majorities on the provincial and Communal councils, the provincial administrative juntas and the executive councils of the various Ministries, and of a reform of the electoral laws that would enable Catholics really to assert themselves, breaking the stranglehold of local *paternalismi*, of those influential families which under the constitution of the Kingdom disposed of seats in Parliament, either reserving them for their own members or trading them for various concessions: such families in Sicily and the South had in many cases been subject for two generations to masonic domination. Nor is it surprising that he approved of that concept of decentralization which had always been part of the tradition of Catholics moulded in an age when—partly because of the *non expedit*—Catholic domination of the State was regarded as unthinkable, whereas it was considered quite reasonable that Catholics should exercise a limited hegemony in certain provinces and communes. This point of view also reflected Sicily's desire for autonomy, which had been strong ever since the island had ceased to be a monarchy in its own right.

Still less is it to be wondered at that ecclesiastical policy in the strict sense of the term was not one of his themes. In Italy no good Catholic enunciates ideas and proposals on this subject without the authority, explicit or implicit, of the Holy See. A priest occupying the prominent position of Don Sturzo could not have spoken on ecclesiastical policy, whatever reservations he might have made, without being regarded as the mouthpiece of the Secretariat of State. For that matter, apart from the solution of the Roman Question (in regard to which any proposal was bound to emanate from the Holy See and could be made public only if a previous understanding had been reached with the Government), it would have been impossible in 1919–20 to conceive of any significant reform of ecclesiastical legislation other than the repeal of the law suppressing the religious associations. For such a development public opinion was by this time largely prepared; but was it worth while arousing controversy and hostility to the new party for this? Probably the Holy See even then had in mind the reservation which it was to express some years later—that Italy should not be permitted to modify her ecclesiastical legislation, to render it acceptable unconditionally to Catholics and to the clergy, by shelving the Roman Question. Moreover, with the disappearance of the old liberals, who had ascribed to the legislation of the Risorgimento an ideal significance far surpassing its practical value and for that reason had believed that it ought to be respected both formally and in the manner of its application, a way had already been found of according the religious Orders the means of legal ownership—namely, by recognizing what were in fact monasteries or convent schools of an Order as missionary training colleges or educational establishments.

The new party cherished high hopes; it set before itself a vast though somewhat vague programme; it was too impatient to act and to reach the hearts of the people to get bogged down at the outset in questions of ecclesiastical policy, which by now were of interest only to a very limited number of Italians.

In the event, the party succeeded in gaining the allegiance of Catholics of every hue, including a number of sonorous names from the old Roman aristocracy. It attracted those Catholics—such of them as still remained in Rome—who had always refused to be presented at Court, who had always respected the *non expedit*, and who referred in their newspapers to 'King Victor Emmanuel' and not to 'the King', because the second designation would have implied the existence of a King of Italy. It attracted those Catholics who regarded themselves merely as a wing, albeit with a distinctive colouring, of the great army of conservatives. It attracted the 'social' Catholics, those who, notably in northern Italy, had shown themselves particularly skilful at creating a fine network of commercial interests, with the result that in certain districts the tradesman, the contractor, the small landowner who needed credit for the development of his property or who had to come to terms with a cheese-manufacturer or a wine-merchant in order to keep himself employed and to sell his produce, were virtually compelled to support these confessional-commercial enterprises. It attracted those Catholics who idealized Toniolo, but who in reality did not so much derive inspiration from the *Rerum novarum* and from the ideology of the professor of Pisa University as conform to the principles of what was later to be referred to north of the Alps as 'technical clericalism'. It attracted the survivors of the 'Democratic League' and of the disciples of Murri, who had been able to pose as rebels, but who were Catholics first, and might well have been said to illustrate Renan's allegory of the bird that flutters round the steeple in which it has made its nest and in which alone it will be able to find repose. And, finally, it attracted those Catholics who saw in its programme the only possible means of satisfying their aspirations, who would have felt like fish out of water in any truly secular party, where religious values counted for nothing.

This breadth of scope, this admission of such disparate elements, certainly represented a weakness in the party: the extreme Left regarded the extreme Right as hopelessly reactionary, while the latter looked upon the former as riff-raff. Yet ecclesiastical discipline, even in the absence of any formal prescriptions or explicit sanctions, is such a potent force that until the rise of Fascism, and until the Secretariat of State's indifference to the Popular Party became apparent, the danger of a split was never regarded as imminent. There could be no place in Italy for two Catholic parties, each for ever at the other's throat, to the great satisfaction of the enemies of the Church.

The Popular Party professed to be non-confessional; and it even welcomed into its ranks *rarissimae aves* who were not Catholics. It was, to be sure, non-confessional in the sense that its local branches were run entirely by laymen, that it did not form part of the framework of the diocesan organizations, that it denied the right of the episcopate to make dispensations affecting itself. It was non-confessional, too, in virtue of the Holy See's assertion that it did not represent the Church and could not commit it in any way and that the Church could not answer for the attitudes adopted by its organs. In reality, however—I believe everywhere, but certainly in Italy—it was necessary to understand in a very special sense the non-confessional character of a party which, proclaiming its fundamental desire to uphold Christian values and to work for their implementation, postulated its moral right to the allegiance of sincere Catholics to whom such values were of paramount concern: a party which during elections necessarily attached peculiar importance to the support of bishops, to the warmth with which parish priests commended its programme to their flocks, and which at such times would have a second electoral office (in reality the more important) in every presbytery. The Popular Party was a non-confessional party: but a difference of opinion between the provincial leaders of such a party and the local bishop was not to be thought of; such a difference, if it arose, would have to be composed—if necessary, by the replacement of the leaders in question. The Popular Party was a party independent of the ecclesiastical authorities inasmuch as the latter in effect dissociated themselves from many of its initiatives and aims; but neither it nor any avowedly Catholic party would find it possible, either now or later, to oppose the Secretariat of State whenever it issued a directive on any question; the power to fix the limits between that which was purely political and that which concerned morality and religion in such a way as to legitimize the intervention of the ecclesiastical authorities would always remain with the last-named. An organization of Catholics which sought to defy the Pope had been for a century at least a contradiction in terms, a practical impossibility.

The party issued its manifesto to the country, thereby announcing its birth, on January 18th, 1919. All the signatories were members or officials of Catholic organizations, and a clear majority were from the north. The political secretary was Don Luigi Sturzo. The appeal to the country was couched in the following terms:

'We support the political and moral programme, heritage of the Christian peoples, previously expounded in the august words of the Supreme Pontiff and to-day championed by Wilson as a basic element of the future world order; and we reject the imperialisms that create dominant nations and provoke violent reactions. Accordingly, we call upon the League of Nations to recognize just national aspirations, to hasten the advent of universal disarmament, to abolish secret treaties, to enforce the freedom of the seas, to urge international acceptance of the principles of social legislation, equal pay for women and, in the religious sphere, individual freedom from all sectarian oppression; and to invest itself with full legal authority and with the means to uphold the rights of weak nations in face of the arrogance of the strong. We wish to see the centralized State ... replaced by a truly democratic State, which will recognize the limits of its authority, respecting the individual personality and the natural units and organisms—the family, the various social classes, and the communes—and encouraging private enterprise.' The manifesto demanded 'religious freedom not only for individuals but also for the Church, so that she may accomplish her spiritual mission in the world; freedom of education, without State monopolies; freedom for professional organizations without sectional bias or distinctions of party; and, finally, Communal and local freedom in accordance with Italian traditions.' It affirmed the civilizing mission of Italy in accordance with the firmly-established principles of Christianity, 'in face of socialist democracies which seek to reduce every idealism to a material level, and in face of the old sectarian liberalisms, which use the strength of the centralized State organism to resist the new emancipatory trends.'

The party's programme demanded the protection of the family by means of the struggle against alcoholism and prostitution, the affiliation of illegitimate children, the protection of the prolific family, and the establishment of family welfare centres. It demanded the return of the elementary school to the control of the Commune and the introduction of State examinations for which pupils both in State schools and in private schools could enter without distinction. It demanded 'that anyone be permitted to open a school without observing bureaucratic formalities or financial conditions . . . [and] that the State's authority over the schools be limited to a responsibility for hygienic and moral welfare similar to that which it exercises, or ought to exercise, in the sphere of public entertainment.' It advocated the formation of numerous trade unions, while demanding legal recognition of professional organizations. It also advocated mixed labour exchanges, adding: 'In the interests of the family budget it will be necessary, so long as female labour continues to be employed in those industries to which on moral, hygienic and technical grounds it is least suited, to assert the great principle of "equal pay for equal work". At the same time, we believe that in the interests of justice the employment of female labour should be subject to certain safeguards and restrictions.' It proposed the introduction of compulsory social insurance, to be realized through the freest and most widely varied organizations; administrative decentralization; fiscal reform on the basis of the progressive tax, with exemption for the lowest income-groups; reform of the Chamber through the introduction of the plurinominal constituency, broadly based and with proportional representation of minorities; votes for women; passage of a law whereby the Senate would become at least in part elective; protection of the small property, especially in the matter of taxation. 'In regions containing latifundia which are subject to normal cultivation on a large scale, these should be split up wherever such action is technically possible. This applies especially to estates situated in the vicinity of towns, which should be ceded or leased to local workers.'

The programme did not envisage any changes in ecclesiastical legislation. It declared, however, that 'it is the duty of the State . . . to ensure full respect for the Christian conscience . . . and since by virtue of their faith believers are living members of a spiritual community which transcends in space and time the narrow limits of the State, the latter will not be able truly to respect the Christian conscience unless it truly respects the Church and leaves it completely free to carry out its mission.' It deplored the fact that the State had shown itself powerless to defend the dignity of bishops and parish priests and to guarantee to them the free exercise of their ministry in the face of ignoble anti-clerical campaigns. It recalled that these principles, whose validity was universal,

> 'have a loftier meaning in Italy, which is the seat of the Roman Pontificate—the most sublime moral force in the world, the champion of justice and civilization in all their aspects, whose glories have always been so intimately bound up with the glory of Italy herself. Finally, these principles have a loftier meaning and a more profound significance if it is borne in mind that an essential precondition of a settlement of the Roman Question not entailing any violation of our country's territorial integrity is a more enlightened Christian consciousness on the part of the Italian people. And it is unnecessary to point out here how much a settlement of that question can contribute to the greatness of Italy herself.'[1]

The party recorded its first great victory at the moment of its birth, as a result of the proposal which the Nitti Ministry put forward and succeeded in carrying through for a change in the electoral law involving the abolition of the uninominal constituency in favour of proportional representation. The elections of November 16th, 1919, enabled it to send 103 representatives to the Chamber.

It had succeeded in enlisting numerous supporters among the bourgeoisie and the rural classes, although the flow of workers into its ranks remained a trickle. In the political and administrative elections it was accorded the votes not only of Catholics but of many others—opponents of the various socialist splinter-groups, which were no longer controlled by their old leaders and in that

---

[1] The non-confessional character of the party, its desire to free itself from the authority of the Church, the 'liberal poison' that was to creep into it, its failure to assume the Catholic label as its distinctive emblem, the lack of an explicit reference in its programme to the absolute freedom, sovereignty and independence of the Pope— all these deficiencies are castigated in the pamphlet by A. Gemelli and F. Olgiati (ecclesiastical founders of Italy's Catholic University, the University of the Sacred Heart in Milan), *Il programma del Partito popolare italiano. Come non è e come dovrebbe essere*, Milan, 1919.

post-war period seemed to constitute a menace; and bourgeois intellectuals who, while animated by a sincere love of the people and by a desire to see the reins of government wrested from their own class, were convinced of the virtue of pursuing their ends by legal methods. The party also attracted the votes of many electors who had grown weary of the war of invective between neutralists and interventionists which had been in progress for nearly five years and showed no signs of ending with the advent of peace. There were many Italians who voted for the Popular Party in November, 1919, because they hoped that it would bring a breath of fresh air into their country's political life. For the older men appeared exhausted; they did not seem to realize that since 1915 things had changed profoundly and the political struggle in Italy could no longer be viewed merely in terms of the distribution of seats at Montecitorio.

In the event, opinions on the Popular Party were to vary, both then and later, not only in accordance with the political orientation of those who formulated them but according to whether they were accustomed to look to the South or to the North. For if they looked at the situation in the region south of Rome it would be possible even for those who had remained hostile to its ideology to say of the party—as men would later be able to say of Christian Democracy, and even of Fascism—that it had achieved beneficial results. Where those parties have been responsible for the destruction of family hegemonies alien to all ideas of political development and based solely on ties of kinship and on the principle of *do ut des*, they have also facilitated the fusion, or at least the reconciliation, of different social classes, and the entry of women into public life.

The party seemed to have been imbued by its creator with that flair for administration, that belief in what can be achieved by means of the administrative machine, which was one of his most notable characteristics. It disappointed the few who had believed that a Christian party should daily invoke utopian ideals, a superior moral law, a moralistic vision of positive justice, and the conduct of life. It was viewed with qualified approval by those who were in favour of peaceful evolution. Like Don Sturzo, its leading men were conscious of the measureless power wielded by the modern State, of the great part played in its day-to-day life by bureaucracy, of the futility of any political affirmation or any bold legislative conception, if the machine of the State is reluctant to translate it into action. The working class furnished the technical ministers who really knew how to run a Ministry of Finance or Agriculture or Industry and were concerned first and foremost to install as many as possible of their own men in key positions. During negotiations between parties and at times of crisis Don Sturzo or whoever spoke in his name used to demand for their supporters posts not only as ministers and under-secretaries but as councillors of State and permanent heads of departments, together with seats on ministerial committees and on the boards of the principal bodies responsible for the administration of the law.

And yet, apart from its success in finally bringing about the entry of Catholics into Italian public life—the official Vatican newspaper of November 10th–11th, 1919, announced that the *non expedit* was now a dead letter—the party disappointed the hopes of its supporters, inasmuch as it failed to compel any notable changes in the civil laws or to bring about any genuine *rapprochement* between the various classes. When it was finally killed by the March on Rome its solitary claim to a place in history rested on the fact that it had provided the archetype of an Italian Catholic party.

To attempt to reconstruct *a posteriori* the causes of success or failure is always a waste of effort. It has, however, been said that the party's anxiety to secure control of the instruments of power, so that it might participate in the work of government under more favourable conditions, led it into the very same error with which it had reproached its adversaries—that of thinking too much of Montecitorio and too little of what happened in the country, and so of pursuing by every means the search for more advantageous solutions to crises and of not addressing itself sufficiently to the people. The result was that it allowed the character of its alliances to be influenced by its plans to secure a larger share of political power and quite neglected to form a single united front in order to resist the advance of Fascism. It is, nevertheless, a fact that its leaders deluded themselves with the belief that time did not matter and that they could realize their programme at leisure—a misconception shared by all the outstanding politicians of the time, who completely failed to understand the nature of Fascism, regarding it as a transient phenomenon which could safely be ignored. According to those who believed in the orderly conduct

of affairs such an attitude played into the hands of the revolutionaries. But socialism's greatest figure, Filippo Turati, was no
whit more perspicacious, and the advice which he gave to his
followers was equally unsound.

However, the extremely limited value of all these post-mortems
is now universally recognized. And the same must be said of the
accusation levelled against the Popular Party of helping to bring
about the fall of the Giolitti Ministry—at the instigation, it was
said, of the Holy See, which opposed the registration of securities
in order to protect the patrimony of the religious congregations—
thereby removing from power those best equipped to wield it; and
also of hindering the formation in February, 1922, of an Orlando
Cabinet based on a broad coalition and contriving that the reins
of government should pass into the hands of Luigi Facta, an
extremely mediocre politician, incapable of opposing the dynamic
initiatives of the Fascists.

Apart from the activities of the Popular Party, which, as we
have seen, ignored the question of ecclesiastical policy almost
completely, a would-be historian of Italian religious life in the
years immediately following the war would find scant material to
work on. For their part, successive governments confined themselves entirely to the work of day-to-day administration. There
was, of course, no lack of men of extreme piety, both among the
clergy and the laity—men such as Father Genocchi, Ludovico
Necchi, and Don Giovanni Rossi, who created in the Paulines a
new type of religious Order destined to make its influence felt in
the world at large, a type that seemed likely to play a great part
in the future history of the Church. But none of these was capable
of impressing his personality on the hearts and minds of his contemporaries, of attracting into the fold, on a vaster scale than was
possible through the medium of individual conversions, people
who had hitherto remained outside it. In the Italian episcopate,
too, front-rank figures of the kind that had emerged during the
pontificate of Leo XIII were becoming fewer. In point of fact,
the cardinal most revered in the lay world was Pietro Maffi,
Archbishop of Pisa and a mathematical scholar.

Italian literature had always lacked, and continued to lack,
authors who aimed at a vast public and who by their mastery of
the writer's art might have brought religious problems back into

the forefront of men's minds. Religion was usually absent, *tamquam non esset*, from the Italian novel and drama. The Catholic novelist *par excellence*, Fogazzaro, was dead—he who in his novels had always expressed the yearnings and the exigencies of the religious life and had consistently represented the triumph of faith over the revolts of the flesh and of undisciplined reason.

The controversy continued to rage between orthodox Catholics and philo-modernists, those modernists who were not rebels but who desired to preserve the essence of the movement. In the pages of *Civiltà Cattolica* Father Rosa persisted in attacking every opinion expressed by Ernesto Buonaiuti, the movement's principal dialectician. He was one of Italy's most brilliant minds but adverse circumstances were destined finally to crush him, with the result that he failed to leave a mark commensurate with the power of his intellect and with his rich store of all those gifts which go to the making of leaders. If he had ascended the Papal throne on the death of Leo XIII in 1903, he might even have become the Newman of Italy. Catholic controversialists condemned every periodical, every intellectual coterie which sought to revive modernist traditions. But these polemics hinged on questions that were of no interest to the general public, to whom problems of ecclesiastical history, problems relating to the origins of the Church, meant less than nothing. The debates between Buonaiuti and the disciples of Gentile on the Catholic position with regard to the idealist philosophy—Buonaiuti remained to the last an uncompromising anti-idealist—had wider, but none the less distinctly limited, repercussions.

If it is true to say that Italian intellectual life has always been weak from the religious standpoint—in the sense that even when the religious historian can point with satisfaction to periods notable for the great number of ecclesiastics and laymen who have excelled in virtue, for the abundance of charitable organizations that have arisen and borne fruit, and for the extreme devotion of countless individuals, he is always obliged to recognize that his luxuriant garden is an enclosed garden and that the mass of the people pass it by without gathering its fruits, without inhaling its perfumes, almost without noticing it—then it may be asserted with equal veracity that these years immediately following the First World War constitute a period of spiritual poverty that is quite exceptional.

Bibliographical Note.

On the bearing and record of the Catholics during the First World War see E. Vercesi, *Il Vaticano, l'Italia e la guerra* (Milan, 1925), and F. Meda, *I cattolici italiani nella guerra* (Milan, 1929).

The story of the attempt at reconciliation made during the Peace Conference in Paris is told by V. E. Orlando in his book *Miei rapporti di governo con la Santa Sede*, 2nd ed., Milan and Rome, 1944.

CHAPTER VI

THE FASCIST ERA

FASCISM grew daily in strength, and became daily more and more a force to be reckoned with. Orthodox thinkers continued to assert that it gave no cause for alarm, that it would destroy itself, that it could accomplish nothing because it 'had no programme'. Much credit was given to those astute Ministers of the Interior who exploited it to restrain the arrogance of the Reds, thus sparing themselves the necessity of enforcing martial law, of opposing the police, of adopting violent measures in defence of law and order—policies which no Italian government has ever found profitable—and who would repudiate it as soon as the Reds had been brought to heel. Those whose opinions were based on intuition rather than on cold reasoning felt that the tide was running in favour of Fascism and were conscious of the lack of any means of stemming it. Such arguments represent the habitual excuse of men who are resolved to follow a given path. These orthodox thinkers revealed a deep-rooted reluctance to accept the challenge, to oppose Fascism, a reluctance prompted by a number of considerations and irrational impulses which in all probability none of them could have analysed. It might perhaps have been summed up in the statement that even for those among them who had been neutralists (and so did not recognize in the Fascists their comrades in the interventionist struggle of 1915 and the opponents of those who would have renounced the fruits of victory), even for those who detested the Fascists' excesses, their bombast, their cult of violence, and most of all their leader, in whom they saw only the demagogue from the Romagna, the rabble-rouser who in 1913 had shown his quality by instigating the most violent civil disorders since those of 1898—Fascism still remained the less of two evils.

In the north of Italy the Reds had given too much offence with their daily strikes, their acts of violence, their vulgar, anti-bourgeois class warfare, as a result of which even the down-at-heel, undernourished little clerk was scowled at in the trams and in the streets because he was a 'pen-pusher' and so not a 'worker'. They had caused the image of the dictatorship of the proletariat to appear for too long in its gloomiest colours. They had cut themselves off too completely from the control of the wise leaders who had made of the Italian Socialist Party a great, powerful, harmonious organism. Their demands appeared too fragmentary, and lacking cohesion, with the result that even the few bourgeois intellectuals who would genuinely have been prepared to support a new order promising greater social justice turned away in disgust when they perceived only disorder and destruction accompanied by no constructive effort. So it was that, in the eyes of every orthodox thinker, every small landowner, every poverty-stricken member of the bourgeoisie whose only wealth consisted in the knowledge that the class to which he belonged was not the lowest of all, no other political ideology could conceivably have been more evil than communistic socialism.

It must, moreover, be remembered that Fascism, setting itself up as an anti-socialist force, declaring itself to be the antithesis of Bolshevism, proclaiming the slogan 'Rome or Moscow' to which it was to owe so much of its success and which it was to bequeath to the party that ultimately succeeded it in power, was able to enter the lists on the crest of a universal wave of political passion. Thus it assured itself of the sympathy, the goodwill or at least the connivance of all, both in Italy and abroad, who had been shocked and terrified by the Bolshevist revolution and its atrocities, which they ascribed to its ideological creed rather than to the cultural conditions, the character, and the history of the country in which it took place.

Although very few people realized it at the time, from 1917 onwards Europe was in a frame of mind reminiscent of, but destined to become even more violent than, that of 1793–1830. Even monarchs and Heads of Governments had shed the attitude of reserve towards the internal politics of other countries which had been *de rigueur* until a few years before. Nicholas I no longer seemed so remote—he who, during a visit to Austria round about 1850, refused to receive the ministers of Franz Josef, whom he suspected of continuing to harbour liberal sympathies, or, if he received them, proceeded to lecture them on the principles of right conduct. When, in May, 1923, George V of England came to

Rome, not only did he personally decorate Mussolini with the Order of the Bath on the very evening of his arrival, but in the course of the reception at the Capitol he recalled the crisis recently surmounted by the Italian people 'under the wise guidance of a strong ruler'. Switzerland strove to reconcile her position as the seat of the League of Nations with the clear preference displayed by her rulers for authoritarian régimes, of which Fascism was the first, and with their aversion to every form of socialism that did not accept the anti-Bolshevist proviso.

Until about 1931, until, that is, the Fascists revealed their imperialistic yearnings, and also until they squandered some of their moral capital on the foolish campaign against Catholic Action, Italians of the middle or upper classes who travelled abroad encountered wherever they went conservatives of their own social standing who envied Italy the strong, energetic man who had brought her back on to the right road. If they replied in deprecatory fashion, denying that the possession of such a man was a fortunate thing for their country, they would be regarded with some suspicion, as traitors to their class, as disguised Communists. An anti-Fascist Catholic, unless he took refuge, while he still could, in the temporalist argument and revealed himself as a survivor from the age of Pius IX, would be looked upon as a kind of miniature Lamennais.

Throughout the twenty-one years of the Fascist era opponents of the régime were, in fact, to be found among the bourgeoisie. But, particularly at the outset, when the threat of a Red dictatorship was still a living threat, a threat but lately dispelled, there were very few who regarded Fascism as a greater evil than Communism.

Fascism was instinctively anti-clerical. The few intellectuals included in its ranks came to it from trade-unionism, or else, via literary channels, from Futurism, and had derived their philosophy, even if indirectly, from Nietzsche and Sorel—sources which made them implacably hostile to the Church. The broad masses of the people lacked any ideological tradition or impulse; but they had a love of violence, they abhorred any form of constriction, they were filled with nostalgia for a war that had ended too soon—a war that had brought to some economic well-being or at any rate immunity from the cares of daily life, to others freedom from the daily round of humble and unwelcome toil; that had revealed to many their true selves, conjuring up in place of the disagreeable picture of the insignificant little clerk or the reluctant workman the shining image, object of his own and others' admiration, of the man who knows no fear, of the soldier who, armed only with a dagger and a hand-grenade, hurls himself upon the enemy machine-gun nest. None of these roads led to a love of the Church. Indeed, between 1919 and 1921 the Church could discern within the ranks of Fascism only indifferents—for whom everything connected with religion was 'the concern of priests' and a source of ennui—and enemies.

Had not the movement's greatest figure himself fought the election of 1919 on the same ticket as Guido Podrecca, editor of *L'Asino*, and F. T. Marinetti, lending his support to a programme that envisaged even the confiscation of the episcopal revenues? And where the Catholics had been able to organize their White leagues and their co-operatives, was not the attitude of the Fascists seemingly identical with that of the Reds? Certainly it was characterized by the same violence, the same destructiveness. In the Fascist Press, in Fascist cartoons, Don Sturzo was treated no better than the exponents of socialism or of neutralism. Even Catholic processions were not infrequently the object of Fascist violence.

But the high priest of Fascism was a man with a rare insight into human nature. Both then and later it was the habit of anti-Fascists to deny Mussolini the possession of any positive quality. By a quirk of fortune—as extraordinary as if a whole canto of the *Divine Comedy* had fallen into place after a box of type had been upset on the floor—a man utterly without distinction, whose like one might have encountered a hundred times in any city street, had suddenly become the despotic ruler of Italy and was later to fill a role of fundamental importance in the history of Europe. Or —another interpretation current in anti-Fascist circles—the rise of Fascism was due not to the exceptional qualities of Mussolini but to the incredible stupidity of his adversaries. The Italian people, it was claimed, had suddenly degenerated into a race of morons, with the result that a man of the utmost insignificance had been able to dominate them.

It is a fact that all Mussolini's shortcomings, which were probably pathological in origin—an inveterate cynicism, a lack of affection for and faith in his fellow-men so profound and complete

N

that it was sickening to contemplate—were counterbalanced by an intuitive understanding of the mob verging on the miraculous. He always knew exactly what demands he could make upon them and how far he could press those demands. He possessed the art of hypnotizing them, of leading them where he willed: that rare art, which the Tempter reveals to few, of addressing himself to their least noble instincts and leaving them with a feeling of self-satisfaction, of urging them into the paths of Satan and leaving them convinced that they are savouring the delights of Paradise. Viewed from a distance, Mussolini's technique may appear monotonous: it somewhat resembled that of the man who brandishes a stick and shouts and threatens until he is given what he asks for. But his peculiar talent consisted in his ability to estimate in advance the resistance of those whom he would threaten, to weigh their attachment to what was demanded of them against their will to fight. He fell only when he was drawn into a game greater than himself and of which he was no longer the arbiter.

Up to the time of the Spanish Civil War, however, the technique had always succeeded both in domestic and in foreign policy. An old martial dynasty had submitted to twenty years of constant humiliation. At the time of the Abyssinian adventure Britain had sustained a blow to her *amour-propre* the like of which she had not experienced for several centuries. So long as he continued to control his country's policy this man never attacked unless he was certain either that his adversary was physically incapable of offering serious resistance or that he would yield.

That he should abandon the anti-clericalism with which he had been imbued from birth, and to which he had clung throughout the first thirty-six years of his life, was the greatest tribute he could pay to the Catholic Church, inasmuch as it signified his appreciation of the fact that the Church would not surrender without a fight, that she would strenuously defend all those values, institutions and principles by which she set most store, that she was not, in short, an adversary he could hope to crush.

Thanks to his intuition, Mussolini had realized as early as 1920 that among the things which he would be able to humiliate, to overthrow and grind into dust, it was not possible to include the Church. Perhaps it was then that, through his contemplation of the classical Roman models, of Machiavelli—a somewhat superficial contemplation, it must be said, even though, before the period of his omnipotence, it had exerted a real influence on his life—he first became attracted to the idea of a Church that would be gradually, almost imperceptibly transformed into an *instrumentum regni*.

Certainly, in the whole of his life he never gave a sign that he had finally become reconciled to the acceptance of Christian values. On the contrary, one always detected in his demeanour a resistance, an ill-concealed rancour, almost a sense of shame on the rare occasions when he was obliged to pay lip-service to Catholicism. In this reaction, in this ill-concealed rancour, lies the explanation of his harsh strictures on the Holy See in speeches delivered at the time of the ratification of the Lateran Treaty. So, too, on the occasion of the official visit which he was forced to pay to the Pope after the reconciliation, he was at pains to make it known that he had been exonerated from the hand-kissing ceremony; and when, following the visit, protocol required him to go down to St. Peter's and pray at the tomb of the Prince of the Apostles, he took his place at the faldstool only after he had had the lurking photographers evicted: photographs of Mussolini kneeling in prayer were unthinkable. He liked to pose as the defender of Christendom against the forces of Bolshevism, just as he had liked to pose as the defender of Islam. But the image of the devout son, the penitent, the son at prayer was not an image of himself that he could accept. Moreover, his intuition told him that it was not an image of himself that he could present to his faithful followers, of whom the most fervent and the most reliable were warlike, unregenerate barbarians.

None of the men who were really close to him—and these never included the Nationalists, his hated allies—revealed any genuine disposition to accept religious values or at any moment of their lives gave the impression of being imbued with the spirit of Christianity. A fundamental anti-clericalism was always apparent in the Fascist hierarchy, whose members at all times regarded the Church with the deepest suspicion. The Party had to be the true Church, it had to be all-embracing, every need had to find its satisfaction in the temple of Fascism. A little parish theatre, a diocesan cultural circle, an association of Catholic students— these things were manifestations of heresy; they represented attempts to seduce the faithful from the true Church.

And yet, from the moment of his speech in the Chamber on June 21st, 1921, until the end, Mussolini remained firm enough in his resolve not to join issue with the Church, never to unleash an offensive against it, to keep it, if possible, on his side.

The Catholic attitude towards Fascism was far more complicated. In the context of their mutual relations it is much easier to speak of the Fascists (excluding the Nationalists and those who came late to the feast) as a united body than it is of the Catholics.

Here it is at once necessary to distinguish the small minority of survivors from the 'Democratic League' who had come to the Popular Party with a mature political consciousness orientated towards an openly anti-conservative economic programme very similar to that of reformist socialism, and who were never attracted to Fascism. With these must be grouped some of those organizers of White leagues who had seen their handiwork destroyed by Fascist violence as well as a certain number of men of rigid moral principles, upholders of the maxim: 'Do your duty, happen what may', Catholics in whom no consideration of expediency or convenience could outweigh a natural aversion to a movement constituted by refugees from trade-unionism and revolutionary socialism who had always hated the Church and continued to proclaim eminently anti-Christian principles; beneath whose present moderation it was impossible to discern the faintest glimmer of spiritual enlightenment. But these, I repeat, were a minority.

At the opposite extreme were those who for decades past had prophesied a rush of Catholics to join a great new conservative party, those who had naturally experienced, and detested, the violence of the Reds and who saw in the doctrines of socialism the subversion of that rule of order, of that social hierarchy, which in their eyes represented the very essence of Catholicism. Fascism attracted them not only because of its success in destroying the Red organizations and overthrowing the forces of socialism, not only because it proclaimed its championship of patriotic values and its respect for property and for the traditional social order—already men of title were beginning to join its ranks, and already the consideration there accorded to an illustrious name was becoming more apparent—it attracted them also because at the outset it professed itself in favour of limiting the State's functions to administration and the maintenance of law and order, and at the same time promised to restore complete freedom to industry and commerce. (After the March on Rome this policy was at once abandoned; and in the years that followed, the Fascist Government's whole economic policy was openly opposed to the principles of free trade.)

Between the two extremes there existed in the years 1920–22 a vast body of Catholics, substantially lacking any political orientation, who had no illusions as to the anti-Catholic and anti-religious character of the movement. Up to the last moment these Catholics would have welcomed an alliance of constitutional parties—with the Popular Party occupying the place of honour—strong enough to keep both Fascists and socialists under control, failing which they would even have approved of the re-establishment of order by martial law imposed by a military Government. In practice, however, they were to do nothing, partly because of a lack of fighting spirit and of any machinery with which to organize resistance. If forced to make a choice, many of them, though not all, would even have opted for a new, unknown force in which they could place their hopes rather than for a return of socialism or social-communism. The forces of social-communism had been strengthened—alas, too late—by an accession of intellectuals who would willingly have abandoned all the vociferous and vulgar anti-clericalism that was in the tradition of the movement. The journal *L'ordine nuovo* had recognized that priests and monks had a function to fulfil, and had conceded their right to practice their vocation. Of the new leaders, none would have pledged himself to uphold the traditions—in this respect, the Jacobin traditions—of the old. Young men such as Togliatti or Gramsci felt nothing but disgust for Podrecca's *L'Asino*. But here too, time no longer permitted of any kind of evolution, and the image of socialism imprinted on the minds of its enemies remained essentially the same as it had been for twenty years past.

One may ask oneself whether the Italian clergy did not include men who perceived the radical inconsistency between Fascist doctrine and practice—which at this stage were to all intents and purposes identical—and the principles of Christianity: one of those absolute inconsistencies which, when the Church defines them, exclude all possibility of compromise. The answer to the question must be: No.

True, Fascism exalted violence, war, and those doctrines of irrationality and opportunism, of undisciplined self-expression and the rhetorical gesture, which are diametrically opposed to the doctrine of Christianity—that Christianity which in its rationalistic fervour has fitted the whole world of the divine into a rational framework—indeed, into a completely logical system— and which exalts self-denial, patience, meekness, humility, the individual who conquers and transforms himself, the man who, when his enemy smites him, turns the other cheek. Fascism indeed exalted the Fatherland above all things; it rejected the idea of justice when one of the parties to a dispute was the Fatherland, because the Fatherland was always right. There was no longer any question of good or evil when its interests were at stake, and it was the duty of the citizen at all times to maintain his country's cause. Christianity on the other hand stands for the universal law whereby all men are brothers and distinctions of race and nationality cannot prevail against the principle of universal brotherhood and the duties that derive therefrom. The injunction to love the Creator more than the creature carries the implication that no bond of kinship, no allegiance to any man-made organizations, can warrant neglect of the principles of justice or support of an evil action. All this was indisputable.

It was also clear, to those who had eyes to see, that unlike liberalism, which attracted very few party-members, exerting its influence for the most part indirectly, by propaganda rather than by discipline, and which made only very limited demands even on those few—Fascism, like Bolshevism was itself a Church, claiming the whole man, in all his waking moments and in all his activities. Even in art and literature it prescribed what he must condemn and what he must admire. It had its uniforms, its epistolary style, its formulas, its gestures of salutation, its rites that accompanied the party-member to the grave: the summons to the burial service, the Roman salute with which the Blackshirt greeted even funerals, even religious processions. (For many years the anti-Fascist was easily recognizable by the way he saluted a hearse and by his behaviour when passing a cemetery, by his recourse to the traditional forms of greeting and his refusal to adopt the Fascist salute.) As the parish church and its presbytery are a focal point of the activities of the good Catholic, so was the local party headquarters a place of meeting, recreation, and medita-

tion: a place where the new faithful forgathered in the evenings
and on feast-days, where all initiatives, whatever their object,
had to originate, and where—after 1935—a bride would often
go immediately after her wedding to exchange the gold ring
which the priest had just blessed for a ring made of iron. The
party was a Church that persuaded its zealots to renounce all
other interests: a Church that did not concern itself with the life
to come, because in the Fascist *Weltanschauung*, as in the Communist, every aspiration has to be fulfilled in this world and there
is no place for a future life in which earthly injustices may be set
to rights.

That this fundamental conflict of ideals existed was undeniably
true; but it was also true, especially in Italy, that the Church and
Fascism had some common enemies. The Italian clergy had been
reduced to a state of poverty which often no attempt was made
to conceal—something that to its present members, who had
never known better times and were nearly all of humble origin,
did not in fact signify a great deal. Its representatives had been
dismissed from positions of authority, and had been subjected to
an endless succession of pin-pricks and petty humiliations. The
liberals had not behaved generously and, having won their battle,
had never been at pains, while not renouncing any of their
principles, to mollify and conciliate the enemy, or respect his
amour-propre. They had failed to repudiate in time that part of
their legislation which all had felt to be justified only by the
exigencies of warfare. They had not even had the wisdom to
declare that in the matter of ecclesiastical legislation all necessary
precautions had now been taken and that the question was no
longer one of devising fresh laws hostile to the Church but rather,
if anything, of repealing some of those already in force. Latterly,
indeed, they had even taken to uttering veiled threats. But what
had irritated the clergy and their most faithful lay supporters even
more than this legislative activity and the threats of new measures
had been the ceaseless petty humiliations of civic life, the constant
pin-pricks in connection with the nomination of the administrative
councils of charitable institutions and the allocation of premises
for religious instruction. A movement which claimed to represent
a reaction not merely against socialism, not merely against
liberalism, but, going even further back, against Jacobinism and
Girondism, against encyclopaedism and illuminism, against the

values and affirmations of the French Revolution, could hardly appear to Catholics to be irreconcilable with their faith.

Nor did the extreme nationalism of the Fascists give any cause for alarm. The dividing line between nationalism and fanatical patriotism is almost imperceptible. It is not necessary to cast one's mind back to the beginnings of the Christian era or to invoke Tertullian; one need only probe the conscience of any enlightened Christian to realize how painful it is to all who remember that Christianity is a universal religion, a religion of peace, and that only just wars have received the sanction of Catholicism, to be reminded of the spectacle that confronted them at the outset of both world conflicts: the spectacle of the bishops of all countries not merely blessing the departing soldiers and their colours but praying for their victory—and then, when the struggle was at its height, extolling without a qualm not only the soldier who had perished in a righteous cause but even men who had volunteered for the most sanguinary missions, such as the bombing of cities or the sinking of merchant ships.

But a study of human events down the ages confirms the fact that military values, with which patriotic values are, by a freak of history and certainly for no logical reason, closely interlinked, have very often marched hand in hand with religious values. Thus, men have viewed the age of chivalry as a golden age of Catholicism, they have regarded as exponents of the purest Catholic idealism those terrible protagonists of classical Spanish literature who do not turn the other cheek to a blow but are obliged to kill in order to wipe out the shame of a betrayal or of an insulting word, who do not look upon every man as a brother but consider that the nobleman, the plebeian, the *marrano*, the man who has a drop of Jewish or Saracen blood in his veins, represent so many different species of humanity. Entire national traditions, from the *Gesta Dei per Francos* to the *Voyage du Centurion* of Ernest Psichari, have sanctified this identification of the good Christian with the man of violence. The anti-chivalrous attitude of the primitive Christian, who did not scruple to appear a coward and to violate all the rules of human society so long as he kept the commandment of God, is remembered to-day almost with embarrassment. In Wiseman's *Fabiola* we still meet the figure of the Christian youth, soon to become a martyr, who does not react when a schoolfellow slaps his face and prefers to be stigmatized by his companions as a coward rather than break his vow of humility; but we shall not find a similar scene in any modern Catholic novel.

A man such as Déroulède, who spent his whole life trying to precipitate France's war of revenge, has always been regarded by French Catholics as one of themselves, even if they have considered him a trifle eccentric because of his penchant for duelling. It is a sad thought; but there is consolation in the words of Benedict XV, who, faced with a war in which the issues at stake were not universal principles or forms of civilization but questions of frontiers, braved unpopularity by daring to speak of 'useless slaughter'.

In all fairness, however, we must bear in mind that all those who in our time have risen in protest against militarism, against nationalism, against the acceptance of war as an instrument of policy, have been enemies of the Church. If, towards the end of the nineteenth century, the Catholic fixed his gaze on the current manifestations of anti-militarism—on the socialists, on those organizations for peace whose every pronouncement betrayed the influence of the masonic lodge, or on that most illustrious writer, Tolstoi—he found nothing to give him the smallest ground for complacency.

All these things represent, so to say, the human dross left in the Church by two thousand years of history, yet they must be borne in mind—painful though it may be for a Catholic to recall them—if the attitude of enlightened Catholics and of the majority of the clergy to Fascism is to be understood.

So far as can be ascertained, the March on Rome received no support whatever, either material or moral, from any section of the Catholic clergy. The latter's conduct in that hour of decision contrasted violently with the treachery of the police and of the Army, which openly ranged itself against the lawful Government, and with the equivocal, vacillating attitude of the civil service. The ecclesiastical hierarchy remained aloof and apprehensive. Apart from a few isolated incidents the March was not characterized by any acts of violence directed at ecclesiastical personages and sacred objects, and the first Fascist Government included in its ranks a number of deputies of long-standing Catholic traditions who were members of the Popular Party.

With the assumption by the Fascists of the reins of legal

government a number of illusions were shattered. The momentous event served to reveal the naïveté and fallacious reasoning of those conservatives who had supposed that Fascism represented a transient phenomenon, or better still a happy expedient for overcoming the stubbornness of the socialists, as well as the emptiness of the theory that once his rule was established Mussolini intended to return to constitutional normality, to a 1914-type régime, perhaps even to a régime of that strictly constitutional kind for which Sonnino had pleaded twenty-six years before in his article *Torniamo allo Statuto!*

The Duce's famous inaugural speech at Montecitorio, containing the memorable sentence: 'I could have transformed this drab, silent hall into a bivouac', was designed first and foremost to humiliate the Monarchy, which, declared the speaker, was no more arbiter of the situation to-day than it had been yesterday, and would have been incapable of preserving the integrity of the country's institutions even if it had wished. It embodied the statement destined to be repeated on countless subsequent occasions (for example, on the eve of the ratification of an electoral law, when the nation was reminded that whereas revolutions have many times overthrown constitutions, the ballot-box has never yet revealed the power to suppress revolutions), that a semblance, a façade of constitutional forms might be kept by the Italian people so long as they clearly appreciated that their political energies must henceforth be directed into a single channel. In the division which followed that speech (November 17th, 1922) the votes cast for the Government by the popular group totalled 306, compared with the 116 hostile votes registered by the extreme Left.

Thus the Popular Party earned the right to participate in the Fascist Government.

The suppression by the Fascists of Catholic societies and of co-operatives and popular leagues became a daily occurrence. The dissolution of the White trade unions, the Catholic labour organizations and the working men's co-operatives (but not of the small banks and the friendly societies, not of the wine-shops and the cheese-factories: it was only the labour organizations that were disbanded in this initial phase) proceeded inexorably. The Communal elections were contested with great bitterness, always amid scenes of violence. Communal councils in which non-

Fascists constituted a majority were frequently compelled to resign. In June, 1923, the Communal council of Turin, a council born of a coalition of 'national' forces (and also, it seems, of a last-minute violation of the ballot-boxes which was said to have snatched the reins of local government from the grasp of the Reds), was forced by the local Fascist organization to resign, on the pretext that as the price of its support Don Sturzo's party had demanded an unduly large number of seats. The Prefect said that Mussolini approved of the local organization's action. A little earlier, the Government had dismissed the popular mayor of Schio for making a speech on the anniversary of the foundation of the City in which he extolled Christian Rome at the expense of pagan Rome, declaring that the latter's ephemeral greatness and splendour had had their origins in fratricide, had reached their peak amid oppression, and had dissolved in a welter of persecution, matricide and incest. But from the moment of their entry into the Government the moral position of the Popular deputies was difficult, almost intolerable.

In February, 1923, the *Lavoro d'Italia*, principal organ of the Fascist corporations, asserted that it was impossible for the traditional subversive trade union organism to continue to exist side by side with that of the Fascists except in an atmosphere of hostility and conflict. It went on to advocate the suppression of the White leagues ('as if these had not fought Bolshevism before Fascism was ever heard of', commented *Civiltà Cattolica*). In March of the same year the secretary of the Fascist Party declared that he regarded the Popular Party as an equivocal organization harmful to the nation's life, and that he could not see the necessity for a popular trade union movement.

On April 12th the fourth congress of the Popular Party was held at Turin. The party had a Right Wing which advocated complete and whole-hearted collaboration with the Fascist Government and repudiated the Left Wing, which it accused of seeking 'an alliance with demagogic parties incompatible with the need for national reconstruction based on a reconciliation of the various classes and on respect for the country's unitarian institutions'. In fact, this Left Wing, of which the animating spirit was Guido Miglioli, an organizer of White leagues in the country districts of Lombardy, was opposed to any further collaboration with a Government hostile to parliamentary forms and to the principles of Christian democracy. The party had a Right Centre, and it also had a Left Centre, under Don Sturzo, which affirmed the necessity of preserving party unity and of making collaboration with the Government conditional upon the maintenance of its individuality and of its role as a critical and restraining element.

Don Sturzo, the party's political secretary, was substantially victorious in the battle for its future. He justified the continued existence of the party, which, he said, was the only political group that still represented the Italian people's Catholic conscience. He claimed for it that it had always combated socialism, and denied that it was hostile to Fascism, even though it reserved to itself the right to criticize and to exert a restraining influence. It offered collaboration, not a series of blank cheques. The party approved the policies propounded by Don Sturzo and by the Trentine deputy Alcide De Gasperi, who for his part advocated the continued participation of Popular deputies in the Government, committed the parliamentary group to a whole-hearted defence of the principle of proportional representation, and insisted that the party maintain its autonomy and its individuality.

But while the representatives of the party were on their way to the Turin congress an old Catholic, the Honourable Cornaggia Medici, launched an appeal-cum-programme for a 'National Union' of those Catholics who did not intend to adhere to the Popular Party. The appeal called for 'a closing of the ranks by all those Italians, old and young, who have always cherished and who cherish still the twofold ideal of an august and powerful Fatherland and a free and universally respected religion'. It referred to the Utopia of the International, of 'demagogy in different colours', of the 'equivocal religion of those who claim to enjoy a monopoly of the faith'. 'To the alien Utopia of the International' it opposed 'a healthy national consciousness'. It demanded the creation of an army prepared 'to be the rallying-point of a nation armed for its defence'. It called for a decentralized State affording full scope for private enterprise. 'We ask that Italy first among the Catholic countries should uphold in the councils of the nations the interests of the Church and of the faithful.' The official Volta Agency gave great prominence to the appeal, declaring that it had not lacked the sanction of exalted ecclesiastical circles; but the *Osservatore Romano* denied that the Holy See had played any part in the constitution of the 'Union'.

Polemics ensued between popular newspapers and anti-popular
Catholic newspapers. But they amounted to little. All were by
now conformists, all tended to overstress the patriotic and anti-
socialist note. The Marchese Cornaggia had no fear of being
reminded by anyone that neither Jesus of Nazareth nor Paul of
Tarsus ever evinced 'a healthy national consciousness' or an
enthusiasm for armies.

Then came another bombshell from the Palazzo Chigi.

The Turin congress had not yet ended when it was officially
announced that Mussolini had sent for those members of the
Government who belonged to the Popular Party. The Duce had
discerned in the speeches and debates at the congress a criticism
of his Administration; accordingly, he thanked the ministers and
under-secretaries in question for their services and restored to
them their freedom of action.

The party did not know how to take the blow. It did not understand that the bombshell from the Palazzo Chigi was connected
with Cornaggia's appeal and with the Right Wing's avowed
intention of repudiating the Left. It wanted to persist in its
alliance with the Government. Don Sturzo declared that he could
not understand Mussolini's intransigent attitude, because the
Turin vote had reflected 'a clear, genuine and unmistakable
desire for honest co-operation with the Fascist Government'. (He
had not yet grasped the dynamics of totalitarianism.) The *Osservatore Romano* expressed the hope that a crisis would not follow.
Other deputies from Don Sturzo's party gave assurances of their
continuing loyalty. The party's parliamentary group approved by
a large majority a resolution reaffirming its confidence in the
Administration. 'The Popular deputies' co-operation with the
Government', ran the statement, 'will be inspired, as in the past,
by an absolute loyalty to the Head of the Government and by a
fidelity to the party in keeping with the latter's aims and with
their own firm consciousness of their duty as Catholics and as
Italians.' One of the deposed ministers, Cavazzoni, communicated
the resolution to Mussolini. In his reply the Duce asserted that
the vote did not satisfy him. The Grand Council, he wrote,
'declares that the Fascist policy of re-establishing religious and
moral values in no way depends on the approval or disapproval
of those parties which set themselves up as sole guardians of the
nation's Catholic conscience.' Mussolini's paper, the *Popolo*

d'Italia, stated categorically that a prerequisite of any agreement was the expulsion of 'Left Wing elements' from the party and the removal from his post of Don Sturzo.

The withdrawal of the Popular Ministers from the Government was an inglorious episode. In consenting to take office they had not been actuated by personal vanity nor by a love of power—slight though that power turned out to be. They had hoped to protect Catholic interests, deluding themselves that their participation in the Government would spare the various Catholic organizations from persecution. Yet the fact remained that they had tried to cling to office and had been dismissed for their pains. Three Right Wing deputies had not waited for the crisis to come to a head before leaving the party.

Henceforth the party no longer enjoyed the support of influential members of the ecclesiastical hierarchy. On the morrow of the resignations *Civiltà Cattolica* wrote:

'We, who are in no way tied to the Italian Popular Party—to which, indeed, we might have seemed opposed whenever we have deemed it our duty to criticize or to express reservations about its conduct—do not blind ourselves to the danger that a reconciliation of conflicting attitudes may come too late for the nation's life to be rebuilt on a firm foundation. Meanwhile, the most impetuous and thoughtless adherents of Fascism—on the fringe of the party at least, if not at its centre—will easily be able to find in the present state of affairs an excuse for reverting to the abominable technique of violence. They will identify with the Popular Party, if only in the excitement of the moment, Catholic circles and associations which neither have, nor should have, any common bond with groups or parties of whatever political orientation, even though these may consist predominantly of Catholic men who profess to be inspired by Christian principles.'

Catholic newspapers exhorted Don Sturzo not to do anything that would embarrass the ecclesiastical authorities.

The expulsion of the 'Left Wing elements' had its sequel.

On June 30th there appeared in the streets of Rome a Catholic-sponsored manifesto which stated that 'in this hour of the nation's political evolution and spiritual crisis' Catholics intended to proclaim their 'complete accord' with the Fascist Government: an accord 'determined by the fact that Fascism, through the Government, which is the movement's sole authoritative medium of expression, openly recognizes and honours those religious and social values which constitute the basis of any sound political system, seeking to establish within the State, to the detriment of outmoded democratic and sectarian ideologies, a régime based on discipline and a hierarchical social order such as may accord with the religious and sociological doctrines proclaimed from time immemorial by the Church.' The Vatican newspaper *Osservatore Romano* made it clear that this initiative had not the support of Catholic Action.

Don Sturzo resigned from the post of political secretary to the party.

Meanwhile, the Chamber was debating the electoral law. The Popular Party had decided to support a motion of confidence in the Government, but to oppose the second reading of a Government bill which would have conferred such overwhelming advantages on the dominant party as to reduce its opponents' seats to a minimum. Mussolini, however, delivered a powerful speech which achieved a notable success. While even outstanding liberal parliamentarians resolved, in token of their relief at the relaxation of tension, to abstain rather than vote against the motion, the party proceeded to reconsider its policy. As a result, its members reaffirmed their confidence in the Government and, by a majority of 41 votes to 39, resolved to abstain instead of voting against the second reading of the bill. In conformity with this decision De Gasperi requested that the motion calling for a second reading should be made the subject of two separate votes, so that deputies might be able to express their confidence in the Government without necessarily approving the second reading. A few hours later, however, nine Popular deputies repudiated the party's decision and, instead of abstaining, voted in favour of the second reading. They were expelled from the party in consequence.

In the last days of July five senators left the party. Two were nonentities, but the other three—Grosoli, Crispolti and Santucci —were men of considerable eminence.

If there was anyone who had failed hitherto to divine the secret thoughts of the Holy See, all knew now that, notwithstanding every official declaration of neutrality, the Vatican regarded the

Popular Party as an obstacle to the maintenance of Catholic interests.

It must be understood that all, 'Rightists' and 'Leftists' alike, were true Catholics; all were obedient to the Holy See, Rodinò and De Gasperi no less than Grosoli and Crispolti. If the Pope had sent a trusted emissary to De Gasperi or Don Sturzo ordering them to dissolve the party and not to reveal the Pontiff's responsibility for the initiative, carrying out the order with an air of spontaneity, De Gasperi and Don Sturzo would have obeyed without hesitation. But the Pope was not in the habit of issuing such orders. Moreover, in every hierarchy, in every human organization there are degrees of obedience, degrees of loyalty. There are those who obey and who make it plain that their convictions remain unaltered; there are those who obey and who allow nothing of what they think or feel to appear on the surface; there are those who obey with overflowing hearts, rejoicing in their sacrifice; there are those who never put themselves in the position of really having to obey, because they smell out, divine, anticipate the wishes of their superiors and carry them out in advance. Now, those who were acquainted with the Italian Catholic world knew full well that Don Sturzo, De Gasperi and Rodinò were exponents of differing traditions, that they represented respectively the wealthy Sicilian clergy, the Austrian Catholic party, and the Catholicism of the South—where, if the laity was distinguished by its complete submission to the high clergy, the episcopate had produced during the Risorgimento a cardinal (d'Andrea) and a certain number of anti-temporalist prelates—and that they were disposed to obey, but not to anticipate the wishes of their superiors. The Marchese Crispolti, on the other hand, personified the tradition of post-Risorgimento Catholicism established by Pius IX, in which there was no longer a trace of that independence, of that idiosyncrasy of feeling—sometimes entailing a divergence from the strictest canons of Roman orthodoxy, but never degenerating into outright disobedience—which had characterized the Catholicism of Tommaseo, of Manzoni, even of Cantú and d'Ondes Reggio. As for Giovanni Grosoli, the story of his life might well have been embodied in a hagiology. His friends spoke of him, and would continue to speak of him, as of a saint. In his devotion to the Holy See he had already accepted a whole series of humiliations without blinking an eyelid. Finally, Carlo Santucci, in whose house the Popular Party had been born, personified the tradition of the world of Papal Rome, the Rome of the consistorial advocates and the procurators of the sacred palaces. No one acquainted with the Catholic world could doubt that, if Grosoli, Santucci and Crispolti had left the party, they had done so in the sure knowledge that they were translating into action the unexpressed thought, that they were anticipating the wish, of Pius XI.

The 'Rightists', Cornaggia and Pestalozza, seemed rather to have lost their sense of proportion when they asked Mussolini to permit members of the 'National Union' to join the Fascist Militia, the armed guard of the revolution. The same could not yet be said of the greatest Catholic newspapers. For example, in an article published on August 4th, 1923, *L'Unità Cattolica* noted that 'initially there was no mass opposition to the idea of supporting the Fascist movement in its work of reconstruction, and that the present 'controversy regarding the degree' of that support 'has been artificially provoked'. This article received the blessing of *Civiltà Cattolica*, which in its always well-informed Notes of the Day observed how the various sections of the Popular Party had in general remained loyal to the party leadership, thanks largely, no doubt, to Fascist lawlessness in the provinces; but 'the ranks of the loyalists are in danger of becoming confused, partly because of the personal followings commanded by the expelled deputies . . . and partly because of the activities of the National Union, headed by the Marchese Cornaggia and seemingly supported by the Government.'

At the end of the year the National Committee of the Popular Party approved by 28 votes to five a resolution which declared that the internal situation continued to be disturbed by lawlessness and local acts of violence. At the same time it decided to fight the coming election without resorting to coalitions either of the Right or the Left. For their part, the senators and deputies who had resigned from the party issued a statement in which they reaffirmed their intention of supporting the Government, feeling as they did 'that its vigorous attempt to rescue the nation from the moral and material decadence of the post-war years, its bold policy of reconstruction, reflecting a contempt for the old dogmas of liberalism and the sectarian factions, its just regard for Catholic rights and its loyal and practical recognition of the educative power of the religious principle have been, and continue to be, symptomatic of a profound desire to re-establish the nation's life on a fruitful basis.'

On January 26th, 1924, the Popular Party threw itself into the electoral struggle, reaffirming its programme of Christian democracy and declaring that it was descending into the arena with the object of co-operating in the restoration of public life 'to constitutional normality and of opposing all attacks on parliamentary institutions and on the political liberties of the nation'. It now inserted in its programme provisions for the reform of ecclesiastical legislation, the abolition of the *exequatur* and the *placet*, and the restoration of the legal status of the religious corporations.

In the elections the party polled 645,090 votes—a large number by comparison with the 448,058 of the Unitarian Socialists, the 348,540 of the Maximalists, the 304,682 of the Communists, and the 241,685 of the Liberals, but insignificant when set against the 4,593,690 of the Fascists.

On the eve of the Matteotti outrage the party—the direction of which Don Sturzo had finally relinquished—refused to join a united front of opposition groups. Subsequently, however, its representatives joined with those of the Left Wing parties in abstaining from all parliamentary activity—a course of action which it was wrongly assumed would induce the King to intervene in order to ensure respect for the Constitution.

But on November 9th, 1926, the Chamber declared that the survivors of the so-called 'Aventine Group' had not fulfilled their parliamentary mandate inasmuch as they had *failed to observe the explicit prescription of Article 49 of the Statute—namely that the function of deputy should be exercised with the sole aim of promoting the joint welfare of the King and the Country.*

Such were the reactions and the fortunes of the Popular Party up to the time of the Matteotti outrage.

But what was the attitude of the clergy—in particular the episcopate—and of the mass of Catholics who had remained outside active politics, and so had not participated in the life of the Popular Party? One may answer without hesitation that it was substantially favourable to the Fascist Government, although, as was natural, the signs of favour varied in intensity, being more pronounced in places that had experienced several years of outright socialist domination (or, as some put it, of Red tyranny), and less pronounced, or imperceptible, in places where the advent of Fascism had wrested control of the local councils from the hands of Catholic elements. I believe that this favour reached its peak in Emilia and the Romagna, where the clergy compromised their principles more openly than elsewhere.

With the disappearance of that respect for the individual which had been shared alike by liberals, radicals and socialists there ensued in the smaller centres, in the villages, a revival of the old traditions. This development was favoured by the fact that Fascism lacked cadres of sufficient size to enable it to fill all the key posts; in places where it had supporters of proved loyalty these posts were entrusted to them; where such men were lacking, it had recourse to local squires and noblemen, who thus regained a lustre they had lost. In this way it gave back power to those elements which, even if perhaps they lacked a true religious faith, had continued to foster certain traditions. The mayor, clad in the black shirt and the sash, took the place of honour in processions and made the votive offering in church in accordance with a centuries-old tradition which had been interrupted only a decade or so previously. The Communal Council reclaimed the honour of guarding a relic which had remained in its custody for centuries and which a socialist council had returned twenty years before to the ecclesiastical authorities. These were small things, but they meant a great deal to the local clergy—who, it must never be forgotten, had endured pin-pricks for half a century past—and to their parishioners.

Once again the blessing of the bishop and the priest was invoked at all public ceremonies; once again the bishop became an influential public figure, to whom official visitors from Rome went to pay homage on their arrival in the city and whose recommendation was worth almost as much as that of the local deputy in the Prefectures and Ministries.

A few highly popular priests—men such as Father Ermenegildo Pistelli and Father Semeria—prompted by patriotic fervour, by a heightened national consciousness, had strayed somewhat from the paths of Christian universalism. (For close on a century this failing has been by no means uncommon among the Catholic priesthood and laity; but it is not regarded as a mortal sin.) The writings and utterances of these men of great intellectual and moral stature—Father Semeria especially was passionate in his devotion to good works and to the pursuit of charitable aims—earned Fascism no inconsiderable prestige among the faithful. Another great religious figure of the time, Father Agostino Gemelli, maintained in the early years of Fascism an attitude of reserve combined with a diplomatic shrewdness and he availed himself of the privilege granted to ecclesiastics who taught in schools or universities of abstaining in their academic capacity from swearing allegiance to the régime. None the less he belonged to that category of men who are by temperament builders and organizers, who feel that they have a goal which they must at all costs attain. Such men are incapable of admitting defeat, of leaving it to a succeeding generation to fulfil what they conceive to be their task. Father Gemelli's goal was the foundation of a great Catholic university which in his imagination was to have been the chief university of Italy; and in Italy no project that conflicted with Fascist policy was any longer feasible. His comparative coolness towards the régime in its early years gave way to the enthusiastic support expressed in his articles and speeches of the years subsequent to 1930.

When taking possession of his diocese in March, 1923, the Archbishop of Messina, Mgr. Paino, made a speech which according to the *Giornale d'Italia* had the blessing of the Pope, but which according to the Catholic Press limited itself as an exposition of ecclesiastical policy to the statement: 'I feel it my duty to send my greeting also to him who is leading Italy along the right road, to him who is imbuing the Nation with new vigour—I mean, to the Head of the Government.'

Meanwhile, Fascism waged a ceaseless campaign of proselytization. It was not until much later, during Italy's most tragic years, that the phrase about the stick and the carrot was coined. But it could have been applied most fittingly to the methods adopted during the early years of the régime, when the disbandment of Catholic societies and the beating up of priests alternated with acts of homage to the Church, both in Rome itself and in the provinces.

As early as December 28th, 1922, the Council of Ministers decided to hand over to the Vatican the Chigi Library, which the State had acquired along with the Palazzo itself in 1918. (The bureaucrats of Rome could afford to smile; they knew that for some time past, whenever permanent under secretaries and heads of departments had wanted to make more room for themselves, they had been in the habit of consigning quantities of books to the cellars. At the root of the gesture there was only a desire to have another floor available; but the gesture remained.) A few days later the Minister of Education, Gentile, revealed in an interview the Government's intention to make religious teaching in the schools compulsory. Moreover, in the first days of 1923 the Council of Ministers resolved to make a grant of three million lire for the restoration of churches damaged in the war and to distribute among them six hundred pictures on religious subjects; and already there was talk in official circles of increased subsidies for Italian schools abroad run by religious communities. The Fascists secured the resignation of the Communal Council of Rome and the appointment as Royal Commissioner of the ex-mayor Filippo Cremonesi, who, taking office on March 12th, 1923, immediately paid a courtesy visit to the Cardinal Vicar Pompili.[1] During the same period the crucifixes that had been removed twenty-seven years before were solemnly restored to the wards of the Rome General Hospital. In March, 1924, the Council of Ministers confirmed and broadened the scope of the provisions relating to clerical stipends and announced a wholesale exemption of ecclesiastics from military service.

Great Christian spirits steeped in the teaching of Him whose sternest rebukes were reserved for the Pharisees and who taught that piety should never be flaunted, that God is truly venerated in the heart, and that the principal outward sign of His worship is love of one's neighbour, would probably have found these ostentatious measures distasteful. But great Christian spirits have been rare in every age. There was certainly no lack among the clergy of men who perceived the grounds for dissatisfaction which undoubtedly existed.

With the establishment of a single-party totalitarian régime the Church had been forced to abandon its dream of a political party which would have been ostensibly non-confessional and free, but whose leaders at all levels would nevertheless have regarded the wishes of the Secretariat of State or of the local bishop, on whatever subject they were expressed, as tantamount to an order.

---

[1] The *Osservatore Romano* of March 14th, 1923, states that the visit, which had been announced in advance, was officially regarded as private; but the juridical question remained unclarified, as it had done after September 21st, 1870.

But in the less enlightened strata of society there has always existed, apart from all political preferences, an aversion to a plurality of parties, to controversies that divide opinion. Along with it has gone a naïve prejudice in favour of the notion of a single party of honourable men that would concern itself not with politics but with good administration (as if any government could operate effectively without basic policies and aims, and the latter were not good or bad according to the principles, the concepts of social justice, that inspired them). The totalitarian State exploited this predilection to the full. For their part, the more enlightened members of the community recalled that in the State of the *ancien régime*, the ideal State under which the Church had experienced its best days, political parties and struggles had been unknown. There was undoubtedly one aspect of the totalitarian State which churchmen viewed with less approval, and that was its insistence on assuming responsibility—in a far more radical way than the liberal State had done, and with a very different attitude to the question of imposing its stamp on youthful minds—for the education of the young. In this sphere, as is well known, some most serious conflicts arose. Nevertheless, even the most ardent churchman could find some positive signs that might serve to lull his conscience. Thus, equality of status was granted to private schools —and in Italy the expressions 'private school' and 'Church school' are in practice identical in meaning—on a scale hitherto undreamed of. The *balilli* and the other Fascist youth organizations had their own chaplains, celebrated their own Masses in camp, had their pennants blessed, presented themselves to the world at large in a Catholic, not a secular guise. Even in study-groups of university students or graduates demonstrations of anticlericalism were frowned upon, respect for the Church and its institutions—even if only of a passive kind—was *de rigueur*.

The Fascists' success in winning a certain measure of support from Catholics during the first six years of the régime, and the attitude of Italian Catholics and clergy in general to Fascist ideology, must be borne in mind if one is to understand how the Concordat ultimately came to be signed. According to the constitution of the Church all power is derived from God; the will of the bishop is not a manifestation of the will of the faithful; the will of the Pope does not reflect the desires and aspirations of Catholics. All this is undeniable. And yet, in the Church, as in the absolutist States of an earlier age, it would be difficult in practice for those who fill posts of authority to ignore completely the will and desires of those who are expected to obey. To be sure, this has sometimes happened: in 1905 a referendum among French Catholics, or even among the episcopate, would have indicated widespread disapproval of Pius X's denunciation of the Law of Separation and of the rupture on which he subsequently decided. In the Catholic Church, as in every other organization, the leader does not normally send his forces into battle against their will.

There was another and more radical consideration which, then and subsequently, was to thrust the fundamental conflicts between the Church and Fascism into the background: a consideration which had begun to take shape long before the Fascist era and which would continue to weigh after its ending. I refer to the change in the ruling class, the change in its mentality and its interests.

The conflicts between Church and State which persisted throughout the nineteenth century, as they had done for considerable periods during the centuries that preceded it, were concerned pre-eminently with questions of theory, with juridical questions. To the nineteenth-century jurist, as to the eighteenth-century magistrate, it mattered less that a greater or smaller number of new ecclesiastical organizations should come into being than that it should be clearly understood that the legal status of each such organization should be derived exclusively from the State, as a reflection of the latter's sovereignty; and that, as some of the nineteenth-century jurists were to put it, this status should be created, and not merely recognized, by the State. Thus the politician, learned in the law, would be disposed to attach significance not so much to what the Pope might say as to the assurance that his decisions would not be promulgated nor become an effective part of canon law without the sanction of the State; not so much to the question of who the bishops might be and what they might do as to the assurance that they would not be able to take lawful possession of their sees without governmental approval, and that they would even be obliged to obtain such approval in respect of the honorary titles which they might enjoy, of the insignia which they and their fellow ecclesiastics might be authorized to wear. As we have seen, there would remain under consideration the question of the introduction of a law whereby the civil marriage ceremony would take precedence over the religious, and also that of the limitations which the State should be able to impose on the Church's exercise of its punitive powers.

Such a juridical mentality, in this sphere as in every other, was destined to fall into decay when the bourgeoisie ceased to be the ruling class *par excellence*, when it changed its character—when its pre-eminently juridical culture, with its substratum of classicalism and philosophy, gave way to a less syllogistic habit of thought, to a culture based rather on the exact sciences—and above all when its main centre of interest shifted from the law to economics.

Those questions of 'principle' by which the ruling class of the nineteenth century set so much store were destined to appear of small account to the ruling class of the ensuing century, which was permeated with pragmatism and regarded everything in the light of the practical results in view. Furthermore, whereas the nineteenth-century man had thought in terms of individuals, had been capable of reacting emotionally to single cases, had found it intolerable that civilized peoples should connive at a colossal injustice—I think of the Dreyfus case: among my childhood memories is the wave of indignation that swept over Europe because *one* innocent man had been wrongly sentenced—the twentieth-century man was to think in terms of the community, was to accept without protest the sacrifice of the one for the benefit of the many.

Conversely, the Church was to persist in that nineteenth-century attitude of mind which attached immense significance to outward forms, to questions of principle, to the formulation of rules of conduct. She would continue to set a higher value on questions of law than on questions of economics. She would continue to give weight to that which in the eyes of the politicians had ceased to count. And she would continue to attach the highest importance to the question of her relations with the State, to the manner in which she was affected by the latter's laws and ordinances; while the State for its part would pay less and less regard to questions of ecclesiastical policy. Not only in Italy, but everywhere, the place occupied by problems of ecclesiastical policy in parliamentary debates, by relevant monographs on the shelves of libraries, by dissertations on such themes in the annual catalogue of academic theses, would diminish rapidly from decade to decade. In Italy the volume of literature on the Lateran Pacts is less than one-tenth of that on the Law of Guarantees.

The agreement of 1929 was facilitated by the fact that what had great significance for one of the two parties meant little to the other: we readily concede that which in our eyes is of small account. The Church was to win almost without striking a blow many of the battles which she had fought in vain all through the nineteenth century; but the price of her victory would be a slackening of public interest in all that concerned herself, a straying of political parties into paths from which she was excluded, an eager concentration of public opinion on problems which concerned her not at all.

The formula of the two parallels became topical once again, though now it had a new significance: that of a Church and State whose interests were mutually exclusive, so that conflicts between them became impossible, not as a result of the good will or the co-operative spirit of men but through sheer force of circumstance.

A few more immediate indications of the way in which the activities of the Fascist Government were viewed in ecclesiastical circles may not be without interest.

To begin with the most august voice, that of the Pontiff: in 1923 Pius XI does not appear to have made any direct reference in his pronouncements to the Government and the political life of Italy. However, in his consistorial allocution of March 24th, 1924, the Holy Father spoke of the joy with which he had welcomed the reintroduction into the primary schools of Christian teaching, together with the reappearance of the crucifix (which in fact had never been removed). He went on to deplore the violence which continued to characterize the country's internal struggles, pointing out that the victims were often organizations which, though not religious *per se*, were closely connected with religion and with the Hierarchy and, remote from the political battle, sought only to persuade men to feel and live as Catholics: '*Quod enim perspicue atque plus semel ediximus, nulli prorsus licere, ad consilia dumtaxat politica vel ad fovendam partium quarumlibet causam, cum auctoritate sacra, tum catholica actione abuti,—idque ne fieret pro facultate prohibuimus—, idcirco impositas Religioni iniurias aut vim personis, rebus institutisque cum ea coniunctis, per speciem publicarum rationum, adhibitam iure optime conquerimur atque improbamus.*'

The Pope then reverted to two events which had given the Holy See much satisfaction—the reform of the law relating to charitable institutions, and the decision to maintain the increases in clerical stipends. But in this connection His Holiness could not by his silence allow the opinion to take root that the Holy See renounced its rights in those ecclesiastical matters *'quae ad se unice pertinent, itemque, quicquid concessum concedendumve in futurum tempus, alio id nomine, quam inchoatae restitutionis in acceptum imputare posse.'*

A year and a half later, in his allocution of December 14th, 1925, in which he reviewed the Holy Year, the Pontiff gave notice that the rulers of Italy had done all they could to ensure the success of the pilgrimages. He also expressed his gratitude for what they had accomplished in the interests of religion—adding, however, that their efforts did not suffice to repair the damage that had been inflicted on the Church and on religion in the past, and that the Pontiff's present position was not in keeping with the dignity of his office. Pope Pius went on to say that he appreciated all that was being done to allay domestic strife and to induce all Italians to unite in seeking to promote the common good; *'illud tamen displicet, quod, cum in re oeconomica et sociali, quam vocant, novae hisce diebus leges conderentur, visum est, plenam haberi rationem non posse et catholicae in hoc genere doctrinae et actionis catholicae, cuius partes sunt ut hanc ipsam doctrinam explanando evolvat atque in usum deducat, in eo quidem campo, in quo utraque, et doctrina et actio, est in primis necessaria ad salutaris.'*

But the passage in the allocution which attracted most attention was that in which, after referring to the absence of civil disorders during the period of the pilgrimages, the Pontiff observed: *'Atque is rerum civilium ordo ne tum quidem defecit, cum nefarium illud tentatum est facinus, cuius ipsa Nos recordatio hodieque perturbat, nisi quod ob superatum Dei beneficio discrimen et dolorem laetitia commutavimus et debitas Deo gratias egimus: quod utrumque, vel dolere vel laetari eo magis Nos decuit, quo Nos celsiore in loco constituti conscientia apostolici muneris admonemur "reprobare malum et eligere bonum".'*

This is a reference to the projected attempt on Mussolini's life by Tito Zaniboni. And the Pontiff's words are unexceptionable: what Catholic could fail to deplore an attempted assassination and to rejoice in the knowledge that it had failed? It is nevertheless worthy of remark that Papal allocutions do not normally make any mention of attempts that are made on the lives of Heads of Governments, especially when these have proved abortive. The passage in question therefore constituted a mark of special regard for Mussolini.

On October 31st of the following year the Duce was passing through Bologna in the midst of a procession when the sound of a revolver-shot was heard. The bullet missed him by a hair's breadth, actually singeing his clothes. Mad with fury, the crowd immediately set upon and proceeded to lynch[1] a fifteen-year-old boy, of whom it may be said that even to-day strong doubts remain as to whether he in fact fired the shot. (Many people, indeed, were of the opinion that it had come from quite a different source.)

All over Italy there followed the customary reprisals. Opponents of the régime were beaten up, advocates' chambers and even a number of Catholic clubs were wrecked, although neither the boy nor his family had ever had any Catholic connections.

The boy's entire family was arrested. After a lengthy trial, in the course of which the magistrates retired, later to declare that there was not a shred of evidence against the family, the father and an aunt of the dead lad were sentenced to thirty years' imprisonment. After a few years they were pardoned; but the sentence had been widely publicized and the news of the release was hushed up. At the same time, the authorities made a point of warning any who might be disposed to throw away their own lives that a merciless vengeance would be taken on their relatives.

On December 20th the Pontiff delivered his customary allocution to the Sacred College—an allocution that was particularly important for its condemnation of *Action française*.

After deploring, as was his wont, the difficulties of the times and the disorientation for which they were responsible, Pius XI continued:

'To those who solicit Us for clear and precise directives ...
We must in the first place point out that in practical matters
it is not always possible to give a general answer with complete
clarity and precision. In the second place We declare that what
we have said and written ... already contains ... maxims and

---

[1] Thus the official report. But in the popular version it was one of the most notorious and bloodthirsty members of the Fascist hierarchy who leapt from one of the escorting vehicles and slit the throat of the alleged gunman with a weapon which he was to display, still stained with blood, that same evening in a city café.

indications making both for sound doctrinal judgment and for right conduct. We would add in conclusion, for those who may still need the warning, that it is not lawful for Catholics to lend their moral or material support to a programme or doctrine that sets politics above religion and makes the latter serve the former, nor to expose themselves or others, particularly the young, to trends or influences that constitute a threat to faith and morals, to Catholic education and training.'

Since one thing that may be said with certainty is that Fascism had always assigned a secondary place to religion and that prominent posts in the Fascist hierarchy were filled by men to whom the Catholic tradition meant less than nothing, the passage was presumably intended to signify that it was not lawful for Catholics to lend their moral or material support to Fascism or to encourage the young to join its organizations. But any who interpreted it in this way must have remained perplexed not only by the comments of a large section of the Catholic Press but also by the subsequent part of the allocution.

This, in fact, recalled that Italy, like other States, had recently passed through a period of storm.

'First there was the storm of indignation and horror at the insane attempt on the life of the man who rules the destinies of the Country with such energy that whenever his person is endangered one may justly feel that the Country itself is in peril. Thanks to the prompt and almost visible intervention of Divine Providence that first tempest was immediately followed by a veritable hurricane of jubilation, rejoicing and thanksgiving, occasioned by the escape from danger, by the complete and, it may well be said, miraculous preservation of him who was to have been the victim of the outrage. As We were among the first to receive news of the fearful peril through which he had passed and which he had so fortunately surmounted, so Our prayers of thanksgiving were assuredly among the first to ascend to the Lord of life and death, Who from on high rules and governs all things and all men, both individuals and peoples. But lo! even while We, and with Us the Bishops, Priests and all good Catholics, have been offering prayers of thanksgiving and supplication in recognition of the inestimable benefit conferred on the nation by its leader's miraculous preservation, behold!

another storm has burst over Italy, a storm of violence and destruction, directed against persons and property, against institutions and the buildings in which their work is performed; a storm which spared neither the sanctity of the temple, nor the venerable dignity of the Bishop, nor the sacred character of the priest. This blind fury seemed to identify with the enemies of order those good and faithful Catholics whose very faith and religion makes them the best friends and guardians of that same order; and, with an evil discrimination sought out the best among the Catholic faithful in order to subject them to harsher treatment—themselves and their choicest works and organizations, which are of religious, cultural, economic and social benefit to all. . . .

'It seems that a dark menace, a menace betokened by a vast cloud of suspicions, intrusions and difficulties, is poised and suspended above the works and organizations, especially those which concern the young, of "Catholic Action", the apple of Our eye; and it seems also that danger threatens the Christian training and education of the young, which is the most exquisite part of the Divine prescript *Euntes docete*. It seems that once again there is being revealed and enunciated a conception of the State which cannot be the Catholic conception, so long as it makes of the State the end, and of the citizen, of the individual, merely a means, causing all things to be monopolized and swallowed up by the State. It seems that a veritable dualism of powers and functions is continuing to transform into executors and often arbitrary interpreters of orders that are in themselves salutary and prudent provincial officials who, though serving under new colours and new names, are still the same sectarians, still the same enemies of society and religion, as of yore.'

Apart from the fact that it exemplifies that too frequent desire to attribute natural events to Providence which was characteristic of Pius XI, the allocution is in itself unexceptionable. The reader at once perceives that while at the beginning the Pontiff has stressed the note of deference to Mussolini in order to heighten the effect of the subsequent protest, he has nevertheless sought to make that protest acceptable by drawing a distinction between the salutary and prudent orders which emanate from Rome and the factious and sectarian officials who interpret them in the provinces.

It is not, to be sure, one of those documents in which the Papacy expresses itself in its loftiest and most exalted tones; but more than once when confronted by tyrants the successors of Peter have been at pains, in the interests of the flock entrusted to their care, to ward off greater evils, to find those accents of humility which never ill become him who speaks beneath the sign of the Cross.

What may grieve the dispassionate reader is not that which is said, but that which is left unsaid.

Civiltà Cattolica in its impartial account of the episode records that the body of the fifteen-year-old boy revealed signs of strangulation, fourteen deep stabs and a wound caused by a revolver-bullet; and it expresses criticism, albeit moderate in tone, of this so-called summary justice. That there should be no mention of this circumstance in the Pontiff's allocution is a fact which one cannot but deplore.

I have mentioned *Civiltà Cattolica*; and, in view of the wealth of relevant material which they contain, its comments are perhaps of greater interest to the student than the occasional oblique references to political events embodied in official Papal utterances. In fact, this journal has never been disowned by the Vatican, and it has always interpreted the thoughts and desires of the Pope. Its commendation of an individual or of an action has never failed to neutralize the effect of criticisms emanating from other Catholic sources, and every campaign which it has waged against a particular doctrine has heralded an official condemnation of the latter by the Holy See.

Its comments on current affairs have always been comprehensive and honest. It is, of course, only natural that it should give much prominence to acts of violence directed against ecclesiastical personages, exponents of Catholic Action or Catholic societies; but similar acts at the expense of others also receive publicity.

It goes without saying that the news columns of *Civiltà Cattolica* record every act of homage rendered by the Government to religion and to the Church; and reading between the lines of its commentaries on events one senses a gradual acceptance of that distinction which the dissident 'Rightists' of the Popular Party were the first to formulate: the distinction, that is, between the Government, which seeks to promote order and discipline, and the party, which for a while is made the scapegoat, and to which every evil action is to be imputed. Thus, any act of violence will be the work of 'vulgar malefactors armed with membership-cards of the Fascist Party'; but the impunity which they constantly enjoy will be treated with reticence. In the account of Mussolini's visit to Sicily in May, 1924, a reference to the 'changed political climate'—a phrase actually coined by a member of the opposing camp—is introduced when describing how the President of the Council and the Minister of Marine, together with their suites and the crew of the *Dante Alighieri*, landed at Catania for the purpose of attending Sunday Mass in the Cathedral.

In March, 1923, *Civiltà Cattolica* published an article entitled *Fascism and Trade-Unionism* which had some harsh things to say about the Fascist unions. These, it declared, following the negative and anti-proletarian action taken by the original *squadristi*, had established as their main objective 'the negation of the pernicious Marxist dogma of the class struggle'; looked upon the national interest as the stimulus, law, and goal of economic activity; and regarded the intellectual worker as superior to the manual worker. 'Just as in the political sphere the fundamental points in the Fascist programme for Italian reconstruction are borrowed from the programme of the Popular Party (reform of schools, reintroduction of religious teaching, reform of the bureaucracy, decentralization, constitution of technical councils of labour), so in the field of trade-unionism Fascism has derived its principle *directives* from the White unions.' However, 'the weakness and the fallacy' of the Fascist system consisted in the fact that it differed from White trade-unionism both in method and in spirit. 'If we read the writings and listen to the speeches of the Fascist organizers we are struck by a reckless tendency to *over-simplification*, whereby it would appear that all economic and social differences and causes of friction can be eliminated overnight, as by a miracle, at a peremptory word of command from a Fascist official.' The article also expressed scepticism about the mixed corporation, in which the Fascists firmly believed. 'The bourgeois ruling class is certainly not distinguished by its exquisite moral and religious sense. Agnostic on religious questions, materialistic, at any rate in practice, corrupted by the evil principles of liberalism, it provides even to-day a ceaseless flow of recruits to freemasonry and anticlericalism. Is it possible—without speaking of other grave problems, such as *big business* and the Marxist mentality of a large section of the proletariat—for such a delicate plant as the mixed corporation to flourish in this pestilential atmosphere?' Furthermore, continued the article, Fascist trade-unionism's condemnation of all the Internationals was a sign of its poverty of ideas. 'Let them hurl anathema at the Moscow International, which, when all is said and done, is only a short-sighted expedient of Soviet foreign policy . . . ; let them even condemn the Amsterdam International, which seeks to impose itself on foreign States and to fight them; but let them not condemn the White International.' And among other things to be deplored was the spirit of violence and 'the purely socialistic mentality of the working masses' who were enrolled 'willy-nilly' in the various Fascist organizations.

To the same year belongs the article *Liberalism in Travail*, which rather reflects the satisfaction of a journal originally founded in order to combat liberalism and which for three-quarters of a century had regarded it as an enemy. 'The services rendered by liberalism to the cause of fighting Fascism, of which the entire liberal Press speaks in such grandiloquent and boastful language, are real enough, but they are also prompted to some extent by self-interest.' The liberals had counted on exploiting the forces of Fascism against the Reds before grafting them on to their own stock. But their calculations had gone awry: it was the victorious Fascists who were now bending everything to their totalitarian yoke.

'We consider—without, however, allowing ourselves to be so blinded by passion as to condemn the entire history of liberalism out of hand—that fundamentally the anti-liberal attitude of Fascism may be quite legitimate. . . . If one is to be consistent, one cannot be an implacable enemy of socialism and of its doctrines without at the same time rejecting its first principles and the premises on which those doctrines and the movement's political and economic initiatives were originally based. Liberalism, whatever its votaries may think of it, represents the premise of socialism, the tree on which this poisonous fruit has grown to maturity. . . . The fundamental concept of liberalism, in its dominant form at least, is the atheistic or monistic concept. . . . Another branch of liberalism, without going to the monistic extreme, without denying categorically that the life of Man is subject to any kind of religious influence, professes indifference to the positive forms of religion, upholds the tenets of theism, acknowledges the existence of a natural moral law. . . . Another principle, one that has constituted the main centre of attraction for the masses, is the principle of "equality" . . . , which transplants the fundamental equality of human nature into the material world, where there exists in fact only an infinite disparity' Italian liberalism 'was at once demagogic and anti-clerical'.

'The Fascism which has proclaimed its intention of re-establishing order, discipline and a hierarchical social system, and which thus aims to restore to Authority its old force and meaning; the Fascism which intends to reaffirm religious values, particularly the most sublime among them, spiritual elevation, and the Catholic inspiration of the country, finds itself faced with the necessity of combating liberalism. . . . Comical indeed is the position of the liberals, who yesterday in their arrogance did not scruple to oppose the Popular Party by every possible means, even the most ignoble, on the ground that it was too meddlesome and voracious, and who to-day find the new, victorious party worthy of eulogy, even while it destroys all that they have built up over the years, and in addition covers them with contempt, blatantly declaring itself to be *illiberal and anti-liberal*. How true it is that with vicious, stubborn children the rod is more persuasive than reason!'

And in the commentary *Cose italiane* for August, 1923, we read: 'Contemporaneously with the eclipse of socialism, the weakening of the Popular Party and the progressive enfeeblement of the other parties, Fascism continues to increase in strength and vigour, taking root in all the centres of the nation's life. Backed as it is by the authority of the Government, flanked by a militia that is ever ready to defend it, who can wonder that up to now it has captured altogether 1,556 communes, not to speak of the 1,785 on which it is represented? And it is easy to foresee that this figure will be increased very shortly, when new elections are held in the not inconsiderable number of communes whose councils have been forced by the local Fascist organizations to resign. And yet, for all its strength, even Fascism has its Achilles' heel,' represented by the dead weight of its criminal elements. These elements 'largely serve to explain the lawlessness which still breaks out sporadically in the peninsula in the form of acts of violence which do no credit to Italy or to civilization'. And the journal noted the extent to which Catholic societies and even ecclesiastical personages continued to suffer from Fascist lawlessness and violence.

After the celebrations in honour of the first anniversary of the March on Rome *Civiltà Cattolica*, in its last issue of 1923, acutely observed that one might have discerned in the celebrations 'a well-concerted series of political manoeuvres—a veritable essay or treatise on human wisdom—by a man who, shrewder than the professional diplomats and more resolute than the statesmen of former years, understands and dominates the psychology of the crowd; with the result that even the highly complex *organization* of the celebrations has its prescribed place and its practical function in the grandiose design of the Government, in the *Fascist programme of reconstruction*'. But the writer of the article could not discern 'any clear evidence of salutary social reconstruction' except in the solution of the problem of State and people—a solution long since suggested and illustrated by the Christian ethic, let us say rather by Catholic practice and teaching, as handed down to us and defended in all their transparent sincerity by the Church and its organs of education and government'. Because 'they returned—at least in part, and albeit under the pressure both of circumstances and of a clearly perceived national interest—' to this source, 'the new rulers have enjoyed for a year now a success which, even if perhaps their enthusiastic admirers extol it excessively, impartial observers recognize and we too are glad to praise impartially. And we praise it all the more because in the good that is derived from it we find not merely a confirmation of what has been said but also—and this is universally true— an exposure of the false *ideologies* and the methods of the old liberalism, true source of the new anti-clerical socialism, down to Communism and the most tyrannical Bolshevism. For if liberalism is now receiving its just deserts, and has cause to bewail the severity and the despotism of the *dictator*, it can only blame itself, and would do well to remember that the rigours of the present are mild by comparison with the acts of tyranny and violence of which it was itself guilty in the age of "liberty" and under the rule of "liberalism".' And the article concludes by urging Fascism to seek its inspiration in the *Diuturnum* and the *Immortale Dei* of Leo XIII.

Symptomatic of contemporary Catholic feeling is a series of articles, published in 1923–24 under the title *Patria e patriottismo*, which develops a theme destined to be elaborated on innumerable occasions by Catholic writers in the future. It is a mistake (declares the writer) to suppose that State frontiers can be abolished and that the nations can combine to form a single empire. Such an ideal conflicts with Man's present mood; it is incapable of realization. The Church stimulates and reinforces patriotism, represses selfish instincts and bends and subordinates them to the common good of the country. Certainly the ultimate goal of the Christian lies outside this world; but 'the Christian conception of a future homeland, far from being opposed to the ideal of a homeland on earth, is rather its surest defence'. It is true that the Church is essentially an international institution and that it does not tolerate any form of exclusiveness. 'But charity, like the sun, sheds a greater warmth in proportion as the radius of its beams is restricted.' The universalism of the Church does not obliterate the frontiers of States, but it is a corrective to exaggerated nationalism.

Cronache italiane, 1924:

January: 'Ample reservations can, and indeed should, be expressed with regard to the methods adopted [by Fascism] for the purpose of seizing the reins of government; but one cannot deny the Duce credit for the wise intention of ensuring that the *reconstruction* of the nation's life should be characterized by respect for Catholic feelings and by the assertion of *spiritual values*. This intention is all the more praiseworthy in that it has already been given practical expression through the maintenance of the principle of the indissolubility of marriage, the reintroduction of religious education, and other similar measures.'

February: It is recognized that the essence of Mussolini's speech in the debate on electoral reform is contained in the following passage: 'In practice, if not in theory, we subscribe to the belief that parties resemble individuals in that they either allow themselves, like the nationalists, to be absorbed completely by Fascism, in which case there is peace, or else they are not prepared to send their respective shirts post-haste to the dyer, in which case there is more or less open war.' But what is the reaction of Catholics? 'Some turn to the Fascist, some to the Popular Party, depending on whether they consider the declared purposes and the measures already taken by the one to be more favourable to religion or whether the policy explicitly professed by the other seems to them more genuinely inspired by Christian motives. Agreed as to principles, agreed on their objectives, they disagree about the methods to be employed.' The ecclesiastical authorities leave them complete freedom of choice.

March: 'The errors and the anti-clerical fury of not a few of the adherents of Fascism should not, however, lead one to overlook the efforts that are being made at a higher level to give a new turn to relations between the civil and the ecclesiastical authorities.'

But Fascism was intolerant of criticisms or reproofs.

When, in April, the Cardinal Secretary of State remitted to the president of Catholic Action half a million lire assigned by Pius XI to the centres, clubs and institutes which had been damaged by the hooliganism of the past weeks, the entire Fascist Press rose in protest. The *Popolo d'Italia* made a personal attack on the Pontiff. His gesture, it declared, was a 'provincial extravagance. Frequently, amid the vicissitudes of their daily life, those who occupy the most exalted posts forget to be *universal* in their outlook and become merely *parochial*'.

March, 1925: At the dinner given in his honour on March 1st, 1925, by the journal *L'Impero*, F. T. Marinetti made a speech in which he expressed sentiments far from respectful to the Holy See. Giunta, a far more influential personage than the creator of futurism, followed with a speech in which he explained his admiration for Marinetti as the man who had first demonstrated the need for violent action.

Civiltà Cattolica commented severely on the Regazzi case[1] and on the defence of the political crime put forward by Farinacci—one of the Fascist Party's most violent deputies, and one of its first political secretaries—declaring that some people were in danger of forgetting the very meaning of the word 'justice', which it defined as *fundamentum regni*.

Violent debates were conducted by the Catholic Press about an article by Giovanni Gentile published as a statement of policy by the new review *L'educazione politica*. Gentile demonstrated the religious character of the present struggle, invoking the biblical phrase 'I came not to send peace, but a sword'. The *Corriere*

---

[1] One of the many scandalous trials conducted under the threat of reprisals by the *squadristi*, the Regazzi case culminated in the triumphant acquittal of a Fascist who was guilty of the murder of a socialist.

d'Italia observed that in using this quotation from the Gospel to justify his equation of Fascism with religion the writer had been guilty, even if unwittingly, of blasphemy.

November, 1925: Comments on the sequel to the Zaniboni outrage—a crime which, 'planned with the object of overthrowing the Government, only succeeded in bringing it closer to the people'. However, *Civiltà Cattolica* found it distasteful that 'the citizens of Bologna should be regaled with the spectacle of a university professor and former under secretary in the Ministry of Education offering to act as the executioner of those who had been arrested'.

January, 1926: Comment in *Civiltà Cattolica* on the conditions which Mussolini had declared on January 17th, 1926, must be fulfilled by the deputies who had walked out of the Chamber in protest against the murder of their colleague Matteotti (the 'Aventine Group') before they could resume their parliamentary functions. 'An authentic case of the application of the law of retribution—"an eye for an eye, a tooth for a tooth". And the applause that punctuated and followed the extremely short speech made it clear that, even if they decided to return to Montecitorio, none of the members of the Aventine Group could avoid passing through the Caudine Forks. The victory of Mussolini over his adversaries accordingly appeared decisive—not so much, however, because those who had first raised the moral question and imposed the terms of surrender were now hoist with their own petard as because the relative positions of deputies and Government had been reversed; for whereas in the past the former, even when in a minority, had been able to make a Minister's life a nightmare, now it was the Government that disposed of the parliamentary lives of more than a hundred deputies, in the full knowledge that none of those present, not even the liberals, would dare to utter a word of protest. . . . But if the rude blow was aimed primarily at the Aventine Group, it fell most heavily on the Popular deputies who had provoked it'—by trying to re-enter the Chamber while tributes were being paid to the memory of the late Queen Margherita. Nor did the various deputies who had at the last moment dissociated themselves from the Aventine Group find themselves in a much happier position after Mussolini's speech; and during the sitting of January 22nd Anile (formerly Minister of Education), Di Fausto and Scotti were obliged to make a *solemn and public* recantation, thereby earning for themselves not, indeed, forgiveness for their past errors, but only a grudging tolerance.'

The traditional Italian subtlety of mind must have been quite dead if, after perusing this half ironical, half complacent comment, any reader of the authoritative *Civiltà Cattolica* could still doubt the extent to which the stock of the Popular rump had fallen in high places.

Towards the end of 1925 the same journal had published a remarkable article entitled *Politica e cattolicesimo*. After noting the political dissensions that existed among Italian Catholics, the writer observed that the latter never supported or allied themselves with parties that were non-Christian or, worse still, positively anti-Christian.

'The Catholic co-operates with such a party *only in so far as* it actually promotes the welfare of all, that is to say of the entire community. In this way he is really supporting not the party *per se* but the *nation*, in the persons of its sole current representatives, the members of the lawfully constituted Government which rules it in fact and is alone capable, in the prevailing circumstances, of promoting the public good or at least of averting the greatest ills.'

Those who were the victims of Fascist attacks did not always have cause to complain, 'because when in power themselves they had acted equally badly, if not worse; and, if their past conduct is any guide, they would proceed to accomplish new acts of vengeance should they ever return to power'; and also 'because it was they who, with their monopoly of education and the Press, propagated these false doctrines and moulded the persons who now practise them. . . . If we condemn the negation of justice, freedom and public morality in the form which we have come to associate with liberalism in all its gradations, down to the most logical of all, namely socialism and Bolshevistic Communism, we do not approve of it when it appears under a diametrically opposite type of régime, to which the first gives rise by its very disorder, be it a military directory or a popular revolution. We do not approve of it if it is vitiated by the same fundamental error, albeit not in a worse way, nor with graver injury to the Church and to society, than was the case under earlier anti-Christian Governments. In other words, the new form of government—following on the heels of what has been variously described as a "liberal", "parliamentary" or "constitutional" régime—may have, and has in practice, its drawbacks, like every other form of government. Indeed, its disadvantages are indubitably grave, inasmuch as it is based on some of those erroneous principles, like the prevailing one of the glorification of the State. It follows from this that Catholics cannot embrace or praise it without reservation, setting it above all others, i.e. conniving at those of its features which are least compatible with or are diametrically opposed to Catholicism. But it does not follow that they should set it beneath all others, as if its drawbacks were more fatal, more pernicious than those of any other form of government, past or possible; for error too has its gradations.'

This article—in which the echo of Father Taparelli's thought is clearly perceptible—provides every serious-minded man with food for sober reflection. For it undoubtedly poses a practical and tremendously agonizing problem, which no abstract formula can ever alleviate: the problem of how one should conduct oneself in the face of a tyrannical or sacrilegious Government, above all if one sees no hope or possibility of escape; the problem of whether, for all men and at all times, the ideal course consists in an absolute refusal to compromise, in standing aside, in 'not defiling oneself', in refusing even to recognize the men in power, or whether there can be a Christian course which consists in seeking to mitigate the evil and to win good from it. Finally, what concessions is it permissible to make in order to carry this second policy into effect? Many saints have entered the palaces of the most cruel tyrants, not with invective on their lips but in the hope of persuading them to grant some favour (the chief distinguishing mark of the rightful course is an absence of self-seeking: none of these saints obtained honours or positions of trust from the tyrant). It is a moral problem of the most agonizing kind. Even the man who chooses one horn of the dilemma owes a measure of respect to him who, disinterestedly, with a pure heart and empty hands, prefers the other.

But what really makes the spirit rebel is this equation of Fascism with the old liberal Governments. For even a man whose knowledge of Italian history, past and present, was derived exclusively from the column *Cose italiane* in *Civiltà Cattolica*—in itself, a sufficiently comprehensive and substantially impartial column—would have appreciated that political murders committed with complete impunity had never been known under any previous Government, either before or after the unification, either during or since the Risorgimento, either under Victor Emmanuel II or under Umberto I. The review had had to record so many. Don Minzoni and Giacomo Matteotti had fallen. These murders had been glorified by the Fascist Press. At the ludicrous trials, action squads bivouacked in the corridors and courtyards of the Palace of Justice. Opponents of the régime had been beaten up on the very steps of Montecitorio. Catholic clubs and printing-presses had been systematically wrecked.

The Italy of these years was the Italy of the anti-Risorgimento. To suppose otherwise would be to misread the facts of history.

The deputies expelled from the Chamber had lost their immunity; the 'Reds' had nearly all been sentenced to *confino*. For members of the Popular Party the treatment was milder: usually it was limited to banishment from public life, or, in the case of prospective barristers, to the periodical sacking of their chambers. The Fascists did not prevent them, however, from continuing to languish in the obscurity of the episcopal chancelleries, from serving as directors of companies or as clerks in Catholic banks. The last secretary of the party, Alcide De Gasperi, was the only one to be victimized. On the evening of March 11th, 1927, at the instance of the Rome police, he was arrested at Florence station, in company with his wife, while on his way by train to Bologna. On being searched he was found to be in possession of a ticket from Orvieto to Trieste, together with a writ summoning him to appear as a witness at a trial which was due to take place at Trieste, made out in the name of De Rossi, and two Touring Club vouchers for himself and his wife made out in the same name. He at once gave correct particulars about himself, said that he was travelling under the name of De Rossi for fear of being molested by political enemies, that he knew the writ was false—it had been sent to him by a friend as a joke—and that he was going to Trieste for a holiday and possibly to look for a job. The Rome Tribunal in its judgment of May 28th, 1927, pointed out that the drafters of the existing law of public security 'have aimed, with an exquisite sense of political wisdom, to protect, among other things, the State and the nation from the effects of the baneful activities of citizens who, by seeking asylum in foreign countries, can do untold harm to the interests and the good name of their rejected homeland', and sentenced him to a long term of imprisonment for clandestine emigration prompted by political motives and for forgery of an official document. The Court of Appeal found the second charge unproved but endorsed the first. The Court of Cassation rejected the appeal addressed to it, likewise pointing out that the existing law of public security, 'with the aim of repressing and ending the scourge of political emigration, whose exponents persisted in carrying on abroad a reckless and pernicious propaganda campaign, highly injurious to the interests and prestige of the nation, had introduced a new and grave class of crime', that of clandestine emigration.

Only with the conclusion of the Concordat—as the result of a secret clause it has been alleged, probably without foundation— was De Gasperi to regain his freedom.

Fascism's efforts to reach an understanding with the Church became increasingly strenuous. Having consolidated its position at home, and aspiring as it did to a world-wide political influence, the régime felt instinctively that it must win the support of the Vatican and the sympathy of the episcopate and of Catholic parties throughout the world. Mussolini was fated never to shake himself lose from the fanatics and the men of violence—the elements who he felt were closest to him and for whom all his sympathies continued to be reserved. But as time went on it became more and more dangerous for a man of ambition to play the leading role in any anti-clerical episode.

Gentile, who after July 1st, 1924 ceased to be a minister, was destined for many years yet to represent the still, small voice of secularism which continued to throw out a challenge to Fascist orthodoxy. He was to fill a variety of posts, retain his seat on the Grand Council, but never again held government office. On January 9th, 1925, the portfolio of Minister of Education passed into the hands of Pietro Fedele, a determined worker for conciliation who was ready to concede anything to the Holy See. It was during his three-and-a-half-year term of office that Ernesto

Buonaiuti, Professor of Religious History at Rome University, was dismissed from his post. It was in his name that Bodrero declared, at the opening of the fourth International Congress of Moral Philosophy: 'The Italian national Government considers that the only possible form of moral education is that prescribed by the Gospel of Christ, in the interpretation, tradition and teaching of the Catholic Church, from the Ten Commandments of God to the Catechism.'

Meanwhile, however, there began to unfold the series of events which was to culminate in the Concordat.

At the beginning of 1925 a committee of three canons from the patriarchal basilicas of Rome was set up to consider a reform of the ecclesiastical laws. Even though they had been appointed directly by the Government, no one could have supposed that these eminent ecclesiastics had consented to serve on such a committee without the approval of the Holy See; and it was even possible to believe that the latter had nominated them. For their part, however, the *Osservatore Romano* and *Civiltà Cattolica* confined themselves to observing that although these worthy prelates had no 'official mandate' to negotiate in the name of the Holy See, they were nevertheless 'well qualified on the score of intelligence and ability to interpret and to protect the interests of all the Roman and Italian clergy'.

Before embarking on its work the committee was addressed by Rocco, Keeper of the Seals, who, while not attempting to trace the lines of the projected reform, emphasized the change in the spiritual climate that had occurred since the period of the Risorgimento and asserted that the conflict between Church and State had by now become not merely nonsensical but injurious to Italy. The committee concluded its work by formulating a plan of which the main points were as follows: the grant of legal status to the churches of the religious organizations suppressed by the legislation of the Risorgimento; legal recognition of the religious Orders and their institutions, subject to the proviso that the civil authorities would be entitled to insist on the conversion of immovable ecclesiastical property and to withdraw legal recognition from institutions which, although specifically informed of the restrictions imposed on them, persisted in carrying on activities incompatible with their declared aims, or which committed acts contrary to the State's laws and institutions or prejudicial to public order; abolition of the *placet* and substitution of the *exequatur*, with the proviso that all episcopal appointments would be subject to the approval of the civil authorities; renunciation by the State of the right to appropriate the revenues of vacant benefices; and fiscal reliefs. Except in Catholic circles, where it met with general approval, the project aroused no public interest. It represented a lopping of dead branches, a jettisoning of regulations which no longer had any meaning.

Public interest began to awaken when the *Acta Apostolicae Sedis*, in its issue of March 1st, 1926, published—and the daily Press reproduced—a letter, dated February 18th, from the Pontiff to Cardinal Gasparri on the subject of the proposed reforms.

'From the fact that learned ecclesiastics were invited to serve on the Committee ... some have wished to infer that the proposed reform was itself studied and drafted in collaboration with the Holy See.' This was not so. 'Now that it is proposed to translate the suggested reforms into law, and therefore of necessity to introduce legislation affecting matters and persons that are subject, basically at least, to the sacred power entrusted to Us by God, the duties inherent in the Apostolic Ministry, for the exercise of which We are responsible to God Himself and to God alone, require Us to say and to declare that We cannot concede the right and the power to make laws affecting such matters and persons to others unless they have first entered into proper negotiations and concluded valid agreements with this Holy See and with Us.'

A moment of suspense followed.

Would the Government react? It might, and perhaps violently; but it might equally well continue to follow its chosen path, cutting off these dead branches of the legislation of the Risorgimento, introducing a code of ecclesiastical laws that would be entirely satisfactory to Italian Catholics and would arouse the envy of the Catholics of other countries, and paying no regard to the Pope's words. But the Holy See probably knew already that this possibility, which from its own point of view was the more dangerous of the two, would never be realized. In fact, the Keeper of the Seals respectfully declared that in view of the Pontiff's letter he was temporarily shelving the question of the reform, with the idea of tackling it afresh from a new angle at a later date; and it then emerged that, if the pontifical letter had not actually been drafted after consultation with the Government, the latter had certainly been notified of its contents, which had only been published in the knowledge that such a procedure would not displease Mussolini. It was realized that the letter provided a basis for negotiations on the subject of a concordat.

Nevertheless, the majority continued to take a sceptical view of the possibility that the Holy See would agree to settle the Roman Question and to negotiate a concordat with the Fascist Government.

The idea of a Pope shut up in the Vatican, brooding over a grievance which all knew to be without substance, was by now so deeply rooted in the minds of Italians that they could not conceive of the possibility that the situation might change—not least because they were prevented by a kind of mental inertia from thinking of the settlement of the Roman Question as a purely juridical settlement, and thought it should be accompanied by a radical change in the very character of the life of the Papal Curia, by the emergence of a Pope who would travel freely about Italy and about Europe.

It seems, moreover, that up to the last moment Pius XI likewise continued to be a prey to doubts and hesitations.

Certainly the fact that a concordat was being negotiated remained known to only a very limited circle of people. It was one of those rare cases of an important political development which the authorities managed to keep secret until diplomacy had done its work.

The signing of the treaty, announced on February 11th, 1929, came as a genuine surprise to the whole Italian nation and also, it seems, to the Foreign Ministries of other countries. The Press gave the news of the event together with almost the complete text of the agreements.

The reactions of the public could not be gauged from the newspapers, which had already lost every vestige of independence and could only applaud the development. It may be said, however, that they were on the whole favourable.

There were, of course, none of those scenes of delirious enthusiasm which would have greeted Pius IX if, after the events of 1870, he had come out into St. Peter's Square to bless Italian

Rome. To the overwhelming majority this termination of the seventy-year-old conflict between Church and State, this formal settlement of a difference which had in fact already been composed, was of no importance. The Fascist Government's success was of the same order as a moral success gained at a great international conference. Its value was to be judged in terms of prestige, and of the hopes which it engendered for the future.

Nevertheless, the public at large recognized the moral success which the settlement of the Roman Question, the removal of this last juridical obstacle to Italian unity, undoubtedly represented.

Among Catholics there was a stronger feeling of satisfaction, though this was by no means universal. There were those who were sincerely attached to the party of Don Sturzo and were convinced that it would aspire within a few years to the position of the ruling party, who believed that democracy and Catholicism would ultimately be reconciled and that the one would help the other to conquer the world, and who could not resign themselves to defeat. Even more acute, perhaps, was the distress of certain Catholics who, though fervent in their convictions and rigorous in their observance of religious forms, had remained outside the various Catholic organizations, even outside Catholic Action, and were therefore less accustomed to disciplining themselves and to submitting without question to the decisions of the Pope. Such Catholics were in this respect like survivors from an earlier age; they belonged in spirit to the seventeenth or to the eighteenth century. They regarded Mussolini and his Fascists with a kind of horror, looking upon them as a gang of bloodthirsty ruffians. Their religious susceptibilities were offended by any eulogy of the dictator, whose marital infidelities were paraded quite openly and shamelessly. They recalled the parable of the tree and its fruit; they were incapable—and here too they were survivors from an earlier age of Catholicism—of distinguishing the man from his works or of differentiating between his good and his evil actions. One of them was to say that on hearing the news of the Concordat he had had the same impression as a mediaeval man would have had if an Honorius or a Boniface had entered the Lateran patriarchate in conversation with a devil complete with horns and tail and had patted him between the horns and said to him: 'I know you aren't really such a bad devil at heart.' But—and in this too he was like the mediaeval man—although he suffered, he did not lose faith. He had had to ring his Catholicism about with new ideological trenches and shelters, but he had not deserted the fold.

Such men, however, represented only a tiny minority. The great majority of Catholics—by which I mean, of course, those who were Catholics not only in virtue of the fact that they had been baptized and had recourse to the sacraments, but also by reason of their adherence to the Church on the political level—were delighted with the Pacts. Apart from the ostentatious enthusiasm of those Catholics who had not irremediably compromised themselves with Fascism but had hitherto maintained an attitude of frigid reserve, and now seized the opportunity to 'climb on to the band-waggon', there was the real joy of those who had found even the memory of the rift oppressive, not only because of the occasional embarrassments and equivocal situations in which it was still liable to involve them, but also because in their eyes a flag not blessed by the Pope was in effect a flag that yielded in dignity to other flags. Many of these Catholics clung, perhaps unconsciously, to the old, traditional idea that Italy occupied a special position, that she had intimate links with the Holy See which not only imposed upon her peculiar obligations, but also afforded her expectations and benefits of an unusual kind. In their eyes the Lateran Pacts ought to have had the effect of reviving a tradition a thousand years old. Hence—though there was in their attitude a hint of sentimentality, a tendency to identify themselves in spirit with a very remote age, with the age of Adrian I and Leo III— they were inclined to share the view of the many who saw in the Lateran Pacts above all a card, that of the political influence of the Papacy and of Catholic parties abroad, placed at the service of future Italian foreign and colonial policy, and who had high hopes for that policy.

For among the educated class, among that section of the community which in any other country would have constituted the ruling class, there was a feeling that the significance of the Lateran Pacts consisted not in what they had erased of the past, but in the guarantees which they afforded for the future.

The card of temporalist pretensions, or merely of protests against the events of 1870 and the unilateral solution represented by the Law of Guarantees, had lost its value, had been rendered null and void by prescription. By this time there was hardly a corner of the world where Catholics still believed that the Pope had been placed in an intolerable position, that the Holy See had suffered any loss of freedom or prestige; and the Italian State was no longer embarrassed by a refusal on the part of the Vatican to acknowledge its existence. To have traded the confessional character of the State against that card would have been the greatest of follies. The fact remained, however, that the moral and political influence of the Holy See had been steadily increasing, that Catholic parties everywhere were renewing their strength, that the support, active or merely passive, of the Holy See in the realm of international politics and colonial rivalries could be of the utmost value to Italy.

In the public mind the treaty held pride of place (and naturally the Fascist Press laid great emphasis upon it, on the fact that Mussolini had succeeded where all others, beginning with Cavour, had failed). Only comparatively few—the jurists and the die-hard liberals—were left with a bitter taste in their mouths, not because of the Concordat itself, but because the State had abandoned its claim to exercise jurisdiction over the marriage ceremony, because this modicum of secular authority had been conceded to the Church.

But on that 11th of February there were others too—not jurists, not heirs to the liberal tradition, but the anti-Fascists—who felt greatly embittered. These, it must be admitted, were in a minority; but anyone who had penetrated into their conclaves would have heard phrases of a slightly rhetorical character that recalled a past age. One that sticks in the memory described the Pope as the man who had driven the last nail into the coffin of Italian liberty.

However, even staid anti-Fascists, men who retained their sense of proportion and were sufficiently objective to give the enemy credit for his successes, acknowledged that the Pacts represented a victory for Mussolini. 'This will prove to have been the peak point of his career'—such was the prophecy made to me at the time by a Bolognese colleague who a few years later was to be driven by the racial laws to seek asylum in Latin America. And indeed, in the story of Mussolini's life those days might well be said to have had the same significance as the days of the Congress of Paris had in the life of Napoleon III.

Either of these men had it in his power at that moment to alter his course, to enter upon the path of safety. For Napoleon III it was the moment when the Great Powers finally ceased to mistrust the former *carbonaro*, the man who had tried to overthrow the order established in 1815, the intruder among the crowned heads of Europe. Possibilities of inaugurating a conservative policy, of accomplishing a work of peaceful mediation among the Great Powers, Austria, Russia and Great Britain, were opening up before him. In the same way, Mussolini might have set himself up as the champion of a policy of Catholic conservatism, calculated to win him the confidence of all the moderate elements in Europe on a scale so vast as to embrace not only Catholics of long-standing legitimist traditions but also those moderate socialists who were ready to applaud his social policy. But neither of the two men was able to control his impulses. A most noble demon—the old idealism of the young man of 1830, his love for an Italy that remained for ever ungrateful to him, combined with a feeling of compassion for Poland—prompted Napoleon III to alienate the Papacy, to embark on the war with Austria, to incur the distrust and rancour which, especially after 1863, Alexander II harboured towards him. A demon whose origin was probably pathological prompted Mussolini, without a reason in the world, to destroy, on the very morrow of the Lateran Pacts, that confidence which the Pope had only just begun to repose in him.

On February 13th Pius XI received in audience the professors and students of the University of the Sacred Heart. He talked to them at length about the Lateran Pacts; and his address included the following well-known passage: 'We have been nobly assisted by the other side also. And perhaps the times called for a man such as he whom Providence has ordained that We should meet: a man who lacked the prejudices of the liberal school, in the opinion of which all those laws, all those instruments of order, or rather of disorder—all those laws, We say, and all those ordinances were so many fetishes and, after the manner of fetishes, were as intangible and as venerable as they were ugly and ill-proportioned'; and he extolled the Concordat, which 'is certainly among the best that have so far been devised; and it is with profound satisfaction that We express the belief that through it We have given back God to Italy and Italy to God'.

In every quarter of the Catholic world the refrain was taken up, and Mussolini was hailed as the man who had restored not only social order but religious and moral values. In this respect his position corresponded exactly to that in which Louis Napoleon found himself at the end of 1849.

But now what hidden spring, what recrudescence of his violently anti-clerical boyhood and youth, what memory of his father and his kinsfolk, of the region from which he derived his very name prompted him to make such bitter speeches, to utter words that seemed to constitute his defence against an anti-clericalism which had become inarticulate, which had seemed now to be a thing of the past?

In a speech in the Chamber on May 13th he declared:

'In the State, the Church is not sovereign, nor is it even free. . . .' The Christian religion 'originated in Palestine, but it became Catholic in Rome. If it had remained in Palestine, it would in all probability have become one of the countless sects that flourished in that torrid environment, as, for example, those of the Essenes and the Therapeutae; and in all probability it would have died out, leaving not a trace of itself behind. . . . We have not revived the temporal power of the Popes, we have buried it.' (Thus the official text; but the newspapers of May 14th included another sentence, one that, as so often in the Duce's speeches, contained an echo of his youthful reading: 'We have left them with as much territory as would suffice for them to bury its corpse.') 'Another régime, a régime different from our own, a liberal-democratic régime, a régime of the kind that we despise, might deem it expedient to disclaim responsibility for the upbringing of the younger generation. Not so Fascism. In this matter we are inflexible. Education must be *our* liability. These children must be brought up in our religious faith, but we must complete their upbringing, we must give these young men a sense of manhood, of power, of conquest. Above all, we must imbue them with our faith, and fire them with our hopes. . . . The Régime is vigilant, and nothing escapes it. Let no one think that the most insignificant rag circulating in the most remote parish does not at some time come beneath the eye of Mussolini. We shall not permit the resurrection of parties or organizations which we have destroyed for ever. Let all remember that when the Fascist régime engages in a battle it fights on to the end and leaves behind it a desert. . . . The Fascist State

R

categorically reaffirms its ethical character. It is Catholic, but it is Fascist—indeed, it is exclusively, essentially Fascist. Catholicism sets the seal upon it, and we say so openly; but let no man seek, on some philosophical or metaphysical pretext, to change the cards that we have laid on the table.'

Above all, the concept of Christianity—a Palestinian sect, a Hebraic idea which Rome had purified and elevated to the status of a universal force—was a very old concept, which Fascism had taken up anew and reinvigorated and which had exercised the minds of authoritative doctrinarians of the régime.

This part of the Duce's speech elicited an immediate retort from the Pope. In the course of an audience accorded to the students of Mondragone College he declared, obviously in answer to Mussolini:

'We for Our part shall never accept the thesis that for the State to accomplish its task in the sphere of education it is necessary, fitting, or expedient that it should breed a race of conquerors, that it should imbue its youth with an appetite for conquest. That which was done in a single State might be done throughout the world. And if all States were to imbue their youth with an appetite for conquest, what would happen? Such a policy would make not for universal peace, but rather for a universal conflagration.'

Moreover, on May 30th Pius XI addressed to Cardinal Gasparri a chirograph in which he deplored the Duce's

'harsh, cruel, drastic words' and in particular his 'heretical, and worse than heretical, comments on the very essence of Christianity and Catholicism. Efforts have been made to repair the damage; but they do not seem to us to have been successful. To distinguish (as is seemingly the intention) between historical affirmations and doctrinal affirmations would be in keeping with the most pernicious and abominable modernism';

and he claimed for the first beginnings of the Church and of the apostolic mission the quality of universality. He also deplored the fact that the speaker had evoked the Risorgimento and its legislation without criticizing the latter, asserting, indeed, that the events and laws of that period had 'paved the way for the recent rapprochement—as if it could seriously be claimed that oppression and war contain the seeds of justice and reconciliation'. In the Concordat, wrote the Pontiff, two completely sovereign States had composed their differences; and

> 'it is scarcely necessary to add that the objective dignity of the ends determines no less objectively and necessarily the absolute primacy of the Church. . . . It is not for the Catholic body in Italy to submit to the authority of the State, even under the most favourable conditions. It is rather for the Supreme Pontiff, the paramount and sovereign Authority of the Church, to determine what, in his opinion, can and should be done for the greater glory of God and for the greater good of the souls of men.'

And the chirograph went on to insist that, even though other religions were 'permitted' or 'admitted' or 'tolerated', only the Catholic religion was officially recognized by the State—

> 'with all the logical and juridical consequences that flow from such a situation in the field of constitutive law, notably as regards propaganda. . . . A more difficult question is posed by these persistent references to 'undiminished freedom of conscience' and to 'full freedom of discussion'. It is unthinkable that the speaker should have meant by this latter term *absolute* freedom of discussion, including, that is, those forms of discussion which may easily deceive listeners whose understanding does not match their good faith, and which may easily become disguised forms of a propaganda no less easily capable of causing injury to the religion of the State, and hence to the State itself—namely, to what is most sacred in the tradition of the Italian people and most essential to its unity. It seems to Us even more unthinkable that he should have meant to give an unqualified guarantee of *absolute freedom of conscience*. This would imply that the creature is not subject to the Creator, this would legitimize any orientation, or rather any deformation, of the conscience, however criminal and socially disastrous. If he means that conscience is not subject to the authority of the State, if he is merely acknowledging, as Catholics everywhere acknowledge, that in matters of conscience the Church and the Church alone is competent, in virtue of her divine mandate, then he is acknowledging by implication that in a Catholic

State freedom of conscience and of discussion must be interpreted and exercised in accordance with Catholic law and doctrine. And logical necessity leaves him no choice but to acknowledge also that full and absolute authority in the field of education belongs not to the State, but to the Church.

'*A Catholic State*, he says, and repeats, *but equally a Fascist State*. We accept this without any special difficulty, indeed willingly, since it undoubtedly means that the Fascist State, both in the realm of ideas and doctrines and in the realm of action, will admit nothing that does not accord with Catholic doctrine and practice; for otherwise the State would not and could not be Catholic.'

The chirograph ended with a series of *prises de position* regarding the interpretation of the Lateran Pacts. It was not true, declared the Pope, that the Concordat had reserved to the State the right to veto ecclesiastical appointments. It was not true that ecclesiastical organizations had to apply to the State for legal recognition. It was not true that legally no one could compel a Catholic to be married by a priest, because the Church not only could but did do so. It was not true that Article 5 of the Concordat, relating to priests who abandoned their vows or incurred the censure of the Church, did not apply retrospectively. In particular, the idea that the Treaty and the Concordat could be separated, that the one could remain effective while the other lapsed, was inadmissible.

The Pope's reply had been most skilful.

At the same time, the general tone of the chirograph had revealed him in the guise of the old and dignified grandfather who, with a slightly disdainful air of superiority and compassion, seizes upon and denounces, one by one, the extravagances of speech and conduct of his grandson. Moreover, Mussolini's statement had given him an opportunity to reiterate in vigorous language the most radical historical affirmations of the Church's pre-eminence, to define the Holy See's interpretation of certain passages in the Concordat, and above all to enunciate his thesis on the indissolubility of the Treaty and the Concordat. But for Mussolini's speeches the Pontiff would have had no justification for repeating those affirmations. Had the Duce remained silent it might have seemed provocative to stress the primacy of the Church, to emphasize the rights which that primacy gave her over the State, to repudiate, or at any rate to qualify, the notion of freedom of conscience and discussion. But now it was the Pontiff who had been provoked; and after Mussolini's speeches many who in the absence of such provocation would have been moved to protest accepted his words without question.

The reply was skilful also because it did not reopen any old wounds. The Pontiff knew the men with whom he had to deal. He knew that the Fascists—great and small, leaders and rank and file, men of culture and ignorant officials—would never feel impelled to join issue with the Church on the subject of freedom of discussion or of the treatment to be accorded to minor religious sects, on historical problems, on abstract questions or questions of principle. To their way of thinking the only vital points concerned the absorption of the workers into the trade unions and the enrolment of children and adolescents in the youth organizations. Now, on the first point the pontifical chirograph said nothing to which they could take exception. On the second, it contained a categorical reaffirmation of the Church's right to assume responsibility for education, of the dominant role that it must fill in this field; but it contained no threat to seduce Catholic youth from the régime's para-military organizations, to prohibit their enlistment in the *balilli* or in the *avanguardisti* or in the Fascist equivalent of the 'Brownies'. And it was these organizations, not the State school as opposed to the Church school, not the philosophical curricula based on idealistic texts or on texts conforming to the scholastic tradition, that were closest to the heart of the Fascist Party.

The pontifical chirograph was received calmly; it did not provoke any significant reactions.

So that the ratification of the Pacts should have a more solemn character it was deferred until after the election of a new Chamber.

Those who preferred to shut their eyes to reality, and continued to think in terms of the *paese legale* and the old constitutionalism, could even maintain that the Government had conformed scrupulously to the constitutional tradition by appealing to the country, by summoning the people to the polls so that they might elect the Chamber that would have to ratify the Pacts.

But for four years political parties in Italy had been a thing of the past. The elections of the spring of 1929, like those of the spring of 1934, were a travesty: in nearly every constituency the voting was open. The two ballot-papers, 'for' and 'against', were everywhere identifiable. Everything was faked—even, probably, the few tens of thousands of hostile votes which were intended to prove the spontaneity of the avalanche of 'ayes'. It is likely that in a free referendum the Pacts would have been approved just the same, because the values of liberalism were now obsolete, as the two sure reference-points, the periods 1919–21 and 1945–47, clearly demonstrate. But the elections of 1929 in themselves proved nothing.

There was no doubt of any kind that the Pacts would be triumphantly vindicated in both Chambers; and it would naturally be the Duce who would decide what form the debate should take, and which points should be emphasized.

The whole proceeding was to be conducted at lightning speed. It was necessary to show that the age of parliamentary government, of the 'paper warfare', as the Fascists called it, of interminable oratory, was past and gone, that everything was now attuned to a march rhythm. In the interests of speed the Chamber was to debate and approve simultaneously the Pacts—consisting of three parts, namely Treaty, financial convention and Concordat—which could only be approved or rejected *en bloc*; the marriage law, which impinged upon the rights of the family at their most sensitive points, those which every legislator had always approached with the utmost circumspection; and the law relating to ecclesiastical organizations and to the departments of State responsible for Church affairs, which also contained features on which legal experts would have been able to argue at length. But it did not matter: the Chamber's function was not to debate, but to acclaim.

In 1929 Hitler was still an insignificant figure; the forces of Anti-Europe, Anti-Enlightenment and Anti-Risorgimento were still in the embryo stage. Eight years later the principal occupation of orators was to consist in deriding liberalism and in demonstrating that the Pacts had sounded its death-knell; but in 1929 Fascism preferred, by one of those countless falsifications of history to which parties are never averse, to point to the Pacts as the consummation of the policy of the Risorgimento. There would even be the ceremony of the olive-branch laid on the tomb of

Cavour at Sàntena. A few years later Mussolini would not deign to be compared with anyone but Caesar or Augustus. But in 1929 the evocation of the name of the Piedmontese statesman did not provoke official displeasure, inasmuch as it carried the implication that Mussolini had succeeded where Cavour had failed.

The Chamber of Deputies was on the whole vastly inferior, in moral calibre, in political experience and in the administrative flair of its individual members, to the Chambers of Giolitti's day; but it still included, particularly among the jurists, a significant nucleus of men of solid worth. Had the Government been willing to allow serious discussion of the marriage law and the law relating to ecclesiastical organizations, the speeches of the legal experts might well have produced a debate not inferior in quality to those which had taken place at the time of the introduction of the civil marriage bill. But any possibility of serious discussion was excluded from the outset.

For its deliberations on the bill sanctioning the Pacts, on the marriage bill, and on the bill relating to ecclesiastical organizations the Chamber was allowed two days, May the 10th and 11th. Mussolini was to speak on the 13th, Rocco, the Minister, and Solmi, the relator, on the 14th, and then the vote would be taken.

In this way there was foisted upon the country the most chaotic and anomalous marriage law that could possibly be imagined, embracing a system of preliminary formalities which everyone would be free to observe or to disregard without needing to worry about the consequences, together with a clause on the subject of late registrations whose purpose no jurist would ever succeed in comprehending, and another clause, providing for the total annulment of paternal authority at the whim of any parish priest, which was enough to make any Catholic Minister of 1814 turn in his grave: for the 'system', though no one had realized the fact, amounted to this—that if a girl of fourteen ran away from home, so long as she could find a parish priest willing to marry her she would become completely independent of the authority of her father, who would be left with nothing but the responsibility for her maintenance. But juridical questions were no longer of any interest. Who could afford to bother his head with such trivialities?

The deputies—jurists and men of learning as well as all the rest—had but one function, and that was to applaud. Who among them would have dared gainsay the Duce when, speaking of the State boundaries of the Vatican City, he declared that 'it would be rather absurd if the front of a building were fixed as the boundary of a State', or if, on taking a stroll within the precincts of the Vatican, he had been confronted with the palace wall nearly everywhere he went? And who would have dared to point out to him that his citation of Article 3 of the Bavarian Concordat as a justification of Article 5 of the Italian, which made a pariah of the priest who abandoned his vows or incurred the censure of the Church, had been singularly inept, since the Article 3 in question merely laid down that lecturers in theological faculties and religious instructors would be replaced should their bishop pronounce them unsuitable for grave reasons connected with their teaching or their moral conduct, and not only did not prejudice their status as citizens, but explicitly guaranteed their rights as State employees? So, too, when Mussolini shortly afterwards published his speeches under the imprint of the *Libreria del Littorio*, supplementing them with texts of comparative law, who would have dared to point out to him that the man who had assembled those texts was a dilettante, because he had not perceived that he was confusing two different matrimonial systems: that which left the regulation of marriage entirely in the hands of the Church, and the system based on the Austrian code, which limited the Church's role to the actual solemnization, while assigning to the State the task of formulating the substantive law and settling all controversial questions?

Naturally, the main emphasis in the speeches was laid on the Treaty, which represented the concrete achievement of the Government, the Concordat being thrust into the background. Historical memories, many of them second-hand, were quoted *ad infinitum*. Every speaker had his dig at the anti-Fascists. One deputy declared: 'The Vatican on the one hand and Fascism on the other utter a warning to these various categories of mental defectives—a warning which may seem rhetorical, but which in this case is not really so: "Woe to you whose cheeks are not touched by the palpitating wings of history in the making; woe to you who are not enveloped by the ideal flame of unfolding destiny!" ' Another declaimed: 'To all those blind, cowardly, wretched men who continue to prate about the so-called egoistical and tyrannical violence of a Fascism that perverts men's consciences, spreads oppression, and disturbs the peace of the nations we repeat that, while on the one hand the Pact has raised the Cross of Christ on its lawful Throne still higher above the World, it has also made it possible for the Imperial Eagles of the new Italy to spread their wings'; and the same speaker also referred to the 'toothless Cassandras of a defunct liberalism'. Another deputy, an old Catholic who had been among the first to desert from the Popular Party when it assumed an attitude of resistance to Fascism, spoke contemptuously of those 'who accepted the Reconciliation under protest', branding them as 'anonymous blackmailers of the most despicable kind' whose names he could not bring himself to utter because 'by naming in this place Italians who are no longer Italians I should be insulting both myself and you'.

Ercole, a historian who shortly afterwards became Minister of Education, disparaged the Cavour formula, the concept of separatism and the Law of Guarantees, but went on to assert that it was 'in the belief that the freedom and unity of the Country are not ends in themselves, but the instruments of a mission of secular leadership which it is the destiny of Italy to accomplish in the world, that Fascism, unitarian and anti-democratic, identifies and associates itself with the thought of the federalist Gioberti and the democrat Mazzini'.

Cantalupo, a former nationalist whose philosophy had inspired him with a profound sympathy for that French conservatism of which the foremost exponent was Paul Bourget, found that the way to the reconciliation had been prepared by the anti-modernism of Pius X. 'Modernism did not originate in Italy. It was one of those extremely potent foreign poisons which often penetrate into Italy, and which at a certain point encounter resistance in the form of the good sense and the native character of the Italian people. . . . Modernism was nothing but a form of subversion, one of the means which subversive elements devise to destroy all that has been built up in the past at the cost of immense effort—to destroy it, moreover, without creating anything in its place.' But Italy, through Fascism, had rid herself of this foreign poison; she had rid herself 'of materialism, rationalism, atheism and all the other "isms" that used to pass for sciences or philosophical systems . . . of that way of thought which was not ours, which did not spring from Italian culture, but was borrowed from a democratic culture not our own, and which is losing its hold even in the country of its origin.' Another old Catholic declared: 'They have taught me to look with mistrust at the human products of 1789, at men such as Leo XIII and Georges Sorel. Fascism, with its straight, sharp sword, has administered the *coup de grâce* to the *ideology of* 1789—an ideology which represented a foreign intrusion into our political life and our juridical thought.'

One of the country's most distinguished advocates and university professors, de Marsico, felt that the Concordat also had struck a crippling blow at individualism and democracy. It 'proclaims that the rights of the individual are gradually yielding place to the rights of the mass (whether State or people is here irrelevant), that the concept of individual rights is being superseded by the concept of national missions. It proclaims, in short, the ineluctable necessity of an international organization that shall be not only juridical, but ethical and religious. The religious problem no longer presents itself to States as an adjunct or as an integral part of the legislative problem, but imposes itself on their attention as one of the fundamental problems of human life, one that can no longer be thrust into the background or disguised. An essential aspect, this, of the democratic defeat.' So there emerges, if only in vague outline, the image of the ancient State, with its national gods, an essential element of its constitution, whom no man can repudiate without failing in his duty as a citizen.

Another speaker emphasized that the Concordat had only been made possible by the Fascist revolution. The State which Fascism had established was a 'religious State, openly religious and Catholic, no longer non-confessional, still less atheistic'; but 'it is also a State that invests its secular might and authority with an absolute character, with a mystical power of expansion, with the mark of a transcendental mission'. And he concluded by posing the alternative of Rome or Moscow, of a world only Fascist or only Bolshevist. Those who had defended the West against Asia in remote times would defend it again, should the need arise. The old Roman Empire had preserved it in the past, 'the new Roman Empire will save it in the future. . . . To-day there stands at the Duce's side the figure of Alighieri, who, in fulfilment of his inspired prophecy, sees the signs of the Eagle and the Cross at last preparing a new life for Italy and for Humanity.'

As a spectacle, the debate in the Chamber had been a trium-

phant success. Among the speakers were representatives of every
shade of opinion: nationalists, *squadristi*, old Catholics, a representative of the younger generation of the Garibaldi family,
historians, jurists, idealist philosophers. Everything was perfect.

Would things go off equally well in the Senate? The régime
had been in power for less than seven years; the Senate still
consisted for the most part of men nominated by Giolitti, by
Orlando, by the liberal Governments. The outcome, of course,
was not in doubt. But it seemed likely that the debate would
produce some heated arguments.

The chairman and relator of the central committee of the
Senate was Paolo Boselli, now aged ninety-one. A veteran socialist,
one of Crispi's ministers from 1889 to 1891 and between 1893 and
1896, a minister again under King Umberto and King Victor
Emmanuel III, he had seen his political career crowned in 1916–
17 by his appointment as leader of the National Coalition Government. After the March on Rome he had quickly been converted
to Fascism. His report would have represented a masterly carica-
ture of the old-fashioned breathless style of rhetoric but for the
fact that it was written in all seriousness. 'The God Who guides
the Nations,' he thundered, 'marked the propitious hour, and that
hour came to an Italy purged and uplifted by the Heroic War: an
Italy which the revivifying genius of the Duce, far-seeing in
thought and action, restored to that sense of reality which fortifies
the peoples: an Italy in which He opened the way to the historic
event, and in which the Lictorial Fasces, uniting the Nation in
social peace, intensifying its patriotic fervour, inspire, stimulate
and strengthen the Italian resolve to meet the challenge of the
new age. The Supreme Pontiff perceived in his heart the desire
of his people, and in his lofty imagination saw that it was consistent with the aspirations of the Universal Church. . . . The
Peace of the Lateran causes the twin Suns which Dante so
prophetically descried to shine on our land. And Rome to-day is
incomparably more beautiful than the Rome which the Venusian
bard declared to be without an equal in all the world.'

A nationalist senator took issue with the Pope on his address to
the students of Mondragone College, in which he had proclaimed
the rights of the Church in regard to the education of the young.
The gist of his speech was as follows: In no country in the world
had the State entrusted the education of its youth to the Church.

'What would happen if in Italy alone the education of the young were directed exclusively to the conquest of the Kingdom of Heaven, what time all other nations are equipping themselves both mentally and militarily for physical conquest, for the acquisition of the material things of this earth?'

The attention of all was riveted on Vittorio Scialoja when he rose to speak. Scialoja was one of the most notable figures in the intellectual life of Europe—an eminent Romanist, an illustrious teacher of at least two generations, for several years Italy's representative at the League of Nations. He was the son of Antonio Scialoja, the Neapolitan exile who had been a minister during the reign of Victor Emmanuel II; his name recalled the finest traditions of the Risorgimento, the Turin of the *émigration*, which was his birthplace, and also the Ricasoli Ministry and the laws relating to the confiscation of ecclesiastical property. He had filled the office of Keeper of the Seals, and had been Minister without Portfolio in the Government of national unity in 1916–17. He had been a member of the Rome Communal Council in the days of the popular coalition, during the mayoralty of Nathan. He had thrown in his lot with the Fascists, to the sorrow of his anti-Fascist admirers. But the attitude which this lean, refined septuagenarian adopted towards Mussolini and Fascism was strangely reminiscent of that of the great aristocrats—Talleyrand, for example—who had rallied to the support of the First Consul and the Empire. He regarded Mussolini, and spoke of him and the Fascist hierarchs, in the same way as a French duke who had accepted an embassy from the First Consul would have regarded and spoken of him and the generals who surrounded him, in 1802–03. Caustic to a degree, a great coiner of *bons mots* and inventor of charades, neither the King nor the Duce nor the institutions of the régime escaped the lash of his tongue. It is hard to say why he was not numbered among the opposition, this famous teacher, this supreme advocate, this completely disinterested *grand seigneur*, who could hope to obtain from the régime nothing that life had not already given and who in fact accepted from it nothing of any value. Because he had misgivings? So that, by collaborating with the party, he might insure himself against the consequences of possible errors? So that he might effect, as effect he did, the rescue of a few men or minor institutions? No one can tell.

The speaker immediately before Scialoja had been the old champion of political Catholicism, of Catholic organizations, of what was now called Catholic Action, Filippo Crispolti, who had seen fit to remind the Chamber that he was 'a man who belongs to a family (and I remain absolutely loyal to it) in which, on the evening of September 20th, 1870, tears were shed'.

Vittorio Scialoja began: 'You have just been listening to an old and very dear friend and opponent of mine, Filippo Crispolti. At the end of his speech Senator Crispolti declared to you, with the sincerity that has always characterized his words, that September 20th—the ever-memorable September 20th of 1870—was for him and his family a day of mourning. One might add that for many others it was the same. But in *my* home it was a day of exultation.' The official transcript, which records that Crispolti's speech provoked 'lively comments', indicates that Scialoja's words were greeted with 'enthusiastic and prolonged applause'. It was the last tremulous whimper of the liberal conscience of the Assembly.

Scialoja did not cast any stones at liberalism. He defended the Law of Guarantees. He ridiculed the criticism that it was a one-sided law—as if in 1871 any other settlement would have been possible. 'The political instinct of those who sponsored and voted in favour of the Law of Guarantees was astonishing. They responded to the negative attitude of the Pontiff with deeds. "See", they said, "we are giving you what you have never demanded. We are offering you a dignity superior to that of any other man: the dignity of a spiritual Sovereign. We promise you security; we shall exercise no control over your ministry. This is the essence of the Law of 1871. But the Pope would not recognize that Law. Nevertheless, we have kept our promise faithfully to this day". He would associate himself with the ratification, because the Pacts had to be ratified *en bloc*; but he knew that the Concordat had its good and its less good parts, and that what mattered most was the manner of its application. Of the part relating to marriage he preferred not to speak.

The Greek scholar Gerolamo Vitelli elicited from the Head of the Government an assurance that higher education would retain its independent character. He had asked to speak so that he might reaffirm the merits of the Law of Guarantees, but Scialoja had forestalled him.

The only hostile speech came from Benedetto Croce. The

celebrated philosopher did not object to the reconciliation or to the Treaty, but he maintained that in subscribing to the Concordat the State was abandoning completely a tradition which had lasted for centuries. 'Once again there will be agonizing and futile conflicts of opinion about unalterable facts; there will be a renewal of pressures and threats and fears, and the souls of men will be poisoned by those pressures, threats and fears.' There were those who thought that the Concordat 'is a stroke of political genius, to be judged not in terms of ingenuous ethical ideals but in terms of politics—in the light of the well-worn saying that Paris is well worth a mass'. But 'alongside, or facing, those who consider that Paris is well worth a mass are others to whom freedom of choice as to whether or not they hear a mass is worth infinitely more than Paris, because it is a matter of conscience. It would be a sad thing for human society, for human history, if men with such a different outlook had been lacking in the past, or were lacking to-day!'

Despite its moderation, and the fact that it contained no personal attacks, this single hostile speech[1] angered Mussolini, who the following day made a violent and ill-mannered attack on Croce. 'Besides the column-dodgers of war,' he declared, 'there are the column-dodgers of history, who, being unable for various reasons, and perhaps not least because of their creative impotence, to shape events, in other words to make history before writing it, get their revenge later by belittling the political achievements of others, often without objectivity and sometimes without shame.' (And the Duce's words were to have repercussions: students and professors of Turin University, called together by a meek and mild Franciscan professor named Umberto Cosmo, who had the courage of a man with a crystal-clear conscience, drafted a letter to Croce in which they declared: 'No, you are not a column-dodger of history. . . .'; and the letter was intercepted, and there were judicial inquiries and prison-sentences. . . .)

The passage of the bill followed by a majority of 317 votes to six. Those who voted in favour of the Pacts included a number of

---

[1] For a record of the sitting see B. Croce, *Quando l'italia era tagliata in due* (*Quaderni della Critica*, March, 1947, No. 7, p. 103): 'A senatorial rabble who had collected in some corner of the Chamber and a journalistic rabble in the Press gallery kept interrupting me with unseemly abuse. I let them vent their spleen, and went on repeating what I had to say until I won the battle, and they resigned themselves to letting me continue without disturbing me further.'

old radicals, anti-clericals and members of popular coalitions, as well as several men who had been accused in the past of free-masonry. They included Francesco Scaduto, who, as professor of canon law in the Universities of Naples and Rome, had upheld the jurisdictionalist tradition (in 1913 he had engaged in a polemic with Francesco Ruffini in which he denied that there could be full religious liberty in a State unless the same juridical treatment were accorded to all religious confessions, while two years later he had written articles urging that the Law of Guarantees be suspended for the duration of the war). They included all the Jewish senators present. They included all the judges and university professors, among whom was a certain professor of medicine who fifteen years before had been spoken of as an *avant-coureur* of free-masonry in the universities. They included even Galimberti, who in his time had been sacrificed through the Gentiloni Pact to the vengeance of Giolitti. They included some princes of the blood, who had come to the Palazzo Madama specially to support the bill, thus breaking a tradition extending back to 1848 whereby princes were members of the Senate by right of birth, but did not participate in its work. Only six senators voted against the Pacts: the journalist Alberto Bergamini, for so many years editor of the *Giornale d'Italia*, who had been guilty of extreme pro-Fascism between 1919 and 1923, when his paper had repeatedly asserted that a distinction must always be made between the violence of those who were traitors to their country and that of the defenders of the victory, but who after 1925 had become a resolute anti-Fascist, and only opposed the bill because of his hatred of the régime (seventeen years later, in fact, he was to defend the inclusion of the Lateran Pacts in the Constitution of the Republic); Benedetto Croce, Francesco Ruffini and Luigi Albertini, the three men who continued to represent all that was best in the liberal tradition, who kept alive a faith in the values affirmed by Cavour and Minghetti, and who embodied in their persons what little remained of the homelier traditions of the Risorgimento; the old Marchese Emanuele Paternò, who had sat in the Senate for nearly forty years; and Tito Sinibaldi. (In the secret ballot the number of hostile votes was to rise to ten against ratification of the Pacts and to 17 against the marriage bill.)

It had been felt that the introduction and discussion of a bill dealing with permitted religions before the Pacts had passed into law would have been disrespectful to the Holy See. But the bill in question was tabled in the Chamber on April 30th by the Keeper of the Seals, Rocco.

It was relatively liberal in tone. 'While reserving, as is just,' ran the report, 'a special juridical position for the Catholic Religion, which is the Religion of the State, it is essential to permit, in accordance with the principle of freedom of conscience, which no modern State could repudiate, the free exercise of all those religions whose doctrines or whose rites do not constitute a threat to public order or to public morality.' But it was added that, even if the phrase 'permitted religions', which had been included in the legal code for the past fifty years, continued to be used, it 'does not, from the juridical viewpoint, differ substantially in meaning from the phrase "tolerated religions" embodied in the Statute, although it is rightly less provocative'.

In Article 5 of the bill was reproduced the formula of the Law of Guarantees ('Discussion of religious matters is subject to no restrictions'), and in Article 4 that of the old law of 1848 ('Religious nonconformity does not constitute a barrier to the enjoyment of civil and political rights, nor does it affect the eligibility of candidates for civil and military posts'). A clause was introduced whereby the appointment of ministers of permitted religions would have to be approved by the Government. The ministers in question would be allowed to celebrate marriages provided they obtained the necessary authority, which would be granted in respect of each individual case by the appropriate civil officer; but such marriages would be regulated in all respects and for all purposes by the civil laws.

The bill passed without amendment both in the Chamber and in the Senate. But the reports of the Committees were by no means favourable to the permitted religions. That of the Committee of the Chamber declared:

'In the course of your Committee's deliberations reference has been made to cases—of which there have been echoes in the Press and in Parliament—of audacious pseudo-religious propaganda by certain Protestant organizations, whose activities have clearly threatened the unity and solidarity of the spiritual and political forces of the régime. The suspicion has been voiced that after what has happened, sectarianism, which is ever on the watch for opportunities to do injury to Fascism and Catholicism, is using the reaffirmation of religious freedom as a pretext for intensifying, by all the means at its disposal, an insidious and fraudulent campaign of anti-Fascist propaganda. There are some statistical data (drawn from the census of 1911) which emphasize in curious fashion the success achieved in the field of proselytism, through the propagation of ideas and elevated discussions, by certain non-Catholic sects in areas of the Realm not always particularly susceptible to penetration by religions of exotic origin. According to the census of 1911 the Italian cities containing the greatest numbers of Evangelicals or Protestants are Turin (as the principal centre of Waldensianism), 19,558; Bari, 9,178; Milan, 6,863; Rome, 4,624; Caltanissetta, 3,934; and Naples, 3,190. For the single administrative district of Barletta the figure is 7,619, and for that of Terranova (Sicily) 3,675. It cannot be doubted that the authorities concerned will know how to be vigilant.'

And the report of the special Committee of the Senate (of which the chairman and relator was Boselli) stated: 'Criticisms and fears were expressed by members of your Committee with regard to the propaganda which some of the permitted religions seem to be in the habit of disseminating.

'To be sure, as regards the practice of such religions free and unrestricted preaching in church or chapel ranks as legitimate edification and as the main bulwark of a particular faith. Outside, however, it can easily provoke public disorder and can undermine the faith of others, the more so if propaganda is freely disseminated among ignorant and unthinking elements of the population whose lives are darkened by desperate poverty and by secret misery and suffering of the most shameful kind.

'There were among the members of your Committee those who would willingly have introduced into the bill an additional clause designed *to prevent illicit attempts to proselytize orphans of Catholic parentage or distressed, helpless or simple-minded persons*. But it seemed sufficient to bring this recommendation to the notice of the Hon. Minister, who will know how to reconcile the freedom and vitality of the permitted religions with the integrity of the religion of the State and of the Italian family and school, and how to eliminate what is the greatest menace

s

of all—the menace of a propaganda that is alien in its origins, its tone and its aims.

'If it were true that a pernicious propaganda was circulating among military recruits it would be urgently necessary to repress it effectively in order to safeguard the religious unity of our people, which constitutes the basis of our national unity. Not least because of the part it has to play in the spiritual education of Italian youth, the Army is a school whose inviolability must be jealously maintained.

'For the rest, the Government, in permitting the constitution of Corporations, will define their religious and social functions and will devise the machinery for their conduct.'

In the event, the freedom of the permitted religions was limited by special regulations, under which all sects were required to seek authority for the opening of churches and chapels, such authority being granted only where they were found to be essential to the needs of substantial bodies of believers; and it was the judiciary—in particular the Criminal Court of Cassation—and the police that dealt the hardest blows at these religions. Distributors of Protestant Bibles and Evangelicals who assembled in private houses to pray together or to sing hymns were fined or imprisoned. Being a Protestant meant in practice exclusion from political office and from all important posts.[1]

And since there is a logic which governs all the actions of a régime, Fascism was anti-liberal even when it came to prescribing internal rules for individual sects. In organizing the Jewish religion it penalized the reforming elements in the interests of the strictly orthodox: the Jew who did not pay his tribute to the community could not be laid to rest beside his kinsfolk in the family tomb.

But among the members of the permitted sects courage was as rare as it was elsewhere. Their newspapers welcomed the law as the *Magna Charta* of their liberties, while the Union of Jewish Communities struck a gold medal which was presented to Mussolini.

---

[1] When, in the course of the Second World War, Italy annexed the province of Ljubljana, the High Commissioner, Grazioli, issued a decree dated June 24th, 1942, suppressing the Old Catholic Church and prohibiting its members from practising their religion in public.

The Lateran Pacts had been in force for less than two years when the Fascist newspapers launched their offensive—which like all such offensives was characterized by violent incidents—against Catholic Action, accusing it in particular of forming a league of workers opposed to the Fascist trade unions and of offering positions of authority to old members of the Popular Party who had remained uncompromisingly hostile to the revolutionary Government.

The reasons underlying this offensive—which to the man in the street seemed an act of sheer folly—are not easy to determine. There was, perhaps, in the depths of the Fascist mind a nagging consciousness of a continuing opposition to the régime, an awareness that, despite the enslavement of the Press, despite the removal of every vestige of organized resistance, there were considerable areas of the national consciousness that remained hostile and impenetrable. There was the persistent feeling that every campaign initiated by Fascism must be carried to a victorious conclusion, must culminate in the total destruction of the enemy. Perhaps there was the thought, clearly formulated by only a few but vaguely present in the minds of more than one ardent Fascist, that in order to ensure its survival, whatever the subsequent course of events, the régime must first make a clean sweep of every organization hostile and extraneous to itself, so that enemies and indifferents alike would at some time find themselves faced with the dilemma: 'Either Fascism or anarchy and chaos.' The régime's hostility to any confessional organization that was not strictly religious and liturgical, that set before itself aims of a social character, that entrusted key posts to laymen, was inspired by the thought that it might constitute a way of escape from this dilemma.

The salient episode in the offensive against Catholic Action was a speech delivered at Milan in April, 1931, by Giuriati, President of the Chamber. This was accorded the unusual honour of a reply—for in such cases it is difficult for the Pope to reply directly, mentioning the author of an action or of a speech, especially if the author is not Head of a State or Head of a Government—in the chirograph which Pius XI addressed on April 26th, 1931, to Cardinal Schuster, Archbishop of Milan.

This chirograph, besides reaffirming the virtues of Catholic Action and insisting on the protection of which it was assured by the Concordat, reaffirmed the 'peculiar and specific competence and authority' of the Church in the field of education.

'The régime', it declared, 'has the duty not only of respecting the Mandate which God has entrusted to her in that field, but also of facilitating its exercise.' The Church recognized that the régime and the State were totalitarian; but this signified that 'in everything that falls within the competence of the State—a competence determined by the latter's particular functions and aims—all the subjects of the State, all its citizens, must bow to the State and to the régime, acknowledging their sovereignty; hence, a totalitarian quality, which We will call "subjective", may certainly be attributed to the State and to the régime. But one cannot speak in the same context of an "objective" totalitarian quality, in the sense that all the citizens must bow to the State and look to it ... for everything that is or may become necessary for their existence viewed in all its aspects—individual, domestic, spiritual and supernatural alike.'

Nor could difficulties arise from the corporative character of the State, granted 'that the corporative system assumes in practice the form of a special, peaceful organization of the different categories of citizens, subject to varying degrees of intervention by the State, by the law, by the judiciary, in the field of work, production, etc., such intervention being, of course, restricted at all times to the natural and civil sphere'; whereas Catholic Action confined itself to the spiritual and supernatural field, although it had the right to intervene 'in the industrial and social field also, not in order to usurp the functions or to disrupt the work of the trade unions or other such bodies, whose activities are outside its jurisdiction, but in order to safeguard and to promote, always and everywhere, the love of God, the good of men's souls, and the spiritual life, with all its attendant benefits.' Not even the Fascist character of the State need create any difficulties. 'Fascism professes and wishes to be Catholic. Now, in order to be Catholic not only in name but in fact, in order to be truly and devoutly Catholic, and not Catholic falsely so-called ... it is necessary to fulfil one condition only, one that is, however, indispensable and unalterable: it is necessary, in short, to obey the Church and her Head, and to be in sympathy with the Church and her Head.'

In the speech which he delivered on May 31st, on the occasion of his pronouncement *super virtutibus* of the Servant of God Glicerio Landriani, Pius XI deplored the

'tempest of intrusions, appropriations, sequestrations and depredations' which had been unleashed against the youth associations and federations of Catholic Action. These shameful incidents had been 'preceded, with the connivance of the civil authorities, first by a Press campaign compounded of false-hoods, insults and calumnies, then by a campaign, conducted in squares and streets, of insults and improprieties, of acts of violence and oppression, not seldom involving bloodshed and very often committed by large numbers of malefactors against small, always unarmed groups of Our sons, and even of Our daughters.'

And the Pontiff recalled that he had always held out his hand to the Government, that he had always been at pains in his pronouncements to emphasize the good things it had accomplished. Only a fortnight before, the encyclical *Quadragesimo anno* had contained 'a benevolent allusion to the trade-union and corporative institutions of Italy which none can have failed to discern'.

The atmosphere grew more and more heated, and when, on June 29th, 1931, the Pope issued the long encyclical *For Catholic Action* it was rumoured that the Holy See had even reckoned with the possibility that the encyclical would be seized by the civil authorities and had taken all the necessary precautions to ensure that whatever happened it reached the bishops.

The encyclical contained a further protest against the dissolution of the youth and student associations of Catholic Action, the

'severities and acts of violence, involving even physical assaults and bloodshed, and the offensive words, deeds and newspaper articles directed against things and persons, not excluding Ourself. . . . And all this tragic sequence of insults and acts of violence was to be accompanied by such widespread intervention of uniformed party elements, by such a chorus of approbation echoing from one end of Italy to the other, and by such passivity on the part of the Authorities and the police, as inevitably to create the impression of an officially-inspired campaign.' It also protested against the calumnies disseminated by the 'hostile Party Press, which alone is free, and is often virtually ordered to make all kinds of brazen assertions', and embodied 'in a statement, which, it must be said, has no official backing'. This statement referred among other things to the 'black ingratitude' of the clergy towards the party which had been a living guarantee of religious freedom for the whole of Italy. 'The Clergy, the Episcopate and this Holy See itself have never been slow to recognize what has been done during all these years for the benefit and to the advantage of Religion— indeed, they have frequently expressed lively and sincere gratitude because of it.' But all too soon 'systematic attacks' had been launched 'on the most precious and most salutary free-doms of Religion and conscience—for example, the attacks on Catholic Action. . . . But if one wishes to speak of ingratitude, the most glaring instance has been, and remains, that shown towards the Holy See by a party and a régime which, in the judgment of the entire world, derived from their amicable relations with the Holy See, both at home and abroad, an accession of prestige and credit which some in Italy and elsewhere considered inordinate, just as they regarded the favour and the trust evinced on Our side as unduly generous.'

The encyclical took issue with the statement to the extent of denying the political character of Catholic Action, disputing the assertion that its leaders had been prominent figures in the now defunct Popular Party, and contesting the argument that even the activities of the youth and student associations were outside the sphere of religion and Christian charity. Later, it asserted that 'the battle now being fought is not political, but moral and religious—exquisitely moral and religious. . . .' Under cover of a whole series of pretexts, 'what the enemies of religion wished and what they had attempted to do was to seduce from Catholic Action, and so from the Church, the whole of the country's youth'. They had revealed 'the intention—already so largely fulfilled—of monopolizing the young completely, from their earliest childhood until they reached maturity, for the sole and exclusive benefit of a party, of a régime, on the basis of an ideology which declaredly resolves itself into a veritable pagan glorification of the State, wholly at variance no less with the natural rights of the family than with the spiritual rights of the

Church.' In short, they wished to prevent the young from being reconciled with Christ.

Those who presumed to teach the Pope what should 'suffice for the Christian training and education of human souls' could not call themselves Catholics. It was a 'most grave and pernicious error ... to foster the belief that the work accomplished by the Church through the medium of Catholic Action has been superseded or rendered superfluous by religious instruction in the schools and by the Church's ministration to the youth associations of the party and the régime. Both are most certainly necessary: without them the schools and the said associations would become, inevitably and very quickly, by a remorseless logical and psychological process, wholly pagan. They are necessary, then, but they are not enough in themselves': for through them the Church does not deploy 'more than a fraction of her spiritual and supernatural forces, and these in a field and in a milieu not subject to her jurisdiction and concerned with many other aspects of teaching and with completely different activities, subject to the immediate control of authorities who are often largely or entirely hostile and who not seldom exert an adverse influence by their words and their personal example. . . .

'To a Catholic, a political philosophy which makes the young completely and unreservedly subordinate to the State from their earliest childhood until they reach maturity is irreconcilable with Catholic doctrine, and even conflicts with the natural rights of the family. . . .

'Men are Catholics only by baptism and in name . . . if they adopt and carry out a programme that embraces doctrines and principles so contrary to the rights of the Church of Jesus Christ and of human souls, a programme that discounts, combats and persecutes Catholic Action, which is to say all that is universally known to be dearest and most precious to the Church and to her Head. At this point You will ask Us, Venerable Brethren, what thoughts and judgments remain to be expressed, in the light of what precedes, about a form of oath that obliges even boys and girls to execute without question orders which, as We know by observation and direct experience, may entail, in defiance of all truth and justice, the violation of the rights of the Church and of human souls, which formerly were held to be in themselves sacred and inviolable; and to serve with all their strength, even at the cost of bloodshed, the cause of a revolution which seduces its younger elements from the Church and from Jesus Christ and teaches them hatred, violence and irreverence, from which even the person of the Pope is not immune, as recent events have clearly demonstrated.

'When the question is put in such terms there can be, from the Catholic, and even from the purely human, point of view, only one answer; and We, Venerable Brethren, merely confirm the reply that You have already made in Your hearts— namely, that such an oath, as it stands, is not lawful.'

What, then, would all the party members who had taken the oath be expected to do?

'Knowing the manifold difficulties of the present hour, and knowing that many are obliged to join the party and to take the oath of allegiance merely for the sake of their careers, merely to secure their livelihood, We have sought a policy that may serve to restore tranquillity to the consciences of Catholics, while reducing their material problems to a minimum. And it seems to Us that such a policy might be for those who are already members to make individually, before God and their consciences, the reservation: "saving the laws of God and of the Church", or "without prejudice to the fulfilment of the duties of a good Christian", coupled with a firm resolve to express such a reservation openly, should the need arise.

'We would wish, moreover, that Our prayer, the prayer of a Father who desires to safeguard the consciences of so many of his children in Jesus Christ, might move the hearts of those from whom the orders and dispensations in question proceed: in other words, that the same reservation might be introduced into the form of the oath, unless those in authority are willing to do something better, far better, namely, omit the oath, which is *per se* an act of religion, and is surely out of place on the membership card of a political party.'

But even now the hand of conciliation remained outstretched.

'We would add that in all that We have said so far We have not wished to condemn the party and the régime as such. We have sought to indicate and to condemn those features of their programme and actions which We have seen and found to be contrary to Catholic doctrine and practice and therefore irreconcilable with the name and profession of a Catholic. We believe, moreover, that We have at the same time rendered a service to the party itself and to the régime. For what interest, what material purpose can they have in continuing to embody in their programme, in a Catholic country like Italy, ideas, principles and practices that are irreconcilable with the Catholic conscience? In the long run the consciences of peoples, like those of individuals, always revert to type and seek again those paths which for a longer or shorter period they have lost sight of or abandoned.'

And the encyclical ended by expressing the sure hope that God 'will be willing to illuminate men's minds with truth and to bend their wills to good, so that, as the Church of God seeks to usurp from the State nothing that is within the competence of the State, so the State may cease to dispute the Church's responsibility for the Christian training and education of the young, which has been entrusted to her not as the result of any human dispensation but by Divine command, and which, therefore, she always must and always will assert, with an insistence and an intransigence which nothing can curb or weaken, because she owes it not to any human decision or calculation, not to any human ideological system (for such systems vary at different times and in different places), but to an inviolable dispensation of God.'

The dispute had now reached a critical stage. On the one hand, it was clear that the Pope would not give way, that he would not disavow the work of Catholic Action. On the other, there was no disposition on the part of the State to renounce the advantages of the Lateran Pacts and the glory which their conclusion had earned the Duce.

It seems that the difference was finally composed as the result of a meeting between Mussolini and Cardinal Pacelli. The reconciliation took concrete form when it was decided, among other things, to exclude from posts of authority in Catholic Action anyone who had assumed in active political life an attitude hostile to Fascism. (The State, however, did not promise for its part to find a scapegoat; but in fact the fortunes of Giuriati, the man who had compromised himself more than any other, declined sharply from that moment.) And it was sanctioned in the new constitution of Catholic Action, approved by the higher authorities of the Church on December 30th, 1931. By the terms of the constitution Catholic Action was placed under the immediate jurisdiction of the ecclesiastical authorities, its associations were forbidden to fly any flag other than the national one, its members could not be organized in professional groups for the purpose of pursuing trade-union ends, but only for religious, moral or cultural reasons.

'Since the professional groups as such have no trade-union functions, those members of Catholic Action who belong to any of the legally recognized trade-union organizations will help to ensure that the latter conform ever more strictly to the principles of co-operation between the classes and to the social and national aims which in a Catholic country the State seeks to promote.'

A compromise peace, then, with neither victors nor vanquished. A dignified peace, which the Church was able to conclude without misgiving, conscious, as she needed to be, that the formative influence of her schools, associations and clubs was far greater than that of any trade union, local Fascist organization, or 'century' of *balilli*. In reality, the danger threatening the very concept of Christianity, in all its aspects, consisted in that nationalistic *mystique*, in that exaltation of the irrational, in that myth of force, that cloud of neo-paganism which for forty years at least had darkened the Christian sky, and of which Fascism was only one expression.

Fascism, on the other hand, lacked men capable of moulding youthful minds; it lacked teachers, educators, men who could attract the young by setting themselves up before them as ideal models.

There followed the years which opponents of the régime would always remember as the most grievous of the entire Fascist era. They were the years in which Hitler established himself in Germany, the years that saw the humiliation of the Democracies, their terrified submission to the will of the dictators.

During this period the position of the Fascist Government could not have seemed more secure. There were no longer any serious incidents between Church and State, only occasional local clashes, minor in character and devoid of any significance. To militant Catholics the world of pure politics had become a stable world, with which they no longer needed to concern themselves. They had no obvious political problems to contend with; they had only a religious task to fulfil. So it was that men of transparent piety had not the smallest scruple about editing Catholic daily newspapers in which three pages out of four bore the unmistakable imprint of the Ministry of Popular Culture, being filled with the *bourrage des crânes*, with all the obligatory hate-propaganda directed against the Democracies, with eulogies of the warlike spirit and so forth, while the fourth page was devoted to pious reflections and religious gossip. They never suspected for a moment that they were doing anything wrong, and they would never realize why, sixteen years later, a few anti-Fascists with long memories were wont to eye them with suspicion, unable to understand how others failed to discern even the shadow of a dividing line between them and the men of the old Popular Party, the Catholic anti-Fascists who had never yielded an inch.

Even those Catholics who evinced the utmost political orthodoxy, who genuinely believed that what had happened since October 28th, 1922 was all for the best, were very far removed in sentiment from the true-blue Fascists, who worshipped the Duce and had a blind faith in him. A whole mentality was reflected in the episode of Egilberto Martire, who was among the first to turn his back on the Popular Party when the latter began to incur the displeasure of the régime, whose speeches were all politically ultra-orthodox and ultra-deferential, but who was eventually sentenced to *confino* because, in February, 1939, on the death of Pius XI, he let slip in the lobby of the Chamber a jesting remark about what would happen if Mussolini died, a remark which a fanatical Fascist deputy hastened to report to his master.

However, among the Catholic laity and clergy there was no lack of sincere admirers of the Duce, at any rate until he set himself in opposition to the Holy See. So long, in fact, as relations between régime and Church remained amicable, the profound difference in outlook between the Catholic who supported the Government and the true Fascist was obscured. Often, indeed, the sentiments voiced from the pulpit did not differ overmuch from those expressed in the local *Casa del Fascio*; and even cardinals identified themselves in letters and speeches with those who saw the future of the world in terms of the dilemma 'Either Rome or Moscow', where Rome was at once the city of the Pope and that of the Duce.

These were the years in which it seemed that the values of the Risorgimento, the values of liberalism and of democracy, had been discarded for ever.

October 2nd, 1935, saw the outbreak of the Abyssinian War. In a brief statement the *Osservatore Romano* asserted that Catholics could not accept the thesis that the need for living-space justified a war of conquest. But Catholic bishops blessed the departing regiments and their colours, and Catholic newspapers adopted the romantic fiction about the Catholic faith following the Italian flag into new lands. When in due course sanctions were imposed, Catholics and Catholic newspapers were not the least vehement in proclaiming their iniquity. Britain, who had promoted them, was Protestant Britain; the opposition to Italy's plans came from Protestantism, the ally of freemasonry. On the specially-proclaimed 'Day of Faith' priests and Catholic men and women were not the least zealous in collecting gold and silver. In a number of churches some of the *ex-voto* offerings, the oldest and most dilapidated, were handed over to the State. More remarkable was the fact, which the Press was able to record without deviating from the truth, that in all countries the attitude of Catholics, parties and episcopate alike, was favourable to Italy. Support for sanctions, for the adoption of a stern policy, came only from socialists and adherents of Left-Wing coalitions and from masonic lodges. 'Right-thinking' people everywhere were on the side of Italy.

Less than a year later came the Spanish Civil War. It was easy to give it the appearance of a crusade in defence of the ancient Faith and the freedom of the Church against the emissaries of Moscow. This time the clergy had no inhibitions; this time they bestowed their blessings on the legionaries without compunction.

The passing of the racial laws disturbed the fundamental cordiality of the relationship between the régime and the clergy and shook the confidence hitherto reposed by the Catholic masses in Fascism, a confidence which, if not blind or very profound, was genuine enough.

By their very nature the new measures offended a deeply-ingrained sense of civilization, of universality, common to all

Italians without distinction of faith or party. But above all, they were an unmistakable symptom of Italian subservience to Nazi policy. The ingenuous hope, fostered more or less consciously by a number of priests and Catholics of the old school, of a gradual transformation of the political structure of Europe, of the emergence of a type of State not very different from those of the *ancien régime*, with no political parties and with a strong confessional flavour, the hope—already somewhat shaken by the murder of Dollfuss and the overthrow of the Austrian Republic—that Italy, Spain and Portugal were merely a beginning, the model of a future Europe, was now fading. It was, indeed, possible, perhaps even probable, that the old democratic Europe, the old liberal State, had had its day. In that event, however, the type of régime likely to become fashionable on the Continent was not Catholic, but National Socialist. Now, National Socialism was not, perhaps, Enemy No. 1—that title was still reserved for Communism—but it remained Enemy No. 2: it had engulfed Austria—an Austria which from the point of view of political Catholicism had been orthodox, bound to the Holy See by a Concordat refashioned on the Italian model, an Austria infinitely preferable to the Austria of the Habsburgs. National Socialism did not concede as much to the Church as Fascism had done. More ostentatiously than Fascism, it set itself up as a régime-cum-Church, as a universal system, whose universality completely absorbed the functions of the Church proper. Under a National Socialist régime the Church had no hope of being permitted to assume responsibility for matrimonial legislation, of enjoying complete liberty in the sphere of education, of obtaining recognition of the clergy's right to express themselves with absolute freedom in the pulpit, or of maintaining a clergy that was genuinely subordinate to Rome and not rather to the civil authorities. On the other hand, the attitude of the old democratic régimes was well known. In their case, experience had revealed the nature and extent of possible compromises; it had shown how, in the normal way, and apart from brief periods of conflict, the Church was able to discharge virtually the whole of its task. As between these régimes and National Socialism, therefore, the choice, for Italian Catholics and clergy and for the Holy See, was not in doubt.

Nevertheless, rather than being directed specifically at the Government's legislation—and the action of the régime in

depriving mixed marriages of their civil validity certainly conflicted with the interpretation invariably put on the Concordat
by Catholics—the Holy See's protests were limited in the main to
an assertion of the Catholic doctrine that recognizes no ethnical
distinctions and rejects the notion of 'superior' and 'inferior' races.
In fact, no evidence of any official protest to the Government is
to be found either in the acts of the Holy See or elsewhere.

But the tension was rapidly increasing; and it was with a kind
of fearful expectancy that the nation looked forward to a speech
which it was said the Pontiff would deliver on February 11th,
1939, the tenth anniversary of the Concordat. However, at dawn
on February 10th, after a short illness, Pius XI passed away.

Then and subsequently many Catholics were of the opinion
that the Pope's death had deprived them of the spectacle of a
great gesture. Pius XI, like all men, had been moulded by his
environment. Coming from the well-to-do conservative middle
class of the Lombardy of the last decades of the nineteenth century,
he had taken, round about 1898, an unfavourable view of the
socialistic Catholicism of Don Davide Albertario. His conservative
background had certainly influenced his policy. But he had always
been a man of great piety; many stories are told of him which
demonstrate how his profound and vital Christianity transcended
all questions of doctrine, all considerations of expediency, not only
political but disciplinary. Had he lived, it is likely that February
11th, 1939 would have produced the great and edifying spectacle
of a Pope confessing that he had erred, in a matter wholly political
and human, in a factual judgment of men and of a party, and
challenging the earthly powers in the name of the Christian
law.

Nothing of importance occurred to mark the beginning of the
new pontificate, unless one counts the return visit paid by the
Pope to the King and Queen of Italy at the Quirinal on December
28th, 1939, which created an unfavourable impression in Fascist
circles because, not being followed by a visit to the Duce at
Palazzo Venezia—for ceremonial purposes the Vatican always
regarded the Duce as the Prime Minister, not as Head of the
State—it destroyed in the eyes of the people that illusion of
diarchy in virtue of which the honours should have been divided
equally between the Sovereign and the Duce.

However, there was no lack of effort on the part of the Fascists to woo the Vatican, as when, in November, 1941, the title of prince was conferred on the Pontiff's nephews.

With the outbreak of the European War in September, 1939, the desires—and probably the efforts, even though up to now documentary and other proofs are lacking—of the Holy See were directed to keeping Italy outside the conflict. The Vatican's attitude may have been inspired, in this as in the earlier World War, by a natural Christian charity to which the spreading of bloodshed cannot but be repugnant, coupled with an anxiety about the difficulties which Italy's entry into the war would raise for the Holy See; or it may have been determined by the considerations that the neutralization of Italy would have signified the end of her subservience to Nazi policy and a return to the situation of the years before 1938, and that there would even have been a possibility of auspicious future developments if the Catholic countries—Italy, Spain, Portugal and the republics of South America—had banded themselves together and formed a single, independent *bloc*.

Italy's entry into the war evoked the usual reactions from the local ecclesiastical authorities—propitiatory ceremonies, special prayers, pastoral letters—all of which testified to the political loyalty of the clergy. But one no longer sensed the upsurge of genuine enthusiasm which had characterized the similar demonstrations of solidarity five years before, when the troops were leaving for the war in Africa.

There was no point of resemblance between this Second World War and its predecessor of 1914–18. True, the latter also had represented a struggle for political hegemony between the Great Powers. But then the peoples involved had been able to believe that their mode of life, and even the extent of their political liberties, would remain substantially the same whether the victory went to the Central Empires or to the Allies. Now, on the other hand, it was only too clear that the issue lay between two incompatible ways of life, and that the man did not exist who was so remote from politics, so isolated, so cut off from the life of organized society, that he would not feel, even in his own family circle, the impact of the victory which one side or the other must surely win. In the first war a compromise peace had always appeared an objective possibility, and it was only the tenacity of the Allied leaders, the belief in victory to which they continued to cling even in the darkest hours, that had prevented such a peace from being concluded. Then, the Pope's appeals for a cessation of hostilities, his attempts at mediation, had not seemed altogether unreasonable. Indeed, the fact that they had given so much offence to those, both in France and in Italy, who were in favour of continuing the struggle until victory had been achieved was due specifically to the just appreciation which they constantly reflected of the factors operating in 1916–17. These factors might be summed up in a few words as the even balance between the rival forces, the enormous sacrifices which every day of war entailed, and the possibility of a settlement based on the principle of 'neither victors nor vanquished'. In the Second World War it was clear from the very first day that the struggle could only end in the complete victory of one of the two sides. A compromise peace never appeared possible. Either the Nazis would impose their creed as a universal law—had not the armistice of 1940 meant for France the immediate introduction of a totalitarian régime, the enforcement of racial laws, the loss of her political liberties?—or they would be crushed beneath the heel of the conqueror. Consequently, this time there were no attempts at mediation on the part of the Pontiff. Instead, there were speeches and appeals for peace, invocations of the principles of justice, touching reminders of the sufferings of the peoples—for three centuries the civil populations of Europe had not known that war could bear more heavily on them than on the soldiers—appeals to the rulers of the world not to ask too much of victory but to content themselves with a just peace. All this left the Pope's audience rather cold, since all knew well that this was a fight to the death between two completely irreconcilable philosophies of life, each of which was under the necessity of destroying the other in order to ensure its own survival.

All the official pronouncements of the Papacy were characterized by the strictest impartiality. The Holy See never took up and endorsed the accusations of brutality and of breaches of international law which, in this as in the preceding World War, the belligerents hurled at one another with great frequency. Acts of mercy, assistance to prisoners and internees, and attempts to keep families informed of the fate of their loved ones were fairly divided between the two sides.

This time the Holy See was no longer a guest on Italian territory.

Formally at least it was now a State in its own right. But the State in question was completely enclosed by a single quarter of Rome. For this reason it was obliged to participate in those security measures—in particular the black-out—which were essential for the protection of the Italian capital against enemy air attacks.

The existence of this territory served, however, to simplify the position of the representatives of countries at war with Italy who were accredited to the Holy See. Under the terms of the Law of Guarantees the diplomatic representatives of the Central Empires and their allies would have been entitled to remain in Rome in their various embassies and legations; but in 1915 they moved to Switzerland. Similarly, under the terms of the Lateran Treaty the representatives of the Allied Governments could have remained in their official residences on Italian territory. But now too the rule would have been difficult to apply. Accordingly, the diplomatic staffs concerned sought accommodation on the territory of the Holy See. On June 5th, 1944, the British, French, Belgian and Polish representatives emerged from the Vatican and the German Ambassador moved in.

The neutrality of the tiny State was in the main respected—except that aircraft of disputed nationality flew over it on a number of occasions. During the German occupation of Rome the Holy See took somewhat elaborate precautions in order to ensure that no pretext was given for the violation of this neutrality. A careful watch was kept at the gates of the Vatican City to prevent escaped prisoners of war or German deserters from entering. At one time even admission to St. Peter's was made conditional upon the production of evidence of identity. But—I repeat—the State's neutrality was substantially respected.

Somewhat less complete was the respect accorded to those buildings situated in Rome which belonged to the Holy See and which under the terms of the Lateran Pacts enjoyed so-called extra-territorial rights. In effect, these were the buildings most used by Roman prelates (under the indulgent eye of the Holy See, which in fact authorized the practice, while officially ignoring it), for the purpose of sheltering political and Jewish refugees. The most notorious case of a breach of the convention was the search of the Abbey of St. Paul extra Moenia conducted by the Fascist police during the German occupation.

T

The Italian 'Social Republic' established by Mussolini was naturally not recognized by the Holy See (it was not even recognized by Spain), although diplomatic relations with Italy were maintained, until the occupation of Rome by the British and the Americans, through the Counsellor of the Embassy, who had assumed the title of chargé d'affaires.

In northern Italy a number of clashes occurred between the civil and the ecclesiastical authorities; but these never assumed a dramatic form.

Mention may be made of the statement issued on April 20th, 1944, by the Episcopal Conference of the Venetian Region, presided over by the Patriarch, Cardinal Piazza. This deplored 'the activities of the handful of priests, both secular and regular, who, casting aside the restraints of ecclesiastical discipline, take advantage of their priestly status and of the prestige deriving therefrom openly to make propaganda of a purely political nature which, whatever the intention behind it, is incompatible with the exclusive and proper mission of a priest'. It denounced the weekly *Crociata italica*, edited by Don Calcagno, a fervent supporter of one of Fascism's most fanatical exponents, Farinacci, as being tainted with doctrinal errors and inspired by 'a savage and rebellious spirit, neither priestlike nor even Christian'. It also deplored the 'moral and physical violence' of the forced arrests and deportations of individuals, whose fate was frequently unknown.

The statement was attacked by Farinacci's paper. But it did not provoke the Government into taking repressive measures, nor did it give rise to any official protests.

Numerous cases are recorded of bishops who insisted on going in person to offer the consolations of religion to condemned political prisoners. Among these was Mgr. Bortignon, Bishop of Belluno, who, when fifty partisans were about to be hanged, insisted on ascending the scaffold and embracing them one by one, at the same time holding up their executioners to reprobation.

Naturally, the ecclesiastical authorities condemned, as they were bound to do, the murders and outrages perpetrated by groups of patriots. Cardinal Schuster celebrated mass at the funeral of a party official who had been executed by partisans.

No one who contemplates with a dispassionate eye the general picture of relations between the Church and the Fascist Government during the eleven years that elapsed between the conclusion of the Concordat and the spring of 1940 can fail to recognize that they were extremely cordial, and that they were characterized by a spirit of compromise and co-operation.

The Church succeeded above all in ensuring that the laws relating to the Concordat were given the widest possible interpretation, that which corresponded most closely with her desires. Credit for this was due chiefly to the judiciary, which showed itself ever more inclined to favour all the aspirations of the ecclesiastical authorities—thanks in some measure to the personal influence wielded by the first president of the Court of Cassation, Mariano d'Amelio, a man of ardent Catholic faith—but it was also due in part to the Government.

The complex and heterogeneous marriage law became very simple in the interpretation placed upon it by the judiciary. This said in effect: 'What the Church does is well done; the bonds that it recognizes are valid for the State, those which it declares obsolete are obsolete for the State.'

Every foundation, every institution, now qualified for recognition as an ecclesiastical organization, even if by the standards which had prevailed hitherto its aims would have been considered purely secular. The works departments of cathedrals, which the Church had always viewed with disfavour on the ground that they represented an intrusion on the part of the civil authorities, were for the most part abolished. Nearly all the confraternities were recognized to be exclusively or mainly religious in purpose so that they might no longer be subject to the surveillance of the State. As a result of jurisprudential regulations and decisions the exemption of ecclesiastical organizations from payment of taxes became the almost invariable rule. Attempts to disseminate Protestant propaganda were resisted and the persons responsible punished.

All these concessions, which reflected a genuine desire on the Government's part for co-operation, were facilitated by their insignificance as factors in a policy whose sponsors were indifferent to such commonplaces of the nineteenth century as questions of principle, vague affirmations of the sovereign rights of the State, defence of the laity and of the few rights hitherto conceded to it under the constitution of the Church, and so forth. They were facilitated also by that general indifference to problems of ecclesiastical policy to which reference has already been made, and by the fact that, within two generations, experts on ecclesiastical law whose outlook was invariably secular and somewhat anti-clerical, men of the kind who occupied Italian university chairs between 1890 and 1920, had been succeeded by others with manifestly Guelphic sympathies. It would be comforting to be able to say that they were the result of a wholesale conversion of Italian intellectuals to the values of Catholicism, but this was not the case. In fact, they were due to the fundamental indifference with which ecclesiastical law, like politics, was now regarded by all those who were not militant Catholics. Ecclesiastical law was a branch of study with which only Catholics now concerned themselves.

But the Church also obtained even greater concessions in the field of education. Not only were its schools granted equality of status, but it was agreed that they should have their own boards of examiners for children seeking admission to gymnasia and technical colleges, and that such boards should always be composed of sympathetic elements. In the modern State the goodwill of the Administration counts for more than that of the legislator; and this the Church enjoyed almost continuously. I do not believe that an appeal by the Nuncio to a minister ever went unheard. Money was always found by the Treasury to meet ecclesiastical requests. There were even cases of churches being built and provided with sacred fittings out of the funds earmarked for land-reclamation, the Government treating this work as an integral part of the programme, which thus assumed a 'comprehensive' character instead of being limited to drainage and cultivation.

The federal secretaries knew that if they came to Rome they could obtain with comparative ease the head of an intractable prefect, a procurator general, or a financial administrator; but they were advised to be patient with the Bishop, even if he did not always respect their wishes. Only in the inflammable zone adjoining the Jugoslav frontier was an archbishop forced to abandon his see as a result of friction between himself and the party hierarchy.

But the Government gained far more from this co-operation than did the Church—among other things, a sense of legality, almost of divine prescription, such as no Government had ever enjoyed in the past: and that not merely as a Government, but as a régime. It might have seemed of small account that in their processions the boys of Catholic Action walked in threes, in imitation of the Fascist militia, and not in fours, as they had done up to 1922; that they carried their flags with the staffs resting on their stomachs, again in imitation of the Fascists, and not on their shoulders, as had been the custom before the March on Rome; that even the most obscure parish magazines and journals of religious associations showed the year of the régime alongside that of the Christian era; and that Catholics habitually observed all the outward forms of Fascism, beginning with the Roman salute and the conversational use of *voi*, abandoning, because the Duce so willed it, the age-old use of the third person as the polite form of address. These things might have seemed unimportant, but they were not. Thus, only thus, by drawing a veil over the past, by keeping lowered the curtain which divided the Fascist world from all that lay beyond its frontiers, could the Government assert itself as a régime, as *the* régime: not merely as a system of government, but as a philosophy of life; one might well say, as a Church.

Nor was it a matter of indifference that the Houses of the Fasci, the shrines of those who had given their lives for the Fascist revolution, were invariably blessed by the local bishop; that no party initiative which sought to create a new way of life, a new outlook, ever lacked the co-operation of the clergy; that a course on the *mystique* of Fascism could be inaugurated with a speech (albeit of strict religious orthodoxy) by a cardinal.

All this went far beyond the idea inherent in the precept 'Render unto Caesar', far beyond respect for and co-operation with the lawful Government. All this was a sanctification not of the Fascist Government but of the Fascist outlook, the Fascist way of life. The non-Fascist, the anti-Fascist, was approaching a point at which he would have to ask himself whether the parish church was still *his* church; he was now having to go to mass early in the morning if he wished to avoid the sermon, which too often comprised a full-scale attack on all the democratic, masonic Governments which were opposing the providential plans of the Duce.

And, after 1929, one would have been hard put to it to find a bishop's pastoral or sermon, an inaugural speech at a dioscean conference, that did not contain the word, the invocation, the blessing, the epithet appropriate to the Duce. And the epithets chosen became progressively more sonorous, and the person invoked tended more and more to assume the likeness not of a Head of Government, but of the pioneer of a civilization.

But it was above all in the realm of international politics that the alliance with the Church seemed advantageous to the régime.

Simultaneously with the March on Rome, instinctively, without any prompting from above, the sympathies of the majority of Europe's Catholic clergy had gone out to this new régime and to the man who was its personification. Scions of the Bourbon and Habsburg families, die-hard exponents of legitimism in every country, looked with extreme favour on this victorious champion of a dynamic movement which sought to destroy without distinction socialism and freemasonry, liberalism and the memories and values and symbols of the French Revolution, and the last vestiges of encyclopaedism and illuminism. Grand Masters of ancient orders of chivalry reserved to the possessors of sixty-four quarters of nobility begged him to accept their coats of arms.

After the Concordat, as the régime launched its battle-cry 'Rome or Moscow!' and took its stand not only against Communism but also against all forms of socialism, against organized labour, against all the European democracies, these sympathies steadily increased. We have already seen how, during the Abyssinian War, during sanctions, during the Spanish War, the Italian newspapers could truthfully report in their foreign news-columns the efforts which all the Catholic episcopates of Europe were making to boost the Italian Government, and the expressions of support for that Government which Catholic newspapers, sometimes alone in their particular countries, repeatedly published.

Peace yielded its fruits to the Church as well as to the régime.

Was this peace based on a profound mutual trust? Assuredly not.

Among those who filled important posts under the régime there were hardly any sincere Catholics of long standing, hardly any daily communicants, hardly any members or supporters of Catholic Action, of Conferences of St. Vincent de Paul, of religious confraternities or other pious organizations. The high

Fascist official usually had his own marriage and those of his children solemnized in church; he took part in religious processions wearing party uniform; he welcomed the Bishop on the occasion of his pastoral visit or the Papal Legate when he came to preside over a regional council or to crown a sacred image. But he was a stranger to his local ecclesiastical organization; he was not a devout son of the Church. To her truly devout sons, the men of the diocesan organizations and of Catholic Action, he was an outsider: courteous, sometimes even obliging, but an outsider. Not seldom he had been identified in his first youth with the most uncompromising anti-clericalism. Frequently he had trade-union, sometimes even anarchistic antecedents. Often he was a man of modest education. Nearly always he had the air of one whose will is law, one who will accept no negative response to his requests. Even though he knew he could never engage in a struggle to the death with his bishop, clashes between the two were not infrequent. There is no Italian town whose annals do not record one or more such cases.

The Catholic of long standing, the member of a diocesan council or of a Conference of St. Vincent, wore the miniature shield of the Party in his button-hole, yet he was no more than a camp-follower of Fascism. At best he filled the humblest of posts, such as the chairmanship of a small recreational and educational club.

By the same token, bishops and parish priests wished to have in their organizations men whom they trusted implicitly, men who did not repeat at the local party headquarters everything they heard, all the conversations they listened to (conversations which might be critical of the régime, even if only mildly so), and who did not divulge the Church's plans prematurely.

Co-operation, then—but of a highly selective character. Either a man had the confidence of the local party organization and of the federal secretary, or he had the confidence of the local Catholic organization and of the bishop. Any priest who allowed himself to be carried away by his enthusiasm for the régime did not, indeed, run the risk of censure and punishment; but he soon came to realize, however vaguely, that he no longer enjoyed the regard of his bishop.

Can one accuse the clergy of having failed to discharge what was manifestly their duty, namely to draw the attention of the faithful to all that was profoundly anti-Christian in Fascist doctrine and practice?

The question is not an easy one to answer in a monosyllable. It can be admitted straight away that any heretical principle, any proposition contrary to Catholic dogma, historical orthodoxy or ethics that had been so much as hinted at by Fascists or Fascist journals of any standing was immediately refuted by the Papacy or by the most authoritative ecclesiastical reviews or by the *Osservatore Romano* with the energy and precision, the theological and juridical wisdom that distinguish the servants of the Church.

Those who for twenty years listened eagerly to any voice that sought in the face of Fascist excesses to reaffirm the values of Christianity remember perfectly the condemnations of totalitarianism, the assertions of the rights of the individual and the family—as well as, of course, the Church—the replies made to the allegation that the Catholic Church was the heir to the spirit of Imperial Rome far more than to the preaching of the Prophet of Nazareth, and the condemnation of the thesis that the need for living-space constituted a justification of the war of conquest. They remember everything, including the condemnation of the doctrine that it is lawful to equate the attempted crime with the crime itself—a condemnation implicit in the headline of the *Osservatore Romano* announcing the death-sentence passed on the anarchist Schirru, who had been found guilty of 'intending' to kill the Duce.

If one wished to defend the Church against the charge of having given way or kept silent on some point in face of noxious Fascist doctrines one could produce a well-documented case in support of the contention that the rightful doctrine was at all times expounded and upheld.

And yet one would be telling the truth, but not the whole truth; just as one would be telling the truth and not the whole truth if one were to say of a counsel for the defence that he had adduced all the arguments favourable to his thesis, but that he had failed to add a comparison between his current defence and others for which he had been responsible, that he had failed to say whether on the day in question he had been equal or superior or inferior to his normal self.

Fanciful analogies apart, it is not possible to evaluate the Church's defence of Christian doctrine against the assaults of

Fascism without comparing it with the anti-liberal polemics of the preceding generation and with the contemporary campaign against Bolshevism.

All that has been written by Catholic pens in condemnation of Fascism would scarcely fill a small bookshelf. What has been written during the same period in condemnation of Communism would fill a library. It is, however, not the difference in quantity that is striking, but the difference in tone. In Communism everything is condemned—doctrines, methods, actions, individuals. The authors concerned are not even willing to make any distinctions; they will not allow a Catholic to be a Communist even if he explicitly rejects the doctrine of dialectical materialism. When two alternative interpretations are open to them they never choose the more favourable, they never say of a speaker or writer that his words may possibly have outstripped his thought, that his intention may possibly have been good. In Fascism, on the other hand, only certain specific points of doctrine are condemned, never the Movement, never individuals. The critics always try so far as possible to assume that the intention of the writer or speaker was good. No one remembers a Fascist writer ever being asked to recant on his death-bed, not even one of those writers who, especially during the critical period 1929–31, expounded the most heretical opinions—for example, that if Christianity had not spread beyond the borders of Palestine it would never have been more than an oriental form of Bolshevism.

Such an assessment demands some kind of explanation. Does it imply that the ecclesiastical authorities were guilty of excessive prudence? A negative answer is at once suggested by the fact that their attitude did not change even after the collapse of Fascism, even when the reaction against it was at its peak.

Rather should it be borne in mind, as has already been said, that the Church's authoritarian constitution does not render it immune from the effects of a rule that is fundamental to every man-made organism: the rule whereby the topmost strata are subjected to continual pressure from below. When issuing directives to the faithful of a country about the attitude they should adopt towards the Government there established, the Pope and the Episcopate cannot disregard the views and desires of the faithful in question. Now, in Italy the number of genuinely anti-Fascist Catholics who would have welcomed a struggle between the Church and the régime, willingly accepting all its painful consequences, was infinitesimal. As we have said, the most fervent Catholics, those most intimately connected with the organs of Catholic Action, were lukewarm towards Fascism and rather mistrustful of it; but they were not at all anxious to fight it. The great mass of Catholics—those who were such in virtue not only of baptism but also of the frequency with which they partook of the sacraments—were among the orthodox majority who genuinely approved of the régime, who had been sincerely 'Concordat-minded' even before 1929, who desired, in other words, the closest possible co-operation between Church and State. At the two moments when a conflict between Church and State appeared least improbable—in 1931, year of the episode of Catholic Action, and in 1938–39, when the racial laws came into force—dispassionate observers asked themselves in anguish how many Catholics would, in the event of a clash, resist the threats and violence of the Government, refusing to abandon their faith; whether even the clergy would range itself entirely on the side of the Pope against the Government, whether even the Episcopate would not offer the spectacle of a few defections.

Italy lacks, as she has always lacked, Catholic writers who—if not for the masses, at any rate for the cultured Catholic middle class—are at the same time moulders of opinion; Catholic writers who, albeit at a different level, support the ministration of the clergy. Italy possesses no equivalent of François Mauriac or the late Georges Bernanos, or of a philosopher and writer such as Jacques Maritain. But the two or three Italian Catholic writers with a large following never departed from political orthodoxy in their attitude to the régime. The one who achieved the greatest popular success, Papini, went if anything too far in this direction.

The support accorded to Fascism by the mass of the faithful and even of the clergy was largely due, as has been said, to the fact that they had common enemies, to certain concessions, albeit of a superficial character, made by the régime to Catholic sensibilities, and to the favourable response of Catholics to certain of Fascism's declared aims, such as the defence of the family, of property, and of the country.

It may be asked whether there were not those who perceived the profound distortion which Christian values had undergone in the crucible of Fascism. Motherhood is certainly a Christian value: the cult of the Virgin Mother has induced many to transfer their allegiance from Protestantism to Catholicism; it is rooted in the heart of every Catholic. But Christian motherhood is the noblest, the most spiritual type imaginable. The sainted mothers of hagiology urge their sons to suffer martyrdom rather than deny their faith; the Christian sons of degenerate mothers pray for their conversion. Mothers and sons look upwards to the Kingdom of Heaven; the mothers rejoice in the good works of their sons, they bear them and educate them 'for heaven', in other words for the Christian life. The Christian mother bears no relation to the prolific mother, who is extolled by Fascism for the number of sons she has borne, without ever being asked whether they have proved virtuous or otherwise. This exaltation of the prolific mother, with the related news-items in the papers about births of twins and triplets, with the rewards for large families, has nothing in common with the Christian cult of motherhood. But many failed to perceive this. Others, while admitting that the cult of the prolific mother was really the cult of the creator of cannon-fodder, nevertheless told themselves that it might prove effective as a propaganda-weapon against Malthusian practices.

Those open-air masses, those religious parades of unbelievers, those votive offerings by Fascist officials whose immorality and lack of faith were often notorious, aroused no indignation even among sincere believers. He who contemplates the life of the Church from without will never see it in the way believers see it. To them, the importance of example as a stimulus to religious practice is profound. That a régime under which an exaggerated regard for public opinion has caused many to stay away from church in defiance of their natural inclinations should be succeeded by another under which it becomes at times a civic duty for the young to go to church, even if they have no urge to do so, is a great step forward. The believer will be guided not so much by those laws of experimental psychology according to which outward appearances create the emotional tone and habit creates the need, as by his belief in an instinctive human religiosity, in religious practice as a natural activity, as an effect of nature that reveals itself only when the obstacles in its path—of which an exaggerated regard for public opinion is itself an example—have been removed. He will likewise be impelled to accept the idea of a limited *compelle intrare* by his belief in the sacrament, which is efficacious *ex opere operato*. Without doubt, it is sacrilege for anyone who does not believe in the real presence to receive communion; but the doctrine which postulated that a good communion requires a peculiar fervour, a special frame of mind, was a Jansenist doctrine. The fruits of the spirit will not be withheld from him who approaches the Lord's table without meditating on theological questions, without inwardly professing his acceptance of the Church's teaching.

A régime that does not hinder and in some ways encourages the practice of religion could hardly be opposed by the Church, particularly if the Church were afraid that it might be succeeded by another which in this respect pursued a directly contrary policy.

Generally speaking, the Church has made a stand only against régimes that have persecuted her, that have hindered her teaching, that have sought to interpose themselves between her and the Faithful. The fact that régimes have been atheistic or have had a non-Christian vision of the world has not greatly disturbed her, so long as they have neither directly nor indirectly opposed her ministration. It is for the Church, not the State, to define the nature of good and evil, to formulate the laws of morality, to explain the Christian vision of the world. That the State should clothe itself in a mantle of pseudo-Christianity is not a great evil, so long as the Church is not hindered in her task of revealing the essence of true Christianity.

Finally, if, after determining the real nature of the relationship between the Church and the Fascist régime, one wished to justify the conduct of the ecclesiastical authorities, one might well point also to that Christian indifference to political régimes which the Church has displayed throughout her history, to her practice of trying to wring some concession, some act of mercy, from even the worst tyrants—one thinks of the visit paid by St. Antony of Padua to Ezzelino da Romano; and during the Fascist era the ecclesiastical authorities interceded frequently and not without success for the victims of political persecution—to her spirit of peace and prudence, above all to her constant endeavour to avoid giving offence. A would-be apologist for the Church might even assert, not without justification, that, if her attitude during those years embittered and shocked a limited number of Catholics (not, indeed, alienating them from the Faith, but undermining their filial respect for and trust in the Hierarchy), a condemnation of Fascism, a conflict with a régime that protected the family, property, the country and religion, would have shocked a far larger number of people: people whom we for our part may term, a little ironically, 'orthodox thinkers', but whom the priest could only regard as souls entrusted to his care. And he might conclude that the Church, faced with the painful necessity of offending one side or the other, acted wisely in preferring to offend the minority, who were also the more adult in spirit and were better able to weigh the factors involved.

Such might be the defence of our hypothetical apologist: a defence which all are free to accept or to reject as they think fit.

Bibliographical Note.

This period is dealt with in the following works: L. Salvatorelli, *La politica della Santa Sede dopo la guerra* (Milan [1937]); *Pio XI e la sua eredità pontificale* (Turin, 1939); and *Vent'anni fra due guerre* (2nd ed., Rome, 1945); and S. Jacini, *Storia del Partito popolare* (Milan, 1951).

The literature on the subject of the Lateran Pacts (which does not seem to me to include any work of major significance) is listed in three essays by A. Giannini published in the *Rivista internazionale di scienze sociali* (January, 1930, November, 1931, November, 1933), and in R. Giustiniani's *Bibliografia degli Accordi lateranensi*, in *Il diritto ecclesiastico*, 1934, pp. 101–129.

Of the numerous writings on the Lateran Pacts by A. Giannini, the short work *Il cammino della Conciliazione* (Milan, 1946) is particularly noteworthy, among other reasons because it contains some personal reminiscences which are not without importance.

Some hitherto unknown facts, albeit of no very great importance, emerged with the publication of C. A. Biggini's *Storia inedita della Conciliazione* (Milan, 1940). What purports to be the text of the Holy See's original proposals relative both to the Treaty and to the Concordat will be found at the end of M. Missiroli's book, *Date a Cesare* (Rome [1929]). I have no means of determining whether or not this document is genuine. However, I have been unable to trace any official or unofficial denial of its authenticity.

Conspicuous among all the other writings on this period for its general hostility to the Concordat is E. Orrei's *La Conciliazione* (Rome, 1942), which does not confine itself to the subject of the Italian Concordat.

G. Castelli's *Il Vaticano nei tentacoli del fascismo* (Rome, 1946) is apologetical in character.

CHAPTER VII

AFTER FASCISM

ON the conclusion of the Concordat, and later during the various manifestations of cordial co-operation between the Holy See and the régime, anti-Fascists had times without number been heard to exclaim:'What folly! What a compromise of principle! From now on the Holy See must consider itself tied to Fascism and must share its fate. A collapse of Fascism would inevitably be accompanied by a savage outburst of anti-clericalism.' But nothing is more futile than such attempts to anticipate the course of history.

Neither on July 25th, 1943, nor following the establishment of the first coalition Governments at Salerno, neither on the liberation of Rome nor on that of northern Italy, did the predicted outburst of anti-clericalism ever appear probable. Neither Benedetto Croce nor Palmiro Togliatti ever proposed the suspension of the Lateran Pacts or any other measure hostile to the Church. Not only was there a tacit agreement to defer a solution of the problem of relations between Church and State until all the constitutional issues had been settled, but in this matter also there were not even any of those *prises de position* which one noted in connection with other problems of the future Constitution. The question did not seem at all urgent. It was not one of the Italian people's major preoccupations.

In point of fact, the interval of approximately two years between the overthrow of the Fascist régime and the liberation of northern Italy represented the period when friction between the clergy and politically-minded Catholics on the one hand and the extreme Left on the other was reduced to a minimum. It was the only period during which the belief in the minds of Catholics that Communism must always be regarded as the arch enemy appeared to be weakened if not eradicated, shaken if not completely dead. It was the only period during which the possibility seemed to exist of a fairly extensive collaboration between parties based on programmes from which all questions of ecclesiastical policy had been excluded, perhaps for a very long time to come: on programmes which did not raise any questions of principle and which almost represented, not an impossible reconciliation, but a by no means wholly negative armistice, between the champions of *laissez-faire* and the advocates of collectivism. Such an armistice might have taken the form of the nationalization of certain key-industries and the granting of economic freedom to other industries.

In fact, there was a genuine desire on the part of all members of Left-Wing parties not to return to the old errors of anti-clericalism. A potent factor in this change of heart was their sincere gratitude for everything that the clergy had done, all over Italy but especially in Rome, during the period of the German occupation, on behalf of the victims of political persecution—sheltering them, hiding them, providing them with forged papers and food-coupons, and running grave personal risks for their sake. This humane work had been carried on by the secular and regular clergy and by members of the male and female Orders on an almost universal scale. Through this work sincere and intimate bonds of friendship had been forged between ecclesiastics—including prelates of the pontifical Departments of State and rectors of great Roman seminaries—and eminent representatives of the extreme Left. But besides this fortuitous and highly personal aid to conciliation there was another, less positive perhaps, but no less important. I refer to that 'spirit of secularism' on which we have several times had occasion to dwell at length, that overriding preoccupation with economic problems which later prompted the leader of an extreme Left-Wing group to declare that in his view any trade-union question was more important than a great abstract question, such as whether the Lateran Pacts ought to be incorporated in the Constitution.

During these two years I do not think there was a single act of administration, either national or local, to which the ecclesiastical authorities could reasonably have taken exception. The three successive Ministers of Education—drawn respectively from the Action Party, the Liberal Party, and the Democratic Labour Party—were unanimous in refusing to allow Ernesto Buonaiuti to resume the chair of Religious History in the University of Rome, even though his jurist friends demonstrated to them that such an interpretation of Article 5 of the Concordat, the article that debars priests who have renounced their cloth or who have incurred the Church's censure from holding teaching posts or public offices, was less liberal than that placed upon it by Benito Mussolini (who had guaranteed the acquired right of priests who were already professors in 1929). 'The Nuncio has been to see me . . . ,' one of these Ministers used to reply to such representations, signifying thereby that no juridical consideration would have entitled him to settle in a manner contrary to the desires of the Holy See a question in connection with which the Nuncio himself had seen fit to climb the stairs of a Ministry.

The demonstration of gratitude to the Pontiff staged in St. Peter's Square on the morrow of the liberation of Rome had been attended by Socialists and Communists; and perhaps for the first and last time the people of the city had witnessed the spectacle of red flags adorned with the hammer and sickle being waved in a gesture of greeting to the Pope as he stood at his window.

It must, however, be said that all men of Catholic sympathies, even those who later filled high political offices and who revealed the maximum inflexibility on the question of the incorporation of the Lateran Pacts in the Constitution, appeared to everyone who spoke to them during this period to be imbued with a true spirit of moderation, conciliation and goodwill. Their programmes and opinions were genuinely liberal in tone. They sought freedom for the Church, not privilege. No one during this period saw fit to question either the equality of all confessions in everything that concerned their rights in the field of preaching and worship, or the incompatibility with the principles of a liberal State of the above-mentioned article of the Concordat which sought to debar the priest who had renounced his cloth or who had incurred the Church's censure from public employment and from the pro-fession of teaching (and the interpretation placed upon the article by the Prefects emphasized its harshness, making of the priest a pariah, ineligible for any office, even though he might be called to it by the trust and confidence of his fellow-citizens).

How did it happen that this atmosphere of harmony, of true conciliation, was gradually, almost imperceptibly, dispelled?

The most obvious answer (that which historians are wont to give when, thinking of the events of a century before, people ask them why the liberalism of Pius IX, which had given birth to neo-Guelphism, dissolved into nothing) would be that the harmony in question was based on an illusion: that it was both logical and inevitable that the antagonism between Catholics and parties of the extreme Left should reappear in its entirety: that long periods of history cannot be obliterated at a stroke. The Church could not replace in a moment its historical allies, the wealthy classes and that *petite bourgeoisie* of workers and countrymen who were hostile to the parties of the Left not only for economic reasons but even more because they hated change. The latter were attached to their own traditions, to their own way of life, to that pride of caste which in their lives takes the place of the material goods which they lack. With the collapse of the authoritarian régimes, they could not but aspire to assume in full the task of ruling the Italian people, no longer contenting themselves with that with which they had had to be satisfied under Fascism: a series of nominal and juridical privileges which could not disguise the fact that the spiritual leadership of the people no longer rested with the rulers of the ecclesiastical hierarchy.

But these obvious answers, inspired by a historical fatalism and based on a belief in pre-existent forces that impose themselves on the wills of men, always leave the questioner feeling profoundly sceptical.

It can also be argued that the answer lies in the fact that during these two years the nation was in a state of genuine uncertainty with regard to the balance of the opposing forces. The representatives of a heterogeneous collection of parties had assumed power, without having had any opportunity of consulting the people beforehand. Three of these parties were fortified by the knowledge that they enjoyed massive support, of which, however, no one could assess the reliability; and two—the Socialist and the Christian Democratic Parties, in the second of which it was easy to perceive a resurgence of the Popular Party—also had behind them a long tradition. By contrast, the public history of the Italian Communist Party had been brief, inasmuch as its significant activity did not extend back beyond 1919, while after that date its story had been one of suffering, trials, imprisonment by the Fascists, and exile. As for the other three parties, it was very hard to determine the exact size of the forces which they carried with them; all that could be said with certainty was that these did not amount to anything very substantial. But even though one of

U

them, the Action Party, had a new name, all three in essence
represented the old ruling class, the political forces that had
constituted a majority in the Italian Parliament during the First
World War. In point of fact many distinguished survivors of the
old ruling class were distributed among them, although it was the
Action Party that attracted the greatest number of *homines novi*.
Three of these parties—the Communist, the Socialist and the
newly-formed Action Party—had made a particularly significant
contribution to the partisan struggle, just as, with good reason, it
was their men who personified the tradition of active resistance
to Fascism. This resistance had not contented itself with *bons
mots* and with the discerning scepticism that had represented the
answer of so many to orthodox totalitarianism, but it was a
resistance symbolized by the political refugees, by the rows of
defendants in the political trials held before the special court, and
by the volunteers in the international brigades during the Spanish
Civil War. The sufferings under Fascism of those who had
remained outside these three main categories had been only
relative. They had been consigned to oblivion, they had languished
in silence, they had been excluded from all lucrative offices, from
all positions of honour, but they had scarcely ever been subjected
to genuine persecution. The Catholic Party, on the other hand,
represented a framework, an organization that had been preserved
openly in the form of Catholic Action or of philanthropic undertakings. It had been allowed to maintain its own newspapers and
reviews; and although these had been subservient to the régime,
they had not belonged to the party. Nor, for that matter, had the
journalists who worked for them been appointed by the party.
They obeyed the directives of the Ministry of Popular Culture,
the party, the federal secretary and the prefect; they filled three
out of every four pages of their papers with reports of world-
reactions to the Duce's latest speech, with comparisons between
corporative order and democratic anarchy, with eulogies of
autarky and of the grain campaign, with expressions of pity for
the nations that did not enjoy the blessings of Fascist rule; but
they found their true medium of self-expression and self-fulfilment
in the fourth page, the one in which they could write of eucharistic
congresses, of current processes of beatification, of the Pope's
latest speech, of pilgrimages and religious life.

During the Fascist era it had always been said that, if unfore-

seen events had brought about the collapse of the régime, the
only organization that would have survived, seeing that every
political grouping extraneous to the party had been suppressed,
would have been the Church. If Christian Democracy had played
but a small part in the resistance movement, the clergy everywhere had aided fugitives and had not been hostile to the partisans,
while Christian Democrats had served on all the Committees of
Liberation set up during the German occupation.[1]

Now, that state of uncertainty about the true balance of
political forces which prompted all to adopt a cautious and
conciliatory attitude was resolved by the first Communal elections,
which reflected an overwhelming volume of support for the big
parties, and which gave first place to the Christian Democrats.
But the resumption of political activity, even within the limited
field of the Communal councils and, later, of the Consulta, was
still more revealing. In addition to the adherents of the various
parties the voters in these first elections included people with no
political affiliations. These latter were not, strictly speaking,
Fascists, even though they held Fascism's domestic policy in high
regard and deplored only its foreign policy, its colonial adventures,
its warlike fervour and its vast military expenditure. But they were
appalled by the new vitality which was beginning to manifest
itself in Italy: a pre-eminently Southern phenomenon, this, a
resurgence of the pre-1860 South, of the aristocratic families who
had handed on the control of public affairs from father to son and
were suspicious of new ideas, of political ideas that might stimulate
the imagination of scoundrels and cause them no longer to respect
the property of the aristocracy. The attitude of these a-political
elements represented a perpetuation of the notion that a 'man of
honour' does not concern himself with politics. Also among the
voters were whole-hearted Fascists who regretted nothing, who
felt no remorse and were convinced that theirs had been a just
cause. These men had not yet organized themselves into parties
of their own (only the a-political elements were here and there
beginning to declare themselves). Both groups found it natural to
give their votes to candidates of the Christian Democratic Party—

---

[1] The opposition provided during the last years of Fascism by Catholic elements,
drawn largely from the old Popular Party and destined to constitute the main bulwark
of the Christian Democratic Party, and the collaboration of these elements with other
clandestine organizations, are referred to in L. Lombardo Radice's *Fascismo e anti-
comunismo* (2nd ed., Turin, 1947).

the party which in their eyes represented the least of several evils, the party that might be expected to do the minimum of harm, and possibly some good, if certain of the trends which it embodied should prevail. So it was that on the one hand the Christian Democratic Party came to have an exaggerated idea of its own strength, while on the other hand it became aware that the situation which had continued for forty years prior to the First World War, when the very many Catholics who were opposed to the *non expedit* had voted for the conservatives, was now repeating itself in reverse, inasmuch as it was now the forces of the Right who were lavishing their votes on the Christian Democrats. In this way it began to understand that by shifting its centre of gravity to the Right, by setting itself up as the champion not only of the wealthy classes, but of all those provincial and rural elements who detested the innovations of Socialism and Communism, and finally by assuming, as a sop to the Fascists, the task of propounding a policy of 'pacification' that would enable those adherents of Fascism who had not occupied key posts, and who had not compromised themselves irredeemably, to maintain their positions, it could enormously increase its electoral following.

In consenting to such a compromise the party was undoubtedly evading one of its possible tasks, the task which many anti-Fascist intellectuals had assigned to it: that of proving to the Italian people, by its Christian teaching and guidance, that the division between Fascists and anti-Fascists and in particular, after September 8th, 1943, between the supporters of the Committees of National Liberation and those of the Salò Republic, had been not merely a political division; that it was not even comparable to one of those deep political cleavages (one thinks of the conflict between Monarchists and Republicans in the France of 1871, or of that between Bourbonists and Unitarians in the Kingdom of Naples in 1860) which embrace a whole world of values transcending the true and proper sphere of politics; but that the party's rightful domain was that of ethics and religion. For the conflict beween Fascists and anti-Fascists was essentially a conflict between all those basic principles of Christian teaching which regulate the lives of the great social units and what the Fathers of the Church called the teaching of paganism or of Satan. The former may be summed up thus: universality of the human family, with its law of a universal love which transcends all personal antagonisms; refusal to attribute the character of supreme values to the nation and State, whose welfare must always take second place to that of humanity as a whole; the supreme dignity of the individual, who can never become a means or an instrument, and hence the irreducibility of religion and the Church (which are intended to rule men's souls, to influence men at the highest level of their being) to *instrumenta regni*. These principles are incompatible with the notions of a State possessing its own gods, and hence of religion as *instrumentum regni*; with the conception of the Country as the highest good, as the arbiter of moral values, so that good and evil, the lawful and the unlawful, are not such in themselves, are to be judged not by any objective criterion but solely by whether the action under consideration is or is not useful to the Country; and also with the exaltation of war, regarded as something beautiful in itself, with the exaltation of violence, with contempt for the man of peace who turns the other cheek, for the humble man, who in the Gospel is the elect of God.

Those anti-Fascists who are not such merely because Mussolini failed to win the war have always pointed, Christians and non-Christians alike, to this conflict between two scales of moral values, between two gospels. Yet it was clear that the Christian Democrats would be able to speak to the masses in this language with greater moral authority than any rival party, that they would be able to put them on their guard against any revival of Fascism—not least for the practical reason that they addressed themselves pre-eminently to those working-class elements who were not definitely committed to a political ideology irreconcilable with Fascism, and in whose case what appeared most possible, most to be feared, should the appropriate circumstances arise, was a crisis similar to that which in 1922–24 had pushed the majority of the Popular Party's supporters first towards the Catholic Centre and then into the arms of pro-clerical Fascism.

This task could well have been assumed by those Left-Wing elements of the Christian Democratic Party, who had formerly belonged to that section of the Popular Party which had found it quite impossible to come to terms with Fascism. It was, nevertheless, a task of extreme delicacy. Indeed, its fulfilment would have involved criticism of the policy which had found expression in the Concordat. It would have meant passing judgment by implication on all those senior members of the hierarchy who had sung the praises of Fascism. It would have entailed the expulsion from key posts in the party, if not from the party itself, of those Catholics who had seriously compromised themselves under the old régime. It would have meant the loss of votes; it would have ruled out the possibility of alliances with Fascist elements, disguised or otherwise; it would have imposed a moral obligation on the ecclesiastical authorities to put the Faithful on their guard against those Fascists who, resurrecting their old scales of values intact, were now introducing into them a forced, intensified note of clericalism (still based on the hypothesis that religion was to be regarded as *instrumentum regni*, that it was to be looked upon not as a means of perfecting the soul of man but purely as a kind of social and political cement). Finally, since it would have necessitated looking at the past, the present and the future, it would have cast doubts upon the principle that Communism constituted Enemy Number One.

The policy of letting bygones be bygones, of regarding Fascism and anti-Fascism, the Committees of National Liberation and the Salò Republic, as purely political antitheses, to which ethics and religion were extraneous, was thus a matter of expediency. But there are other considerations too.

In terms of hardship, misery and popular disturbances the immediate post-war period in Italy was far less sombre than the prophets had anticipated in 1944. The country displayed a resilience, a capacity for recovery, such as the most optimistic would not have dared to hope for. So far as popular disturbances and crimes with a political or social motif were concerned, no one who recalled what had happened in 1799 or 1815, particularly in the South, or in 1849 in Piedmont, or in 1860–61 in the whole of southern Italy, and who contrasted the small-scale military events of those days with the frightful conflict of 1940–45, could have failed to perceive how comforting was the picture which Italy on the whole presented, and how it demonstrated the high degree of civilization, the humanity, the Christianity of her people. All this would have been apparent to the man of culture; but to the man in the street, who does not draw comparisons, to whom all that belongs to the present is momentous, while the events of the past are unknown or forgotten or insignificant, the evils of the post-war period seemed colossal, the crimes with a political or social motif perpetrated in certain regions of Italy presented a fearsome picture. In the face of these immediate evils the guilt of those who had willed the war was already fading from the ordinary man's consciousness. It was therefore not to be wondered at if that which had happened in Italy and elsewhere after other lost wars—let the reader think of the Bordeaux Assembly of 1871—now repeated itself in the peninsula in the form of a movement which could not be described as conservative, since it was not identified with any concrete idea of conservation, and which did not envisage any programme of reconstruction, but was inspired solely by fear of the forces of the extreme Left.

It was understandable that the Christian Democrats should be tempted to take advantage of the fresh winds that were sweeping the country.

In this matter there was a considerable divergence between the attitude of the Christian Democrats of Lombardy, Piedmont, Liguria, Emilia and Tuscany, who were more deeply committed to supporting the demands of the masses of workers and peasants, and that of the Christian Democrats in other regions of Italy. But the great strength of this party lies in the fact that it is more secure than any other against the danger of internal schisms.

Finally, there have even been those who have explained the gradual dissipation of the atmosphere of harmony as being due to a reminder which the party allegedly received from the ecclesiastical authorities of the fact that it was expected to adopt a policy in line with that of all the forces of Catholicism throughout the world, which could not remain neutral in a struggle, even in a bloodless struggle, against Communism.

In point of fact, all attempts to build bridges between Communism and Catholicism were condemned by the Church. The Catholic Communists who had appeared in Rome and in a few other cities—Catholics by upbringing and tradition and in practice who had accepted the basic principles of Communism while rejecting its doctrine of dialectical materialism—sought to escape censure by transforming themselves into a Christian Left, but even this was forbidden them. When Guido Miglioli, a one-time Popular deputy who in later years had sought asylum in Russia, endeavoured in a book entitled *Con Roma e con Mosca* to demonstrate the compatibility of Catholicism and Communism, he found himself expelled from the ranks both of the Christian Democratic Party and of Catholic Action.

In practice the clergy had already anticipated—for example, by refusing to allow Communists to fill the office of godfather at baptisms or of witnesses at weddings—the regulations which the Holy Office subsequently formulated in the decree of July 1st, 1949, which forbade Catholics to join the Communist Party or to read or work for its newspapers, and branded as apostates, liable to excommunication under a special dispensation of the Holy See, any of the faithful who professed the doctrine of materialistic Communism, and in particular any who defended it or sought to propagate it. These regulations appear not only justified but necessary in cases where the Communist is truly wedded to the Communist conception of life, which is a universalistic conception, totally incompatible with a belief in the transcendency, or indeed with an acceptance of the basic tenets, of Christianity. But they should be considered against the background of life in Italy, where in the elections of 1953 fully a third of the population voted for the Communist Party or for one or other of the parties allied to it, and where at the same time only 1·1 per cent of marriages are celebrated in a non-religious form, while the percentage of unbaptized infants is perhaps even lower. There is, in other words, an enormous body of Communist supporters, including even members of the party, who regard their support (whether justifiably or not is unimportant: but often the Italian proletariat feel that they have no alternative, in other words that there is no other party which they can rely upon to fight wholeheartedly on their behalf) as a weapon in what is an economic rather than a political struggle, and who would be unwilling to see this means of redress taken from them, while at the same time wishing to remain attached, even in the smallest details, to the religious faith of their fathers.

On June 2nd, 1946, voting took place for the election of deputies to the Constituent Assembly and a referendum was held to determine the constitutional form of the new democratic State.

Despite all the efforts of the Dynasty to win its support the Holy See remained neutral. The Christian Democrats were predominantly Republican in the north of Italy, Monarchist in the centre and south of the country. But at the party congress the Republicans had clearly been in the majority. The final speeches delivered by De Gasperi had been essentially Monarchist in tone:

the President of the Council had urged Catholics not to regard it as by any means certain that if the nation voted for a Republic it would be a Christian Republic. It is probable that the votes of the clergy, both secular and regular, were cast mainly for the Monarchy. The neutrality of the ecclesiastical authorities was, however, genuine enough, in the sense that no suggestion was ever made to Catholics that it was their sacred duty to vote for the Monarchy. And Prime Minister De Gasperi, who had been not unjustly criticized for having failed in his last speeches before the elections to reflect the desire for a Republic expressed by the majority of his party, was nevertheless firm in his insistence that the Dynasty should respect the referendum, even though he knew that he was exposing himself to the wrath, and perhaps also to the vengeance, of the Monarchists.

In the elections for the Constituent Assembly the final results were as follows: Christian Democrats, 8,080,664 votes, 207 seats; Socialists, 4,758,129 votes, 115 seats; Communists, 4,356,686 votes, 104 seats; Liberals, 1,560,638 votes, 41 seats; Qualunquisti, 1,211,956 votes, 30 seats; Republicans, 1,003,007 votes, 23 seats.

The positions taken up by the various parties in the Constituent Assembly did not reveal any fundamentally irreconcilable differences of outlook. The men of culture who at the beginning of this new era of Italian life cast their minds back to that wonderful programme (duly carried into effect) which had been expounded nearly a hundred years before by Gioberti in *Il Rinnovamento*, felt their hearts sink within them. Now it was the 'municipalists'—the men of little hardihood, the men with a desire to preserve as much as possible of the past, the opponents of change—who were asserting themselves: almost without opposition, it might be said, for where were the men of 'ample vision', such as Cavour had seemed to the dying Gioberti? All the parties (even the Communist Party, in the eyes of those able to discern the true intentions behind mere words—intentions that are related to practical possibilities and not to the writing of post-dated cheques payable to the next generation) revealed a moderation, a fear of innovation, a dread of upsetting the existing order, a respect for personal susceptibilities, for every manifestation of local pride, for all the most trivial interests, a desire to postpone, to defer, which in the end caused the people to view the proposed new juridical and economic order with a certain scepticism. I think that more than one observer, contemplating the Government and the Constituent Assembly of 1946, justly considered that a favourable opportunity was being missed of rooting out a number of baneful parasitic growths, of creating something new, of instilling into the people a passionate interest in politics, of imbuing them with an austere regard for the public weal and with a consciousness of the sacrifices which it demanded of them. There are moments in the history of a nation when the need is for calm discussion, goodwill and compliance. But there are others that call for the mood symbolized by the Burning Bush.

This mood was certainly lacking now. The Assembly may have had its lively, boisterous sessions, but they were like certain sessions of the carefree legislatures of 1904 and 1909. Their atmosphere could never have been described as torrid.

The question of the relations between Church and State presented itself in the following terms. All were substantially agreed—further evidence, this, of the comparatively small place which problems of ecclesiastical policy occupy in the thoughts of political parties—to the extent of demanding neither the denunciation of the Lateran Pacts nor a new Concordat. The question was simply one of deciding whether the new Constitution should conform to the pattern of other constitutions, which have never sanctified concordats or international treaties by elevating them to the status of constitutional principles, modifiable only after the completion of the most solemn formalities; or, on the other hand, whether the Pacts should be included in the Constitution as an integral part of it; whether their scope should at any rate be limited by some declaration of principle—it would, for example, have been possible to modify Article 5 by stipulating that no citizen could suffer any loss of civil rights as the result of sanctions imposed by a religious authority—or whether even those articles of the Concordat should be deliberately left intact which had most offended those spirits in whom a spark of the old liberalism still survived.

A widespread impression existed that the Christian Democratic Party was pledged to fulfil a mandate entrusted to it by the Holy See. Its Parliamentary representatives, who in 1945 had seemed to be men of understanding, anxious not to 'raise the Alps higher yet'—that is, not to make of the Italian Constitution something fundamentally different from the constitutions of the majority of other European countries, even those of long-standing Catholic traditions—even these appeared in the winter and spring of 1947 to have been transformed into sentries with whom it was not possible to reason. The arguments[1] which they propounded in the debate on what subsequently became Article 7 of the Constitution —the article which gave legal sanction to the Lateran Pacts and which could only be repealed after the completion of the formalities which had to precede any modification of the Constitution —all seemed more appropriate to men with a task to fulfil than to men with a deeply-rooted conviction.

The flames of controversy were fanned by all the resurgent Fascist newspapers, by all the weeklies for which nothing had changed, for which everything was as it had been in 1937, everything had to be started afresh and the ground lost recovered, and for which, therefore, the slogan 'Rome or Moscow!' had a truer ring than ever. These journals were even more pugnacious than the Christian Democrats; they were ready to breathe fire and fury on any who sought to alter a single word of the Concordat.

The Liberal Party appeared henceforth a resolutely, rigidly conservative party, which justified its name by its attachment to economic liberalism. It too was bent on 'pacification', in other words on maintaining all Fascists not of the very first rank in their old positions and on consigning to oblivion even what had happened during the period of Mussolini's Social Republic of 1944–45. A vague, much attenuated, very conciliatory attachment to the tradition of the party in the matter of ecclesiastical policy could be discerned only in the circles closest to Benedetto Croce, which concerned themselves above all with educational problems, with the defence of the secular school.

Already the Christian Democrats had prevailed in the Committee set up to draft the new Constitution, securing agreement to their demand that the Lateran Pacts should be accorded constitutional status. In the general debate on the draft Constitution (March 4th–21st, 1947) this question of the sanctification of the Lateran Pacts did not occupy the prominent position which a similar question would have done in a debate held forty years

---

[1] E.g., *Quieta non movere*. Several of the other formulas proposed were acceptable in themselves, but they ceased to be accepted once the question of the constitutional sanctification of the Lateran Pacts had come up for discussion. Thereafter the Pacts were looked upon as a kind of rightful possession which had to be guarded at all costs because the preliminary Committee had approved the sanctification in question.

before, but it occupied what might be termed a place of honour. The discussion was by no means heated, its tone was always courteous. Those who opposed the sanctification of the Pacts showed the utmost regard for the Church and for religious values, while advocates of the measure spoke of respect for religious freedom and for minority cults.

The opposition speakers included deputies from various parties, most of them being either Socialists or Communists.

Perhaps the most realistic speech was that made by Mancini, who declared that the age-old question of the relations between Church and State was no longer relevant. 'Church and State, secular State, confessional State—the expressions no longer strike a chord. They are distinctions drawn by our grandfathers in the days of the Subalpine Parliament. They are no longer relevant for the simple reason that every one of us intends to stick firmly and resolutely to his own point of view, avoiding risks, steering clear of danger, and taking care not to come into conflict with those whose attitude is diametrically opposed to his own. . . . Very different are the questions which keep the workers in a permanent state of tension and vigilance. The bush is no longer burning. Its flames are quenched. . . . How can you expect the people to concern themselves with the Lateran Pacts, of which they know nothing? . . . Do you seriously imagine that at a moment when their lives are darkened by so many sorrows and privations, by hunger and unemployment, the people of Italy can interest themselves in the Lateran Pacts?'

Pietro Nenni, leader of the Socialist group, asserted that the Socialists were more interested than the Christian Democrats in the preservation of religious peace.

'When one desires, as we desire, to put agrarian reform and industrial reform on the agenda of the nation one does not go looking for butterflies under the Arch of Titus, one does not go about reviving the old bugbear of anti-clericalism. Perhaps such a diversion might interest bourgeois folk who had been brought up on Voltaire, who wanted to consign the most urgent social questions to oblivion. . . . I take the liberty of repeating what I said at the Socialist Congress in Florence: "None of us has any thought of reviving the argument about the Lateran Treaty or of promoting the unilateral denunciation of the Concordat. . . ." The smallest of agrarian reforms is of greater interest to me and to my colleagues than the revision of the Concordat. . . .'

Calamandrei, a renowned professor of law in the University of Florence, protested against the plan to incorporate the Lateran Pacts surreptitiously in the Constitution and thus to ensure the confessional character of the State. He declared that it was impossible to reconcile religious freedom and freedom of conscience with the confessional State, of which the Lateran Pacts were the symbol, and he denied that those Pacts had truly set the seal on religious peace. This prevailed in Italy

'because it is in men's minds, in their hearts; because it pervades the consciousness of the people; . . . because at a certain moment, in the years of most ruthless oppression, we perceived that the sole newspaper which still spoke with the voice of freedom—with the voice of *our* freedom, of the freedom that is common to all free men—was the *Osservatore Romano*; because we know from experience that he who bought the *Osservatore Romano* was exposing himself to the risk of being beaten up; because a free voice found expression under Fascism in the *Acta diurna* of our friend Gonella; because, when the racial persecutions began, the Church ranged itself against the persecutors and took the part of the oppressed; because, when the Germans were seeking out our sons in order to torture them and shoot them, they, whatever their party, found sanctuary . . . in presbyteries and monasteries. . . . It was from these things, and not from the Lateran Pacts, that religious peace sprang. . . . This brotherhood of the humble, the suffering and the oppressed in face of the oppressors . . . has given back to Italy religious peace. That peace is in men's hearts. Do not destroy it, do not endanger it, my Christian Democratic friends, by paltry, pettifogging subterfuges.'

Another speaker proposed the formula:

'The State recognizes the independence of the Catholic Church, with which it will continue to regulate its relations by means of concordats': adding that, if it was desired to mention the Lateran Pacts by name, the following clause should be appended: 'always provided that they do not contravene the existing Constitution.'

Also against the inclusion of the Pacts in the Constitution was the solitary Christian Socialist deputy, Gerardo Bruni, who declared:

'There is a religiosity and, I would say, a Christianity that may be described as apocryphal—I mean the religiosity and the Christianity of clerical, paternalistic, absolute Governments, which allow the grossest social injustices to prevail without lifting a finger. And there is a religiosity and a Christianity that may be termed authentic—namely, the religiosity and the Christianity that consist in a constant and heroic striving to promote an unfettered search for truth and justice.' Only 'the principle of unity and spiritual pluralism in the political field ... can ensure to every citizen full respect for his freedom of conscience, worship and religion. Obviously one cannot speak of these freedoms where there is a *State religion* or where there is a *State atheism*. ... When we find ourselves on political ground, the only way to save the essence of Christianity, which is charity and the spirit of brotherhood, is not by introducing laws which accord exemptions and privileges to the national Church, but by establishing a régime based on equality. ... Naturally, Italian society, being composed for the most part of Catholics, will preserve its spiritual physiognomy. It will do so, however, not in virtue of a confessional jurisdiction exercised by the State, but in virtue of the number and spirit of the majority of its members and of the democratic forms which permit and fully guarantee the public expression of religious sentiments. ... Since neither the principles of logic nor those of honesty can justify the inclusion, *sic et simpliciter*, of this Pact in the text of the Constitution, such an inclusion would assume the significance of a mere act of violence, inspired, if you like, by a distrust of this democratic régime.'

The inclusion of the Lateran Pacts in the Constitution was passionately advocated by the Christian Democratic deputies.

All made the point that the Pacts had not been born of Fascism, but that they represented the culmination of a gradual historical process and the fulfilment of the anguished longings of the Italian people. And nearly all hinted that the Church would consent to some modification of those clauses of the Pacts which seemed most to offend the liberal conscience.

In a speech rich in biblical echoes and ending with an invocation of

'the blessing of God and of the Immaculate Virgin' Giorgio La Pira—for many years a well-beloved Mayor of Florence, who as such shocked conservatives and liberals by his fight against unemployment and by the manner in which he supported strikes and the occupation of factories by the workers when it was a question of preventing their closure, and who to-day represents his city in Parliament, having obtained a larger majority than any other candidate in the last elections in May, 1958—declared that 'if Man has an innate religious propensity, and if this innate propensity necessarily expresses itself in the form of religious communities, then there can be no such thing as a secular State. The only possible State is one that respects this religious propensity and the particular religious organizations through which it expresses itself. . . . There can be no such thing as a secular State, there can be no such thing as an agnostic State. In the same way, we should not create a confessional State, that is to say, a State in which civil, political and economic rights derive from a certain profession of faith. Instead, we should build a State that will respect this innate religious propensity of the individual and of the community and will adapt the whole of its juridical and social structure to it.'

Since no objections had been raised with regard to the substance of the Lateran Pacts, why refuse to incorporate them in the Constitution and so 'strike a blow at the Catholic Church? There are political proprieties and historical proprieties that must be observed'; and he spoke of the good which the Church could do for Italy in the political as well as in the spiritual field.

Another speaker was Stefano Jacini, who in 1926 had been declared ineligible to sit in Parliament together with the other deputies who had boycotted the Chamber as a protest against the murder of their colleague Matteotti, and who shortly afterwards had published an impartial *Storia del partito popolare* which did not minimize the culpability of Pius XI.

'There never has been, there is not now, and presumably there never will be any possibility of an absolute separation of the two powers in a country of Western Europe, least of all in

Italy,' said Jacini. 'There never has been and there never will be such a possibility for the reason that the European conscience is one and indivisible. You can fight the Church. You can persecute the Church. You can come to terms with the Church. But you cannot ignore the Church. That is a fact which nineteen centuries of history confirm. . . . It is in no spirit of intolerance or clericalism that we demand the conservation of the Lateran Pacts. We demand it on historical grounds, because we consider that it affords the only possible guarantee of religious peace.'

Iginio Giordani declared: 'We desire that this [religious] peace should be in no way disturbed. And in order that it may not be disturbed, we consider that it is better to leave well alone, or—as the Tupini put it—*quieta non movere*. This structure, product of the Italian people's political genius, is so delicate, its creation has cost us so many tears and so much labour, that to touch it now, to compromise it now, would be in truth to spoil a masterpiece, to whose advantage no man can say. . . . Why do we wish to incorporate the Lateran Pacts in the Constitution? Because we wish to affirm their immense and unique importance as international Pacts. This is not just an ordinary Treaty between two Powers, between two sovereigns. When one makes a Treaty with the President of an American Republic, it is of little interest to the people to know what manner of man the Head of that Republic is and what sort of a life he leads. They may not even know his name. . . . But *this* Treaty has been concluded with a Sovereign who is the spiritual Head of our Church, the corner-stone of our religion, and the source of all the authority and prestige of our faith. . . . [If we were now to exclude these Pacts] from the draft of the Constitution we should lessen their effect, and that is only the first consequence that would flow from our action. . . . If we were now to reject the proposal that has been submitted to us by the Committee it would be said that these Pacts had been robbed of much of their force and that their future was in the balance. . . . It behoves the Italian people to-day *quieta non movere*.'

The Deputy Dossetti delivered what was the most technical of the speeches in favour of the article, maintaining that the Catholic Church was the only religious organism to have evolved a juridical system which could fairly be described as significant and sovereign, and that relations between Church and State could only be regulated by agreements. He derided the dilemma 'secularism *versus* confessionalism' as a historical curiosity. He asserted that true freedom of conscience consisted in 'the realization that certain facts or actions or relationships, though not without importance to the State, are of a highly specialized nature, which differentiates them from everything else that enters into the State's sphere of interest'. Their special position was due to the fact that they originated in 'the most secret and most jealously guarded recesses of the individual mind and conscience. For this reason, the State should admit that it . . . can only regulate them in concert with the spiritual community'. He denied that the adoption of the article in question would mean that the principles of the Lateran Pacts would become principles of the Constitution; but he firmly maintained that no article of the proposed Constitution would derogate from any of the articles of the Pact and, indeed, defended the substance of the article of the Concordat which had given most offence to the opponents of the bill, namely, the one that curtailed the civil rights of the priest who renounced his cloth or who incurred the Church's censure. He also denied that Article 1 of the Treaty implied acceptance of the principle of the confessional State, asserting that it amounted to no more than a recognition of the undoubted fact that the Catholic religion was the religion of the majority of Italians. 'We cannot reject Article 5,' he went on. 'If we were to do so, we should be destroying the soul of our future body politic. If we were to do so, our dream of a political community essentially and not just formally recreated would dissolve into nothing. If we were to do so, we should be founding the new edifice, in this decisive moment—as in that other decisive moment at the outset of our first Risorgimento—on a spiritual conflict, on a mental reservation that might prevent many of us, if not from making our material contribution to the work of reconstruction, at least from devoting to it all our inner resources, that portion of our being of which we are most jealous and by which we set most store.'

But the embodiment of the Lateran Pacts in the Constitution

v

was not defended by the Christian Democrats alone. The measure also had the support of the 'Qualunquisti', whose adherents included all the surviving members of the Fascist Party.

The speakers in this general debate also included the survivors from the pre-Fascist Chamber.

Meuccio Ruini, chairman of the Committee which had drafted the proposed new Constitution, defended the article, seeking to minimize its significance and expressing the hope that the Chamber would hit upon 'a conciliatory formula which, by respecting the fundamental positions of both sides, will avoid the danger of provoking a new religious war, which would be disastrous for our country'.

Francesco Saverio Nitti considered that the French people, and in particular the French clergy and Catholics, had given proof of maturity and wisdom by their acceptance of Article 1 of France's new Constitution, which declared the country to be a Republic, indivisible, secular, democratic and social. (But he subsequently voted in favour of the article.)

V. E. Orlando, who had been Prime Minister at the end of the First World War and during the peace negotiations at Versailles, sought to ascribe the credit for the original conception of the Lateran Pacts to his last Government. (But Cevolotto justly objected to him that in 1919 no one could have envisaged a concordat, least of all the Concordat ultimately concluded.) He declared that he had

'no reservations to make regarding the reference in the draft Constitution to the Lateran Pacts. My misgivings, in fact, are based not on political but on technical considerations, inasmuch as the inclusion of an article repudiating the sovereign right of the State to denounce a treaty would in my view constitute a limitation of sovereignty.... But it is the political factor that weighs most heavily with me.... I earnestly hope ... that a formula may be found which will dispel the technical doubt and permit a favourable vote.'

Benedetto Croce recalled that in 1929 he had been the only man to speak in the Senate against the Lateran Pacts.

'But even then I made it clear that I did not in principle oppose the idea of a reconciliation between Church and State, which had been long desired and frequently sought by our liberal statesmen. My disgust and hostility were directed

specifically against the agreement under discussion, which had
been effected in the name not of a free Italy, but of an enslaved
Italy, by the very man responsible for her enslavement—a man
who, so far from being animated by any spirit of piety or of
peace, had negotiated that agreement merely in order to acquire
new prestige and to reinforce his tyranny. But amid the present
terrible difficulties, amid the agonizing problems that beset the
whole of Italian life, no one, least of all myself, has any thought
of reopening that question. . . . It will be said that the strange
idea of including the Pacts in the Constitution is intended as an
insurance against the future. But when have words like these
ever exerted a restrictive influence on subsequent policy? . . .
If the sanctification of the Pacts, which would be glaringly
illogical and a juridical scandal, would moreover constitute too
flimsy or illusory a bulwark against future eventualities, why
offend that juridical instinct which in Italy has always been so
highly developed and which only Fascism has ventured to
disregard?'

The republican Della Seta, having proposed an alternative
formula, defended it in these terms:

'The State and the individual churches are, each in its own
sphere, independent and sovereign. Relations between the State
and each individual church are regulated by law. As regards
relations between the State and the Catholic Church, it will be
possible to preserve, by the terms of a Concordat, those principles of the Lateran Pacts which do not conflict in letter or in
spirit with the fundamental principles of the Republican Constitution.' Calamandrei and a group of deputies belonging to
the Action Party moved the adoption of this text: 'All religious
confessions are equal before the law. Relations between the
State and the Catholic Church are regulated by the terms of a
Concordat that is compatible with the present Constitution.
Communions other than the Catholic have the right to organize
themselves in accordance with their own statutes. Where these
communions request it, their relations with the State may be
regulated by law on the basis of understandings concluded
between the respective representative bodies.'

Lelio Basso, speaking on behalf of a group of Socialist deputies,
proposed the following amendment, which seemed to him and his

colleagues to satisfy the demands of the Christian Democrats as expressed by Dossetti:

'The Catholic Church is, in its own sphere, free and independent. Relations between the State and the Catholic Church are regulated by the terms of a Concordat.' And he continued: 'Rather than a party vote, which will reopen a religious controversy that for us had ended, and for which the responsibility will not be ours, we would prefer a unanimous vote, a vote which—just as in our memory the name of Don Minzoni is associated with those of Amendola, Gramsci and Matteotti, and the blood shed by the Socialist and Communist partisans is mingled with that shed by the Christian Democratic partisans—will reflect the determination of all Italians to demonstrate on the one hand that Italian democracy has truly outgrown the old shibboleths of anti-clericalism and has opened its eyes to broader horizons, and on the other hand that the Catholic Church has learned from its own experience that religions are defended and strengthened not by legal formulas, not by concessions wrung from dictatorial régimes, but by the maintenance of an atmosphere of freedom and respect for human personality.'

Pietro Nenni expressed himself in somewhat stronger language.

'The Republic which we have founded,' he declared, 'will have a meaning and a significance only if it seeks to preserve, and to surpass, the achievement of the Risorgimento, not if it repudiates that achievement. Its present trend is reactionary rather than progressive, a fact which disturbs us not only as Socialists but also, and above all, as Italians. . . . By humiliating the State you humiliate the Republic and the Nation, which we wish to be strong so that they may be able to fulfil their social and political mission.'

Still others opposed the sanctification of the Lateran Pacts, asserting their right to defend the concept of a secular State without ceasing to be regarded as sincere Catholics. The republican Randolfo Pacciardi observed:

'The Church has not demanded the inclusion of the Lateran Pacts in the Statute of the Republic. . . . Such a demand has never been made on behalf of any State in the world, not even on behalf of so staunchly Catholic a State as Ireland. Why, then, do you seek by force of numbers to impose such an anomaly on the infant Republic of Italy?'

But speeches in favour of the article were made by the Monarchist Bergamini, one of the six senators who in 1929 had voted against the ratification of the Pacts; by Ivanoe Bonomi, another illustrious survivor from that epoch; and by the diplomat Carlo Sforza, who, speaking as one who had spent the years of Fascist tyranny in exile, declared that he felt 'in his heart of hearts' that 'the advantages [to be gained by ratifying the article]—advantages which, I assure the Chamber, will be not merely national but international in character—will far outweight the dangers, which, I am convinced, the future will show to have been wholly illusory.'

A 'Qualunquista' of the extreme Right, Gennaro Patricolo, proposed the following amendment: 'The Catholic Religion is the official religion of the Italian Republic. Relations between the Catholic Church and the State are regulated by the Lateran Concordat.'

The great event of the sitting was, however, the speech of Alcide De Gasperi, who left the seat reserved for the President of the Council to address the Assembly from his place on the benches. The article, he declared, was not designed to

'arrest the course of history', to 'ensure . . . that our relations [with the Holy See] will remain, in all their aspects and for all time, in the state in which they were yesterday or which they entered in 1929. The Constitution ascribes to the Lateran Pacts a fundamental character, but at the same time it declares that they may be modified—modified, moreover, as the result of a simple parliamentary vote, and not under the terms of one of those more solemn and comprehensive guarantees which the Constitution provides for many things, some of them comparatively unimportant. . . . The question at issue is not . . . the fate of one or another of those non-essential provisions of the Concordat which owe their existence to particular historical circumstances, for these can be modified without any revision of the Constitution. . . . Hence, it is not the fate of this or that article which you have criticized or which may become the object of your censure. The question at issue is the fundamental one of whether the Republic is reconciled to the prospect of religious peace which this Concordat offers.'

Basso's amendment would have been acceptable in itself if it had been approved in Committee. But now, after the debate, after judgments had been passed on the Concordat, on the relations between Church and State, it was the duty of the Assembly to approve the article in its original form. The President of the Council spoke with profound respect of the country's religious minorities.

'If necessary,' he said, 'we are ready at the opportune moment to vote with you for the removal from the penal code of any provision that may constitute an affront to the minorities.' The salient passages in his speech were, however, those in which he emphasized that the sanctification of the Concordat would induce the ecclesiastical hierarchy to pledge its material support to the Republic ('Here in Italy our form of government is not so firmly established that we can too lightly disregard such pledges so solemnly given'), whereas an adverse vote would add 'to our woes a further woe, of a kind that cannot strengthen the Republican régime'.

The impression which the Assembly derived from these words was that, if the article were not ratified, the Christian Democrats would support the Monarchists in seeking to submit the entire Constitution to a popular referendum. De Gasperi also appealed to his audience to have regard to the country's international interests.

'We must,' he insisted, 'vote in such a way that we shall gain the sympathy of the free world, that world which I know and declare is watching us. The world that is watching us is anxious that there should be created here a government of free men. The Catholic world at large is anxious that the Italian Republic should establish at the outset peaceful and friendly relations with the Roman Pontiff, who during the war upheld human dignity against tyranny and stretched out his protecting hand over the persecuted of all nations and all faiths.'

Another great speech came from the Communist leader, Palmiro Togliatti. The Communists, he declared, had never had any difficulty in accepting the first part of the article, in which it was affirmed that Church and State were, each in its own sphere, independent and sovereign. They regarded the Lateran Treaty as inviolable; they considered that the Concordat was a bilateral instrument and that it could only be revised bilaterally. They could have wished that, in accordance with the desire expressed by V. E. Orlando, it had been possible to find a compromise formula which would have permitted of a unanimous vote; but such a formula had not been found. In reality the dispute was not between the Christian Democrats and the Left but

'between the Constituent Assembly of Italy and another party, the other contracting and signatory party to the Lateran Pacts. This is the reality, and we must face it squarely. . . . Representatives of all shades of opinion in the Assembly . . . have said that specific amendments to certain provisions of the Pacts, carried out at a specific moment and with due formality, would be desirable and ought to be possible. Here is a unanimous, or an almost unanimous, expression of opinion emanating from the place where the people's representatives transact the nation's business.'

If any but a Christian Democratic Government had been in power it would have represented the authority best equipped to negotiate these amendments with the Holy See. The Government as such had unfortunately failed in its duty. However, the situation was that the Holy See demanded as the price of religious peace the constitutional sanctification of the Lateran Pacts.

'The converse of the term "peace" is "war". It is true that it takes two to make a war and that one of the two sides can always say—as you do, Comrade Nenni—"We do not want war". But it takes only one to *declare* war.'

In view of the Communist Party's heavy political responsibility, due to the fact that 'the majority of the working class allow their course of action to be determined by our party's policy', in view of the fact that 'the working class does not want to see the country torn by religious dissension', in view of the Communists' unwillingness to divide Christian Democratic workers from their Communist and Socialist brothers, the Communists would vote in favour of the article. (Did this speech reflect a Marxist indifference to everything that is unconnected with the class struggle and with economic problems? Or did it reflect the shrewdness of the party man who is actuated above all by the desire to maintain the unity of the General Confederation of Labour? Or even the cunning of the parliamentarian, who foresaw that the article would be approved in any case and did not want its approval to represent a check for the parties of the Left? Certainly it is inconceivable that Togliatti was naïve enough to imagine that the vote would in any way diminish the uncompromising hostility of the Church to Communism.)

The Assembly voted by call-over on the formula:

> 'The State and the Catholic Church are, each in its own sphere, independent and sovereign. Their relations are regulated by the Lateran Pacts. No amendment of the constitution is required in the event of any modification of the Pacts by mutual agreement.'

Socialists, Republicans, Actionists, Labour Democrats and the Christian Socialist deputy voted against the motion; all the rest supported it. Of the old guard, Orlando, Nitti and Ruini voted in favour, while Croce and Ivanoe Bonomi were absent. The motion was carried by 350 votes to 149.

No one who followed the debate dispassionately can have failed to observe the widely varied reactions which the question at issue provoked among the different political groups. The Actionists, the Republicans, the Communists, and a considerable number of Socialists, including a few whose membership of the party dated back to the pre-Fascist era, felt very strongly about it. The 'Qualunquisti' were at pains to appear more royalist than the King, more Catholic than the Christian Democrats. As for the last-named, in their eyes the article represented the very essence of the Constitution, for the sake of which they would have been willing to sacrifice all the rest. There was uproar when one of the most distinguished among them derided the 'secularism *versus* confessionalism' dilemma as a historical curiosity, declaring that, while in his view all other political issues paled before this one, no values were of greater importance than those which the State, as the medium through which citizens were first directed into the paths of religious truth, was in duty bound to uphold.

Once the article had been approved no further reference was

made to those bilateral amendments of single provisions of the
Concordat which had been made to appear so easy of realization,
nor was there any more talk of modifying those articles of the
penal code which assigned a position of inferiority to non-
Catholic religions. Article 5 of the Concordat was destined to be
applied with the utmost strictness: for example, if a priest happened to be elected a member of a Communal Council his
appointment was invariably declared invalid by the prefect.
There remained on the statute-book the law relating to permitted
religions, which deprives non-Catholics of a liberty which they
acquired in Piedmont as long ago as 1850—when Solaro della
Margarita appealed in vain to Victor Emmanuel to prohibit the
erection of the Waldensian chapel—by forbidding any non-
Catholic sect to open a place of worship without first obtaining
the permission of the Head of the State, which will be granted
only after it has been established that the building in question
would meet the effective needs of a substantial body of believers.
Even that decree on the Jewish religion has been preserved intact,
by which Jews of modernizing and liberalizing tendencies have
been forced to come into line with their orthodox and traditionalist brethren, with those Zionists who provoked the one
angry outburst that occurs in the lofty and serene *Lettere dal
carcere* of Antonio Gramsci. All the work in this field of Fascism's
leading jurist and Keeper of the Seals, Alfredo Rocco—codification of ecclesiastical laws, penal legislation and procedure—has
surmounted the hurdle of the Constituent Assembly.

Bibliographical Note.

For what may, in my view, have been the common aspirations of
the small group of men who still upheld the traditions of liberalism
and liberal Catholicism in 1944, I refer the reader to my short work
Per la pace religiosa d'Italia (Florence [Rome], 1944).

For the emphasis laid on the Lateran Pacts in the Constitution, see
the various articles by Father S. Lener in *Civiltà Cattolica* (1947, Nos. 2
and 3) and those—liberal or secular in tone as the case may be—of G.
Calogero, M. Cevolotto, M. A. Rollier, E. Codignola, A. C. Jemolo,
and P. Calamandrei in the review *Il Ponte* (1947, Parts 4 and 5). An
issue of the Milan review *Lo Stato moderno* was also devoted to the
question in 1947.

On the figure of the reigning Pontiff, see P. Bargellini, *Pio XII,
Pastor Angelicus* (Florence, 1948).

CHAPTER VIII

THE FIRST TWELVE YEARS OF THE REPUBLIC

IN the General Election of April 18th, 1948, the Christian Democrats secured a majority over all other parties in the Assembly. But in the elections of June 7th, 1953, which were conducted in accordance with a system designed to reduce substantially the number of seats held by Communist and Socialist deputies, the Christian Democrats, supported by those parties (Liberal, Republican and Social Democratic) which for practical purposes have always been their allies—sometimes, though not always, sharing with them the responsibilities of government, but never in any circumstances opposing them— failed by a small margin of votes to obtain an absolute majority. Thus the desired reduction in the number of Communist- and Socialist-held seats was not effected; and in August, 1953, the Christian Democratic Prime Minister, Alcide De Gasperi, tendered his resignation, having held office since December, 1945—the longest premiership, apart from the interlude of Fascist dictatorship, since the unification of Italy. The government of the country remained, however, in the hands of the Christian Democratic Party, thanks to the co-operation of the parties which call themselves its allies, but which their opponents call its 'satellites'. In the elections of May, 1958, the Christian Democrats polled about 43 per cent of the votes and, with the support of the Social Democrats, were able once again to form a Government, this time under the leadership of Fanfani.

The Monarchist and neo-Fascist Parties continue as always to be without representation in the Government. Both are plagued by recurrent internal crises, which may be said to stem from the conflict between, on the one hand, the very few who genuinely regret the passing of the Monarchy or who really believe in the Fascist way of life and in the possibility of a Fascist revival and, on the other hand, the many for whom 'Monarchist' and 'neo-Fascist' are merely convenient labels, enabling them to exploit ultra-conservative positions and affording them a medium of exchange in their dealings with the party in power. For some years, too, the Liberals, who have adopted an unequivocally conservative line and who favour a *laissez-faire* economy, and the small Republican group have withheld their support from the Christian Democrats, without, however, actively opposing them.

The relations existing between all these parties are regularly discussed by the various party newspapers and reviews, but they leave the mass of the people substantially indifferent. Until a couple of years ago the latter perceived that among the organized political parties—which is by no means the same as saying among Italians endowed with a political consciousness—there is only one irreducible division: that between the Communists and Socialists on the one hand and the remaining parties on the other.

The hostility which parties other than the Socialists and Communists periodically reveal towards the Christian Democrats has always been motivated by the desire to effect a change of Government, never by a wish to destroy the prevailing order.

The broad agreement on matters of principle that still exists between all the parties other than the Communists and the Socialists is particularly noticeable in the south of Italy during Communal elections or elections for the Sicilian Region. The Christian Democratic Party, as the dominant party and the one that controls the political game, allies itself in turn either to the three parties that assist it in the work of government, or to the Monarchists, or, with a reluctance that is somewhat more marked but has never yet proved insuperable, to the Monarchists and the Fascists simultaneously. In elections of minor importance which do not attract a great deal of public attention alliances between all parties other than the Socialists and the Communists are quite usual. If circumstances change it is possible that the Social Democrats—who still invoke the principles of Marxism—the Republicans and the Liberals will cease to participate in the coalition; but they would never dream either of organizing a popular front or of resorting to the 'desperation' policy of urging their supporters to vote for the 'Reds', or simply to abstain from voting, if this entailed any risk of a Communist victory. All these parties continue to agree on at least one thing: that the Communists and Socialists represent the chief enemy, and that no betrayal of abstract principles or of time-honoured traditions is inadmissible if its effect is to deprive the 'Reds' of control of even the most insignificant Communal Administration.

Since the suppression of the Hungarian Revolution the Socialist Party has become increasingly estranged from the Communist Party, even if there is no lack of Socialist elements who are reluctant to break what they call the unity of the labour front. Naturally, all the Christian Democratic newspapers, and with them those of the Social Democrats and the Liberals, tend to deny the estrangement and continue to speak of the 'Social Communists'. To-day no one can tell how the situation will develop or whether the Socialist Party will succeed in becoming the rallying-point of all those forces which remain equally opposed to Communism, economic conservatism and State confessionalism.

It was against this background that, within the framework of a Constitution drafted in 1947 and brought into operation on January 1st, 1948—a Constitution which, though unmistakably democratic and liberal in character, was anomalous in that, as we have seen, it sanctified the Lateran Pacts—the confessional State came into being.

It is necessary, of course, to clarify the meaning of this term, which, like others of the kind, is used to describe régimes of such varying types, régimes that have been introduced at such diverse periods of history.

It is also necessary to refute forthwith the accusations of the Communists, who speak too glibly of a revival of Fascism: which is to say that they forget the true nature of that régime, under which, even when it possessed full legal authority, the most rigorous legislative sanctions against its opponents were always accompanied and supplemented by personal violence, beatings and shootings on the part of the *squadristi*, who were fortified by the knowledge that their misdemeanours would remain unpunished. Communist and Socialist books and newspapers are printed and sold freely and openly, and, hitherto, the dismissal of a teacher or official for expounding heterodox ideas in print or in speeches would be unthinkable. Criticisms—even fierce and unjust criticisms—of the Government are tolerated in the publications mentioned, and caricatures of Ministers are a commonplace. The largest trade-union organization is controlled by Communists and Socialists; and it prints its own manifestos, supervises strikes, and drafts industrial contracts. There is nothing in all this that is in any way reminiscent of Fascism.

Having exposed the injustice of such a comparison, in what sense can one speak of the new Italy as a 'confessional' State?

The juridical system that finds expression in the Constitution embodies a Concordat with the Holy See, in virtue of which it is impossible for the State to introduce its own independent ecclesiastical legislation (a fact that is of little importance, since no one in Italy objects to the recognition of religious associations, parish boundaries, or religious foundations); together with undertakings on the part of the State (1) to leave it to the Church to pronounce, through its legislative, administrative and judicial organs, on everything that pertains both to the right of citizens to contract Catholic marriages and to the validity of bonds so forged: the State for its part admitting any person—including even priests and religious—to the rites of civil marriage without questioning them as to their faith; (2) to admit priests to public employment only with the approval of their bishops and to dismiss them if such approval is withdrawn, besides, of course, excluding the priest who has renounced his cloth or has incurred the Church's censure from the teaching profession and from any post that would bring him into contact with the public; (3) not to reduce clerical stipends below the figure prescribed in 1929, due allowance being made for the reduced purchasing power of the currency; and (4) to provide religious instruction in a strictly Catholic form, subject to episcopal supervision, in primary and secondary schools (with the proviso, however, that children may be exempted from such instruction if their families wish it).

But this same juridical system also prescribes complete freedom for all religions—indeed, it prescribes equality of status for all religions, Catholicism among them, in everything that pertains to freedom of expression, including propaganda—and envisages agreements between the State and individual communions on the basis of which the regulations governing each of the latter would be formulated. The question of how such a régime should be designated, of whether or not it should be labelled 'confessional', is of concern only to theoreticians and doctrinaires.

It is interesting, however, to note that the State has fulfilled all its obligations towards the Catholic Church but not towards the other communions, and, in particular, that common law has evolved within a far ampler framework than statute law, on which it has exerted a considerable influence.

A superficial study of the Italian penal code at once reveals the confessional character of the law which prescribes penalties for vilification of the Catholic religion but not of other religions, and which makes the severity of the punishment imposed for offences against ministers of religion and for the creation of disturbances at religious ceremonies dependent on whether the misdemeanours in question are committed at the expense of the Catholic religion or of other religions. It is easy to discern a religious motive behind the law that prescribes penalties for all forms of Malthusian propaganda and that which prohibits the advertisement of any species of pharmaceutical contraceptive. A cursory glance at the corpus of Italian law immediately confirms that the State has exceeded its formal obligations towards the Church, in the sense that it continues to accord it economic aid over and above the amount promised, providing subsidies for the building and repair of churches which, though certainly not very large in relation to the State budget as a whole, are generally considered substantial enough in view of the conditions in which the poorer classes in Italy are condemned to live. Students of administrative practice with experience of administrative life are aware that this is only half the story: they know that in every programme of public works sponsored by the State much prominence is given to plans for the erection of churches and presbyteries, that where there are areas to be reclaimed or transformed the authorities always accord priority to ecclesiastical building, that the organizations responsible for agrarian reform have contrived to allot holdings on expropriated land to religious associations so that they may found schools of agriculture. But it is the picture of day-to-day life that is of most interest. In an admirable volume entitled *La politique ecclésiastique du second Empire* (Paris, 1930) Maurain has traced the relations between Church and State in France between 1852 and 1859, when the Italian war shattered the idyll between Napoleon III and Pius IX. The contents of those pages, suitably modified in view of the special character of a Latin State of our time, with its intrusion into every sphere of life, might well be applied to contemporary Italy.

As in the France portrayed in Maurain's book, in the Italy of to-day the clergy enjoy a partial immunity, *de facto* if not *de jure*.

Every commissioner of police, every inspector of *carabinieri*, every public prosecutor avoids as much as possible coming into conflict with ecclesiastics, even on questions that are outside their jurisdiction. In the event of a clash it would be extremely surprising if it were not the State official who got the worst of it, even if his fate amounted to no more than being transferred to another district. Thus, no police officer seeing nuns or monks soliciting alms or selling books in the streets or at the front doors of houses would ever dream of asking them if they had a licence or a special permit; no inspector would be over-scrupulous in his inquiries as to whether a meeting or procession sponsored by an ecclesiastic had or had not been authorized. In other countries such things would have no significance; but they have a great deal in Italy, where these same authorities mercilessly repress—and the sentences passed by the judicial authorities invariably vindicate their action—similar activities (distribution and crying of newspapers, collections, meetings) on the part of the Communists. The latter are denied all freedom of action. Sometimes the authorities even try to hinder them from holding private meetings. The proprietor of a café or a restaurant or a theatre knows that if he lets his premises for a Communist-sponsored banquet, meeting or conference he will incur the disapproval of the Prefects and the police, with possibly far-reaching and unforeseen consequences. Of course, the pressure is greater in small towns than in very large ones.

The State has inherited a very considerable amount of immovable property from Fascist organizations, including sports grounds and seaside and mountain holiday-camps as well as the premises of a number of workers' organizations which had been taken over by the Fascists in 1921–23, in many cases by force, from the socialist organizations that had built or acquired them. Although this immovable property always belongs either to the State or to the public companies of a non-denominational character which have succeeded those set up by the Fascists, its use is for the most part reserved to religious bodies. For its own relief work the State makes ample use of the Vatican relief organizations. During the summer months the Italian tricolour and the Papal standard are usually to be seen flying side by side above the massive buildings of the seaside and mountain holiday-camps which are maintained for the benefit of the children of the working classes. The worker who did not wish his children to be exposed to religious influences would have serious difficulty in securing their admission to these camps, which are invariably staffed by ecclesiastical personnel. The Communists have tried to organize camps of their own, financed out of party funds, but in many places these have been closed down by the Prefect and the children sent back to their families. A few years ago I.N.C.A., an organization closely associated with the Workers' Institutes but legally constituted and subject to the control of the Ministry of Labour, succeeded in organizing a few of these lay holiday camps. Recently considerable portions of this property formerly owned by Fascist organizations have been sold by private treaty to bishops of the Roman Church, offers to purchase submitted by Communist or Socialist Communes meanwhile having been rejected.

With the ending of the German Occupation the Workers' Institutes, which are predominantly 'Red', had inherited, in fact if not in law, the buildings formerly occupied by those Fascist organizations, euphemistically known as trade unions, which in theory had been supposed to defend the rights of the workers. In some cases these were their original premises, built in 1898 or 1900 and seized by the Fascists around 1922. In 1954 the Government issued a general order expelling all Communist organizations from premises belonging to public bodies or to the State.

As has been stated several times already, from the period of the country's unification until 1918 the Catholics represented themselves as the champions of decentralization and of the rights of the free Commune, regarded as a natural unit which preceded the State both in time and in the urgency of its needs. There is an entire Catholic literature devoted to attacks on the centralized State. Don Luigi Sturzo, founder of the Popular Party and to-day, at the age of eighty-seven, a life-member of the Senate, emerged during the first decade of the century as the principal advocate of this programme of decentralization. But what seemed an excellent thing at a time when Catholics could hope to dominate a few Communes and provinces, but not the State as a whole, no longer has any relevance now that the situation is reversed, and a Catholic Party dominates the State, but is unable, constitutionally at any rate, to prevent its adversaries, the 'Reds', from controlling a certain number of Communes and provinces. Thus we have what is in practice, if not explicitly, a tendency towards centralization. The Prefects, representatives of the executive in the provinces, have retained virtually intact the powers they disposed of during the Fascist era, powers far wider than those which they wielded up to 1915; and not even Candido would dare to assert that within the limits of their jurisdiction all citizens are equal, all organizations devoted to relief work, charity, mutual aid, and culture have the same standing, regardless of the political ideas of their members. Recent sweeping reforms of the statutes of charitable institutions and boarding-schools have been designed to ensure that, in regions where the Communal Administrations are 'Red', the governors of such establishments shall cease to be appointed by the Local Authority. As a result, the statutes in question now often embody clauses providing specifically for the appointment of ecclesiastical nominees. Sometimes these statutes are completely new; sometimes they are rehashes of old provisions repealed during the period of liberal rule.

A ceaseless struggle is carried on in all the Prefectures against the 'Red' Communal Administrations, its object being to defeat their resolutions, to annul their decisions, and to deprive them of the power to appoint governors to the institutions named.

Legally, the Communes have only one financial liability in the religious field, the responsibility, in the last resort, for the upkeep of churches. Owing, however, to the poverty of most Communal Administrations even this liability is seldom discharged in full. But where the Administration is controlled by the Christian Democrats the Commune regularly organizes religious demonstrations. Sometimes the local inhabitants are consecrated to the Sacred Heart or to the Virgin; special services are held in the presence of the Mayor, during which the Communal labarum hangs above the altar; votive offerings are made on behalf of the citizenry. Public halls are made available for religious functions.

Charitable institutions are generally secular in character, unless their statutes—which in most cases express the will of the founders—require that they should be administered by religious Orders. It would be very difficult, however, to find in Italy a hospital or boarding-school or home for poor children or old people that was not staffed by religious. This is due among other things to the poverty of the country as a whole and of the institutions in particular, which is such that the employment of adequate, properly trained lay staffs would be an impossibility.

W

In practice—and it is a great evil—the religious instruction provided in the State schools is of very slight value. The student arrives at his university completely ignorant both of the most elementary principles of Catholic theology and of the constitution of the Church, nor is he any better informed on those questions which have inspired a number of Catholic moralists, among them Manzoni, to write pages of a nobility unsurpassed in the whole of Italian religious literature. On the other hand, in these same State schools teachers of unorthodox views are bombarded by headmasters and provincial directors of education with requests to accompany their pupils to religious functions, with recommendations to use certain books, and with circulars prohibiting books which have proved unacceptable to the ecclesiastical authorities from being introduced into the class-room. Religious associations have taken ample advantage of the freedom that prevails in the sphere of education to found schools, which the State duly recognizes. Of these, some are good, others not so good; some are even excellent. People are apt to deplore the fact that the State's inspectorial powers are more theoretical than practical: one never hears of an inspection that has resulted in the withdrawal of such a school's 'certificate of equality' (i.e. of the State's recognition of the legal standing of the courses provided). People likewise deplore the fact that when denominational schools have recourse to lay teachers they pay them starvation wages. The impartial observer, however, recognizes that in a poor country such as Italy, where all aspire to secure educational qualifications of a certain minimum standard, but where even the rich would refuse to pay for their children what it costs to provide a first-class education in the Anglo-Saxon countries, and where the economic resources of the scholastic foundations are derisory, it would be impossible to envisage a different situation—either a good State school that provided a worthy education for the great mass of students, or a denominational school entirely staffed with teachers possessing adequate qualifications. In Italy the two types of school are distributed in more or less equal proportions.

The censorship of films and plays is free, in the sense that productions which have been condemned by the ecclesiastical authorities—and these are very numerous—are not automatically denied a government licence; but the licence in question, and above all the government subsidy—both theatre and cinema are generously subsidized in Italy—are withheld if the production is found to have any anti-clerical or anti-religious bias. A film that depicted the evils resulting in a specific case from the indissolubility of the marriage bond, or that portrayed a family condemned to poverty because the parents had brought too many children into the world (not to speak of a film that extolled a priest who had renounced his cloth, or one that depicted a priest who encouraged superstitious practices), could never be shown in Italy. Italians who travel abroad laugh or become impatient when they perceive the mutilated condition in which certain foreign films—for example, the Swedish picture, *One Summer of Happiness*—reach their country's cinemas. Even a Protestant pastor may not be presented in a film in an unfavourable light if any criticism is thereby implied of principles common to all religions. Naturally, the censors' chief preoccupation is with questions involving sexual morality, but at times it would seem that sexual degradation is to be measured in terms of the amount of skin exposed and that the censors are unaware of more subtle provocations.

Where the confessional character of the State is most clearly revealed, and there is an open, undisguised intention to disregard the Constitution, is in the treatment accorded to non-Catholic minorities.

There is no anti-Semitism. But outside the Communist and Socialist Parties, which are a law unto themselves, no Jew has held a political position of importance since a few venerable survivors from the pre-Fascist era ceased to be members of the Senate, and it is inconceivable that a Jew should be mayor of a big town. On the other hand, the authorities reveal an inflexible determination not to allow the ancient Waldensian sect to extend its influence beyond the boundaries of its two small Alpine Communes and not to permit any Protestant propaganda. The most savage persecution is reserved for the Pentecostals, of whom there are many among the poorer classes in the south of Italy. But no minister of a Protestant sect is allowed to carry on his activities outside the handful of non-Catholic churches, dating back to pre-Fascist days, which cater mostly for foreigners and for a few Italian families who were converted to Protestantism mainly during the period of the Risorgimento and have adhered to it ever since. These traditional Protestants are not debarred from posts which have no political connotation; but the conversion of a Catholic to Protestantism to-day would be regarded as a challenge to the existing order. All activity outside the churches is repressed by the police, who resort to methods which in other countries would be unthinkable, intruding into private houses where the Gospel is being expounded or hymns are being sung, closing down huts hired by sects for the purpose of holding services, confiscating devotional literature, the prosecution of any minister who is known to have conducted a baptism by immersion together with those attending the ceremony (the charge being entered under the heading of 'Unauthorized Religious Ceremonies'), and forcing Protestant ministers to leave their parishes and to return to their home towns by a prescribed route (naturally, the Italian Constitution, like that of any other democratic country, embodies an article—No. 16—which provides that 'Every citizen shall be free to move about and to reside in any part of the national territory'). A few pastors who thought they could profit by their American citizenship have been no better treated. It is common knowledge that one such who wished to found an institution for the relief of apostate priests, who in Italy are treated like veritable pariahs, was expelled from the country. The fact that the diplomatic authorities of the United States have done nothing to help these men testifies to the acumen of the American Government, which has come to realize that any Christian Democratic politician would be much less inclined to compromise on this question of Protestant propaganda than on the most intractable question of international policy.

Apart from this, expansion of any kind by Protestant organizations is forbidden. It would be useless for some old-established health organization run by Protestants to offer to provide new hospital facilities for the general public: the necessary development-permit would not be forthcoming.

This failure to comply with the provisions of the Constitution (Article 8: 'All religious confessions shall enjoy equal freedom before the law'; Article 19: 'All citizens shall have the right to profess their religious faith freely and in any manner, individually or collectively, to propagate it and to practise it in private or in public, provided that its rites do not offend against morality') is justified by the whole Catholic Press with the usual arguments about religious unity, the violation of consciences and the rights of the dominant confession in a country where religious dissenters amount to 1·1 per cent (but where the votes cast for parties condemned by the Church exceed 33 per cent[1]), and with the old refrain about truth's right to be protected against error.

It is impossible to cite any relevant provision of the Concordat, because the Concordat does not say a word about other religions. But mention of the Concordat brings one back to the concept of the 'Catholic State', with its inevitable corollary that the latter cannot tolerate propaganda against the dominant confession.

The Constitutional Court has ruled that advance notice of religious meetings to be held in places open to the public (e.g., cinemas, theatres and garages), as distinct from public places (streets and squares), need no longer be given to the police, who formerly could, and usually did, veto such meetings. As a result of this ruling, a pastor who wishes to hold a meeting in a village or township where there is no proper non-Catholic church is no longer under an obligation to notify the police in advance. But as soon as they hear of his intention the authorities hasten to issue an injunction in which, on the pretext of safeguarding public order, they prohibit the meeting. A legal battle is now in progress against such injunctions, the outcome of which is still in the balance.

On the other hand, the courts have always acquitted those Catholic priests and religious (a very small company, be it added: but the Protestant propagandist is also a *rara avis*, and few Italians encounter a single one in the whole of their lives) who have insulted or defamed Protestant propagandists, or even seized and destroyed their stocks of tracts and pamphlets.

Generally speaking, during these years the judiciary has displayed in its judgments a more intense Catholic sensibility than the other organs of the State. It is lavish in granting all the benefits made available under the terms of the Concordat, all the tax reliefs prescribed for ecclesiastical bodies. It rigorously upholds the principle of the indissolubility of marriage, refusing to recognize any annulment by a foreign court of a marriage between Italians contracted in accordance with the Catholic rite. Under its interpretation of the matrimonial laws a secret Catholic marriage may at any time be recognized as valid by the State,

---

[1] 57 per cent if account is taken of the fact that before the last elections the Faithful were instructed by their bishops to vote only for Christian Democratic candidates.

even against the will of the couple concerned, at the request of
the ecclesiastical authorities. (In cases of bigamy, the original,
secret marriage takes precedence of the subsequent, officially-
registered one.) It refuses to keep any check on ecclesiastical
judgments relating to matrimonial questions. It affirms, with no
legal justification, that the final judgment of a court in respect of
incest or any other sexual offence may be invalidated under the
terms of the ecclesiastical dispensation that permits of the con-
traction of a religious marriage between stepfather and step-
daughter or between a father-in-law and his son's widow. It
upholds the interpretation of the law, so dear to Fascism,
penalizing evasion of parental responsibilities by punishing the
husband who abstains from sexual intercourse with his wife.
(Under Fascism the ideal of 'strength through numbers' inspired,
as we have seen, the cult of the prolific couple, as a result of which
abstention from intercourse came to be regarded as a crime. To
all this the authorities succeeded in giving a quasi-religious
appearance, describing it as 'a disciplined fulfilment of the
purposes of marriage'.) In the Italian legal journals there has
been heated discussion of judgments in cases of judicial separation
which have stipulated that if only one of the parties is a practising
Catholic he or she should be given custody of the children of the
marriage.

But the Catholic sympathies of the judiciary are most clearly
revealed in their interpretation of the criminal law. Stern punishment is meted out to all those found guilty of creating disturbances
at religious functions—disturbances which have sometimes taken
the form of someone in the congregation shouting 'That's not
true!' while the priest has been inveighing from the pulpit against
the parties of the Left, describing their errors and omissions—of
any affront, whether verbal or published in the Press, to the
religious feelings of the faithful, or of any disparagement of
religious personages or institutions. Anyone who insults the
Pontiff incurs the most rigorous sanctions, and such persons are
always excluded from amnesties. Those who study the reports of
these cases are sometimes left in doubt as to whether the charge
has been substantiated when they read that the evidence for the
defence has been deemed 'not probative', on the ground that the
witnesses concerned subscribed to the same political philosophy as
the accused. When a journalist was prosecuted for publishing a

book sharply critical of the ecclesiastical policy of the Holy See, the court, unable to find evidence that the defendant had been guilty of vilifying the Faith or of insulting the Pontiff, sentenced him—and the sentence was subsequently confirmed by the Court or Appeal and the Court of Cassation—under the terms of the article in the criminal code which penalizes those who commit acts hostile to a foreign State, of a sort calculated to expose the Italian State to the danger of a war or to disturb its relations with a foreign Government, or alternatively to expose the Italian State or its citizens to the danger of reprisals or retaliations.

By contrast, no Catholic or Catholic newspaper is ever penalized for libelling non-Catholics or 'Reds', whether Italian or foreign.

It is easy to understand how, with the law interpreted in such a way that the ecclesiastical authorities have come to expect from the judiciary the maximum of protection together with complete immunity from punishment, vehement protests and arguments have been provoked by two cases in which different standards of justice have been observed.

The first, which occurred at Messina, concerned a procurator general who ordered the arrest of a priest who had celebrated the marriage of a girl to a man by whom she had been abducted and forcibly detained. (The marriage was subsequently annulled by the Rota Romana.) The procurator general was shortly after-wards promoted to a higher office, while the priest was granted an absolute discharge, the court refusing to admit that his action made him guilty of complicity in the abduction and detention of the girl.

The other case, which gave rise during the first six months of 1958 to violent controversy, was the action for slander brought against the Bishop of Prato by two of his congregation who had been married in accordance with the civil rite only and had subse-quently been branded in an ecclesiastical edict as public sinners. The indictment of the Bishop and his provisional conviction by the lower court evoked a storm of protest from the ecclesiastical authorities, who considered that the Church's freedom had been violated. The Cardinal Archbishop of Bologna went so far as to order the churches in his diocese to be hung with mourning and their bells tolled. The decision was later reversed by the Court of Appeals which ordered the man and his wife to pay the costs of both the trial and the appeal.

To keep the matter in perspective, however, and to avoid distorting the picture, one must add, what has already been intimated, that the Italian of to-day is completely free to discuss all the attitudes adopted on these questions alike by the Government and by the judiciary. He may criticize freely any measures or decisions taken, declare them contrary to the Constitution, even propound this latter thesis *ex cathedra*—all of which would be, or would have been, unthinkable under any of the totalitarian régimes with which we have grown so familiar. Moreover, the higher seats of learning at any rate continue to provide a platform for free discussion, and in universities and academies professors and scholars of differing, even of diametrically opposite, opinions are to be found working side by side. But even in the secondary schools the confessionalism of the State is reflected in isolated incidents rather than in any serious attempt to dictate educational policy: the teaching of philosophy in particular is still inspired by idealism. And even in these incidents, as also in the sentences of the judiciary to which we have alluded, it would be a mistake to see an expression of Government policy (which is reflected, on the other hand, clearly and unmistakably, in the persecution of the Pentecostals). This tinge of confessionalism in the body politic is largely due to the pressure of public opinion, to the prevalence of a 'conformist' tradition, and to the continuance of the mental habit fostered by Fascism, and I believe by all totalitarian régimes, whereby the civil servant and the judge allow their actions to be influenced by the thought of what their superiors may think and how they are likely to react.

In particular, whenever mention is made, even in our field, of an attack on freedom or of a failure to respect some provision of the Constitution, it is necessary to consider the matter against the background not of this isolated field of Church-State relations but of the atmosphere of religious conflict which has prevailed on the continent of Europe ever since 1917, and of the division of Italy into two camps: Communist and anti-Communist. A measure directed against the 'Reds', even if it be inspired by religious motives, may well find a warmer response in the hearts of inveterate free-thinkers, who declare themselves to be staunch Liberals or Republicans and who reserve the place of honour in their homes for the portrait of Cavour or Mazzini, than in those of the clergy.

Reference has been made already to the existence of a 'social' conformism.

The phenomenon is not very easy to apprehend, particularly if one has no clear picture in one's mind of the evolution of Italian society and customs during the last sixty years. It might be said that around 1895 the average Italian was somewhat under the influence of Monsieur Homais, and that to-day he has a horror of being told that he is still living under his spell. Or alternatively it might be asserted that sixty years ago the average Italian with no political affiliations and no conspicuously Catholic background felt a little ashamed of his observance of religious forms, of his spiritual life. Although a believer, he was not deaf to the positivistic clamour of those who averred that religion was in decline and that it was destined to be superseded by science. He was not, as a rule, a courageous Christian; he often excused his observance of religious forms by saying that he must not displease his aged mother, or that he must set an example to his children: the theme of religion as a necessity for women, children and the uneducated recurs often in the conversation of the bourgeoisie of the late nineteenth century. To-day that same average man, lacking any profound religious convictions, subscribing to no clearly-defined political creed, would be correspondingly ashamed to absent himself from a religious function or to be branded as a dissenter. In the crowded tenement-houses of the great cities of Italy there is nearly always someone, either the landlord or a tenant, who sooner or later proposes that the building should be consecrated to the Sacred Heart or to the Immaculate Heart of the Virgin. Very few, even if they are sincere believers, are really affected by a gesture of this kind; but it is rare for anyone, even if he genuinely lacks faith, to object: opposition would smack too much of latter-day Voltairianism. Thus, even unbelievers are married in church, since the contracting of a civil marriage is automatically interpreted as a demonstration of political extremism. In the same way, it is considered bad form to deride or criticize the manifestations of popular religious feeling which for some years now have been a regular feature of Italian life (sacred images that weep or move their eyes), or simply to display scepticism, even though one's attitude to religion may in fact be sceptical.

For—and this serves to explain why even sincere Catholics

maintain an attitude of reserve, and why their appreciation of the disparities between contemporary Italy and the Italy of former days differs so radically from that of the majority of Catholics—one has the impression that beneath this social conformism there is no genuine religious feeling. Religious education is almost entirely neglected. No place is allotted in the curricula of secondary schools to the study of theological questions. In literature and the theatre the portrayal of spiritual dilemmas and *crises de conscience* is less common to-day than it was sixty years ago. It is rare to meet in politics or the professions the truly religious man, to whom every problem poses itself in moral terms, in terms of the quest for the solution—and there can be only one—that corresponds to God's commandment. In certain towns boys and girls from good families invariably attend schools run by religious associations: but by the time they reach the age of twenty their interest in religion has dwindled to zero, and they talk, think and act like their contemporaries from completely godless environments. Those with a clear picture in their minds of the evolution of Italian social life during the past sixty years remember that half a century ago the problem of divorce had a peculiar urgency and was widely debated (we have already had occasion to speak of the bill tabled by the Zanardelli Government in 1902), whereas in the Italy of to-day divorce is never mentioned, and public opinion accepts without question the total ban imposed by the Court of Cassation on those expedients (annulments of marriages by foreign courts, divorces following a change of citizenship) which were still adopted on a considerable scale during the Fascist era. But they remember also how in those days public opinion, the conscience of society, was outraged by any violation of the accepted moral code. The husband or wife who abandoned the domestic hearth in order to go and live with a new partner was aware that—outside certain circles frequented by artists—the price of such indiscretion was invariably social ostracism, and that any children of the union would experience grave difficulties and humiliations, at least throughout the early part of their lives, and would find many opportunities of marriage denied to them. Now all that has changed. For electoral reasons a politician belonging to a clerical party would be asked to avoid giving rise to any scandal (his personal life meanwhile remaining a matter of indifference to his sponsors). But not one Italian in a hundred would dream of turning his back on a couple who were living in open sin.

A reflection of confessionalism, of which it is not easy to determine how much is due to genuine religious feeling and how much to a fear of flouting convention, is also present, this time with a more pronounced political connotation, in the world of industry. There are plenty of industrialists who seek to interfere in the religious lives of their employees, foisting upon them welfare officers whose aims are openly evangelical, organizing religious services in their factories and bringing a certain amount of pressure to bear on the workers to attend (for example, by asking them to state the reason in the event of their absence), and bearing the cost of pilgrimages, which are sometimes crowned by an audience of the Pope. It should be mentioned that in Italy the world of industry is dominated by three organizations: the General Confederation of Labour (C.G.L.), which is controlled by Communist and Socialist elements and attracts the great majority of the workers, including some who are not members of either of the two Left-Wing parties; a Democratic Confederation, which in theory represents the Social Democrats, Republicans and Liberals; and the Italian Catholic Workers' Associations, which are unequivocally denominational in character.

The 'toughest' of these three organizations and the one most bitterly opposed by the employers is the first (it would be inappropriate here to pass judgment upon it, to assert that it protects the interests of the workers more effectively than the other two: there is much truth in the criticisms levelled against its activities, to wit, that it fosters the myth of the strike, and even encourages irresponsible agitation). Sometimes the three bodies co-operate, as when they jointly oppose the closing down of factories; but they spend most of the time quarrelling among themselves, the C.G.L. usually finding itself in opposition to the other two. One has the impression that the Italian Catholic Workers' Associations (A.C.L.I.), which naturally attract those Catholic workers who from their birth have belonged only to religious organizations and who have had no other teacher, no other master than their parish priest, reveal a greater spontaneity and therefore a greater independence vis-à-vis the employers, than the Democratic Confederation, which, in a country with no

Labour tradition and where the non-denominational and non-revolutionary parties of the Centre have always drawn their membership exclusively from the bourgeoisie, has all the appearance of an organization sponsored by the employers, and which only a limited number of workers ever join spontaneously. A few years ago the results of an inquiry conducted among the members of the Italian Catholic Workers' Associations of Milan were published in a 'White Book' entitled *La classe lavoratrice si difende* ('The Working Class Defends Itself'). The inquiry showed A.C.L.I. to be an independent organization with an adequate sense of freedom, a body that condemns acts of tyranny even when they are committed at the expense of the 'Reds', denounces the attempts of many employers to make life impossible for the 'Red' worker, and deprecates certain isolated incidents—such as that of the female activist who was called into the manager's office and forced to stand for two hours with her face to the wall as a punishment for striking—which would be inconceivable in other countries. In view, however, of the fact that these strictures come from an avowedly denominational organization it is noteworthy that one of them is directed against those employers who try to force their work-people to attend religious services. This indicates an awareness of the negative effect of such forms of coercion, a consciousness that in Italy many workers and peasants join Communist unions only because they drive the hardest bargain, only as a retort to the policy of the employers, which is certainly not a policy of conciliation.

How do the political parties react to these manifestations of confessionalism?

Naturally, the Christian Democratic Party does not regard them with disfavour.

This, the dominant party, is in fact an agglomeration of men of the most disparate antecedents, not to say of widely varied tendencies. It might be said that the composition of the Christian Democratic Party varies according to class and age. At the highest level, among the 'politicians'—deputies, mayors or provincial councillors—and among the not-so-young, the tone is still set by the rump of the Fascist Party, by men who, if Fascism had survived, would not, as members of the hierarchy, have displayed any particular interest in ecclesiastical matters and who, if a breach had occurred between the régime and the Church, would have been as violent as any in their anti-clericalism. Alongside these are, by contrast, survivors from the old Popular Party and members of Catholic Action, who have always had the Church's interests at heart and who, in their minds, have always given first place in the binomial 'Church and State' to the Church. Finally, the younger generation is represented by indifferents of the kind who, faced with the necessity of joining a party, would always opt for the party in power, as well as by men of fervent piety, invaluable elements devoted to the study and contemplation of the problems of the State and of society.

The party and Catholic Action are quite distinct one from the other. The party is formally autonomous and secular, Catholic Action is an official organization subordinate to the ecclesiastical hierarchy. The distinction is less clear in fact than it is in theory, since neither the party, nor sections or individual members of the party, could survive as such without the hierarchy's support. Indeed, the party would be finished the day the bishops and parish priests of Italy instructed the electors to vote for other men; and when, as has sometimes happened in obscure Communal elections in the south of the country, the clergy have supported candidates representing the Monarchist Party, which is not allied to the Christian Democrats, the latter have not enjoyed success at the polls (hence their eagerness not to break with the extreme Right). Nevertheless, the distinction exists, and there are many Christian Democrats who do not belong to Catholic Action, and numerous members of Catholic Action who do not support the Christian Democratic Party. Mutual suspicions and rivalries, concealed so far as possible beneath a veneer of extreme affability, mar the relationship between the two organizations. In both it is the youthful elements who inspire the greatest confidence. Excellent reviews are published by young graduates and by students affiliated to the Catholic Federation of University Men and Women; there are circles devoted to meditation, prayer and study that remind one of certain *cénacles* of the Counter-Reformation presided over by men whom the Church has since admitted to the calendar of saints.

These groups of young people reveal a constant preoccupation with social questions, together with an acute sense of the inequitable distribution of the world's goods, of the injustice underlying

the corporate life of a country in which extreme poverty, of a
kind that in other European States has long since disappeared,
continues to exist side by side with extreme wealth, which is not
penalized by the Treasury as it is in all the advanced countries of
Europe and North America. Here the educated section of the
Catholic youth movement is clearly Left-Wing to a man. There
are those who remain sceptical about the significance of this fact,
pointing out that the history of the Church shows, as Dansette
noted in his study of events in France, that the best type of
Catholic has always tended to identify himself with the Left, but
that at decisive moments the hierarchy has always acted in
accordance with the desires of the Right. On the other hand,
there are those who think that, albeit with the gradualness that
characterizes every development within the bosom of the Church,
the phenomenon in question is bound to have its effect.

What it is important to note here is that—unlike the French
Catholic Left, on which the tradition of Montalembert and
Lacordaire exerts a considerable influence—Italian Catholics,
whatever their political colour, never go so far as to protest
against the confessionalism of the State. At times, indeed, it is
precisely those elements which socially are farthest to the Left,
which feel most bitter towards the rich, that are most passionate
in their confessionalism (so that one is reminded of the tradition
of Girolamo Savonarola, within whose historic domain there now
lives one of those Catholic socialists who in recent years have most
attracted the attention of Italians: the former Mayor of Florence,
Giorgio La Pira).

If we glance through the pages of the reviews edited by young
Left-Wing Catholics, the most daring expressions of opinion that
we shall find will be a few reservations about Franco's Spain. We
shall never encounter a word of protest against the persecution of
the Pentecostals.

The confessionalism of the State then, never becomes a subject
of controversy. Instead—depending on the journal and its political
bias—either it is openly approved (as something which the
majority in a Catholic State are entitled to take for granted, as
something that either is specified in the Constitution, or at least is
based upon it, or at all events is not contrary to it), or there is a
disposition to play it down, to ignore or minimize its manifestations, an attempt to justify the persecution of the Pentecostals on

hygienic grounds, as a necessary policy towards a sect that allegedly upsets the mental equilibrium of its adherents. . . . Diocesan and parish magazines, on the other hand, give the maximum publicity to manifestations of confessionalism, not even questioning the assumption that they *must* take place, that the Italian State *must* have this aspect.

A similar attitude, albeit characterized by a greater harshness towards all kinds of religious dissenters, is maintained by the Monarchists, who are ever ready to rebuke the President of the Republic for failing to attend a Papal ceremony, though in fact he frequently appears on such occasions (forgetfulness of history is a prerogative of the political parties; and the Monarchists have completely forgotten the history of the Savoyard Monarchy from 1849 onwards, and regard all the kings of Italy as replicas of Philip II); and by the Fascists, who are always ready to invoke the Lateran Pacts, always disposed to see in the Protestant the hated foreigner, the abominated Anglo-Saxon, and always similarly infected with the poison of anti-Semitism.

The so-called great independent newspapers, which represent big business and high finance, and which are still in great part controlled and edited by journalists who came to maturity during the Fascist era, tend to play down every manifestation of confessionalism. An occasional note of moderate secularism is sounded in the pages of *La Stampa* of Turin, which until a short while ago still numbered among its contributors the old editor of pre-Fascist days, Frassati—a man beloved of Giolitti, who raised him to the Senate and appointed him Ambassador to Germany—and in whose columns the lay voices of Luigi Salvatorelli and Vittorio Gorresio now make themselves heard from time to time.

The very few Republican and Social Democratic newspapers with large circulations continue to make their feeble voices heard, as also does a Left-Wing liberal weekly, *Il mondo*, which has a certain vogue in the world of culture. Liberals of the Right, on the other hand, are resolutely opposed to any criticism of the Government's 'confessionalist' policy. Politically, they favour the formation of a conservative *bloc* which would include the Monarchists, and in which their own function would be to uphold the principle of free trade.

Naturally, the Socialist and Communist newspapers do not remain silent about these manifestations. They comment upon them with their usual intemperance, mingling established facts with pure fabrications. The effect of their intervention is, however, somewhat negative. In Italy too many people prefer to keep silent rather than speak with the same voice as the 'Reds'—a course of action that would lay them open to the charge of being crypto-Communists, with the result that on future occasions no one would listen to them.

But, aside from the parties, do the Italian people, who, like all Continental peoples, still prefer for the most part to remain independent of political groups, approve or disapprove of the Government's policy?

To this question one would be justified in replying without hesitation that they disapprove. But it would be necessary to add that their disapproval is tempered neither with passion nor with indignation.

And here it is necessary to point to a contradiction that strikes every observer of Italian affairs.

If a foreigner travels about Italy and has the opportunity to mingle with different sections of the population, he will constantly receive the impression that the great majority of Italians are the most moderate and level-headed people imaginable, that they desire modest and just social reforms, based on principles fundamentally similar to those of the British Labour Party, and above all that they are resolutely opposed alike to a Communist régime and to a confessional régime. Time and time again the phrases 'Neither priests nor Communists', 'Neither Blacks nor Reds', will resound in his ears. And he will discover how few and far between are those who regret the passing of Fascism and the Monarchy.

But the evidence of the ballot-boxes will show him how abortive have been all the attempts made to form a party that may truly be said to constitute a 'Third Force', to have inherited the traditions of the Risorgimento and of the Resistance. The relevant figures constantly indicate that nearly half the nation's votes are cast for the Christian Democrats and about a third for the Communists (who are absolutely indifferent to the problems of confessionalism, and who always justify their action in voting for the inclusion of the Lateran Pacts in the Constitution) and the Socialists (who are not so indifferent as the Communists to the problems mentioned, but are obsessed by the idea that the only questions that count are economic questions): the rest being distributed among the Monarchists and the Fascists, who are more passionately confessionalist than even the Christian Democrats, and the Social Democrats, the Liberals and the Republicans. The last-named three parties, which are also called lay parties, ought to be the champions of the principle 'Neither Reds nor Blacks'; but they have never been known to object to manifestations of confessionalism, or to make their support of or participation in the Government conditional upon a cessation of the latter's persecution of minor Protestant sects or upon the granting of freedom in the field of propaganda to all Protestant denominations. Nor does one ever read, in Liberal or Social Democratic journals, that the Lateran Pacts are not sacrosanct, that reference was made in the debate on the Constitution to the question of negotiating changes in their wording, that in order to make them acceptable it would be necessary to restore to the State legislative power and jurisdiction in the matrimonial field and to repeal the provision whereby priests who renounce their cloth are prohibited from taking any part in civil life—a provision which no country that had absorbed even a modicum of the liberal tradition would consider admissible.

Our foreign observer of the Italian scene will note, then, that a party which could truly be described as a 'Third Force', which has truly inherited some part of the tradition of the Risorgimento, simply does not exist.

In 1953 there was formed, with an eye to the elections that were to be held in June of that year, a group known as 'Popular Unity', which opposed both the four-party coalition dominated by the Christian Democrats and the Socialist and Communist Parties, with which it considered any understanding impossible. Although it was headed by Ferruccio Parri, one of the noblest figures of the anti-Fascist movement, an acknowledged leader of the Resistance, and for a brief period in 1945 President of the Council; although it was honoured with the support of Piero Calamandrei, one of the greatest of Italian teachers and jurists; and although it had other illustrious adherents, among them a highly popular industrialist, one of the few who have succeeded since the war in promoting Italy's export trade, 'Popular Unity' obtained little more than 170,000 votes and failed to capture a single seat. The group was dissolved in 1958, the majority of its

x

members transferring their allegiance to the Socialist Party, in the hope of helping to widen the rift between that party and the Communists.

In 1957 the Radical Party was formed. Composed in great part of elements who had broken away from the Liberal Party because they disapproved of the latter's conservative tendencies, this too was essentially a 'Third Force' party, which looked for inspiration largely to British Labour and also to the Fabian tradition; but in the elections of May, 1958, it failed to return a single deputy to Parliament.

Is there any explanation of this paradox, of this contrast between the active secularism of which one becomes conscious when talking to the majority of Italians and the evidence of the ballot-boxes?

There are in fact several.

It must not be forgotten that we are living now in the 'economic' age, and that anything which lies outside the sphere of economics arouses scant public interest. To-day it seems to us incomprehensible that during the Risorgimento the economic interests of certain regions of Italy could be sacrificed to the ideal of unification with so little sign of protest, that the development was so faintly echoed in the literature of the time, that the problems to which it gave rise were considered of secondary importance. If a new age of idealism were to dawn now, indifference towards the fundamental problems of the ethical State, towards the supreme question of religious freedom, would appear equally incomprehensible.

As well as being the 'economic' age, this is the age of the vast social unit or group. To-day it is the group that determines the feelings and actions of the individual, to-day it is to the group that the politician addresses himself. Communism appears to have accepted the principle of the beehive, a principle that implies not merely the unconditional and unlimited devotion of the individual to the group, but also the atrophy of all those qualities of the individual which are not useful to the group. I do not know if it has interpreted and anticipated that mysterious element which we term the 'spirit of the age', or if it is itself imposing it even on its opponents. What is certain is that everywhere political groups, even though still very far from conforming to the Communist pattern, are tending more and more to adopt a centralizing system, to intensify discipline and to suppress individuality. In such a world it is obvious that very few people will concern themselves with the truly religious conscience, with which I would couple the truly liberal conscience—in particular, the conscience that is steeped in the great ethical tradition and for which the quantitative factor does not count—whereas the wrong done to a single individual means as much as the wrong done to a thousand. At the end of the nineteenth century all Europe was stirred and shaken by the injustice of which Captain Alfred Dreyfus had been the victim. To-day, numerous cases in which injustice has been followed by atrocious sentence leave public opinion indifferent. Communists may rage about the sentences passed on the Rosenbergs or about the brutalities committed by French parachutists in Algeria; Catholics may fulminate against the sentences imposed on prelates in Communist countries; Catholics, Liberals, Social Democrats and Socialists may denounce the execution of Nagy; but hardly anywhere can one discern the faintest sign of the onset of a crisis of conscience, a crisis of doubt. Only the few Communists who resigned from their party after the suppression of the Hungarian Revolution have stooped to examine their consciences. In a world given to mass thinking, the repression of small religious minorities, the violation of the religious conscience, which is in truth a rare thing, and which is outraged by any form of coercion, by anything that tends to make of religion *instrumentum regni*, cannot interest the party.

I have termed this the 'economic' age, the age of the vast social unit or group. I would go further, and describe it also as an age of feeling rather than of reason.

Renan, Strauss and Loisy appear to us utterly remote figures. The believer who felt disturbed if he found a discrepancy in the Bible, and whose spur was the hope of a reconciliation of science and faith, is remoter still. The believer is such because he needs to believe: his need is so great that it overcomes every logical difficulty. Furthermore, his religion is pre-eminently an aspect of the lyrical sense of life. Now the cult of liberty springs from reason, not from the lyrical sense, not from feeling. The latter is conducive rather to the eclipse than to the preservation of freedom. In the same way, if the passion of love is not dominated and controlled by reason it is apt to degenerate into tyranny.

All these attempts to explain what is now taking place seem

valid and relevant. Nevertheless, we cannot omit to recall how often, when considering the present time in these pages, we have noted—for example in the conduct of certain employers towards their work-people—something that it is always painful to have to say of one's own country, namely that what is happening in Italy could not happen elsewhere. There must accordingly be some additional explanation which applies particularly to Italy.

In this context it must be borne in mind that Italy as a country is poor and over-populated. It would be impossible to overstress the second epithet. It would also be impossible to repeat too often that advocates of dictatorship, both of the Right and of the Left, become uneasy when reference is made to this fact, the first group declaring that 'numbers are a source of strength', while the second, in defiance of all the evidence, stubbornly maintains that Italy could feed even more millions of people. All the published statistics—relating to the number of calories which the Italian absorbs each day with his food, to the consumption of meat and milk, to the number of rooms available for habitation, to the sales of books and newspapers, to the numbers of motor-cars, telephones and wireless sets currently in use—testify to the besetting poverty of the country, which in some regions assumes frightening proportions. But statistics cannot reflect the degree of insecurity which this poverty generates among a great part of the population. Above a certain level security is to be found in the field of public employment. Below it, the labouring classes, those engaged in manual occupations, live in constant fear of losing their means of livelihood. In few countries is dismissal from a job fraught with such tragic significance as it is in Italy, where nothing is harder to find than new employment.

Such an atmosphere is certainly not conducive to freedom.

In Italy poverty is general. But at the same time the stratification of society gives rise to violent extremes of poverty and wealth such as other States have not known for years. Nor—what is far more disquieting—is it possible to discern any change in this tendency. It seems that the poor are destined to become even poorer, that in certain provinces parents who can read and write may well be succeeded by children who are illiterate, and that the rich are destined to become ever richer.

It is also to be noted that the middle classes lack even the very relative unity of orientation that is discernible in other countries.

Beneath an appearance of political homogeneity[1] there is no general attachment, based on instinct rather than reason, to certain fundamental principles. The Italian's much-vaunted individualism takes the form of a defence of his own material interests, not of his freedom—a freedom that has become second nature to other peoples—to judge every course of action proposed to him on its merits and to act accordingly. The movement which we call the Risorgimento was inspired by an *élite*—and the same might be said of all those movements which, in the conventional phrase, have 'changed the course of history'—but it soon lost its capacity for proselytism and expansion. Of the Italian bourgeoisie, then, it may be said that, while on the whole it is accessible to movements of all kinds, no one has yet succeeded in endowing it with stability. Thus, it was without encountering any serious opposition—except from the minority who were truly wedded to socialism or liberalism, and of whom nearly all resided in the north of Italy—that the Fascists came to power; but Fascism never succeeded in imbuing the great mass of Italians with that blindness, with that uncritical devotion, which other totalitarian régimes have succeeded in creating among their populations.

Again, account must be taken of the Italian people's experience of life under a dictatorship. Nations that have never had such an experience do not realize what it is like, what scars it leaves in men's minds. To have seen at first hand that freedom can be snatched from those who have possessed it for three generations, and this with no undue effort, with little or no risk, once the reins of government have been seized; to have seen how men will let their consciences be violated, how the man who to-day has yielded from fear will to-morrow, in order to rehabilitate himself in his own eyes, swear that the course he followed was that which his convictions dictated; to have seen how many supporters success will attract to the most evil of causes—all these things stimulate the desire to repeat past follies. It is true that Fascism was destroyed in the end; but had the issue of the struggle been different, how many professed champions of freedom, how many

[1] In France the Monarchists and legitimists disappeared with the outbreak of the last war, by which time not even the memory survived in Italy of the erstwhile champions of the order that had prevailed before the country's unification. On the other hand, one still encounters in France men who execrate the Revolution and continue to defend all the traditions, laws and customs of *la vieille France*, whereas in Italy the species is unknown.

people who retained even the vaguest notion of what freedom really means, would still have been living at the end of fifty years?

In a country where those who wield the power have not inherited a political tradition requiring that such power should be exercised in the interests alike of the majority and of the minority, that the ruling party should always take account even of the views of its opponents; where the paternalistic tradition, the tradition which says that the master should watch over the very souls of his dependants, is still alive; where wealth is so unevenly distributed, and where neither the fiscal laws nor the laws of inheritance have fostered the idea that wealth should be subject to limitation or that vast fortunes should not be transmitted wholesale from generation to generation—in such a country the experience of dictatorship cannot but leave the strong with a predilection for the sort of régime in which the employer says to the worker: 'If you want to work, if you want to eat, you must read these newspapers rather than those, you must vote in this way, take part in these processions, attend these ceremonies, bring up your children in accordance with these ideas.' And a religious idea which serves to establish the thesis that by acting thus he is serving the best interests of his dependants, and assuring them of 'true freedom', cannot but prove acceptable to an employer.

By way of providing a further explanation of the special conditions which apply in Italy, one might call attention to the form which political parties are bound to assume in a very poor country, where the tradition of liberal government is not deeply rooted and has, moreover, been interrupted by twenty years of dictatorship; in a country where economic controls are in force and no one can do anything, no one can import, export, or even open a shop, without the sanction of the Government. In such a country it is immensely difficult for those parties which do not wield power to survive; it is immensely difficult for those parties which are in opposition and do not command mass support to find the means of life, the wherewithal to maintain a newspaper. Relations between the party in power on the one hand and, on the other, the industrialists' organizations and the extremely powerful Federation of Agricultural Societies which represents the landed interest are necessarily cordial, being based on the principle *do ut des*. Someone has to pay for the electoral campaigns, which are extremely costly and are conducted with a lavishness in the field of propaganda that is unknown in Britain. Moreover, Italian politicians as a class are poor, and many of them would find themselves in serious economic difficulty the day they ceased to hold public office.

All this helps to explain how those parties which ought to be neither 'Black' nor 'Red', which ought to be the champions of freedom and the defenders of lay interests, readily degenerate into mere satellites of the party in power.

In 1944–45 the partisan struggle, which in the cities had its counterpart in the passive resistance of the people to the German forces of occupation, seemed to have revived the spirit of the Risorgimento. With ample justification, groups of partisans assumed the style of Garibaldi Brigades; the heroes of the Risorgimento, the men who plotted against Austria, seemed to have returned to life and to be mingling with the new generation of Italians; the songs of 1848 and 1859 echoed gaily and spontaneously through the countryside; from unknown pens flowed writings that recalled Gioberti and d'Azeglio. Italians were no longer living in the era of economics, they were living in an age in which the fulfilment of duty, the assertion of individuality, the attainment of an ideal took precedence over all else.

In 1948 there was solemnly celebrated the centenary of the national and European movement which had transported the Risorgimento from the field of ideas into that of reality. The celebrations had all the appearance of a requiem. The events commemorated, which many as children had heard described by people who had taken part in them, seemed infinitely remote.

A log fire gives a dying splutter before its flames are finally extinguished. The partisan struggle resembled that dying splutter. The Constituent Assembly which sat in 1947 was the ultimate confirmation that nothing remained but ashes. Even those men who on grounds of age, name, ancestry, or family or party traditions might have assumed the task of perpetuating the values of the Risorgimento took no initiative in this direction. It was not only that in the matter of ecclesiastical policy they proclaimed their support for the Concordat, without reservation and in defiance of the principle that all religions are equal before the State, but in every other field too their one concern was to go slowly, to avoid coming to grips with concrete problems, to change nothing. Their attitude, in short, was the negation of all that Cavour had stood for.

For that matter, a spiritual remoteness from the Risorgimento was truly indispensable if the government of Italy was to be assumed by men who, although distinguished, although devoted to their country, were total strangers to that tradition. The chief among these men, De Gasperi, was a Catholic from the Trentino who had been a deputy in the Viennese Parliament before and during the First World War. The others nearly all came from old families with Catholic traditions, families which had regarded the events of the Risorgimento as a succession of wrongs inflicted on the Pontiff.

In the fullness of time this anti-Risorgimento tradition transformed itself into what might even be called an anti-progressive attitude. The man of the Risorgimento was also the heir to the Enlightenment; he had his own scale of values, he looked to London, Paris or Brussels rather than to Vienna, St. Petersburg or Berlin. (He set his lowest valuation on Spain.) Where a completely different tradition prevails it is quite natural that this scale of values should not find acceptance, that other values should obtain. Whereas an Italian who is imbued with the spirit of the Risorgimento deems it an affront to his national pride that Italy should continue to exclude women from offices to which they are admitted even in Moslem countries, to a Catholic who rejects the ideals of the Risorgimento this is not a source of irritation. Perhaps, unconsciously, he is even glad that Italy has relinquished that 'progressive' tradition which to his mind is synonymous with Protestantism or with unbelief. To Catholic Spain, always less accessible than any other State to the values of illuminism and, more recently, of liberalism, he looks with especial sympathy.

It is, perhaps, in this attitude towards other States that the liberal with sensitive antennae most readily discerns an expression of the anti-Risorgimento tradition. For a hundred years all liberals had subscribed to that scale of values to which reference has been made above, whereas all those of a reactionary turn of mind had entertained an aversion to Britain. This aversion survived the gradual transition from political Catholicism (a traditionalist philosophy, which made no distinction between the England of George III and that of Edward VII) to Fascism:

during the Second World War the Fascist had but one enemy—Britain.

The man of liberal traditions is not by nature servile. He remembers the smiles which all the British Prime Ministers of the inter-war years bestowed on Mussolini. He deplores the fact that British public opinion takes so little account of Italy, that Churchill in his War Memoirs does not accord the partisan movement that place of honour which is its sacred due. He remembers all the recent wounds that Britain has inflicted on Italy, from the episode of the Italian miners who were forced to return home to that of the British general who, faced with the necessity of quelling a riot in Trieste, forgot that the resources which all the police forces of the world have at their disposal to-day are such that it is possible to suppress any disorder without bloodshed. He knows also that if during the first half of the nineteenth century British Governments always gave at least their moral support to constitutional régimes and whenever possible opposed the initiatives of the Holy Alliance, during the first half of the twentieth century they have remained completely indifferent in face of episodes such as Franco's conquest of Spain with the aid of Moroccan and Italian legionaries.

And yet, in spite of everything, he feels that nowhere in Europe does the spirit of freedom remain so vital a thing as it does north of the Channel, that nowhere else has it been found possible to make so many concessions to the desire for social justice without encroaching on individual liberty, that in no other country has the ruling class so willingly sacrificed so many of its own interests for the common good. Above all, he notes that in no other country is there such a keen awareness of the need to defend European values, such a desperate anxiety to avoid a war that would destroy them for ever, that in no other country have men taken such a sane and realistic view of the question of relations between Europe and other continents, reconciling themselves within the space of a few years to that modification of traditional attitudes which had become essential.

A union of Europe with Britain could never represent the final stage in the creation of a giant republic of the type instituted by Franco or Salazar, which is naturally the bugbear of those Italian liberals to whom the word 'liberalism' signifies not the doctrine of a political party but a way of life. Dictatorships assume countless aspects, depending on the temper of the nation concerned. The militaristic, Imperial Roman masquerade of Fascism at once revealed its spuriously histrionic character, and this tickled the Italian sense of humour. That which it concealed of the old, pre-unification Italy, of the most noxious fruits that have matured on the Italian tree, from the inhumanity of the petty tyrants who ruled central Italy at the end of the fifteenth century to the corruption of the Bourbon kings and of the Popes of the early nineteenth century, was the true, the deadly poison that failed to amuse. A republic modelled on the régime of Franco or Salazar might well prove to be a synthesis of all the poisons that have matured on the Italian tree.

The advent of such a republic is feared most of all by the believer, who, although trusting in the promise of the final victory of Christ and His Church, is not blind to the possibility of temporary setbacks, and in this context is afraid less of the persecution of the Church than of the perversion of the Church.

But the believer ultimately finds relief from these torments by putting his trust in the omnipotence of God. The ways of the Lord are in truth infinite. When all roads seem barred, when men no longer have before them aught but a blank wall of despair or a choice between two paths of blood and sorrow, He who opened a way through the waters of the Red Sea to the fleeing Israelites can make possible unimagined solutions, can open up miraculous ways of salvation.

Against the background of the limpid June sky, newly washed by rain, there rises clearly before my eyes the dome of St. Peter's.

There is no image that more surely reaches my heart through my senses than this, which seems to represent the fulfilment of Man's age-old dream of a bridge uniting earth and heaven. It is at once the offering of a humanity reaching out towards God and the symbol of the refuge, of the fold whose hospitality knows no bounds, that will repel no one, that will shelter all who enter it from the wrath of God and from the temptations of the Evil One.

Among the great monuments of Rome it alone is still alive, it alone is still intact, it alone fulfils to-day the same task that was assigned to it on the day of its completion, witnesses the same rites, listens to the same hymns. Yet it shares with all the millenary monuments of the Eternal City in the admonitory task of reminding men how small a thing are their conflicts, how ephemeral is every episode that is measured in terms of human generations. A hundred years. The passions of three, perhaps of four generations; the triumph and the eclipse of the doctrines of liberalism; the unexpected realization of a Guelph State a century after the collapse of neo-Guelph hopes. A fleeting moment, a brief chapter, in the eternal story of man's relations with God.

POSTSCRIPT

The situation has continued to deteriorate during 1958–9.

Developments in France and the advent of General de Gaulle have been interpreted as a defeat for democracy, and make it seem less improbable that there might be set up in Italy an authoritarian regime, not to say a repetition of Fascism without, however, the organized violence which heralded Fascism's triumph—an authoritarian regime which, wearing the appearance of legality, would side-step the Constitution without reforming it.

Fanfani, a minister who represented the left wing of Christian Democracy, and who seemed to be securely established, has had to resign without a parliamentary vote of no confidence because of disapproval shown in some quarters of the papal curia where it was feared (mistakenly as it seems) that he might go to the length of forming an alliance with the Socialist party. There succeeded him a Segni government exclusively Christian Democrat, and although Segni is himself anti-Fascist, the movement to the right has been rapidly gaining momentum. A series of local pointers and of speeches by the most responsible men indicates how the alliance is being steadily consolidated between Christian Democracy and the right wing (Monarchists and Fascists); there are moreover frequent coalitions between the three parties in the administrative elections accompanied by a setting aside of all the values which were extolled during the resistance period of 1944–5.

It seems that Pope John XXIII, unlike his predecessor, may intend to make less use of the authority of the Holy See, leaving to the episcopate more responsibility for political directives. But while the cardinals of extreme right-wing opinions—admirers of Franco's regime—like Cardinal Ruffini, archbishop of Palermo, and Cardinal Ottaviani, secretary of the Holy Office, do not conceal their sympathies, no wearer of the purple and no bishop ever opposes their views (although it is probable that there are several who entertain contrary opinions).

Among Christian Democrats there can always be found many who claim to be leftist. Whoever reads the numerous weekly leaflets issued by the party, or the reports of meetings of Catholic students and graduates, whoever observes the Catholic workers' organizations, forms the impression, today as yesterday, that they have to do with a left wing party. But in fact these intellectual, trades-unionist and youthful elements count for next to nothing; the instructions come from above; their origins are unknown, but judging by results, it is impossible not to believe that they always aim at an understanding with the right wing.

The other parties have not substantially modified their position; the Social Democrats are today in opposition, but it is a feeble parliamentary opposition, which does not in the slightest rouse the country. For them enemy number one comprises not only the Communists but the very Socialists to whom a small group of their own dissidents have gone over.

INDEX